Republicanism

These volumes are the fruits of a major European Science Foundation project and offer the first comprehensive study of republicanism as a shared European heritage. Whilst previous research has mainly focused on Atlantic traditions of republicanism, Professors Skinner and van Gelderen have assembled an internationally distinguished set of contributors whose studies highlight the richness and diversity of European traditions. Volume I focuses on the importance of anti-monarchism in Europe and analyses the relationship between citizenship and civic humanism, concluding with studies of the relationship between constitutionalism and republicanism in the period between 1500 and 1800. Volume II is devoted to the study of key republican values such as liberty, virtue, politeness and toleration. This volume also addresses the role of women in European republican traditions, and contains a number of in-depth studies of the relationship between republicanism and the rise of commercial society in early modern Europe.

MARTIN VAN GELDEREN studied at the European University Institute and taught at the Technische Universität in Berlin prior to his appointment as Professor of Intellectual History at the University of Sussex in 1995. His publications include *The Political Thought of the Dutch Revolt* (Cambridge, 1992) and *The Dutch Revolt* (Cambridge Texts in the History of Political Thought, 1993), and he is currently preparing (also for the Cambridge Texts series) a new English rendition of *De iure belli ac pacis* by Hugo Grotius.

QUENTIN SKINNER is Regius Professor of Modern History in the University of Cambridge. A Fellow of Christ's College, Cambridge, he is also a fellow of numerous academic bodies and the recipient of several honorary degrees. His many publications include *The Foundations of Modern Political Thought* (Cambridge, 1978; two volumes), *Machiavelli* (1981), *Reason and Rhetoric in the Philosophy of Hobbes* (Cambridge, 1996), *Liberty before Liberalism* (Cambridge, 1998) and three volumes of *Visions of Politics* (Cambridge, 2002).

The European Science Foundation (ESF) acts as a catalyst for the development of science by bringing together leading scientists and funding agencies to debate, plan and implement pan-European scientific and science policy initiatives.

ESF is the European association of sixty-seven major national funding agencies devoted to scientific research in twenty-four countries. It represents all scientific disciplines: physical and engineering sciences, life and environmental sciences, medical sciences, humanities and social sciences. The Foundation assists its Member Organisations in two main ways: by bringing scientists together in its scientific programmes, EUROCORES, forward looks, networks, exploratory workshops and European research conferences, to work on topics of common concern; and through the joint study of issues of strategic importance in European science policy.

It maintains close relations with other scientific institutions within and outside Europe. By its activities, the ESF adds value by cooperation and coordination across national frontiers and endeavours, offers expert scientific advice on strategic issues, and provides the European forum for science.

Republicanism

A Shared European Heritage

VOLUME II
*The Values of Republicanism
in Early Modern Europe*

Edited by MARTIN VAN GELDEREN

and QUENTIN SKINNER

 CAMBRIDGE
UNIVERSITY PRESS

PUBLISHED BY THE PRESS SYNDICATE OF THE UNIVERSITY OF CAMBRIDGE
The Pitt Building, Trumpington Street, Cambridge, United Kingdom

CAMBRIDGE UNIVERSITY PRESS
The Edinburgh Building, Cambridge CB2 2RU, UK
40 West 20th Street, New York, NY 10011-4211, USA
477 Williamstown Road, Port Melbourne, VIC 3207, Australia
Ruiz de Alarcón 13, 28014 Madrid, Spain
Dock House, The Waterfront, Cape Town 8001, South Africa

http://www.cambridge.org

First published 2002

Printed in the United Kingdom at the University Press, Cambridge

Typeface TEFFRenard 10.5/14 pt   *System* LATEX 2$_\varepsilon$ [TB]

A catalogue record for this book is available from the British Library

Library of Congress Cataloguing in Publication data

Republicanism: a shared European heritage / edited by Martin van Gelderen and
Quentin Skinner.
          p.   cm.
Includes bibliographical references and index.
Contents: v. 1. Republicanism and constitutionalism in early modern Europe –
v. 2. The values of republicanism in early modern Europe.
ISBN 0 521 80203 2 (v. 1) – ISBN 0 521 80756 5 (v. 2)
1. Republicanism – Europe – History.
2. Republicanism – Europe – History – Case studies.
3. Political culture – Europe – History.
I. Gelderen, Martin van.
II. Skinner, Quentin.
JN9.R46   2002
321.8′6′094 – dc21   2001052547

ISBN 0 521 80756 5 (hb)

Contents of Volume II

Part III Republicanism and the Rise of Commerce

Contents of Volume 1

Acknowledgments

In May 1995 the European Science Foundation (ESF) accepted a proposal to set up a network for the study of republicanism as a shared European heritage. The proposal had been worked out by a group of six scholars interested in different aspects of this theme: Catherine Larrère (University of Bordeaux 3), Hans-Erich Bödeker (Max-Planck-Institut für Geschichte, Göttingen), Ivo Comparato (University of Perugia), Iain Hampsher-Monk (University of Exeter) and ourselves.

We were influenced in our choice of subject by two earlier international collaborations. One of these was the *convegno* held at the European University Institute in 1987 on the place of republicanism in the political theory of the Renaissance. Organised by Gisela Bock, Maurizio Viroli and Werner Maihofer, this meeting eventually gave rise to the volume *Machiavelli and Republicanism* published by Cambridge University Press in 1990. Our other source of inspiration was the ESF programme *The Origins of the Modern State in Europe, 13th to 18th Centuries*. As part of this project, Janet Coleman chaired a group studying many aspects of the relationship between the development of notions of individuality and the formation of the European system of states. The role played by republics and republican values in this process was a subject of discussion in the group, but it was not one of the themes of the ESF programme. It was specifically noted in the discussions of the group that more attention should be paid to the history of republicanism after the era of the Renaissance and outside the confines of Italy. This became our theme, and between September 1995 and September 1997 we devoted four *Arbeitsgespräche*, workshops and *convegni* to discussing it.

We are deeply indebted to the institutions which agreed to act as our hosts on these occasions, and to the individual members of our network who organised our meetings and made them such a success. Our warmest thanks go to Hans Bödeker and the Max-Planck-Institut für Geschichte in Göttingen, where we held our first meeting on 'Republicanism as Anti-Monarchism' in April 1996; to the Netherlands Institute of Advanced Study (NIAS) in Wassenaar, where our meeting on 'Republicanism and the Rise of Commercial Society' took place in September 1996; to Ivo Comparato and his colleagues at the University of Perugia, where we held our third meeting on 'The Political Institutions of the Republic: Discourse and Practice' in April 1997; and to Catherine Larrère and the University of Bordeaux 3, where our fourth meeting on '*Les Mœurs républicaines*: the political culture of Republicanism' was held in September 1997.

We were able to take stock of our findings, and to pursue their implications in new directions, at a final meeting in Siena in September 1998. This additional *convegno*, under the title 'The Historical Perspectives of Republicanism and the Future of the European Union', was organised in cooperation with the Comune di Siena and took place in the Sala della Pace of the Palazzo Pubblico. We are deeply grateful to Siena's *sindaco* Pierluigi Piccini and to Carlo Infantino for their invaluable support and splendid hospitality. We should also like to thank Monte dei Paschi di Siena for contributing a generous grant towards our expenses.

We also wish to express our thanks to Christ's College Cambridge for agreeing to allow our steering committee to hold its meetings there. We initially met in June 1995 to plan our workshops and decide whom to invite to them. We met again in January 1999 to evaluate the activities of our network in company with representatives of the European Science Foundation and to discuss our plans for publication with Cambridge University Press. On both occasions the College made us very welcome and offered us much hospitality.

The academics and administrators of the European Science Foundation have aided us in very many ways. In the planning phase of our network Max Sparreboom offered especially valuable advice. Vuokko Lepisto attended our first two workshops and gave us much help and support. During the latter phases of our project we were especially fortunate to work with Antonio Lamarra, who took a highly scholarly interest in our activities as well as providing us with further generous support. The Chairman of the ESF's Standing Committee in the Humanities, Wim Blockmans, proved willing at all times to offer academic, administrative and good-humoured diplomatic advice on a variety of European academic matters.

The period since our meetings came to an end has been one of unexpectedly heavy editorial work. The business of translating, reshaping, revising and adding to our original conference papers has had the effect of transforming them almost out of recognition, but it has taken us a long time. We are deeply grateful to the editorial staff at Cambridge University Press for their patience and encouragement throughout this period. We owe particular thanks to Richard Fisher, who gave us excellent advice at the outset and has edited our volumes with great good humour and unwavering efficiency. The Press also provided us with a handsome grant towards our translation expenses, matched by a no less handsome sum from the European Science Foundation. We should note that these volumes are not the only fruits of our network's research. Ivo Comparato, Catherine Larrère and Hans-Erich Bödeker are editing a volume of essays on 'Republican Founding and Republican Models' to be published by Olschki in Florence. Meanwhile a number of papers from our *convegno* in Siena have already been published in *Demands of Citizenship* (London, 2000), edited by Iain Hampsher-Monk and Catriona McKinnon.

We end with the expression of our greatest debt, which is of course to our friends and fellow members of the network. We are deeply grateful to our fellow coordinators Catherine Larrère, Hans-Erich Bödeker, Ivo Comparato and Iain Hampsher-Monk, all of whom discussed every aspect of our project with us at numerous meetings in Cambridge, in Amsterdam cafés and in restaurants in Perugia, Bordeaux and Siena. We are likewise grateful to all our contributors, each of whom participated in at least two of our workshops. They succeeded in turning each one of these occasions into a highly successful combination of hard work, intense discussion and exemplary sociability. We are grateful too for their forbearance in the face of our subsequent calls for the revision – and in many cases the complete re-writing – of their individual chapters. As these volumes go to press, we are delighted to learn that there is still time to offer our warmest thanks to our sub-editor Virginia Catmur, who has brought to bear an extraordinary level of skill and meticulousness, and has succeeded in sorting out a very large number of last-minute difficulties.

While our volumes were in final preparation, our friend Eluggero Pii died after a terrible illness stoically borne. It is an honour to publish here his final paper, the last testimony to the depth, breadth and grace of his scholarship.

QUENTIN SKINNER
MARTIN VAN GELDEREN

Introduction

The following chapters stand in little need of introduction, since they are all the work of recognised experts on the history and theory of European republicanism. A word does need to be said, however, about the editorial decisions we have made in respect of the topics we have chosen to cover and the chronological limits of our coverage.

Chronologically our two volumes focus on the period roughly extending from the mid-sixteenth to the late-eighteenth century. This reflects our sense that the earlier history of republicanism in the Renaissance, and the later fortunes of the movement in the nineteenth century, have both been better served in the existing scholarly literature. In particular, it is worth noting that several contributors to these present volumes took part in the production of *Machiavelli and Republicanism* (1990), in which the origins and influence of the Florentine model of the *vivere libero* were extensively surveyed. The basic decision we made in setting up our more recent network was that the period most in need of further study was the one following the demise of the Renaissance city-republics and preceding the recrudescence of republican theory and practice in the era of the French Revolution.

A word next needs to be said about the specific themes on which we have chosen to concentrate. These reflect our sense of how the values and practices associated with European republicanism can most illuminatingly be made to fit together. We accordingly begin, in Part I of Volume I, with the rejection of monarchy. Whatever else it may have meant to be a republican in early-modern Europe, it meant repudiating the age-old belief that monarchy is necessarily the best form of government. We already find this assumption implicitly questioned in some Huguenot political writings of the French religious wars, and we encounter a far more explicit challenge among the enemies of absolutism in eastern Europe, perhaps above all (as Chapter 3 reveals) in

1

Poland. But it was in the Netherlands, and later in England, that the repudiation of monarchy assumed its most dramatic forms. The Dutch abjured their allegiance to their overlord, Philip II, in 1581 and went on to fight successfully for the establishment of a federated republic, while the English executed their lawfully anointed king, Charles I, in 1649 and set up 'a Commonwealth and Free State'. Chapters 1, 2 and 4 of Part I examine the rôle of anti-monarchical sentiment in the unfolding of these unprecedented events.

We turn in Part II of Volume I to the figure of the citizen, the figure whom we take to be pivotal to the republican politics of early-modern Europe. One crucial fact, duly emphasised by all the contributors to this section, is that the image of citizenship projected by the republican writers of our period was largely drawn from classical and 'civic humanist' sources. This generalisation is shown to hold across much of the European map, from England (Chapter 5) and the Netherlands (Chapter 6) to Germany (Chapter 7) and Poland (Chapter 8).

According to the classical authorities beloved of early-modern republicans, the essence of what it means to be a *civis* or citizen is to be in possession of one's liberty as opposed to being a slave. This assumption not only underlies much of what our contributors have to say about the concept of citizenship in Volume I, but resurfaces in Part I of Volume II in the discussions of freedom (Chapter 1) and its connections with empire (Chapter 2). The predicament of the slave, as we learn from the rubric *De statu hominis* in the Digest of Roman Law, was held to be that of someone condemned to living *in potestate domini*, within the power and hence at the mercy of a master possessed of arbitrary powers. As Hobbes was to complain in *Leviathan*, the republican and 'democratical' writers proceeded to extend this definition in such a way as to argue 'that the Subjects in a Popular Common-wealth enjoy Liberty; but that in a Monarchy they are all Slaves'. If we live as subjects of rulers with arbitrary or prerogative powers, they claimed, we are living at their mercy and hence in a state of servitude.

Hobbes was only the most prominent among numerous defenders of monarchy who raised an obvious objection to this line of argument. How can the mere fact of living under a monarchy limit our options and thereby deprive us of liberty? The answer drawn by the exponents of republicanism from their classical and 'civic humanist' authorities was that slavery inevitably breeds slavishness; that those condemned to a life of servitude will find themselves obliged to cultivate the habits of servility. As Sallust and Tacitus had warned, no deeds of manly courage or greatheartedness can ever be expected from such abject peoples. They will be too fearful of attracting the envious attention of their rulers and thereby bringing ruin instead of glory upon themselves. Nor can they be expected to benefit themselves and their country by winning great fortunes from daring ventures of exploration or commerce. Since they know that whatever gains they accrue will always be subject to arbitrary confiscation with impunity, they will scarcely trouble to take the risks or expend the energies required. It accordingly became a trope of republican writing to claim that nothing but torpor and sullen acquiescence can be expected from the subjects of absolute monarchies. We must expect to find them – as a revealing series of neologisms put it – discouraged, dis-heartened, dis-spirited. By contrast, the freedom of the republican citizen was taken to consist essentially in being secured against such arbitrary domination or interference. The republican citizen was consequently said to enjoy something far more substantial in the way of *libertas* than mere *de facto* absence of constraint. He was said to enjoy protection from the possibility of suffering such constraint. Republican citizens could be governed, but not mastered. This was taken to be the most precise way of distinguishing between genuine citizens and mere subjects. The espousal of this exacting vision of civil liberty brought with it some fundamental questions about forms of government. What type of constitution is best suited to upholding both the liberty of citizens and the stability of commonwealths? Under what form of constitution, in other words, will it be possible to ensure that the laws are duly enforced but that citizens are at the same time immune from arbitrary domination or interference on the part of their government? These are among the issues to which our contributors turn in Part III of Volume I, our section entitled 'The Republican Constitution'.

As one might expect, many republicans took it to be obvious that, whatever else is true of such constitutions, they must eschew any vestiges of monarchical authority. This was because, as the English Act of 1649 abolishing kingship put it, there is an inherent tendency for regal power 'to oppress and impoverish and enslave the subject'. Paradoxically, however, the upholding of civic liberty was not invariably taken to require a republican constitution in the strictest sense. Sometimes it was conceded that, if one could have a Doge-like monarch, subject to election and bereft of prerogative powers, this might offer the best prospect of assuring the right combination of public order and civil liberty. This paradox echoes throughout the early-modern period. We encounter it in Machiavelli's question as to whether a *republica* can be sustained 'per via di regno', and we hear it again in Hume's suggestion that the progress of the arts and the maintenance of liberty may often fare better under 'civilised monarchies'.

Whatever view was taken of this issue, it was generally agreed that, in order to avoid the dangers of tyranny, it will always be essential to prevent our rulers from imposing their wills on us arbitrarily and without check. This was taken to follow from the cardinal assumption that subjection to unchecked power is equivalent to servitude. These commitments help in turn to explain why so many republican theorists – as we learn from Part III of Volume I – were preoccupied by two constitutional problems above all. One was the question of how best to frame a mixed constitution, a *respublica mixta*, in such a way as to deploy power to balance power. The other was the associated question of how to ensure that the people are able to make their voice heard – at least by representation – in the process of law-making, so that whatever laws are enacted may be said to reflect their wills as opposed to being arbitrarily imposed upon them. As a number of chapters in Part III of Volume I reveal, these problems were eclectically solved by reference to whatever sources seemed most serviceable, including local custom, classical theory and the exemplary instance of the Jewish commonwealth, a constitution widely believed to reflect God's own political preferences. Republican writers generally agreed that, so long as arbitrary power is duly outlawed and representation assured, we can legitimately claim to be living in 'a free state'. As this terminology reveals, the republicans took as seriously as possible the alleged analogy between natural and political bodies. Just as natural bodies are said to be free if and only if they are moved to act by their own wills, so too with political ones. To live in a free state is to live under a constitution in which the body politic is never moved to act except by the will of the citizen body as a whole.

If we have the good fortune to live under such a constitution, this will not only have the effect of securing our civil rights; it will also emancipate us from the servility that comes of living under any form of absolute government. To put the point another way, the liberty enjoyed by republican citizens was at the same time held to be an inducement to civic virtue. Freed from the dread of the mighty, we can hope to undertake great and courageous deeds. Freed at the same time from any fear that our property may be taken away from us with impunity, we can likewise hope to pursue our fortunes without anxiety and thereby benefit our community as well as ourselves. Just as the subjects of arbitrary power become disheartened and discouraged, so the constitution of a free state helps to hearten and encourage its citizens to expend their best energies in their own and the public's interests. One consequence of these assumptions was that many defenders of free states became proponents of expansionist policies, seeking in James Harrington's words to establish commonwealths not merely 'for preservation' but 'for increase'. As we learn from a number of the contributions to Volume II, however, the question of empire always remained for republicans a vexed and difficult one. On the one hand, a number of free states, including the Netherlands after independence and Britain in the 1650s, took the view that liberty at home should be matched by greatness abroad, and turned themselves into enthusiastic and successful imperialists. But on the other hand, many republicans feared that the acquisition of an overseas empire might undermine the conditions of virtuous citizenship at home. They were worried about the large armies needed for policing extended frontiers, partly because such forces undermined the traditional identity between soldier and citizen, but even more because they offered governments a tempting means of seizing absolute power. But they also feared moral contamination at the hands of the conquered, a fear as old as Sallust's concern that the introduction of what he called 'Asiatic habits' might bring about the corruption of European *mœurs*. We are left pondering the various ways in which early-modern republicans conceived of the relationship between the values of the *patria* and those of other and wider communities.

A further important topic raised in Part I of Volume II concerns the character of the virtuous citizen. As constructed by the theorists of free states, the republican citizen was undoubtedly a figure of powerful energies and commitments. His concern for liberty made him a vigilant critic of governmental encroachment (Chapter 1), while his belief in the equal standing of citizens made him at least potentially a friend of religious toleration (Chapter 3). By the beginning of the eighteenth century, however, we find his limitations as a moral exemplar increasingly exposed to criticism and even ridicule. His vaunted free-speaking and contempt for courtliness were both challenged by new ideals of politeness and urbanity (Chapter 5), while his fierce insistence on the need for independence was overtaken by new conceptions of civility and sociability (Chapter 6).

We bring our volumes to a close by considering in greater detail the two most important limitations of the republican citizen and his system of values. One stemmed from the fact that his virtue was very much the classical *virtus* of the *vir civilis*, and was consequently viewed as an eponymously male attribute. A construction of masculinity undoubtedly underpinned the ideology of 'civic humanism'. What place did this leave for women in the republic? How was the public space of the republic gendered? These are the questions addressed in part II of Volume II, in which we examine the confrontation between the republican image of virtue and the demand for greater sexual equality. The other limitation on which we focus arose in a similar way from the classical sources of republican thought. As we have seen, the ancient moralists believed that freedom acts to release all kinds of energies, including those which enable prudent and courageous men to amass fortunes for themselves. But they also believed that the highest duty of the *vir civilis* is to employ his energies for the good of his community, whether in a civil or a military capacity. This latter commitment prompted most republicans to insist on honour and glory as the proper goals of the *vir civilis*, and this in turn frequently prompted them to speak disparagingly of the acquisition of wealth as a base and even an unpatriotic pursuit.

The ambiguous implications of this inheritance for the relationship between republicanism and the rise of commerce form the subject of our concluding section in Volume II. We end with the figure of Adam Smith, and with the confrontation between republican principles and commercial realities. With Smith's reflections on our theme, we begin to move away from early-modern debates about virtue and commerce and to enter a more recognisably modern world.

One question that cannot be ignored in discussions about our republican heritage is how far we are confronting a usable past. In our own case these discussions gave rise to a further editorial decision which the present volumes reflect. We resolved to exclude such questions as far as possible, and we further resolved to consider them at a separate conference and, eventually, in a separate book. As we note in our Acknowledgments, this additional *convegno* duly took place, and a volume arising from it has already been published. By contrast, our aim in the present volumes has been to stand back from the politics of republicanism and to produce a series of purely scholarly studies aimed at furthering an historical understanding of this aspect of our intellectual heritage.

Part 1

Republicanism and Political Values

1

Classical Liberty and the Coming of the English Civil War

Quentin Skinner

A good place to begin this chapter – and indeed this entire volume on republican values – is with the rubric *De statu hominis* from the opening of the *Digest* of Roman law, perhaps the most influential of all the classical discussions of the concept of civil liberty. There we read that 'the fundamental division within the law of persons is that all men and women are either free or are slaves'.[1] After this we are offered a formal definition of the concept of slavery. 'Slavery is an institution of the *ius gentium* by which someone is, contrary to nature, subjected to the dominion of someone else.'[2] This in turn is said to yield a definition of individual liberty. If everyone in a civil association is either bond or free, then a *civis* or free subject must be someone who is not under the dominion of anyone else, but is *sui iuris*, capable of acting in their own right.[3] It likewise follows that what it means for someone to lack the status of a free subject must be for that person not to be *sui iuris* but instead to be *sub potestate*, under the power or subject to the will of someone else.

While this summary was exceptionally influential, we already encounter a very similar analysis at a much earlier date among the historians and philosophers of ancient Rome, and especially in the writings of Cicero, Sallust, Livy and Tacitus. Anyone in late-sixteenth- or early-seventeenth-century England who had received a university education would have been required to study

---

1. Mommsen and Krueger (eds.) 1970, I, v, 3, 35: 'Summa itaque de iure personarum divisio haec est, quod omnes homines aut liberi sunt aut servi.' (Note that, in this and all subsequent quotations from the *Digest*, I have made my own translations.)
2. *Ibid.*, I, v, 4, 35: 'Servitus est constitutio iuris gentium, qua quis dominio alieno contra naturam subicitur.'
3. *Ibid.*, I, vi, 1, 36: 'Some persons are in their own power, some are subject to the power of others, such as slaves, who are in the power of their masters' ['quaedam personae sui iuris sunt, quaedam alieno iuri subiectae sunt . . . in potestate sunt servi dominorum . . .'].

these texts in their original Latin (Feingold 1997, esp. pp. 246–56), but it is worth recalling that it was exactly at this period that all these writers also became available in English for the first time. Nicholas Grimalde's translation of Cicero's *De officiis* was issued as early as 1556 (see Cicero 1556), but it only became a best-seller when it appeared in a dual-language version in 1558, after which it went through at least five editions before the end of the century.[4] Meanwhile Henry Savile's translation of Tacitus's *Historiae* and *Agricola* had been published in 1591, with Richard Grenewey's versions of the *Annals* and *Germania* following in 1598.[5] Two years later Philemon Holland issued his enormous folio containing the whole of the extant sections of Livy's *History* (Livy 1600; cf. Peltonen 1995: 135–6), while in 1608 Thomas Heywood published his translations of Sallust's *Bellum Catilinae* and *Bellum Iugurthinum*.[6]

Among these writers, it is Cicero who is most interested in formal definitions of *libertas* and *servitus*, freedom and servitude. The fear of enslavement figures as a running theme of his speeches denouncing Marcus Antonius as a public enemy of Rome's traditional *civitas libera* or free state (Cicero 1926: III, 6, 14, p. 202). These so-called *Philippics* became one of the most popular of Cicero's works in the Renaissance, with a dozen or more editions appearing by the middle of the sixteenth century.[7] Cicero repeatedly exhorts the Roman people to reassert the *libertas* they had lost when they fell under the domination of Julius Caesar, and violently attacks Antonius for aspiring to reduce his fellow citizens to a renewed condition of slavery. Not only does Cicero organise his argument around the contrast between freedom and servitude, but he emphasises in a much-cited passage that liberty is forfeited not merely by actual oppression but also by conditions of domination and dependence:

> Do you call servitude peace? Our ancestors took up arms not only to be free, but also to win power. You think that our arms should now be thrown away in order that we should become slaves. But what cause of waging war can be more just than that of repudiating slavery? For the most miserable feature of this condition is that, even if the master happens not to be oppressive, he can be so should he wish.[8]

4. See Cicero 1558. This dual-language version was reprinted in 1568, 1574, 1583, 1596 and 1600.
5. See Tacitus 1591 and 1598 and cf. Peltonen 1995: 124–35 on these translations and their influence.
6. Sallust 1608. But Sallust's *Jugurtha* had already been translated by Alexander Barclay in 1557.
7. Information from British Library catalogue.
8. Cicero 1926: VIII, 4, 12, p. 374: 'Servitutem pacem vocas? Maiores quidem nostri, non modo ut liberi essent, sed etiam ut imperarent, arma capiebant; tu arma abicienda censes, ut serviamus.

As Cicero's closing remark makes clear, to enjoy *de facto* freedom of action is not necessarily to enjoy liberty. If your freedom is held at the discretion of anyone else, such that you continue to be subject to their will, then you remain a slave. To enjoy liberty, in other words, it is not sufficient to be free from coercion or the threat of it; it is necessary to be free from the *possibility* of being threatened or coerced.[9]

Cicero was at least as much interested in his *Philippics* in the contrasting ideal of the *civitas libera* or free state, but for the best-known statement of his views about the meaning of civil or public liberty we must turn to his *De officiis*. We learn in Book II that, as Grimalde's translation puts it, 'libertie be all to shaken' when 'the lawes bee sounke by some mans might' and citizens are made to depend on the will of a ruler instead of on the rule of law (Cicero 1558, fo. 81ʳ). By contrast, as Cicero had already laid down in Book I, free men can be defined as those who are not dependent on anyone else, but are able 'to use their owne libertie: whose propertie is, to lyve as ye list' (*ibid.*, fo. 31ʳ). Summarising in Book III, Cicero left his early-modern English readers to ponder an almost treasonably anti-monarchical inference: anyone desiring to be a king 'alloweth the overthrow of law, and libertie', so that 'it is not honest to raign as king in that citie, which both hath been & ought to be free' (*ibid.*, fo. 149ʳ).

Cicero's analysis is heavily indebted to Aristotle's discussion of freedom and tyranny in the *Politics*, and it is a further striking fact that Aristotle's text likewise became available in English for the first time at the end of the sixteenth century. Louis le Roy's French translation was turned into English in 1598, and in this version we are told that kingship degenerates into an enslaving form of tyranny whenever a king 'dooth absolutely commaund and raigne over such as are equall, and all that are better; respecting his owne, and not the subjects profit, and therefore is not voluntarie: for no person that is free dooth willingly endure such a state' (Aristotle 1598, Book IV, ch. 10, p. 208). Later we are given an account of the 'tokens' of political liberty – an account that Cicero follows almost word for word. According to Aristotle, 'obeying and governing by turns, is one token of libertie', so that we may say that 'the end and foundation of the popular state, is Libertie'. To which he adds that 'another token of libertie is, to live as men list', since 'the propertie of bondage is, not to live according to a man's own discretion' (*ibid.*, Book VI, ch. 2, pp. 339-40).

Quae causa justior est belli gerendi, quam servitutis depulsio? in qua etiamsi non sit molestus dominus, tamen est miserrimum posse, si velit.'

9. For the idea that liberty should be contrasted not with coercion but with enslavement see Pettit 1997, esp. pp. 17-41, 51-73, an analysis to which I am greatly indebted.

Besides drawing on Aristotle, Cicero refers at several points in *De officiis* to the Law of the Twelve Tables, which he took to be the earliest legal code established in the *civitas libera* after the expulsion of the kings from Rome (Cicero 1913: I, 12, 37, p. 40 and III, 31, 111, p. 390). Cicero alludes to the Twelve Tables again in *De legibus*, in Book III of which he outlines an ideal constitution for a free state and proceeds to enunciate two golden rules. 'When giving laws to free peoples', he reminds us once again, we must first ensure that they are never dominated by the wills of their magistrates.[10] We must ensure that they are entirely ruled by laws, so that 'just as the magistrates govern the people, so the laws govern the magistrates'.[11] The other golden rule is the one explicitly stated in the Twelve Tables, according to which the highest duty of magistrates is encapsulated in the maxim *salus populi suprema lex esto*, 'the safety of the people must be treated as the supreme law' (Cicero 1928: III, 3, 8, p. 466).

The Roman historians were less interested than Cicero in formal definitions of freedom and servitude, but they thought of these concepts in very similar terms. Sallust at the start of his *Bellum Catilinae* describes how the rule of the early kings degenerated into *dominatio* and thereby enslaved the Roman people (Sallust 1931: VI–VII, pp. 10–14). But the people managed – in the words of Heywood's translation – to turn this slavery under 'the Government of one' into a 'forme of limited pollicy', thereby establishing 'this form of Liberty in Government' (Sallust 1608: 17 [*recte* p. 7]). Tacitus in his *Annals* provides a contrasting description of how the Roman people were forced back into slavery under the early principate, and likewise equates their loss of liberty with the re-imposition of arbitrary will as the basis of government. As Grenewey's translation puts it, after the ascendancy of Augustus 'there was no signe of the olde laudable customes to be seene: but contrarie, equalitie taken away, every man endevored to obey the prince', so that 'the Consuls, the Senators, and Gentlemen ranne headlong into servitude' (Tacitus 1598: 2–3). Tacitus admits that some later emperors liked to invoke the traditional *praecepta* of the free state, as when Vitellius adjured Meherdates before the Senate 'that he should not thinke himselfe a Lord and maister to commaund over his subjects as slaves; but a guide, and they citizens' (*ibid.*: 158). But as Tacitus's tone continually makes clear, he regards such rhetorical flights as little better than a mockery of the liberty that the Roman people had lost.

In the opening books of his *History* Livy offers a fuller account of both these processes. Book II begins with a much-cited account of the transition

---

10. Cicero 1928: III, 2, 4, p. 460: 'nos autem, quoniam leges damus liberis populis...'
11. *Ibid.*: III, 1, 2, p. 460: 'ut enim magistratibus leges, ita populo praesunt magistratus'.

from the *dominatio* of the early kings to the liberty enjoyed by the Roman people under their 'free state'. Livy equates this transformation with the establishment of the rule of law and the consequent ending of any dependence on the discretion of the king (Livy 1919: II, I, 218–20 and II, III, 226–8). Having expelled the Tarquins, the Romans established 'a free state now from this time forward'. 'Which freedom of theirs', as Holland's translation goes on, was due to the fact that 'the authoritie and rule of lawes' was now 'more powerfull and mightie than that of men' (Livy 1600: 44).

Livy draws on this understanding of freedom and slavery in many later passages, but he illustrates the danger of falling back into servitude most fully in his account of the Decemvirate. The Tribunes initially called for the establishment of these magistrates on the grounds that the rule of the consuls was 'too absolute, and in a free state intolerable', since they were able to 'rule of themselves, and use their owne will and licentious lust in steede of law' (*ibid.*: 87). But within a year of receiving their special authority to reform the laws the Decemvirs seized power for themselves. As a result, the people who in their reforming zeal had been 'gaping greedily after libertie' found themselves 'fallen and plunged into servitude and thraldome' (p. 112). This reversion to slavery, Livy repeats, occurred when they lost the protection of the laws and found themselves subjected once more to arbitrary power. 'The meaner persons went to the wals, and with them they dealt according to their lust and pleasure right cruelly. The person wholy they regarded, and never respected the cause, as with whom favour and friendship prevailed as much as equity and right should have done' (p. 111).

By contrast, Livy always defines the liberty of cities as well as citizens in terms of not living in subjection to the power or discretion of anyone else. When, for example, he describes the surrender of the Collatines to the people of Rome, he stresses that they were able to take this decision because they were 'in their owne power', and hence 'at libertie to doe what they will' (*ibid.*: 28). The same view emerges still more clearly from the much later passage in which he discusses the efforts of the Greek cities to restore their good relations with Rome. To be able to enter into such negotiations, one of their spokesmen is made to say, presupposes the possession of 'true libertie', that condition in which a people 'is able to stand alone and maintain it selfe, and dependeth not upon the will and pleasure of others' (p. 907).

By the time Charles I confronted his Parliament in 1640, after a gap of eleven years, these observations by the Roman historians about 'free states' and the attendant dangers of enslavement had all been turned into works of English political thought. Carrying with them the unparalleled prestige accorded to the wisdom of antiquity, these works provided at the same time an explicitly anti-monarchical perspective from which the English could begin to reflect anew on their political experiences, and in particular on the relations between the liberty of subjects and the prerogatives of the crown. As Thomas Hobbes was subsequently to observe in *Leviathan*, such reflections were bound in the end to have a destabilising effect on the Stuart monarchy (Hobbes 1996, ch. 21, pp. 149–50). Those who felt threatened by the crown's understanding of its prerogatives now had available to them a way of thinking about their grievances in the light of which the crown's attitudes and policies could easily be represented as nothing less than an aspiration to reduce a free people to servitude.

This aspect of the ideological origins of the English revolution has arguably received too little attention from historians,[12] who have placed an overwhelming emphasis on English common law as the main instrument for challenging the extra-Parliamentary powers of the crown.[13] They have often implied that the constitutional debates of the early Stuart period were largely immune from broader legal influences,[14] and insofar as they have discussed the role of Roman law in these debates they have tended to associate its principles with the defence of absolutism.[15] As we shall see, however, one of the most potent sources of radical thinking about the English polity in the years immediately preceding the outbreak of civil war in 1642 was provided by classical and especially Roman ideas about freedom and servitude. Far more than has generally been recognised, the outbreak of the English revolution was legitimised in neo-Roman terms.

We need to focus on two particular groups who made prominent use of classical arguments in the climacteric period between the convening of the Short Parliament in April 1640 and the outbreak of civil war in the summer of 1642. First of all we need to take note of the common lawyers in Parliament, several of whom exhibit a surprising willingness to draw on Roman sources in defending the liberties of subjects. But we mainly need to focus

12. The most important exception to this rule is the account in Peltonen 1995. For valuable surveys of Roman liberty and its revival in early-modern English political theory see also Sellers 1994, esp. pp. 69–98 and Sellers 1998, esp. pp. 7–11, 17–22.
13. The classic work is Pocock 1987c, but for important revisions see Burgess 1992 and Sommerville 1999: 81–104. These assumptions about common law are particularly prominent in Burgess 1992, Burgess 1996 and Cromartie 1999.
14. A point excellently made against G. R. Elton, Conrad Russell and their admirers in Sommerville 1996.
15. It used to be generally agreed that civil law mainly served as a prop to absolutism. See for example Mosse 1950 and Simon 1968. More recently, thanks largely to Levack 1973, it has been recognised that the situation was more complicated. See, for example, Burgess 1992: 121–30 and 1996: 63–90. But even Levack 1973, esp. p. 88 and Burgess 1996, esp. pp. 75, 78 still appear to assume a basic consonance between civil law and royalism.

on the group of malcontents later stigmatised by Hobbes in his *Behemoth* as the 'Democratical Gentlemen' (Hobbes 1969: 26). Hobbes's characterisation is in one way misleading, for it gives the impression that the gentlemen in question were self-conscious exponents of a radical ideology designed to limit the powers of the crown. To read their speeches and pamphlets, however, is to be struck not by their radicalism but by their defensive and even reactionary outlook, by their bewilderment as well as outrage as they confronted what they took to be the crown's assault on their standing in the community, and above all by their determination to exploit any arguments tending to uphold their traditional privileges. Hobbes was undoubtedly right, however, to see that their reliance on classical arguments about freedom and servitude eventually pushed them into adopting a standpoint so radical as to be virtually republican in its constitutional allegiances. Hobbes bitterly summarises the position into which they stumbled as a result of seeking to defend their interests by recklessly drawing on 'the books written by famous men of the ancient Grecian and Roman commonwealths' (*ibid.*: 3). They found themselves committed to arguing that the crown's prerogatives were straightforwardly incompatible with the liberty of subjects, and thus that 'all that lived under Monarchy were slaves' (Hobbes 1996: 150).

We need to distinguish two separate phases of the attack mounted by these democratical gentlemen and their allies. They began by concentrating on what they took to be the crown's continuing disregard for the personal and property rights of individual subjects. How far the holding of lands and goods may be subject to the will of the king became a leading topic of debate from the moment when Parliament first re-assembled in the spring of 1640. The anxiety of the democratical gentlemen stemmed from the fact that, in the course of the 1630s, the crown had extended its policy of raising non-Parliamentary revenues, in particular by turning the Ship Money levy into a general tax. When George Peard, a common lawyer, rose in the Short Parliament to speak against this judgment, he declared that the imposing of non-Parliamentary taxes takes away 'not onely our goods but persons likewise', so reducing us from free subjects to slaves (Cope with Coates (eds.) 1977: 172). But the most powerful denunciation of the policy from a neo-classical standpoint appeared in *The Case of Shipmony Briefly Discoursed*, a pamphlet anonymously issued by Henry Parker to coincide with the opening of the Long Parliament in November 1640.[16] Parker begins by invoking the

16. On the precise political context in which Parker's tract appeared see Mendle 1995: 32–50.

Roman law view of what it means to live in servitude. 'Where the meere will of the Prince is law' we can expect 'no mediocrity or justice', and 'wee all see that the thraldome of such is most grievous, which have no bounds set to their Lord's discretion' ([Parker] 1999: 98). Parker is clear that the mere existence of such discretionary powers, not their actual exercise, has the effect of reducing us to slavery. 'It is enough that we all, and all that we have, are at his discretion', for where all law is 'subjecte to the King's meer discretion', there 'all liberty is overthrowne' (pp. 110, 112). With these general considerations in mind, Parker turns to the Ship Money tax. If we accept that the king has a right to impose this charge, so that 'to his sole indisputable judgement it is left to lay charges as often and as great as he pleases', this will 'leave us the most despicable slaves in the whole world' (p. 108). The reason is that this will leave us in a condition of total dependence on the king's goodwill. But as Parker rhetorically asks, if we have no alternative but to 'presume well of our Princes', then 'wherein doe we differ in condition from the most abject of all bondslaves?' (p. 109).

As the constitutional crisis deepened, the two Houses eventually produced a general statement to the effect that we forfeit our freedom whenever our properties are made dependent on the will of the king. The occasion for this resolution was the dispute that arose in the opening months of 1642 over the decision by Parliament to take into its own hands the royal arsenal at Hull. When the governor, Sir John Hotham, closed the gates of the city against the king, Charles I reacted by accusing him of treason, arguing that as sovereign he possessed 'the same title to His Town of *Hull*, which any of His Subjects have to their Houses or Lands' (Husbands *et al.* (eds.) 1642: 266). The response of the two Houses – in their Remonstrance of 26 May 1642 – was to proclaim this view of the prerogative blankly inconsistent with the liberty of subjects. Arguing that any threat to the property of freemen is at the same time a threat to their living and substance, Parliament went on to speak – in the litany later made famous by John Locke – of an inherent conflict between such prerogatives and our 'lives, Liberties and Estates' (p. 264). Kings are prone to believe 'that their Kingdoms are their own, and that they may do with them what they will' (p. 266). But this principle 'is the Root of all the Subjects misery, and of the invading of their just Rights and Liberties'. It undermines 'the very Foundation of the liberty, property and interest of every Subject in particular, and of all the Subjects in generall'. To say that a king can dispose of these rights at will is to say that they are held by mere grace, which in turn is to say that we are not free subjects at all (*ibid.*).

The need to secure life, liberty and estates against such encroachments continued to be asserted throughout the period up to the start of the fighting in the autumn of 1642. During the opening months of that year, however, the democratical gentlemen and their allies suddenly shifted the focus of their attack, turning to challenge in the name of popular liberty a power of the crown hitherto regarded as sacrosanct by all parties. The prerogative they now began to question was that of the 'Negative Voice', the right of the king to give or withhold his assent to any proposed acts of legislation put to him by the two Houses of Parliament.

The issue over which the democratical gentlemen plunged into this further phase of their campaign was the question of who should control the militia. After the outbreak of the Irish rebellion in October 1641, and after the king's abortive but violent attempt to arrest five members of Parliament in January 1642, the two Houses claimed to be anxious about their own security. Following their decision in January to take over the arsenal at Hull, they proceeded at the beginning of February to draw up a Militia Ordinance which they sent to the king for his assent. Protesting about 'the bloody counsels of Papists and other ill-affected persons', they proposed that 'for the safety therefore of His Majesty's person, the Parliament and kingdom at this time of imminent danger', the control of the militia should be vested exclusively in persons approved by the two Houses of Parliament. They went on to list their local nominees, granting them extensive powers to muster, train and arm the people 'for the suppression of all rebellions, insurrections and invasions that may happen'.[17]

As every good royalist knew, the control of the militia was one of the indisputable 'marks' of sovereignty listed by Bodin in his *Six livres de la république*. Although Charles had hitherto accepted a number of bills limiting his prerogative, this further demand at first elicited from him and his advisers a stunned silence.[18] While the king temporised, however, Parliament made an astonishing move that wholly changed the terms of the debate. Voting the king's delay a direct denial, the two Houses passed the Militia Ordinance on their own authority on 5 March 1642 (Gardiner (ed.) 1958: 245–7), and ten days later pronounced it legally binding on the people notwithstanding its failure to secure the royal assent (Husbands *et al.* (eds.) 1642: 112).

17. Gardiner (ed.) 1958: 245–6 prints the Ordinance of 5 March, but notes that the same provisions already appear in the version sent for the royal assent by both Houses on 16 February. Husbands *et al.* (eds.) 1642: 73–5 print the list (dated 12 February) of those whom Parliament proposed to entrust with the organisation of the militia.

18. See Charles I's temporising response in Husbands *et al.* (eds.) 1642: 80.

'I am so much amazed', exclaimed the king (an unfortunate echo of Shakespeare's *Richard II*) 'that I know not what to Answer' (*ibid.*: 94). As recently as December 1641 John Pym – unofficial leader of the opposition in the House of Commons – had explicitly conceded that the prerogative of the Negative Voice was a pillar of the constitution and beyond dispute. Less than three months later, however, the two Houses had in effect voted to set this prerogative aside. The outcome was an instant and acute crisis of legitimacy. How could Parliament possibly defend its decision to trample on such a fundamental and hitherto unquestioned flower of the crown?

The answer is that the principles in the light of which the two Houses justified their action were entirely drawn from the legal and moral philosophy of ancient Rome. The resulting campaign mounted by the democratical gentlemen and their allies may in turn be said to have progressed in two distinct steps. They began by taking their stand squarely on the fundamental maxim that Cicero had cited from the Law of the Twelve Tables: that, in legislating for a free state, *salus populi suprema lex esto*, the safety of the people must be treated as the supreme law. The vote calling for the Militia Ordinance to be obeyed as a law speaks of 'the safeguard both of his Majestie, and his People' as paramount (Husbands *et al.* (eds.) 1642: 112), while the petition of a week later repeats that none of their plans can 'bee perfected before the Kingdome be put into safetie, by setling the *Militia*' (p. 123). Summarising their grievances in their declaration of 19 May 1642, they repeat once more that the fundamental purpose of government is 'the safeguard both of his Majesty, and his people', the maintenance of 'the good and safetie of the whole' (p. 207).

The upholding of *salus populi*, they concede, normally requires that the two Houses of Parliament should act in concert with the king. We still find this understanding of the mixed constitution unhesitatingly put forward even in the markedly hostile declaration of 19 May 1642:

> The Kingdome must not be without a meanes to preserve it selfe, which that it may be done without confusion, this Nation hath intrusted certaine hands with a Power to provide in an orderly and regular way, for the good and safetie of the whole, which power, by the Constitution of this Kingdome, is in his Majestie and in his Parliament together.
> (ibid.)

The two Houses accept, in other words, that England is a mixed monarchy, and that in normal circumstances the highest legislative authority can be exercised only when king and Parliament act together as the three Estates of the realm and hence as the joint bearers of sovereignty.[19]

The two Houses next insist, however, that the crisis in which the nation currently finds itself is such that this fundamental principle of the mixed constitution cannot be upheld. Although the nation is facing a dire emergency, the king is incapable of recognising the gravity of the situation, so completely has he been hoodwinked by a 'Malignant Party' of evil counsellors.[20] Given this predicament, with one of the three Estates effectively disabled from pursuing the public good, it becomes the positive duty of the other two Estates to act together in the name of *salus populi*, even if this involves defying the sadly misguided king.

With this contention, the two Houses arrive at their revolutionary conclusion that, at least in conditions of emergency, the highest legislative authority lies not with the king-in-Parliament but with Parliament alone.[21] We find this claim to Parliamentary sovereignty unambiguously put forward in the declaration of 19 May 1642. 'The Prince being but one person, is more subject to accidents of nature and chance, whereby the Common-Wealth may be deprived of the fruit of that trust which was in part reposed in him' (Husbands *et al.* (eds.) 1642: 207–8). When 'cases of such necessity' arise, 'the Wisdome of this State hath intrusted the Houses of Parliament with a power to supply what shall bee wanting on the part of the Prince' (p. 208). The need for this power is obvious in the case of natural disability, but 'the like reason doth and must hold for the exercise of the same power in such cases, where the Royall trust cannot be, or is not discharged, and that the Kingdome runs an evident and imminent danger therby' (*ibid.*). But this is to speak of the very predicament in which, as a result of the machinations of the Malignant Party, the nation now finds itself. It follows that in this emergency the two Houses can and must act according to their own judgment, and 'there needs not the authority of any person or Court to affirme; nor is it in the power of any person or Court to revoke, that judgement' (*ibid.*).

By the end of May 1642, the democratical gentlemen and their allies had fully articulated this new vision of the mixed constitution. Even the core prerogative of the Negative Voice, they now argue, can be set aside by

---

19. For other statements of the theory at this juncture see Mendle 1985: 177.
20. This claim is first strongly stated in the petition about the militia presented to the king on 1 March 1642. See Husbands *et al.* (eds.) 1642: 92–4.
21. On this dramatic revision of the theory of the mixed constitution see Mendle 1985, esp. pp. 176–83. As Mendle 1993 rightly adds, this move in the spring of 1642 undoubtedly involved the two Houses in claiming that sovereignty lay with them alone.

Parliament if the safety of the people might otherwise be jeopardised. We next need to note that, in the course of the months that followed, the two Houses proceeded to open up a different and yet more radical line of attack on the government. Moving beyond their simple invocations of *salus populi*, they began to delve more deeply into their classical heritage, and in particular to appeal yet again to Roman ideas about freedom and servitude.

This further development was prompted by the fact that the government had in the meantime succeeded in mounting a damaging counterattack on their initial line of argument. As Charles I and his advisers soon perceived, the control of the militia was constitutionally a side issue. The key constitutional question was raised by Parliament's underlying rejection of the prerogative of the Negative Voice. Responding to this revolutionary move, the king's advisers went vigorously on the offensive. No one, they responded, can be under any obligation to obey a mere Bill or Ordinance, even if it has been passed by both Houses, if it fails to secure the royal assent. This is because, according to the fundamental laws and customs of the realm, the power to make laws is vested at all times jointly in king-in-Parliament. This reading of the constitution is implicit in several of Charles's Declarations of May 1642,[22] but the clearest exposition can be found in the *Answer to the xix Propositions* composed for the king by Viscount Falkland and Sir John Culpeper and issued on 18 June 1642 (Mendle 1985: 6). The *Answer* unequivocally asserts that 'in this kingdom the Laws are jointly made by a King, by a House of Peers, and by a House of Commons chosen by the People, all having free Votes and particular Priviledges' (Charles I 1999: 168). Furthermore, the essence of the king's standing as one of the three Estates is said to derive from the fact that he possesses a Negative Voice.[23] Speaking in his own person, Charles maintains that any attempt to bypass or even question this prerogative would be to 'deny the freedom of Our Answer, when We have as much right to reject what We think unreasonable, as you have to propose what you think convenient or necessary'. By the terms of the mixed constitution 'the Manage of Our Vote is trusted by the Law, to our Own Judgement and Conscience', and 'most unreasonable it were that two Estates, proposing something to

---

22. See Charles's Answer to Parliament's Declaration of 4 May about Hull (Husbands *et al.* (eds.) 1642: 163–4). See also the King's Answer to Parliament's Declaration of 5 May about the militia (ibid.: 175–6). For the adoption of the same vocabulary by royalist pamphleteers after April 1642 see Mendle 1985: 180–2.
23. Charles I 1999: 155. Fukuda 1997: 24–5 sees in this passage the earliest 'Polybian' definition of the English constitution. But the language of the *Answer* closely echoes the Parliamentary Declarations to which it was a response.

the Third' should be able to bind the third to act according to their will (Charles I 1999: 164).

Charles I's *Answer* has sometimes been seen as a concessive and conciliatory document (Weston 1965: 5, 26, 29). But as soon as we place it in the context of the Parliamentary attack on the royal veto, we can see that it constituted an aggressive and powerful counterblast to the democratical gentlemen and their allies. With its unimpeachable account of how the normal processes of legislation actually operate, and with its consequent reaffirmation of the Negative Voice as an indispensable element in the mixed constitution, the *Answer* furnished the crown and its protagonists with an almost unanswerable legal case. As the democratical gentlemen quickly perceived, if they were to sustain the momentum of their campaign, they needed as a matter of urgency to develop some new and different lines of attack.

It was at this moment that the democratical gentlemen sought to regain the ideological initiative by delving yet more deeply into their classical heritage, and in particular by extending their earlier discussions of freedom and servitude. The main credit for engineering this crucial move appears to be due to Henry Parker, whose *Observations upon some of his Majesties late Answers and Expresses* first appeared anonymously on 2 July 1642.[24] The *Observations* is Parker's most important tract, and as we shall see its neoclassical analysis of freedom and free commonwealths exercised an immediate and pervasive influence on other writers in favour of the parliamentary cause.

Parker's is an unusually complex text, however, and it would be misleading to imply that his account of freedom and slavery carries the main burden of his case. Rather he seems to have taken his principal task to be that of lending full support to the radical interpretation of the mixed constitution already put forward by the two Houses of Parliament. He accordingly begins by reaffirming that *salus populi* is 'the Paramount Law that shall give Law to all humane Lawes', enunciating the principle in exactly the terms that Cicero had employed in his *De legibus* (Parker 1933: 169; cf. Cicero 1928: III, 1, 1–3, pp. 458–60). He next concedes that in normal circumstances 'the legislative power of this Kingdome is partly in the King, and partly in the Kingdome' (Parker 1933: 182). But he then insists that 'where this ordinary course cannot be taken for the preventing of publike mischiefes, any extraordinary course that is for that purpose the most effectual, may justly be taken and

---

24. For an account of the context in which Parker's text appeared see Mendle 1995: 70–89.

executed' in accordance with the paramount duty to ensure that *salus populi* is preserved.[25]

For the purposes of the present argument, however, what matters most about Parker's *Observations* is that, in addition to restating this earlier line of thought, he developed a further and explicitly neo-classical attack on the prerogative of the Negative Voice. If this prerogative, he declares, is indeed pivotal to the operation of the mixed constitution, then we cannot speak of the English as a free nation at all. The effect of the Negative Voice is to take away the liberty not merely of individual subjects but of the people as a whole. It converts the English from a free people into a nation of slaves.

This further argument runs as a groundswell throughout Parker's text, but it may be helpful to distinguish two elements in it. One hinges on the nature of the relationship between the king and Parliament presupposed by the claim that the crown possesses a Negative Voice. With this prerogative, Parker objects, the king 'assumes to himselfe a share in the legislative power' so great as to open up 'a gap to as vast and arbitrary a prerogative as the Grand Seignior has' in Constantinople (Parker 1933: 182–3). For he assumes a power to 'take away the being of Parliament meerely by dissent', thereby making it 'more servile then other inferior Courts' (p. 187). To allow the Negative Voice, in short, is to render Parliament dependent on the king and thereby reduce it to servitude.

The other element in Parker's argument flows from his assumption that 'the Lords and Commons represent the whole Kingdome' and 'are to be accounted by the vertue of representation as the whole body of the State' (*ibid.*: 175, 211). If we allow that the king has a Negative Voice, then 'without the Kings concurrence and consent', the two Houses are reduced to 'livelesse conventions without all vertue and power'. But this is to take away the political virtue and power of the people as a whole. Tracing the implications of this disenfranchisement, Parker closely follows two different formulae used by his classical authorities to describe the onset of national servitude. As we have seen, Livy had equated this condition with the substitution by our rulers of 'their owne will and licentious lust in steede of law' (Livy 1600: 87). Parker repeats that the Negative Voice subjects the entire nation 'to as unbounded a regiment of the Kings meere will, as any Nation under Heaven ever suffered under'. For 'what remains, but that all our lawes, rights, & liberties, be either no where at all determinable, or else only in the Kings breast?' (Parker 1933: 175–6). The other formula to which Parker refers is Aristotle's claim that

---

25. Parker 1933: 182. As Mendle 1995: 48 puts it, the argument amounts to a defence of 'full-blown bicameral parliamentary absolutism'.

(as the English translation of the *Politics* had put it) we fall into a condition of slavery whenever we become subject to the discretion of others, since 'the propertie of bondage is, not to live according to a man's own discretion' (Aristotle 1598, Book VI, ch. 2, pp. 339–40). Parker agrees that, if we permit the king 'to be the sole, supream competent Judge in this case, we resigne all into his hands, we give lifes, liberties, Laws, Parliaments, all to be held at meer discretion' and thereby leave ourselves in bondage (Parker 1933: 209–10).

Charles I had complained in his *Answer to the XIX Propositions* that without the Negative Voice he would be reduced from the status of 'a King of *England*' to a mere 'Duke of *Venice*' (Charles I 1999: 167). Parker daringly picks up the objection as a means of clinching his argument about national servitude. 'Let us look upon the Venetians, and other such free Nations', he responds, and ask ourselves why it is that they are 'so extreamly jealous over their Princes'. It is because they fear 'the sting of Monarchy', which stems (as Livy had said) from the power of monarchs to 'dote upon their owne wills, and despise publike Councels and Laws' (Parker 1933: 192). The jealousy of the Venetians arises, in other words, from their recognition that under a genuine monarchy they would be reduced to slavery. It is 'meerely for fear of this bondage' that they prefer their elected Dukes to the rule of hereditary kings (*ibid*.).

Perhaps foreseeing the conflict to come, Parker adds in minatory tones that no self-respecting people can be expected to endure such servitude. He reiterates that, if a nation is made 'to resigne its owne interest to the will of one Lord, as that that Lord may destroy it without injury', this is to say that the nation in question has been made 'to inslave it selfe' (*ibid*.: 174). Once more we hear strong echoes of the English translation of Aristotle's *Politics*, which had warned that 'no person that is free dooth willingly endure such a state' (Aristotle 1598, Book IV, ch. 10, p. 208). Parker similarly warns that 'few Nations will indure that thraldome which uses to accompany unbounded & unconditionate royalty' (Parker 1933: 180). The reason, he adds, is that it is 'contrarie to the supreme of all Lawes' for 'any Nation to give away its owne proprietie in it selfe absolutely' and thereby 'subject it selfe to a condition of servilitie below men' (p. 186). If kings impose this servitude, Parker implies, they must not be surprised if their subjects throw off this unnatural yoke.

While Parker's intervention was of crucial importance, his neo-classical line of argument was not without precedent. The Parliamentary Remonstrance of 26 May 1642 had already contained a warning that, so long as Parliament is dependent on the will of the king and his evil counsellors, the English will be no better than a nation of slaves:

> We shall likewise addresse our Answer to the Kingdom, not by way
> of appeal (as we are charged) but to prevent them from being their
> own executioners; and from being perswaded, under false colours of
> defending the law, and their own Liberties to destroy both with their
> own hands, by taking their lives, Liberties, and Estates out of their
> hands, whom they have chosen and entrusted therewith; and
> resigning them up unto some evill Counsellors about his Majesty,
> who can lay no other foundation of their own greatnesse, but upon
> the ruine of this, and, in it, of all Parliaments, and in them of the true
> Religion, and the freedome of this Nation.
>
> (Husbands *et al.* (eds.) 1642: 263–4)

The Remonstrance ends by calling on the people to reflect on the treasonous designs of the Malignant Party and ask themselves 'whether if they could master this Parliament by force, they would not hold up the same power to deprive Us of all Parliaments; which are the ground and Pillar of the Subjects Liberty, and that which onely maketh *England* a free Monarchy' (*ibid.*: 279).

After the publication of Parker's *Observations*, these neo-classical hints about public freedom and its forfeiture were far more confidently taken up. The Declaration issued by the two Houses on 14 July[26] maintains that the stark choice now facing 'the free-born English Nation' is either to adhere to the cause of Parliament or else 'to the King seduced by Jesuiticall Counsell and Cavaliers, who have designed all to slavery and confusion' (Husbands *et al.* (eds.) 1642: 464). The Declaration of 2 August presents the dilemma in still more lurid terms.[27] We are being invited to 'yield our selves to the cruel mercy of those who have possessed the King against us' (Husbands *et al.* (eds.) 1642: 492), although it is obvious that their aspiration is 'to cut up the freedom of Parliament by the root, and either take all Parliaments away, or which is worse, make them the instruments of slavery' (p. 494). The final Declaration issued by Parliament before the king raised his standard of war on 22 August recurs to the same theme. The leaders of the Malignant Party 'have now advised and prevailed with his Majesty by this Proclamation, to invite his Subjects to destroy his Parliament and good people by a Civill War; and, by that meanes to bring ruine, confusion, and perpetuall slavery upon the surviving part of a then wretched Kingdome' (p. 509).

It would be an overstatement, however, to suggest that these references to slavery and national servitude necessarily reflect any direct acquaintance

---

26. For the date see Rushworth 1692: 756.   27. For the date see Rushworth 1692: 761.

with classical theories of liberty. These Declarations perhaps imply, but they certainly do not state, the distinctive Roman law assumption that the mere fact of living in dependence on the goodwill of others is sufficient to undermine our liberty and reduce us to servitude. We find a very different picture, however, if we turn to the numerous pamphlets and treatises published in defence of Parliament in the weeks immediately following the appearance of Parker's *Observations* at the start of July. A considerable number of these writers reveal a clear understanding of the classical theory of freedom and slavery, and in several instances they put forward this theory as the essence of their anti-royalist stance.

One of the most forthright statements of the neo-classical case can be found in the anonymous tract of 1 August 1642 entitled *Reasons why this Kingdome ought to Adhere to the Parliament*.[28] We are assured that, despite the calumnies put about by the Malignant Party, the two Houses remain the people's 'onely Sanctuary of their Religion, Lawes, Liberties, and properties' (p. 6). Referring directly to Parker's 'most excellent' *Observations* (p. 2), the author goes on to assail the prerogative of the Negative Voice as uniquely destructive of the nation's liberties. If any decision made by Parliament can be frustrated by the exercise of the royal veto, this gives the king 'an unlimited declarative power of Law above all Courts, in his own breast'. But this means that 'the last Appeale must be to his discretion and understanding, and consequently, the Legislative power [is] His alone' (p. 11). If we now comply with this view of the constitution, the effect will not only be to 'forsake this Parliament, and leave it to the mercy of the Malignants'; it will also be to leave our 'Religion, Lawes, Liberties, and properties open to the spoyle and oppression of an Arbitrary Government' (p. 12). It is just this openness to being spoiled and oppressed, however, which serves in itself to take away our liberty. If Parliament allows the king a Negative Voice, 'this whole Kingdome shall consist only of a King, a Parliament, and Slaves' (p. 14).

Less than two weeks later, the two Houses ordered the printing of a similar argument put forward in *A Remonstrance in Defence of the Lords and Commons in Parliament*.[29] The anonymous author calls on the whole nation to adhere to the two Houses, 'who are the eyes, eares and understanding of the Common wealth' (pp. 5–6). If instead we allow the Malignants to obtain the power they seek, this will bring 'the ruine of the Parliament, the destruction of the Kingdome, and the Lawes and liberties of the Subject' (p. 3).

28. The London book-seller George Thomason (whose comprehensive collection of civil war tracts is now in the British Library) notes the date of publication on the title-page of his copy.
29. Thomason notes on the title-page of his copy that this tract appeared on 11 August 1642.

By defending the Negative Voice, the Malignants hope to 'change the forme of Government of this Kingdome, and make it subject to the Arbitrary power of the king'. But to make a kingdom subject to arbitrary power is to reduce it to servitude. The Malignants are in effect planning to 'become masters of our Religion and liberties to make us slaves' (p. 5).

A further plea to recognise that the very existence of the Negative Voice enslaves the nation can be found in the tract published on 17 August 1642 under the title *Considerations for the Commons in This Age of Distractions*.[30] The Negative Voice gives rise to a consequence that 'must needs sound harsh in the eares of a free people'. This harsh consequence is that 'the King withdrawne by evill Councell may at pleasure take away the very essence of Parliaments meerely by his owne dissent, thereby stripping them of all power in matters of judicature that they may not determine any thing for the good and safety of the Kingdome'. If this prerogative is allowed, 'it must needs follow, that its both vaine and needlesse to trouble the whole Kingdome to make choice of its representative body', for whatever decisions it may reach can always be set aside by the mere dissenting will of the king. The reason why this cannot fail to sound harsh in the ears of a free people is that any king who may 'at pleasure' set aside the laws in this fashion is a king of slaves.[31]

Of all these neo-classical defences of Parliament, however, by far the fullest and most sophisticated was the anonymous treatise published on 15 October 1642 under the title *The Vindication of the Parliament And their Proceedings*.[32] The two enemies now confronting each other are said to be the Malignant Party and the two Houses of Parliament. Quoting the Declaration of 2 August, the author first explains that the goal of the Malignant Party is 'to cut up the freedome of *Parliament* by the root, and either to take all *Parliaments* away, or (which is worse) make them the instruments of slavery'.[33] An easy means of attaining this goal lies ready to hand in the alleged prerogative of the Negative Voice. With this prerogative 'the sole power of managing the affaires of the *Kingdome*' belongs 'onely unto the *King*; and nothing at all to *either*, or *both Houses*' (*The Vindication* 1642, sig. C, fo. 2ᵛ). But to grant the king this 'arbitrary power, to rule us, according to the dictates of his own conscience' is to run the risk of turning ourselves into 'most miserable and wretched slaves' (*ibid.*, sig. D, fo. 3ʳ).

30. Thomason notes the date of publication on the title-page of his copy.
31. All quotations from *Considerations* 1642, sig. A, fo. 3ᵛ.
32. Thomason notes the date of publication on the title-page of his copy. Note that, because of the muddled pagination of *The Vindication*, I have given references by signature mark rather than by page.
33. See *The Vindication*, sig. B, fo. 4ʳ and cf. Husbands *et al.* (eds.) 1642: 494.

As the author is at pains to underline, the mere fact that the king possesses a Negative Voice is sufficient in itself to reduce us to slavery. Speaking in Aesopian vein, he reminds us that, as we can readily learn from the birds and their predators, it is all too easy to live in servitude without suffering actual oppression or constraint:

> For as the Crane had better to keepe his head out of the Wolves mouth, then to put it into his mouth, and then stand at his mercy, whither he will bite off his neck or not, so it is better for every wise man, rather to keepe and preserve those immunities, freedomes, prerogatives, and priviledges, which God, and nature hath given unto him, for the preservation, prosperity and peace of his posterity, person and estate, then to disenfranchize himselfe and relinquish and resigne all in to the hands of another, and to give him power either to impoverish or enrich, either to kill him or keepe him alive.
>
> (*ibid.*, sig. D, fo. 3^v)

An absolute ruler may choose to enrich instead of kill you, but you are none the less a slave for that. What takes away your liberty is the mere fact of living at the mercy of someone else.

Although the author of the *Vindication* assures us that he is writing in the hope of averting 'these *Civill Wars* threatning' (*ibid.*, sig. A, fo. 2^v), he concludes that this prospect of enslavement is enough in itself to justify a resort to armed force. The king has surrounded himself with papists and evil counsellors who 'perswade him that it is lawfull for him to doe what he list'. As a result, the choice now facing the people of England is between '*Popery, or Protestantisme*' and between '*slavery or liberty*' (*ibid.*, sig. D, fo. 4^v). But it would be 'unnaturall, that any Nation should be bound to contribute its own inherent puissance meerely to abet tyranny, and support slavery'.[34] From which it follows that a defensive war must now be justified. We must stand ready to take up arms, and not to lay them down until 'we are assured of a firme peace, and to be ruled as becommeth a free people, who are not borne slaves' (*The Vindication* 1642, sig. E, fo. 1^r).

By the time these revolutionary sentiments had reached print, the two Houses of Parliament had already taken a resolution to raise an army and resist the king. The plots of the Malignant Party and other evil counsellors had left them with no alternative, they now proclaimed, but to 'Declare and Ordaine, that it is, and shall be lawfull for all His Majesties loving Subjects, by force

---

34. *Ibid.*, sig. E, fo. 1^r. Here the author quotes Parker's *Observations*, although without acknowledgment. See Parker 1933: 169–70.

of Armes to resist the said severall parties, and their Accomplices'.[35] Those engaging in such acts of resistance will not only be defending 'the Religion of Almighty God' against the aspiration of the Malignant Party to replace it with popery; they will also be foiling their evil designs by defending 'the Liberties and Peace of the Kingdom' against the imposition of arbitrary government (Husbands *et al.* (eds.) 1642: 499).

Historians have claimed that the arguments used to justify this final decision to resist were essentially contractual in character (see for example Salmon 1959: 80–8; Sanderson 1989, esp. pp. 18–21). The king had broken the terms of his covenant with his people, who had never given up their natural right to set down whatever form of government they had originally consented to set up. Such arguments were certainly brought forward at this juncture, and Henry Parker in his *Observations* makes emphatic use of them (Parker 1933, esp. pp. 167–71). But it is striking that Parliament itself and many of its supporters preferred to justify their decision to go to war in neo-classical rather than in contractarian terms. The final Declarations issued by Parliament in August 1642 make no mention of the natural rights of the sovereign people. They speak instead of the need to liberate the people from being mastered and enslaved by the 'Malignant Party of Papists, those who call themselves Cavaliers, and other ill-affected persons' who have deliberately driven the country into civil war:

> The intention being still the same, not to rest satisfied with having *Hull*, or taking away the ordinance of the *Militia*; But to destroy the Parliament, and be masters of our religion and liberties, to make us slaves, and alter the Government of this Kingdom, and reduce it to the condition of some other countries, which are not governed by Parliaments, and so by Laws, but by the will of the Prince, or rather of those who are about him.   (Husbands *et al.* (eds.) 1642: 497)

It is in the name of staving off such arbitrary government and perpetual slavery, they declare, that they have now decided to raise an army under the earl of Essex, 'with whom, in this Quarrell we will live and dye' (p. 498). From the Parliamentary perspective, the civil war began as a war of national liberation from servitude. If there was any one slogan under which the two Houses finally took up arms, it was that the people of England never, never, never shall be slaves.

35. See Husbands *et al.* (eds.) 1642: 499, who date the declaration to 8 August 1642.

2

Empire and Liberty: A Republican Dilemma

DAVID ARMITAGE

At the heart of the shared European heritage of republicanism lay a tension between the competing demands of two overwhelmingly desirable but ultimately irreconcilable goals: liberty and greatness. History showed that liberty gave birth to republics and that republics strove to safeguard that liberty both internally, for the flourishing of their citizens, and externally, for the security and grandeur of the republic itself. Theory reinforced the historical connection between republican government and liberty. The commitment to liberty under the law, but liberty with responsibility for the collective well-being of the community, has distinguished the republican tradition from its classical origins through to its contemporary revival (Pettit 1993: 164–9; 1997: 35–41). Though the Machiavellian branch of the early-modern republican tradition affirmed this central commitment to liberty, it insisted equally strongly on the primacy of greatness (*grandezza*) in defining the character of the commonwealth. There was nothing novel in either of these commitments, as Quentin Skinner has shown, for both can be found in the prescriptive writings on civil life produced in medieval Italy. Seen from the perspective of thirteenth- and early fourteenth-century republicanism, Machiavelli's defence of the two propositions 'that no city can ever attain greatness unless it upholds a free way of life' and that 'no city can ever uphold a free way of life unless it maintains a republican constitution' appears to be 'a wholehearted defence of traditional values' presented 'in a wholeheartedly traditional way' (Skinner 1990c: 141). However, when viewed from the perspective of seventeenth- and eighteenth-century European republicanism, Machiavelli's account of the relationship between liberty and *grandezza* appears much less stable and reassuring and reveals instead some of that 'acute moral discomfort' that comes from his espousal of incompatible but nonetheless indispensable values (Berlin 1979: 70).

Machiavelli began his analysis of *grandezza* historically with the expulsion of the Tarquins from Rome and theoretically from the origins of that greatness in republican liberty. 'It is truly remarkable to observe the *grandezza* which Athens attained in the space of a hundred years after it had been liberated from the tyranny of Pisistratus', he remarked in *Discorsi*, II, 2. 'But most marvellous of all is it to observe the *grandezza* Rome attained after freeing itself from its kings.' The reason for this rapid acquisition of *grandezza* was not far to seek. Only when the good of the commonwealth was paramount would cities become great, 'and it is beyond question that it is only in republics that the common good (*il bene comune*) is looked to properly in that all that promotes it is carried out'.[1]

Machiavelli inherited this equation between greatness and republican liberty from Sallust, the most popular of all classical historians in early-modern Europe (Burke 1966; Osmond 1993). In the opening chapters of *Bellum Catilinae*, VII, Sallust had argued that the establishment of the Republic in Rome had released the talents of the Roman people which had formerly been repressed under the rule of the kings. So great was the popular thirst for glory that it was indeed remarkable (*incredibile*) how the *civitas* grew once it had recovered its liberty (Sallust 1931: 12–14 (VII, 3); Skinner 1998: 61–4). This passage from Sallust became the *locus classicus* for the equation between republican liberty and the greatness of a free state. Augustine cited it in his discussion in *Civitas dei*, V, 12, of the divine favour which had allowed Rome to be the vehicle for the expansion of Christianity; following Augustine, the author of the *De regimine principum*, I, 5. 2–3, also quoted it and remarked further in Sallustian vein that under republican government 'when [persons] see that the common good is not in the power of one, each attends to it as if it were their own, not as if it were something pertaining to someone else'. Closer to Machiavelli's own time and to his immediate political concerns, both Coluccio Salutati and Leonardo Bruni deployed the same passage in praise of the greatness of republican Florence (Augustine 1928–9: I, 212; Ptolemy of Lucca 1997: 70–1; Osmond 1993: 410–20).

This Sallustian and Machiavellian tradition encouraged the belief that the greatness of the republic derived originally from its liberty. However, Sallust's continuation of his narrative showed that the consequences of pursuing such *grandezza* would lead inevitably to the loss of that liberty both for

---

1. Machiavelli 1984: 287 (*Discorsi*, II, 2): 'Ma sopra tutto maravigliosissima è a considerare a quanta grandezza venne Roma poi che la si liberò da' suoi Re. La ragione è facile a intendere, perché non il bene comune è quello che fa grandi le città'; compare *Discorsi*, I, 58. On the Romans' own dating of their civic liberty from the abolition of the monarchy see Wirszubski 1950: 5.

the republic and for its citizens. The martial virtue and concern for the public good that the citizens exhibited when they had been freed from the repressions of monarchy may have propelled the remarkable growth of the Roman Republic, but (as Sallust regretfully reported) fortune then turned against Rome. The virtuous and the courageous became greedy, ambitious and impious, the character of the republic was changed, and the government itself became cruel and intolerable (*Bellum Catilinae*, x, 1–6; Sallust 1931: 16–18; Skinner 1998: 64–5). Sallust located this declension quite precisely in Roman history during the dictatorship of Lucius Sulla. From that point onward, the pursuit of individual advantage replaced the effort to protect the good of the community, the army which had been sent to conquer distant lands became debilitated by luxury, and all of the former virtues that had sustained Rome in its acquisition of territory and greatness were scorned and abandoned (*Bellum Catilinae*, xi, 4–7, xii, 1–2; Sallust 1931: 18–20).

Machiavelli followed Sallust not only in his account of the origins of Roman *grandezza* but also in his analysis of Roman declension. Rome had used two methods to facilitate its territorial expansion. It had armed the plebs and admitted foreigners to citizenship, but these methods had led to tumults and hence to internal instability (*Discorsi*, i, 6; Machiavelli 1984: 77–8). Though Machiavelli's defence of such tumults marked his greatest departure from the attachment of pre-humanist republicans to internal peace, his argument that they contributed to the decline of the Roman republic was merely one part of his analysis of the contribution of expansion towards the destruction of Roman liberty. Rome's *grandezza* could not have been achieved without the necessary extension of military commands, he argued, but this had led directly to servitude (*servitù*) for the Roman people; the liberty which had been won with the expulsion of the monarchy ended during the dictatorships of Sulla and Marius, which in turn provided the precedent for the tyranny of Julius Caesar and the loss of popular liberty under the emperors (*Discorsi*, iii, 24; Machiavelli 1984: 529–30).

Machiavelli's major advance beyond the limits of Sallust's argument was to show that it would be impossible for any state to avoid the compulsions of expansion, and hence to escape the loss of its liberty. Rome could never have achieved *grandezza* without instituting the practical measures that had led to internal dissension and hence to the destruction of its republican liberty; likewise, those states that did not follow the expansionist policies of the Romans rendered themselves vulnerable to conquest by others and would still lose their liberty as their competitors overran them in due course. Machiavelli's counter-examples were Venice and Sparta, the states that had, respectively, refused in the interests of internal harmony to arm the plebs and declined to increase population by admitting foreigners to citizenship. Each had hoped thereby to resist the temptation to expand in order to safeguard the liberty of the commonwealth. Sparta remained stable for eight hundred years until the Theban revolt checked its ambitions to occupy all the cities of Greece; Venice similarly lost its liberty along with all of its territories on the *terraferma* in one day at the battle of Agnadello in 1509 (Machiavelli 1964: III, 1188–1205; Gilbert 1969; Cervelli 1974). 'What will happen to the others if this [republic] burned and froze in a few days only?' Machiavelli asked. 'And if justice and force and union for so great an *impero* did not avail?'[2] The alternatives were stark: a republic could pursue *grandezza*, or it could safeguard its liberty and maintain tranquil but temporary security. Such security could not be guaranteed, because the republic would be forced to expand and all would be lost. Machiavelli's recommendation was unequivocal: *grandezza* was a greater good than stability. 'Wherefore' (in the words of James Harrington), 'you are to take the course of Rome' (Harrington 1977: 330).

Once Machiavelli had shown that attack was the best form of defence, and that Roman *ordini* would be the essential base for a successful martial republic, he defined more precisely the means by which an *impero* should be enlarged, and the conditions that would make expansion possible. A territory could be augmented by leagues of confederacy as the Tuscans had done; by unequal confederations, with the expansive power keeping the headship of any league to itself as Rome had done; or, least effectively of all, by simply annexing conquered territory without confederation, thus bringing instability and collapse upon republics like Athens and Sparta which could not support the weight of new conquest (*Discorsi*, II, 4). To hold such acquisitions, many soldiers and settlers would be needed, so every effort should be made to increase the population. A small root could not support a great trunk, so 'whoever would make any City great, and apt for Dominion (*faccia grande imperio*), must endeavour with all industry to throng it with inhabitants, otherwise it will be impossible to bring it to any great perfection'.[3] The 'true ways of enlarging an empire (*acquistare imperio*)' were therefore to increase the population; to ally with, and not to subject, other states; to

---

2. Machiavelli 1965a, p. 264 (*Decennale*, II, 178–80): 'Che fia degli altri se questo arse ed alse / in pochi giorni? e se a cotanto impero / iustizia e forza e unione non valse?'; Machiavelli 1965b: III, 1461. Compare Machiavelli, *Dell'asino d'oro*, V, 49–60, in Machiavelli 1965a: 287–8.

3. Machiavelli 1984: 301 (*Discorsi*, II, 3): 'Quegli che disegnono che una città faccia grande imperio, si debbono con ogni industria ingegnare di farla piena di abitori'; Machiavelli 1680: 337. I use Henry Neville's English translation of Machiavelli because it was the one best known to British authors of the eighteenth century, and the one most frequently quoted by them.

dispatch colonies into conquered territory; to put war-booty into the public coffers; to campaign by means of battles not sieges; to keep individuals poor in order to increase public wealth; and to maintain military discipline. The only viable alternative to taking the course of Rome would be to rein in ambition, prohibit expansion, adopt a defensive posture, and make good internal laws, like the commonwealths of Germany: 'whoever takes any other course, rather ruines than advantages himself, for new Conquests are prejudicial a thousand ways, and especially when your force does not encrease with your Territory, and you are not able to keep what you conquer'.[4]

Machiavelli's analysis of expansion offered three possibilities. A state could follow the course of Rome and order itself internally to be capable of mastering its external environment. It would be shaken by popular dissent, its life-span would be limited, but it would nonetheless be glorious and would ride the flux of time. The German republics presented the second possibility, that of defensive stability and curbed ambition, which seemed to have been successful, at least temporarily. Finally, the model of Sparta, Athens or Venice could be followed, which guaranteed internal tranquillity and stability, but only if neither necessity nor greed forced the state to expand (*Discorsi*, II, 3–4). Machiavelli's recommendation instead of the *ordine romano* was not unequivocal. The main reason to prefer the course of Rome was not glory but security in a world of change and ambition. The Roman model would incur the cost of dissent between the nobility and the people; most damagingly, the further the marches of the empire extended away from the centre, the greater was the need to prolong military commands. This would lead to partisanship in the army, giving such men as Marius, Sulla and Caesar the means to effect constitutional overthrow. The empire might not have expanded so rapidly without that prolongation of commands, but it would not thereby have fallen so quickly into servitude (*servitù*) (*Discorsi*, III, 24; Machiavelli 1984: 301–7, 530). *Imperio* and *libertà* would, at last, be incompatible.

As Maurizio Viroli has suggested, 'in recommending the Roman model, Machiavelli was actually sacrificing the substance of the *vivere politico* in the pursuit of greatness' (Viroli 1990: 158–9; cf. 1998: 127). Just such a charge was made by one of Machiavelli's most hostile critics, the Venetian Paolo Paruta. Paruta's *Discorsi politici* (1599) dismissed the Florentine's *Discorsi* as 'already buried in oblivion', and asked, contrary to Machiavelli:

4. Machiavelli 1984: 347 (*Discorsi*, II, 19): 'E chi si governa altrimenti, cerca non la sua vita ma la sua morte e rovina; perché in mille modi e per molte cagioni gli acquisti sono dannosi. Perché gli sta molto bene insieme acquistare imperio e non forze; e qui acuista imperio e non forze insieme, conviene che rovini'; Machiavelli 1680: 358. Compare Viroli 1998: 139–42.

> ... who can doubt but that the true end of a City is to have her Citizens
> live vertuously, not the inlarging of her Empire?... the perfection of
> Government lies in making a City vertuous, not in making her Mistress
> of many Countries. Nay the increasing of Territories, as it is commonly
> coupled with some injustice, so it is remote from the true end of good
> Laws, which never part from what is honest. Governments which aim
> at Empire are usually short lived; which denotes their imperfection.
>
> (Paruta 1657: 111, 10)

Machiavelli would have answered Paruta's charge by invoking the inescapable compulsions of *necessità*, *ambizione* and the flux of human affairs (*Discorsi*, I, 6). His crucial insight was to link the strength of internal institutions to the pressures of external policy, thereby to show that '[t]he Conquests of *Common-wealths* that are ill Governed, and contrary to the Mould of the *Romans*, do conduce more to the Ruine, than Advancement of their Affairs'.[5] This was the lesson taught by Venice, Sparta and the Athenian commonwealth; the commonwealths of contemporary Germany had not yet been tested in this way, but the pessimism of Machiavelli's belief that all rulers demand ever larger dominions, however aware they might be of the costs, would ensure that they too would be tried before too long.

Machiavelli's distinction between the stable, defensive yet ultimately vulnerable commonwealth for preservation, and the tumultuous, aggressive, and finally servile commonwealth for expansion drew upon Polybius's discussion of the peculiar fate of the Roman Republic. Polybius had also contrasted Rome with Sparta, wherein Lycurgus's legislation had ensured harmony among the citizens, kept the territory intact and preserved his country's liberty by equally dividing landed property and banning money, as well as by instituting military training. However, Lycurgus had not left any safeguards against territorial aggrandisement on the part of the Spartans, so that 'when the Lacedaemonians attempted to win supremacy in Greece it was not long before they were in danger of losing their liberty'. Polybius's conclusion was therefore the one that Machiavelli followed: 'the Spartan constitution is deficient, and ... the Roman is superior and certainly better devised for the attainment of power'.[6] Rome was best fitted for empire, Sparta for liberty, but in the end neither could endure. Sparta would be tempted to expand, and

---

5. Machiavelli 1680: 357; Machiavelli 1984: 344 (*Discorsi*, II, 19): 'Che gli acquisti nelle republiche non bene ordinate, e che secondo la romana virtù non procedano, sono a ruina, non a esaltazione di esse.'
6. Polybius 1979: 344 (*Historiae*, VI, 48–50); on Machiavelli's debt to Polybius see especially Sasso 1967.

Rome would be debilitated by the seductions of petty competition for public office and the pleasures of indolent luxury. Machiavelli faced this pessimism squarely, but saw no alternative to the servitude compelled by over-ambitious expansion: that way destruction lay, but at least the bitter pill of servitude would be sweetened by the brief taste of glory that came with *grandezza*.

The Machiavellian compound of Sallust's moral account of Roman decline and Polybius's constitutional analysis provided an enduring model for later republicans to understand the competing pressures of liberty at home and expansion abroad. British republicans, in particular, attempted to reconcile the convergent, but antagonistic, claims of empire and liberty, particularly in the context of European war, mercantilist political economy and the creation of the British Empire in the period between the Elizabethan *fin-de-siècle* and the end of the Seven Years War. The Machiavellian typology of republics for expansion and those for stability first appeared as a tool to analyse English policy in 1594 when Richard Beacon, the disaffected former Queen's Attorney for the Irish county of Munster, published his Machiavellian 'Politique Discourse' on the state of Ireland, *Solon His Follie* (1594). Beacon argued that a 'peaceable & permanent' commonwealth should follow the example of the Spartans and not admit foreigners, and that of the Venetians, in fortifying a naturally defensible site; however, 'such as shall ayme at honour and glory' must take the course of Rome, and naturalise foreigners, arm the people, and make alliances. Yet neither form of commonwealth 'may be founde so happy and permanent, but at the last . . . they fall with their owne weight and poyse to the ground', the difference being that the state aiming at honour (or, in Machiavelli's terms, the commonwealth for expansion) 'leaveth the image of true glory, as a lively picture, to invest a perpetuall memory of a worthy and excellent Institution'. In these terms, to be a commonwealth for preservation was fit only for 'servile commonweales', like Pisa, Cremona or, implicitly, Ireland when held under English subjection. The dilemma was which form of state to imitate, and hence in the end which form of destruction or decline to face.[7]

One solution to the problem Machiavelli presented was the possibility that he had presented a false opposition, and hence that his dilemma was not a dilemma at all. If it were possible to combine the longevity and stability of a commonwealth for preservation with the glory and *grandezza* of a commonwealth for increase, then it might be possible to combine the liberty characteristic of the free state with territorial expansion. 'But may not one

---

7. Beacon 1996: 86, 87; on Beacon's debt to Machiavelli see generally Peltonen 1994 and specifically on his debt to *Discorsi*, I, 6, Peltonen 1995: 99–102.

selfesame common-weale, ayme at the one and the other?' asked one character
in Beacon's dialogue: 'No verily', replied his interlocutor brusquely, before
paraphrasing *Discorsi*, II, 3: a commonwealth for preservation was like a tree
with a slender root – it could not stay upright for long if it extended itself
too far and too fast (Beacon 1996: 87).

The challenge of combining liberty and empire was, however, taken up
half a century later by James Harrington in *The Commonwealth of Oceana*
(1656). The Machiavellian distinction between Rome and Sparta (or Venice)
was fundamental to Harrington's presentation of the options facing the
British republic under the Protectorate. Harrington paraphrased the whole
of Machiavelli's discussion from *Discorsi*, I, 6, on the grounds that 'he that
will erect a commonwealth against the judgment of Machiavel, is obliged to
give such reasons for his enterprise as must not go on begging' (Harrington
1977: 273–4). The *Oceana* constituted an attempt to break free from compulsions of the Machiavellian categories that afflicted both static and expansive
republics by proposing measures that could maintain the internal stability
of an externally expanding commonwealth. Harrington proposed measures
to prevent the kind of strife between the plebs and the nobility that had
destroyed Roman liberty, thereby making Oceana 'a commonwealth for increase . . . upon the mightiest foundation that any hath been laid from the
beginning of the world'. Harrington's solution was, like Machiavelli's, based
upon the Roman model of unequal leagues, in which the metropolitan state
retained the leadership, rather than the subordination of conquered territory
(like the Athenians or the Spartans) or confederation on the Tuscan model.
To 'take the course of Rome' would ensure the maintenance of liberty and
the achievement of *grandezza*; Oceana might then become what Harrington
(*contra* Machiavelli) thought Rome to have been, 'a commonwealth . . . both
for increase and preservation', as he put it in *The Prerogative of Popular
Government* (1658) (Harrington 1977: 160, 446).

Harrington's solution to Machiavelli's dilemma was not sufficiently convincing for his successors to abandon the typology of expanding and non-
expanding commonwealths, to ignore Machiavelli's own account of the
methods and results of expansion, or to cease looking for their own solutions
to the problem of reconciling liberty and empire (Worden 1991a: 466–8).
As I have argued elsewhere, Sallust and Machiavelli provided English republicans in the 1650s besides Harrington with the means to understand the
military successes of the Rump in Britain, Ireland and Europe, as well as
with a series of warnings regarding the consequences of territorial expansion for hard-won republican liberty (Armitage 1992, 1995). Marchamont

Nedham, for instance, took the victories of the Rump to be further evidence that the acquisition of liberty rendered a liberated people peculiarly courageous, and cited Sallust frequently to affirm his point. However, by the time of the Protectorate, he put those successes, and hence liberty itself, firmly in the past tense, and implied that the inevitable declension from liberty through expansion to debility and corruption had occurred in four short years (Nedham 1969: 1, 116–17; 1656: 19, 58). In this assessment, he seems to have been supported by John Milton, who had similarly cited Sallust in the aftermath of the regicide, and had seen the great actions of the Rump as evidence that the Commonwealth had been infused with the ancient spirit of republican liberty, but came to lament the failure to create 'another *Rome* in the west', largely because the rule of Cromwell – an English Sulla – had extinguished liberty and allowed for the return of the monarchy (Milton 1953–82: III, 190; VII, 357; Armitage 1995: 210–14).

After the Restoration, this analysis of the declension of the Commonwealth was shared by Milton and Nedham's fellow-republican, Algernon Sidney, who rehabilitated Machiavelli's typology during the mid-1660s in his *Court Maxims* (*c.* 1663–4). Sidney's spokesman for republicanism in the dialogue judged the condition of England to be 'without discipline, poor, discontented . . . [and] easily subdued', and hence peculiarly vulnerable to Europe's aspiring universal monarch, Louis XIV. In such a condition, any nation that could not aspire to hegemony must resist it at all costs, for '[f]reedom is the greatest advantage next to dominion'. The spokesman for the court argues that it is not dominion alone that should be sought but rather that 'enlargement of dominion and increase of riches and power by conquest' together benefit a nation, to which the commonwealthman makes the Machiavellian reply that only a nation that is constituted for enlargement can profit, even temporarily, from expansion; moreover, 'if government be constituted for other ends, that in a society we may live free, happy and safe', conquest would only be an advantage if it promoted those quite precise goals. Conquests destroyed Sparta and put an end to its 'liberty and glory'; Venice and the Swiss Confederation would be vulnerable if they expanded; even the Spanish monarchy had been 'weakened, dispeopled, and ruined by its own conquests'. Only conquests that do not tend to corrupt the manners of a nation could be justified. Once again, Rome was the great historical example. In the 'fullness of liberty', the law safeguarded the freedom of individuals, since '[t]he Roman virtue was the effect of their good laws and discipline', and Rome's enemies proved no match for it. Nevertheless, '[l]ess glory might have been more permanent', and 'success followed with a prodigious affluence of riches, introduced ambition and avarice, raising some citizens above the power of the law. Then did that victorious people turn its conquering hand into its own bowels, and fell by its own sword' (Sidney 1996: 78, 155, 15–16, 136–7).

Sidney's resuscitation of Machiavelli's warnings about the moral dangers of expansion without adequate constitutional precautions was intended less to school the readers of his manuscript in the best methods to acquire a territorial empire, let alone a universal monarchy, than to affirm the necessity of upholding fragile liberty in a world dominated by reason of state politics. When Sidney returned to the problems of liberty and empire in the *Discourses Concerning Government* (1681–3), he refused to judge between states that found 'felicity . . . in the fullness and stability of liberty, integrity, virtue and the enjoyment of their own' (like Sparta) 'rather than in riches, power, and dominion over others' (like Rome). This could be illustrated by the history of the commonwealths of Italy that fought so valiantly against Rome before they were absorbed into the Republic: '[t]he power and virtue of the Italians grew up, decayed and perished with their liberty', but once 'they were all brought under the Romans, either as associates or subjects, they made the greatest strength that ever was in the world'. Sidney also repeated the Sallustian maxim that the institution of republican liberty in England would lead to the same outburst of courage and industry that the ancient republics had experienced on the recovery of their liberty: 'Men would have the same love to the publick as the Spartans and the Romans had, if there was the same reason for it' – witness the English Commonwealth in the early 1650s, the Swiss Confederation and the Dutch Republic (Sidney 1990: 213, 216).

Despite his admiration for classical republics, Sidney accepted one of the major tenets of modern reason of state that trade provided the sinews of war: 'the best judges of these matters have always given the preference to those constitutions that principally intend war, and make use of trade as assisting to that end', since 'those only can be safe who are strong' (Sidney 1990: 204–5). As commentators noted from the late seventeenth century, the admiration of earlier republican theorists for Sparta – which had banned negotiable currency under the laws of Lycurgus, in order to prevent commerce – was now unsustainable in a world where commerce was a major reason of state. As the political economist Nicholas Barbon argued in 1690, '*Livy*, and those . . . Antient Writers . . . have been very exact in describing the several forms of Military Discipline, but take no Notice of *Trade*; and *Machiavel* a Modern Writer, and the best, though he lived in a Government, where the Family of *Medicis* had advanced themselves to the Sovereignty by their Riches, acquired by Merchandizing, doth not mention *Trade*, as any way interested in the Affairs of State' (Barbon 1690, sig. A3^{r-v}). Writing fifty years later, David Hume agreed: 'There is not a word of Trade in all Matchiavel, which is strange considering that Florence rose only by Trade'.[8] This remark is found among Hume's early memoranda, sandwiched between quotations from Cicero's *De officiis* and Sir Josiah Child's *A New Discourse of Trade* (1665), as if Hume were passing intellectually from the old world of republican mores to the new compulsions of commercial society. That transition had been under way in the British republican tradition at least since the work of Algernon Sidney, for whom trade would provide the sinews of war, and war the means to greatness. What distinguished British republicanism in the two generations before David Hume was the belief that commerce had so altered the maxims of republican politics that the Machiavellian dilemma might either be resolved or, at least, overcome in ways that the Florentine could not possibly have imagined.[9] However, even in this context, he could be rehabilitated as a guide to colonial policy, as James Oglethorpe, the founder of the Georgia colony, lamented in 1732 that the '*Florentine* Historian' had not written extensively about colonies, but nonetheless skilfully excerpted the *Istorie fiorentine* (II, 1), the *Principe* (III, x) and the *Discorsi* (I, 1, 10, 11; II, 6, 7, 19) to illustrate Machiavelli's compatibility with the new maxims of mercantilism enshrined in Sir Josiah Child's *Discourse Concerning Plantations* (1692).[10]

The political economists of the 1690s agreed that European states, whether republics or monarchies, could no longer afford to choose whether they would be self-sufficient or expansive, nor whether they should be trading or war-making commonwealths. They were all now interdependent, so that the Spartan option of economic autarchy was no longer viable. War and trade were now inextricably linked in ways that challenged some of the most cherished tenets of the republican tradition, but might yet allow the reconciliation of liberty and empire. Charles Davenant, for one, expressed the moralistic concern that commerce would bring in luxury, and luxury, debility, but recognised that the commercial conditions of contemporary Europe rendered trade a 'necessary evil' for every state. Commerce would now be the only guarantee of either stability or greatness, and since a nation

---

8. National Library of Scotland (hereafter NLS) MS 23159, item 14, fo. 16, in Hume 1948: 508; compare Hume 1985: 87–8.

9. However, for passing remarks on the subject of trade see Machiavelli 1989: 79 (*Principe*, XXI); Machiavelli 1984: 300 (*Discorsi*, II, 2); Machiavelli 1988: 361 (*Istorie fiorentine*, VIII, 36).

10. [Oglethorpe] 1732: 5–17 (= Machiavelli 1680: 22–4, 201, 213, 268–9, 281, 283, 293–4, 341, 342, 357), 31–40 (= Child 1692: 178–94).

could no longer be a Sparta, it should take the course of Venice (and other commercial republics) in order to reach the eminence of Rome – but with one major proviso, that it should not lead to the military expansion that had caused the collapse of Roman liberty: 'if trade cannot be made subservient to the nation's safety, it ought to be no more encouraged here than it was in Sparta: And it can never tend to make us safe, unless it be so managed as to make us encrease in shipping and in the breed of seamen.' An empire of the seas could provide *grandezza* without the need for large armies, extended military commands, or the takeover of civilian government by over-mighty generals. Instead, maritime empire could enrich the nation, render it stable in the arena of international power politics, and offer greatness without endangering liberty (Davenant 1771: I, 30; II, 275).

The empirical observation that republics like Florence, Venice and the Dutch Republic had been so economically vibrant in the early-modern period strengthened the theoretical connection between republican liberty and commerce. For instance, Henry Parker in his *Of a Free Trade* (1648) had attributed that connection to the influence merchants had over the administration in 'popular states', while later Davenant argued, with a crucial revision of Sallust's analysis of the origins of greatness in liberty, that 'industry has its first foundation in liberty', and that the absolute monarchies of contemporary Europe would fail in achieving commercial greatness just as their predecessors in ancient times had failed to gain the glory of *grandezza*: 'They who are either slaves, or who believe their freedoms precarious, can neither succeed in trade nor meliorate a country' (Parker 1648: 3, 4; Davenant 1771: II, 35; 1701: 288). John Trenchard and Thomas Gordon expressed this argument in classic form in *Cato's Letters* (1720–3). The title of the essay in which Trenchard elaborated it most fully captured its modern form precisely: 'Trade and Naval Power the Offspring of Civil Liberty only, and cannot subsist without it'. Trenchard agreed with Davenant that the whole commercial infrastructure of an absolute monarchy was precarious because it was not protected from the depredations of the monarch by laws that secured property, and he also argued that the luxurious demands of the court necessarily distorted the productive capacity of the nation. However, in a commonwealth where law did safeguard liberty, property would be secure, republican moderation would drive consumption, and the demands of trade would ensure that the nation's military needs were upheld not by soldiers (who might be the tools of tyranny) but by sailors, who presented no threat to the liberty that their duty defending commerce could only promote. For these reasons, liberty would guarantee success in the competition for commercial *grandezza*, because 'despotick monarchs, though infinitely powerful at land, yet could never rival Neptune, and extend their empire over the liquid world' (Trenchard and Gordon 1995, I, 442, 445–6, 447). In his 1728 translation of Tacitus, Gordon reaffirmed the value of 'States formed for peace' (or, in Machiavellian terms, commonwealths for preservation) such as Sparta and Venice: 'The former lasted eight hundred years, and the other has lasted twelve hundred, without any Revolution: what errors they both committed, were owing to their attempts to conquer, for which they were not formed' (Tacitus 1728: I, 124).

The most influential assessment of Britain's mercantile commitments in the context of the argument about the relationship between empire and liberty came in the concluding pages of Bolingbroke's *The Idea of a Patriot King* (1738). Bolingbroke had consistently maintained the classical republican contention that liberty was only secure under law, and that one is 'free not from the law, but by the law'.[11] He also followed the Sallustian and Machiavellian narrative that located the origins of Roman greatness in the acquisition of liberty after the expulsion of the Tarquins, but warned that '[a] wise and brave people will neither be cozened, nor bullied out of their liberty, but a wise and brave people may cease to be such; they may degenerate' (Bolingbroke 1997: 111). In light of such a possibility, it would be necessary to erect a constitution that could prevent such corruption by protecting popular liberty, while bearing in mind the compulsions of mercantilist political economy. This was the task that Bolingbroke set himself while writing *The Idea of a Patriot King*. In that work, Bolingbroke proposed a model of kingship in accord with the mirror-for-princes tradition and the moral advice of Cicero's *De officiis* that also upheld the programme of national unity promoted by the opposition to Sir Robert Walpole and that accorded with the blue-water commercial and colonial policies espoused by English Tories in the aftermath of the Glorious Revolution and the War of the Spanish Succession (Bolingbroke 1997: xx–xxii). The Patriot King would hold the balance between Britain's political parties in order to prevent the corruption of Parliament that Bolingbroke had argued throughout the early 1730s would threaten liberty by denying popular political participation, would undermine property rights in pursuit of invasive taxation and would raise the spectre of permanent standing armies that might be turned against the British people rather than their enemies. The Patriot King's external policies would be consonant with these internal procedures by acknowledging the interests of Britain as an island nation, and hence as a commercial republic, thereby providing the foundations for

---

11. Bolingbroke 1733: 4; Bolingbroke 1997: 196. On the Roman origins of this conception see Wirszubski 1950: 7–9.

prosperity and the survival of liberty. The sea was Britain's natural element, and a navy its natural defence force. Continental commitments in Europe would only encourage the growth of a standing army, while concentrating resources upon the navy would render Britain 'the guardian of liberty' throughout Europe. The sources of greatness would be commercial, not territorial: 'To give ease and encouragement to a manufactory at home, to assist and protect trade abroad, to improve and keep in heart the national colonies, like so many farms of the mother country, will be the principal and constant parts of the attention of such a prince.' Bolingbroke concluded that if such a prince could be found – or trained – nothing could be more inspiring than '[a] king, in the temper of whose government, like that of Nerva, things so seldom allied as empire and liberty are intimately mixed, co-exist together inseparably, and constitute one real essence'.[12]

Bolingbroke's solution to the republican dilemma of empire and liberty was historically speculative and theoretically unstable. It was speculative because it depended so heavily on the unreliable reversionary interest of the heir to the throne, Frederick, Prince of Wales; moreover, it was unstable because it required the emergence of a monarch committed above all to the public good, who would hence be that republican oxymoron, a patriot king. Though the authority of monarchs was never deemed decisively incompatible with a neo-Roman conception of liberty, later British thinkers within the republican and neo-Roman traditions found it increasingly difficult to identify a patriot king or to endorse any particular monarch for their Nerva-like combination of empire and liberty (Skinner 1998: 53–5; Armitage 1997). Future appeals to the compatibility of empire and liberty within British political discourse would henceforth seem either doomed or paradoxical: when Bolingbroke's admirer, Disraeli, repeatedly asserted their amalgamation, Gladstone could cynically reply that he meant only 'Liberty for ourselves, Empire over the rest of mankind' (Koebner and Schmidt 1964: 46, 160; Taylor 1991). Bolingbroke's attempt to reconcile what had been classically irreconcilable failed.

More influential, though yet hardly decisive, as a solution to the dilemma of liberty and empire was Montesquieu's. In the *Considérations sur les causes de la grandeur des Romains et de leur décadence* (1734), he had argued, along recognisably Sallustian and Machiavellian lines, that the collapse of Rome was due

---

12. Bolingbroke 1997: 278, 277, 293; compare Tacitus, *Agricola*, iii, 2: 'Nerva Caesar res olim dissociabiles miscuit, *principatum* et libertatem', crucially revised by Francis Bacon in the *Advancement of Learning* as 'divus Nerva res olim insociabiles miscuisset, *imperium* et libertatem' (Bacon 1730: ii, 439): my emphasis.

to the extension of the empire. While Roman sovereignty extended only as far as Italy, he argued, the republic remained stable, as every citizen could be a soldier. Once it had expanded beyond the Alps, soldiers identified not with the Republic, but with their commanders, beginning with Sulla, Marius, Pompey and Caesar. The offer of Roman citizenship to newly conquered peoples diluted Roman patriotism, and made the deliberations of the *comitia* ever more tumultuous: 'The grandeur of the republic was the only source of that calamity, and exasperated popular tumults into civil wars.' Rome had been founded for *grandeur*, and successfully so, but the speed with which it acquired greatness was fatal to liberty: 'She lost her liberty, because she compleated her work too soon.'[13] However, when Montesquieu came to write the *Esprit des lois*, he argued that the compulsions diagnosed by Machiavelli were no longer applicable to modern politics: 'One has begun to be cured of Machiavellianism (*Machiavelisme*), and one will continue to be cured.' Princes had gradually abandoned this *Machiavelisme* as they realised that only moderation brings prosperity, and that commerce was now the sole source of such prosperity. Trade, for Montesquieu, not only rendered Machiavelli's maxims outdated; it made his principles harmless. In line with arguments developed by British republican theorists during the previous century, Montesquieu held that Britain was the only nation in Europe whose constitution was constructed to promote liberty – just as Rome was built for expansion, Sparta for war, Israel for religion, Marseilles for trade, China for natural tranquillity, and Rhodes for navigation. The separation of powers between the executive and the legislative branches of government prevented any danger of arbitrary rule, and the citizens rested secure in the knowledge that they had nothing to fear from one another, so that the tumults that had propelled Rome's destruction need not be feared. Britain retained its liberty at home by constitutional separation, and maintained its integrity abroad by eschewing overseas conquest, instead planting colonies 'to extend its commerce more than its domination' which would be defended by a navy, not by a standing army. If its terrain were fertile, then the people would be self-sufficient, not ambitious for conquest, and hence secure in the liberty their constitution guaranteed for them. Liberty would foster commerce, and Britain could become everything that the aspirant universal monarchies of seventeenth-century Europe were not, and could not be – an empire for liberty.[14]

13. Montesquieu 1752: 150, 153; 1951: II, 119 ('Ce fut uniquement la grandeur de la République qui fit le mal et qui changea en guerres civiles les tumultes populaires') II, 120 ('Elle perdit sa liberté parce qu'elle acheva trop tôt son ouvrage').
14. Montesquieu 1989: 389 (XXI, 20), 156 (XI, 5), 157–65 (XI, 6), 328–9 (XIX, 17).

Scottish republicans like Hume and Smith reverted to the anxiety transmitted from Sallust to Machiavelli and beyond. In this respect, at least, both Hume and Smith remained firmly within the confines of the republican tradition (cf. Robertson 1983b). Though Hume repeatedly doubted the applicability of Machiavellian politics to the world of commercial modernity, he shared Machiavelli's interest in the pathology of territorial expansion. As he put it in an early note (*c.* 1740) which he later cannibalised for the conclusion to his later essay 'Of the Balance of Power' (1752):

> There seems to be a natural Course of Things, which brings on the Destruction of great Empires. They push their Conquests till they come to barbarous Nations, which stop their Progress, by the Difficulty of subsisting great Armies. After that, the Nobility & considerable Men of the conquering Nation & best Provinces withdraw gradually from the frontier Army, by reason of its Distance from the Capital & barbarity of the Country, in which they quarter: They forget the Use of War. Their barbarous Soldiers become their Masters. These have no Law but their Sword, both from their bad Education, & from their distance from the Sovereign to whom they bear no Affection. Hence Disorder, Violence, Anarchy, Tyranny, & Dissolution of Empire.[15]

Hume rejected the argument that luxury had been responsible for the decline of the Roman commonwealth: the cause of the 'disorders in the ROMAN state' was constitutional not commercial, and 'really proceeded from an ill modelled government, and the unlimited extent of conquests' (Hume 1985: 276 ('Of Refinement in the Arts')). Commerce may have fundamentally altered reasons of state between the classical and the modern periods but Hume maintained the argument that territorial empire presented the greatest threat to liberty, even in modern Europe, at least until the spectre of French universal monarchy had been exorcised by Britain's victories in the Seven Years War (Robertson 1993: 351–6).

At the end of the 'this war', in the spring of 1763, Adam Smith lectured his students at Glasgow on the respective fates of 'a defensive republick' and 'a conquering republick'. He followed Machiavelli's typology in the *Discorsi*, and judged the Greek city-states to be defensive, while Rome and Carthage were conquering republics. Defensive republics declined in strength and power as the arts, commerce and, consequently, refinement and politeness

15. NLS MS 23159, item 14, fo. 27, in Hume 1948: 517–18 (corrected); cf. Hume 1985: 341 ('Of the Balance of Power').

shrank the numbers of willing and available soldier-citizens: 'All states of this sort would therefore naturally come to ruin, its power being diminished by the introduction of arts and commerce.' Moreover, conquering republics 'must hold by a various precarious tenure; not indeed that they are in danger from externall enemies, but as their liberty is in danger by its own subjects' who refuse to serve once they are softened by 'arts and luxury'. A succession of mercenary armies accelerated Rome's slide towards imperial autocracy and hence military monarchy that had begun with the dictatorship of Sulla (who had at least allowed republican government to remain for thirty or forty years after he held the office), gathered pace under Pompey and Julius Caesar, whose perpetual dictatorship paved the way at last for the principate of Augustus: 'And the same will be the case in all conquering republicks where ever a mercenary army at the disposall of the generall is in use.' Athens did not admit foreigners to the citizenship, and hence 'never increased in its power so as to be able greatly to extend its conquests'; meanwhile, Rome, which did extend its citizenship to conquered peoples, 'increased vastly in power and opulence, which at last brought the common wealth to ruin'.[16]

Hume and Smith revised the Sallustian and Machiavellian explanation of declension in light of the new maxims of politeness, political economy, commerce and refinement, but each emphasised their relevance for the world of commercial modernity and imperial expansion. Hume took the end of the Seven Years War as a decisive sign that universal monarchy, on the neo-Roman model, would no longer pose a threat to the liberties of Europe, but continued to hope that Britain's burgeoning territorial empire in North America would be shattered by revolt. Smith may have been more apprehensive of the costs of commerce and conquest in the months when the Peace of Paris was being negotiated, but he, too, had reason to applaud the revolt of the Thirteen Colonies which provided the immediate occasion for the publication of his *Wealth of Nations* (1776). Hume, in his essay on the 'Idea of a Perfect Commonwealth' (1752), proposed an imaginary model of government to combine the stability of the classical republic for preservation with the expansiveness of the modern territorial state. Such a scheme would give the lie to the contention (particularly associated with Montesquieu) 'that no large state, such as FRANCE or GREAT BRITAIN, could ever be modelled into a commonwealth, but that such a form of government can only take place in a city or small territory'. It might be less easy to erect such a government over a large area but, once created, 'there is more facility . . . of

16. Smith 1978: 230, 228–9, 229–33, 233–4, 235 ('Report of 1762–3', IV, 74–5, 75–87, 88–91, 93);
    cf. Smith 1978: 411–13 ('Report Dated 1766', pp. 37–42); Winch 1978: 60.

preserving it steady and uniform, without tumult or faction' (Hume 1985: 527
('Idea of a Perfect Commonwealth')). This, of course, was just the argument
taken up by Madison in the *Federalist Papers*, x. Madison agreed with Hume
that democracies were naturally turbulent and factious, but that in a post-
classical world of representative, rather than direct, democracy such colli-
sions of interests might protect rather than threaten the stability of the
republic. The very expansiveness of an extended republic would multiply,
and thus ameliorate faction, so that empire itself would be the safeguard
of liberty: 'In the extent and proper structure of the Union, therefore, we
behold a republican remedy for the diseases most incident to republican
government.'[17] The new republicanism of the late eighteenth century drew
upon the classical and neo-Roman past even as it looked towards the future
of the modern, extended, commercial republic (Shklar 1990). Within this
tradition of republicanism, federalism offered the distinctly modern solution to the ancient dilemma of liberty and empire, but only for an extended commercial republic under the rule of law – an appropriate lesson for
contemporary Europe to derive from the shared heritage of republicanism.

17. Madison, Hamilton and Jay 1987: 126, 128 (*Federalist*, x); the connection between Hume's 'Idea
of a Perfect Commonwealth' and *Federalist*, x, was first noted independently by Marshall 1954:
255–6, and Adair 1957: 348–57.

3

Republicanism and Toleration

SIMONE ZURBUCHEN

1. Introduction

Toleration is not a concept usually associated with the history of republicanism. The emergence of a 'modern' concept of toleration, which implies the permanence of religious diversity, is commonly linked with the idea of the natural, i.e., inalienable, rights of men and is attributed to the tradition of Lockean liberalism. In this view, the individualistic model of toleration was fully developed in the Enlightenment period, when natural rights were invoked not only to legitimise liberty of worship, but also to advocate the liberty of thought and expression on which the development of the Enlightenment project depended. Not toleration, but rather the idea of 'civil religion' is considered to be a peculiar achievement of republican theory. It is well known that Rousseau introduced the term 'civil religion' to describe the civil 'profession of faith' that he modelled on the national religions of the ancients. Although republican conceptions of religion exercised an extensive influence mainly in the second half of the eighteenth century, especially in France, they can be traced to the re-articulation of republican ideals in the aftermath of the Glorious Revolution. This has been demonstrated by Justin Champion, who rightly insists that, in the period between 1680 and 1720, political issues cannot be separated from religious ones. His analysis of the relation between republicanism and deism leads to the conclusion that anti-clericalism played a crucial role in the republican analysis of the problems of civil government. However, he stresses that anti-clericalism did not imply irreligion. Republicans did not question the idea of true religion, but aimed at reforming corrupted Christianity. Adopting the traditional language of Erastianism, they created 'an idea of the national Church as a civil religion' that they opposed to the Anglican establishment (Champion 1992: 179).

In this paper I propose to further explore the relation between national religion and toleration. I will try to demonstrate that the generation of republicans who transmitted the ideas of their predecessors to the eighteenth century (sometimes also called 'neo-Harringtonians' or 'commonwealthmen') elaborated a concept of toleration that was in a crucial respect different from that of Locke's. Although they shared the latter's insistence on liberty of conscience, they were ready to accept a national establishment. Their defence of Protestantism as the national religion of England has to be viewed as the result of the 'dilemma' that they experienced after the Glorious Revolution. As Blair Worden has pointed out, republicans needed for the first time since 1651–2 to be on the government's side if they wanted to gain public respect and influence the politics of the day. For that reason they had to be at least outwardly loyal to the new régime and thus 'to cloak radical arguments with a conventional deference to the existing constitution' (Worden 1994c: 176; Worden 1991b) (§ II). This strategy of accommodation best explains why authors such as Molesworth, Moyle, Toland, Trenchard and Gordon claimed to support the established church, while at the same time launching vigorous attacks on 'priestcraft' and 'superstition'. As I will try to demonstrate, their theory of toleration also attempts to reconcile the demands of the profession of conformity with the intention of subversion (Worden 1991c: 265). While the defence of a 'national religion' could be used to demonstrate acceptance of the Anglican establishment as part of the post-revolutionary settlement (§ III), full liberty of conscience was advocated not only in support of religious minorities, but also to legitimise 'free thinking' in matters of religion and politics (§§ III–IV).

The tension between an appeal to the republican ideal of a 'free government' and accommodation to the post-revolutionary régime is reflected in ambiguities as well as apparent inconsistencies in many of the republican writings on religious liberty and toleration. In the work of John Toland this tension is manifested in the contradictions between his political and his philosophical writings – contradictions that are at the core of the debates about the proper interpretation of his work. While in his political writings he professed his loyalty to the established church and defended Protestantism as one of the two 'unshaken pillars' of the English monarchy, in his philosophical writings he defended 'pantheism' or 'Spinozism' as the true religion of the philosopher and denounced the clergy of the Anglican Church for deceiving the people and oppressing their liberty (§ v). To resolve these contradictions, Toland developed a new strategy of reform that he claimed to be consistent with the professed moderation of contemporary republican thought (§ VI). However, despite acknowledging his efforts to reconcile the double roles that he played as a political writer on the one hand and a 'Spinozist' philosopher on the other, I conclude that Toland's writings on religion and politics reveal the intrinsic ambiguity of the republican concept of toleration (§ VII).

II. The Republican Ideal and the English Monarchy

Every attempt to examine how the republican ideal of the seventeenth century was adapted to the post-revolutionary government has to begin with the editions of the works of Milton, Sidney, Harrington and Ludlow between 1697 and 1700, 'the most important years for the establishment of the Whig canon of ideas about political liberty' (Skinner 1974b: 114). Toland's preface to Sidney's *Discourses Concerning Government*, the *Lives* of Harrington and Milton, as well as *Amyntor: or a Defence of Milton's Life*, provide ample evidence of his key role in the transmission of the republican ideals of his predecessors to the eighteenth century. As has been noted (Carrive 1995: 235–8), Toland's opposition to Cromwell's usurpation explains why he marked his distance from Milton, whereas he considered Harrington to be 'one of the greatest *Republicans* that ever liv'd in the World' (Toland 1701a: 59) and praised *Oceana* as 'the most perfect form of popular government that ever was' (Harrington 1980: ix). Despite his admiration, he hastens to add that by the publication of Harrington's works he does not 'recommend a commonwealth', because the English government 'is already a commonwealth, the most free and best constituted in all the world' (p. viii). The tension between his appeal to the republican ideal on the one hand, and his praise of the English monarchy as a free government on the other, is present in all of Toland's major political works (Giuntini 1979: 182–90). Accused of defending democratic principles, he repeatedly asserts that the republicans of his days support the monarchy. In *Anglia libera* (1701), in which he explains and justifies the limitation of the succession to the crown in the Protestant line, he insists that the republicans, had they lately not made common cause with the royalists, 'ought to have past for a Pack of Enthusiasts that were fond of Names and ignorant of Things, or rather of seditious Fellows that cover'd an ill Design under a fair Pretence' (Toland 1701a: 88–9). He declares that he means 'by the word *Commonwealth* not a pure Democracy, nor any particular Form of Government; but an independent Community, where the Common Weal or Good of all indifferently is design'd and pursu'd . . .' (p. 92). In *The Art of Governing by Partys* (1701) Toland distinguishes among different forms of commonwealths. When the administration belongs to the people, it is called a democracy; when it lies in the nobility, it is an aristocracy; 'but when 'tis shar'd between the Commons, the Lords, and the supreme Magistrate . . . 'tis then a mixt form'. Referring to Polybius and 'many Judicious Politicians among the Ancients' he declares the mixed form of government to be 'the most equal, lasting, and perfect'. He asserts that 'in this sense *England* is undeniably a Commonwealth, tho' it be ordinarily stil'd a Monarchy because the chief magistrat is call'd a King' (Toland 1701b: 32–3).

Toland was not the only one who praised England as a 'commonwealth'. It was common tactics of the republicans in William III's reign to ignore Harrington's opposition to mixed monarchy and to stress the distinction between 'absolute' monarchy on the one hand, and 'free governments', either monarchical or non-monarchical, on the other. Like Algernon Sidney, who had insisted on the resemblance between the Gothic constitution of England and republics, Robert Molesworth accepted mixed or limited monarchy as 'free government' (Worden 1994c: 178–80). As is evidenced in *Cato's Letters*, written by John Trenchard and Thomas Gordon, these tactics were still telling in the reign of king George I. Drawing on the distinction between 'arbitrary' and 'free' governments (Trenchard and Gordon 1995: I, 413–20), the authors establish the principles on which 'free monarchical constitutions' have to be built. Having demonstrated that men living in society 'can not otherwise preserve their liberties' than by frequent elections of the people's representatives, they state that 'the joint concurrence of the crown and of the nobles . . . and of the body of the people' is the proper constitution of a 'limited monarchy'. They then go on to praise 'our most excellent sovereign King George' as a prince 'who owes his crown so entirely to the principles laid down . . . that it is impossible to suspect, either from his inclinations, his interest, or his known justice, that he should ever fall into any measures to destroy that people, who have given him his crown . . . or that he should undermine, by that means, the ground upon which he stands' (pp. 421–4).

However, the protestations of the republicans that they were no longer democrats but had joined with the royalists were not without ambiguity. As Worden has pointed out, their acceptance of mixed or limited monarchy had much to do with the fact that political writers who aspired to public respect and hoped to influence politics needed to demonstrate their loyalty to the new régime. For that reason 'they had little room for maneuver' (Worden 1994c: 180). Among the subversive strategies that were used to criticise arbitrary power, two will be singled out in the context of religion and toleration. The first was the use of indirect arguments that consisted in comparisons between the English constitution and the constitution of republics, either ancient or modern. Discussing 'the generation of the Roman commonwealth' in his *Essay upon the Constitution of the Roman Government* (1699), Walter Moyle observes that 'changes of government are often derived by imitation into the humours and customs of a nation'. For that reason the example of Rome's neighbouring states of Greece and Italy, 'who were generally republics', are numbered among the 'accidental causes' of the Roman commonwealth. Moyle also remarks that 'the late revolutions in England were in some manner owing to the example of Holland, and other foreign commonwealths' (Robbins (ed.) 1969: 229). This strategy could also be used in the opposite way by investigating, using the example of absolute monarchies, how liberty was lost. Thus Robert Molesworth, in the preface of his *An Account of Denmark* (1694), pointed to the importance of travel as 'a great Antidote against the Plague of Tyranny' (Molesworth 1738: xii). The second subversive strategy of post-revolutionary republicanism was based on the assumption that the present constitution could be perfected. Pointing to the blessings of the 'best constitution' it was possible to demand constitutional changes by way of reform. As Worden put it, the republicans' 'gradualism' enabled them 'to present 1688 as merely the beginning of the journey to liberty' (Worden 1994c: 181).

Before I examine the application of these two strategies in the domain of religion, it must first be established on what grounds republicans accepted the Protestant succession to the throne. The most striking formula was coined by Toland when he defended Protestantism as one of the 'two unshaken pillars' on which the liberty of England reposed after the Glorious Revolution (Toland 1717a: 4). In *Anglia libera* he states generally that it is 'natural' for every government to have a national religion, i.e. 'som public and orderly Way of worshipping God, under the Allowance, Indowment, and Inspection of the civil Magistrat' (Toland 1701a: 95–6.). As for England in particular, Anglicanism is best suited to be established as the national church because it allows more latitude than each of the numerous sects in the kingdom and is 'most accommodated' to the government. Moreover, Protestantism is 'already and so long establisht' that it would be the 'highest Folly as well as Injustice' to change or abolish it (pp. 97–8). However, the greatest advantage of establishing Protestantism as a national religion is the securing of toleration, which Toland considers to be 'a truly Protestant principle' (Toland 1717a: 21; see also Toland 1698a: 80).

It is important to note that the justification of Protestantism as the 'national' religion of England was placed in a European perspective. As

Molesworth observed, one of the advantages brought about by William III's reign was that the English make 'a greater Figure in the World', whereas they were formerly kept 'narrow-spirited' by their kings. As a result, they have 'more foreign Alliances, are become the Head of more than a Protestant League, and have a Right to intermeddle in the Affairs of *Europe*' (Molesworth 1738: vii). England's new role in Europe, which was related to the Protestant alliances, was of even greater concern by the time Toland composed his *Anglia libera* (1701). The spokesmen of the Protestant interest in Europe, led by the Huguenot refugees, were deeply worried about the status of Protestantism in the German Empire. The ambiguity of the Treaty of Ryswick[1] had further confirmed their anxiety over the danger of 'Popery'. For that reason they took the outbreak of the War of the Spanish Succession in 1701 as an opportunity to propagate the defence of Protestantism as one of the goals of the anti-Bourbon coalition (Boles 1997: 1–7). Toland shares their fears about the 'gradual Loss' of the Protestant Religion (Toland 1701a: 184). However, unlike many of the Huguenot refugees who 'wished to take the Grand Alliance, and specifically England and the Dutch Republic, back to the overtly-sectarian armed struggles of the sixteenth and early seventeenth centuries' (Boles 1997: 5), Toland considered the defence of the Protestant interest to be a means of securing liberty. Taking England as the 'worthy Example' for the other European states 'in maintaining, recovering, or inlarging our Liberty' (Toland 1701a: 189), he declares the settling of the crown in the House of Hanover to be 'the likeliest way' to enable England to restore the 'Balance of Europe' and in this way to protect the liberty of foreign states. The Act of Succession was the 'finishing Stroke' in making the English 'the Arbiters of *Europe*' (pp. 140–2), as the crown of England descended to one of the most powerful families in Europe, attaching all the Protestant states to England. Besides supporting the goal of maintaining the balance of power in Europe, Toland considers keeping England '*the Head of the Protestant Religion all over the World*' to be another of the country's maxims (p. 148). In his opinion, the success of the Protestant religion depended, 'Politically speaking', 'on the Liberty of the several States of *Europe*' (p. 185). In this perspective, Toland proposes that England and Holland establish 'a common Deputation' (p. 157) to defend Protestantism against France and Spain, after the example of the states in ancient Greece that formed a union against the '*Persian*

1. It was a specific requirement of the 'religious clause' of the Treaty of Ryswick that Roman Catholicism be observed exclusively in the territories ceded back by Louis XIV to the Empire. To the Protestants this amounted to 'a plain invitation to lawfully assault their religion elsewhere in the Empire' (Boles 1997: 7).

Monarch, whose Designs against all free Governments were the same with those of the *French* King in our Age' (p. 15).

III. Public and Private Religion: The National Church and Dissent

The above account of the relation between Protestantism and liberty helps to explain why the republicans did not question the national establishment, although they identified the Anglican Church as the main cause of the oppression of liberty of conscience. In this regard their concept of toleration is distinct from that of Locke and proves to be indebted to the republican tradition. For it has been argued convincingly that the *Letter Concerning Toleration* was ultimately 'a call for the end of the Anglican establishment and a demand that the Church of England take its rightful place alongside other churches' as a free and voluntary society (Schochet 1992: 163; see Locke 1963: 33), whereas the republicans claimed that a national establishment was consistent with the liberty of conscience. When they speak of toleration, they are concerned exclusively with the relation between public and private religion.

As noted above, after 1689 republicans applied different strategies to advocate their cause. In the introduction to his *Account of Denmark* Molesworth recommends not only travel, but also 'good Learning' as an 'Antidote against the Plague of Tyranny', more specifically the writings of the ancients, that are 'full of Doctrines, Sentences, and Examples exhorting to the Conservation or Recovery of the Publick *Liberty*, which was once valued above Life' (Molesworth 1738: xii). This recommendation was taken up by Moyle, who used his *Essay upon the Constitution of the Roman Government* to draw an analogy between republican Rome and the English monarchy of the times. In his analysis of the religion of the Romans introduced by Numa Pompilius he demonstrates the conditions in which a national religion can be consistent with toleration. His main advice is contained in the observation that Numa 'prevented all factions and divisions in the church' by introducing only two fundamental articles of faith: the first consists of the belief that the gods are 'the authors of all good to mankind"; the second states that to obtain this good, the gods have to be worshipped. For that reason Numa 'instituted a ritual, which directed the priests in the solemn ceremonies and services of religion' (Robbins (ed.) 1969: 211). Although Moyle admits that the Romans were 'very cautious of introducing any new rites into their national religion', he insists that this order 'did not extend to regulate the opinions or devotions of private men'. Indeed, Numa allowed in the particular forms of divine worship 'a general liberty of conscience'. According to Moyle, the institution of a 'universal liberty in religion' depended on 'this single cause' that 'the government of the national religion was lodged in the senate and people'. The subordination of religion to the civil magistrate had two different aspects. First, the institution of rites and ceremonies that contradicted the established religion were either prohibited or approved by the senate. Toleration of new forms in religion did not depend on the priests, but was granted by the senate. Second, 'the supreme power of religion' belonged to the people. For 'the whole order of the high-priests were subject to the jurisdiction of the tribunes of the people'. In this way the clergy of the Roman religion was 'interwoven into the general interest of the state', instead of forming 'a separate independent body from the rest of the community' (pp. 213–15).

In Moyle's view, this is 'a constitution which the modern policy has overlooked . . . or neglected'. In the modern world the priesthood is endowed with 'unlimited power' or is at least independent of the civil power by virtue of its 'great possessions and endowments'. As the analysis of the national religion of the Romans demonstrates, the constitution of the church as an independent body is inconsistent with a 'free government'. Persecutions 'are generally only encouraged by tyrants and priests' who join their interest 'to enslave the world' and 'to share the booty between them'. Fearing that changes in the national religion will ruin their privileges and revenues, the priests will never grant toleration. Although in a cautious and indirect way, Moyle also recommends how the moderns might bring about the subordination of the church to the civil magistrate. For he remembers the fact that in Rome, under the government of the kings, 'the priests had a very large jurisdiction'. Their power only declined 'after the subversion of the monarchy'. He then observes that the question of how 'the civil power wrested the government of religion out of the hands of the priests' is 'difficult to determine', because it has not been answered by the ancient writers. However, it seems probable to him 'that the usurping the right of electing the high priest, after the expulsion of the kings, was the leading step to the invasion of all their other privileges' (Robbins (ed.) 1969: 213–16).

Whereas Moyle uses the example of the Romans to elucidate his theory of toleration, Toland recommends the teachings of Harrington. In *The State-Anatomy of Great Britain* he argues that 'as the conviction of a man's private Conscience, produces his private Religion; so the conviction of the national conscience, or of the majority, must every where produce a National Religion'. Although no country can possibly be without a national religion, every man should have the choice of his own religion, 'since nothing is more consistent than a Publick Establishment and Liberty of Conscience' (Toland 1717a: 27–8). To justify this assertion Toland invokes the authority of Harrington. A national church does not exclude liberty of conscience, 'for a National Religion must not be a Publick Driving, but a Publick Leading, says Harrington, to whom every man is oblig'd who writes on this subject'. Toland obviously refers here to *A System of Politics*, where Harrington declares that in religious matters most people ask for public guidance. For that reason he thinks one must conclude that 'they are debarred of their liberty of conscience' if they are 'debarred of their will in that particular'. But Harrington also insists that liberty of conscience is only guaranteed in a democracy. This applies to the form of government as well as to the organization of the church. Whereas a 'hierarchical clergy' is a 'monarchical ordination', in a democracy the clergy is ordained by the people. Moreover, in a democracy a council is responsible 'for the maintenance both of the national religion and the liberty of conscience' (Harrington 1980: 474–6).

As Toland's use of Harrington's theory of toleration demonstrates, his claim that England was already a 'free government' was not unambiguous. Rather, it has to be seen as part of a strategy of 'gradualism' that takes the post-revolutionary settlement as a starting point to establish religious and civil liberty. Against this background it seems plausible that Toland declared his readiness to approve of the established church in order to gain support for parliamentary reform. This is well documented in a series of political pamphlets by which he hoped to encourage an alliance between the low clerics of the Anglican church and the Dissenters. He praises the position of the low churchmen 'who approve of Episcopacy, the Liturgy, and Discipline establisht by law; but who believe the Protestant religion may subsist (tho not so well) without them'. Whereas the low churchmen 'have a brotherly charity and communion with all other Reform'd Churches' and 'join with them in the defence of the same doctrines against the Papists', Toland accuses the high churchmen of treating Protestants abroad and Dissenters at home 'as no Christians' and of 'compelling the Dissenters in particular to conformity, by penal Laws, Censures, and Incapacities'. As they 'maintain the order of Bishops to be of Divine Institution' they generally support the arbitrary power of the prince, because it conforms to their jurisdiction over the ecclesiastics in the church (Toland 1717a: 24–5). According to Toland, they do not belong to the Church of England, but to that party which 'under pretence of being the flower of this church' oppresses the liberty of conscience and opposes civil liberty (p. 29). He even considers them to be the greatest danger to the Church of England, because they aim 'at erecting the worst part of Popery here at home', i.e. 'the Independency of the Church upon the State'. To denounce this 'spiritual tyranny' he speaks of 'English Popery' or 'Protestant Popery' (pp. 34–5).

Toland's critique of 'Protestant Popery' echoes the arguments already used by Moyle and Molesworth. Based on his analysis of the Lutheran Church in Denmark, the latter takes it to be a great mistake 'that the Popish Religion is the only one, of all the Christian Sects, proper to introduce and establish Slavery in a Nation'. According to Molesworth, whoever takes pains to visit the Protestant countries abroad will soon be convinced 'that it is not Popery, as such, but the Doctrine of a blind Obedience, in what Religion soever it be found, that is the Destruction of Liberty, and consequently of all the Happiness of any Nation' (Molesworth 1738: 164–5). In similar vein it is observed in *Cato's Letters* 'that most of the different religious institutions now subsisting in the world, have been founded upon ambition and pride' (Trenchard and Gordon 1995: I, 468). Although the authors consider 'the Pope's yoke' to be 'more grievous than that of any Christian prince upon earth', they also state that many Protestant countries, 'where there is much miserable ignorance, and much bitter and implacable bigotry', have lost their liberties since the Reformation. However, as regards the Anglican Church, they point to the growing spirit and interest of liberty and express their hope that 'most of the bishops, and many of the inferior clergy' will soon become 'thorough advocates for publick liberty' (*ibid.*: 471).

Toland launched his appeal to the low churchmen in order to gain their support for full toleration of Dissent. As the so-called Toleration Act of 1689 merely suspended the penal laws, the civil disabilities installed by the Test and Corporation Acts had remained in place. Following the accession of Queen Anne in 1702, High Church clergy attacked in Parliament what they considered to be the two main abuses of the Toleration Act: the practice of occasional conformity (by which the Dissenters evaded the sacramental tests in order to hold political office) and the growth of dissenting academies. During the last four years of Queen Anne's reign, when the Tories were in power, the Occasional Conformity Bill (1711) and the Schism Act (1714), which made the separate education of Dissenters illegal, became law (Wykes 1990: 70–5).

In 1705 Toland elaborated a reply to James Drake's *Memorial of the Church England*, in which – as he was later to explain – the Dissenters were represented 'as unworthy of any toleration, since by their principles they wou'd neither tolerate any else, nor even one another' (Toland 1717b: 44). In the following year he composed a letter by which he attempted to invite the Dissenters publicly to declare their adherence to the doctrine of toleration. The publication of the letter in *The Second Part of the State Anatomy* was meant to further encourage the abolition of the sacramental test, a measure that he thought to be 'seasonable' by 1717, because the experience with the latest Jacobite Rebellion had demonstrated that a union of all Protestants was necessary to oppose 'the artifices of the Papists and their accomplices'. Moreover, during the rebellion the Dissenters proved again, as they had on many previous occasions, that they were 'most zealous for the King, the Government, and the Reformation' (p. iv). Together with the more general analysis in *State Anatomy*, these documents provide a clear account of how Toland conceived of toleration and of the concrete measures that he thought the government ought to enact.

In the letter, which he sent to some of the denominations of Protestant Dissenters, he refers to two of the key arguments that Locke had introduced in the *Letter Concerning toleration*. He first asserts that liberty of conscience does not extend to 'licentiousness in morals', but to actions that are indifferent and to doctrines or opinions that are not destructive of society and religion, but consist in 'bare speculation' (Toland 1717b: 54–5; see Locke 1963: 77–9). He then insists that toleration does not mean 'indifference', but that the promotion of truth is strictly limited to 'Arguments, Exhortations, and exemplary Living' (Toland 1717b: 56; see Locke 1963: 81). With regard to the status of the Dissenters in Great Britain, he distinguishes between 'entire' and 'partial' liberty of conscience. The former obtains 'where a man according to the dictates of his own Conscience, may have the free exercise of his Religion, without any impediment to his Preferment or Imployment in the State', whereas the latter renders a man who does not exercise the national religion 'incapable of Preferment or Imployment in the State' (Toland 1717b: 27). There is no doubt that Toland considered the requirement of a sacramental test before appointment to any place of trust or power in the state as an unjustified 'imposition'. For a religious test is 'a Political Monopoly', it is 'Dominion founded in Grace'. Enjoying merely partial toleration, the Dissenters are not only punished for that which is no crime, but they are deprived 'of their native rights'. For that reason Toland demands the abolition of the Act of Occasional Conformity and the Schism Act and expresses his hope that 'in the last place to complete this glorious work ... the Sacramental Test may be abolish'd with regard to all Protestants in England and Ireland, as well as of all Scots-men in England' (Toland 1717a: 30–2).

IV. Toleration and Free-thinking

As we have seen, the claim that national religion is consistent with liberty of conscience could be used to demand the subordination of the church to the civil magistrate after the model of the ancients (Moyle) or to advocate parliamentary reforms designed to realize full toleration of religious dissent (Toland). However, the appeal to liberty of conscience was also applied to justify those who defended the right to think freely in a more general sense. Indeed, the right to judge according to one's own conscience in matters of religion was considered the essential achievement of a free government. As Matthew Tindal argued, based on Locke's *Letter Concerning Toleration*, the use of one's reason to discover truth is the duty of man as a creature endowed with reason. As the use of reason demands examination of the proofs and arguments of others and their comparison to one's own notions, it is 'Mens mutual Duty to inform each other in those Propositions they apprehend to be true, and the Arguments by which they endeavour to prove 'em' (Tindal 1709: 295). The duty to make use of one's reason thus presupposes freedom of printing. Restraining the press is unlawful, because 'Men have the same right to communicate their Thoughts, as to think themselves; and where the one is deny'd, the other is seldom us'd, or to little purpose.' According to Tindal, freedom of thinking and printing is the only means to eradicate superstition. Thus he observes that the degeneration of learning and knowledge chiefly in Catholic, but also in Protestant countries such as Denmark and Sweden, 'is owing only to that Priestcraft which forbids all Freedom'. He invokes the counter example of Rome, 'where to think on what one had a mind to, and to speak one's thoughts as freely as to think 'em, was esteem'd one of the chief Blessings of a Free Government' (pp. 299–300)[2].

In similar vein, Toland observes that that the liberty of the understanding

> is yet a nobler Principle than that of the Body . . . and where there is no Liberty of *Conscience* there can be no civil Liberty, no Incouragement of Industry, no proper means of rendring the contry populous, no possibility of Men's freely informing themselves concerning the true Religion, nor any Refuge or Protection for the Distrest, which is the greatest glory of free Governments.
>
> (Toland 1701a: 100)

2. Despite this allusion to the example of Rome, Tindal should not be numbered among the 'republicans'. For he bases his concept of toleration on the arguments that had been used by Locke.

Whereas Tindal's and Toland's statements support the right to think freely in matters of religion, *Cato's Letters* defend the people's right 'to judge of their governor and government' in order 'to preserve themselves from publick destroyers, falsely calling themselves governors'. As there is no common established power between the magistrate and the people to which both are subject, 'every man . . . must act acording to the light and dictates of his own conscience, and inform it as well as he can'. As the authors argue, this was common practice with the 'honest ancients', who 'following for their guide that everlasting reason, which is the best and only guide in human affairs, carried liberty, and human happiness, the legitimate offspring and work of liberty, to the highest pitch that they were capable of arriving'. The opinion that subjects were not to judge of their governors is considered as an 'absurdity' fostered by 'dreaming Mahometan and Christian monks', who made themselves 'directors of all things; and bewitching the world with holy lies and unaccountable ravings, dressed up in barbarous words and uncouth phrases, bent all their fairy force against common sense and common liberty and truth, and founded a pernicious, absurd, and visionary empire upon their ruins' (Trenchard and Gordon 1995: 1, 407–10). Contrasting liberty with slavery in a more general sense, the authors state that 'true and impartial liberty is . . . the right of every man to pursue the natural, reasonable, and religious dictates of his own mind; to think, what he will, and act as he thinks, provided he acts not to the prejudice of another . . .' They even consider the 'love of liberty' as 'an appetite so strongly implanted in the nature of all living creatures' that to many men it is 'beyond the love of life' (p. 430).

Freedom to think and to publish had most prominently been advocated by Spinoza, who considered it as 'one of the chief elements in the entire debate about toleration' (Israel 2000: 109). Jonathan Israel views Spinoza's defence of the *libertas philosophandi* as a peculiar achievement of his theory of toleration that he labels – in contradistinction to the theological notions of toleration of Locke, Episcopius and van Limborch – 'anti-theological and republican' (p. 103). The first essential element of Spinoza's theory is his conception of a state religion, which is 'an idealized philosophical religion', not Christianity, but what Spinoza calls a 'very simple, universal faith', in which 'worship of God and obedience to him consists solely in justice and charity, or love, towards one's neighbour'. As the second characteristic feature of the seventeenth-century republican tradition of toleration, Israel identifies the 'drastic weakening of ecclesiastical authority and the merging of it as far as possible into the political sovereign' (p. 105). As the above account of the English republican argument demonstrates, it was composed of the same elements. Like Spinoza, republicans took a public or national religion as the basis of toleration, which they claimed to be consistent with liberty of thought and expression. However, they did not invoke the authority of Spinoza, but preferred to point to the example of Rome or to refer to Harrington's distinction between public and private religion. This is certainly no surprise, given their 'dilemma': wishing to demonstrate loyalty to the post-revolutionary régime while proposing radical reforms. However, even these outward pressures aside, it remains doubtful whether the English republicans went as far as to conceive of national religion as an 'idealized philosophical religion'. As Champion argued, one has to distinguish between an English and a continental tradition of free thinking, between 'radical republican attacks on the Anglican High Church' and the 'continental culture of the *libertins érudits*' (Champion 1996: 340). Whereas the main concern of the former was to reform corrupted Christianity, the latter combined arguments of the *libertins érudits* with the new doctrines of Hobbes and Spinoza to question the truth of revealed religion.

However, it is unclear whether this general observation also applies to Toland's concept of public religion. The question of how his republicanism was linked with Spinoza and 'Spinozism' has to be answered on the basis of a closer examination of some of his philosophical writings, in which he defended 'pantheism' as the 'true' religion of the philosopher. As I will argue in the next section, there are reasons to establish a more direct link between Spinoza and English republican concepts of toleration.

v. Toland the Heterodox

More than any other republican of his day, Toland was suspected of being heterodox. Indeed, from the days when he studied in Scotland and later in Holland, he was reported to be a person of dubious origin and reputation (Heinemann 1952: 39–42). After the publication of his *Christianity not Mysterious* in 1696, he was frequently associated with heresies such as Socinianism (Sullivan 1982: 82–108), 'free thinking', and 'pantheism' or 'Spinozism' (Schröder 1989). The way in which Toland's philosophy was linked with Spinoza and Spinozism can be elucidated in connection with the French literary circles in Holland that were formed mainly by Huguenot refugees. Benefiting from the liberty of the press, they published various periodicals and, in the course of using their presses to combat the political and religious persecutions of Louis XIV, also began to distribute a subversive and clandestine body of literature (Vermij 1996a: 241–5). These circles were also responsible for the publication of the *Traité des trois imposteurs* that is now considered a classic of the radical Enlightenment (Paganini 1998: 158–67). Despite much speculation about the issue, it remains unclear whether Toland played any part in the publication of the *Traité*. However, there is no doubt that his literary activities owed much to the liberal culture flourishing in Holland, where he took up more or less permanent residence between 1708 and 1711. At least some of his writings belong to the corpus of clandestine literature which, moreover, he actively helped to circulate (pp. 145–6).

To discuss the question of how Toland's republicanism was linked with pantheism and Spinozism, I will focus on the first letter of the *Nazarenus* that circulated in manuscript form before it was published in 1718. The letter aims at reconstructing the 'original Plan of Christianity', based on a 'Turkish Gospel being father'd upon *Barnabas*' that Toland had discovered in Amsterdam in 1709 (Toland 1718: ii–iii). Toland employed the Gospel of Barnabas as evidence of the continuity of Judaic, Christian, and Islamic theology. Using the historical framework of the succession of reforming prophets, he examined the relations between Judaism, Christianity, and Islam on the one hand, and 'true' religion on the other[3]. The Gospel of Barnabas confirmed Toland in his opinion that the Nazarenes were 'the Primitive Christians most properly so call'd' (p. iii). Their history demonstrated that there existed two kinds of Christians, 'those from among the Jews, and those from among the Gentiles'. According to the 'original Plan of Christianity' these groups united 'into one body or fellowship', although the Jews still observed their own Law, whereas the Gentiles 'who became so far Jews as to acknowledge one God' did not observe Jewish Law. The two groups were united 'in that part of Christianity particularly, which . . . requires the sanctification of the spirit, or the renovation of the inward man' (pp. iv–v). As the Jews 'generally mistook the means for the end' and confounded political with religious performances (p. v), they are forever bound to the law of Moses that comprises both moral law and Levitical law, which was 'essential to the being of their Theocracy or Republic'. Toland thus took Jewish ceremony and ritual to be 'no less national and political than religious and sacred: that is to say, the expressions of the history of their peculiar nation' (p. 38). For that reason the Gentile Christians who lived among the Jewish Christians were only obliged to follow moral law and 'the Noachic precepts of abstinence from blood and

3. For a general account of *Nazarenus* see Lurbe 1995b; Palmer 1996; Champion 1992: 124–32; Champion 2000.

things offer'd to Idols'. It is thus the moral or natural law that was 'both then, and before, and ever will be, of indispensable obligation to all men'. Toland identifies moral law with 'sound Reason, or the light of common sense' and declares it to be 'a catholic and eternal rule, without which mankind cou'd not subsist in peace or happiness one hour'. It is 'the fundamental bond of all society, where there is or there is not a reveal'd religion'. Moreover, it is 'the only thing that's approv'd by the most opposite Revelations'(pp. 65–6). The main design of Christianity was to improve and perfect the knowledge and observation of this law.

As Champion has argued convincingly, Spinoza's *Tractatus theologico-politicus* 'formed some of the central premises of Toland's *Nazarenus*'. The latter shared Spinoza's conviction that Moses was a legislator who introduced ceremonies and rituals into his commonwealth for the temporary prosperity of the state, and that Mosaic institutions like circumcision explained why the Jews had been able to preserve their government.[4] However, Champion denies any link between Toland's 'original Plan of Christianity' and 'pantheism'. Identifying political anti-clericalism and the elaboration of a 'civic theology' as the main concerns of English free thinking between 1670 and 1720, he states that Toland, in accordance with his English predecessors, declares that Christianity of the times is inherently corrupted, but that he is nonetheless convinced that it is based on a pure and divine religion (Champion 1995: 267). Based on these assumptions he argues that Toland's defence of pantheism, which he introduced in the *Pantheisticon* as the 'true' doctrine of the philosophers, must be explained on the basis of his distinction between public and private religion. He thus concludes that Toland's 'real' intention was to reform the Anglican Church, while conceiving of pantheism as the private doctrine of philosophers, a teaching that was never deemed by Toland to be the 'true' religion that he hoped would replace Christianity (pp. 271–8).

However, Champion's demand that the 'purpose and meaning of Toland's pantheism should be subject to radical revision' (Champion 1995: 269) is not consistent with Toland's own account of pantheism and Spinozism. He argues in his *Origines Judaicae* that Moses established ceremonies and ritual to accommodate the people, while in fact 'he was a pantheist, or, to say it in a more usual manner, a Spinozist'. He also states that the pantheists are

---

4. Champion 1992: 130–2. Toland must have been familiar with the *Tractatus theologico-politicus*, although he does not explicitly mention the work. For a general discussion of Toland's relation to Spinoza see Lurbe 1990. For the reception of Spinoza by English authors see Simonutti 1995 and 1996.

convinced that 'there is no Divine Being different from matter and this universe, and Nature itself, the entirety of things, is the only and highest God' (Toland 1709: 117). This account of pantheism and Spinozism had already been established indirectly in the fourth and fifth *Letters to Serena*. Toland pretended to demonstrate that Spinoza's system of philosophy was 'without any Principle or Foundation' (Toland 1704: 131), because he never defined motion or rest. Based on this criticism Toland develops his main thesis that motion is essential to matter. As scholars have repeatedly observed, it can hardly have been Toland's intention to put forward an authentic refutation of Spinoza's philosophy, because a 'refutation of Spinoza, as commonly understood, entailed the exposure of his objectionable, irreligious ideas' (Vermij 1996b: 283). In fact, the view that motion was essential to matter 'was generally identified with libertinism, atheism, and therefore, with "Spinozism"', and was rejected by the orthodox by proving that motion depended on something outside and above the material world. Instead of attacking what the orthodox called 'Spinozism', Toland in fact upholds Spinozism (p. 286). Describing the secret doctrine of a private society of philosophers, Toland presents in his *Pantheisticon* a more elaborated version of pantheism consistent with his earlier account of Spinozism.[5]

The main problem with Champion's interpretation of the *Nazarenus* is that he never elucidates what it is that Toland understood by 'true' religion. He thus misses the opportunity to discuss the relation between republicanism and pantheism that Toland seems to establish in the first letter of the *Nazarenus*. Writing of the 'admirable Economy of the Gospel' of which the 'union without uniformity' between Jewish and Gentile Christians consists, Toland remarks that the Gospel 'consists not in words but in virtue', and that it is 'inward and spiritual, abstracted from all formal and outward performances'. As a consequence, 'something else besides the Legal Ordinances, most of 'em political, was necessary to render a Jew religious'. It was 'Faith, which is an internal participation of the divine nature, irradiating the soul; and externally appearing in beneficence, justice, sanctity, and those other virtues by which we resemble God, who is himself all Goodness' (Toland 1718: 5). As scholars have pointed out, this paragraph is at least consistent with a pantheistic reading of 'true' religion (Palmer 1996: 82–4). The suggestion that Toland identified true religion with pantheism is further confirmed by his description of a society of pantheists. As we have seen, in the *Nazarenus* Toland identifies moral law with 'sound Reason, or the light of common sense' and declares that the main design of Christianity

5. For a critical discussion of the secret doctrine of the pantheists see Iofrida 1983: 35–64.

was to improve and perfect the knowledge and practice of this law. In the *Pantheisticon* he identifies the law of the society of pantheists with 'right reason' that corresponds to nature and is innate in all men (Toland 1751: 84). Moreover, the link between theoretical conceptions of God and the universe and moral law that Toland establishes in the *Pantheisticon* corresponds to the account of his own religion in the preface to the *Nazarenus*. Here he announces that he will 'give a more distinct account' of his religion, 'stript of all literature, and laid down in naked theorems . . .' He further asserts that it will consist in nothing but 'reasonable worship or unaffected piety' and that there will be 'more object of practice than of belief in it; and nothing practis'd but what makes a man the better, nor anything believ'd but what necessarily leads to practice and knowledge: yet nothing that does not concern people to know, or that they cannot possibly know at all' (Toland 1718: xiv).

If the proposed interpretation of the *Nazarenus* is correct, we have to conclude that Toland in fact adopted, like Spinoza before him, an 'idealized philosophical religion' as the model of a national religion consistent with liberty of conscience. As he gave pantheism a ritualistic expression, when he described a private society of pantheists, Margaret Jacob has argued that pantheism was for him an alternative to Christianity that served as the metaphysical basis of his republicanism (Jacob 1981: 72–83). However, if it was Toland's real intention to replace corrupted Christianity by pantheism, it seems impossible to reconcile the radicalism of his philosophical writings with his professed loyalty to the Anglican Church as well as the programme of reform he advocated in his political writings. This is why Champion demanded that Jacob's interpretation of Toland's pantheism should be subject to radical revision. In contrast to Champion, I will argue that, towards the end of his life, Toland elaborated a new strategy of subversion that provides the key to resolving the apparent contradictions between his philosophical and political writings. As this strategy aimed at reconciling the demands of radical criticism of religion and of moderation, it proves to be consistent with the manoeuvres of post-revolutionary republicanism that have been described above.

vi. Truth and Imposture: The Philosopher and the Priests

Toland claimed that he had always pleaded for liberty on behalf of his fellow creatures as well as on his own behalf (Toland 1720: xx). He perceived himself as belonging to those 'who . . . oppose all arbitrary impositions on the Understanding or Consciences of men, from a generous affection to their own species, out of a right knowledge of human nature, and for advancing the flourishing state of the commonwealth . . . Not from temporary ends and politick accommodations, but from a deep and just sense of impartial, full, divine, and eternal liberty.' However, those who defend liberty against the monster of superstition fall victim themselves of 'such [sorts of men] as are guided more by prejudice or custom, than by reason and convenience' ('The Primitive Constitution of the Christian Church', in Toland 1726: 1, 26–7). He accuses the 'corrupt and interested Priests', whose 'ultimate designs . . . are to procure to themselves Riches, and consequently Power and Authority', of 'train[ing] up their hearers in Ignorance, and consequently in Superstition and Bigotry' (Toland 1718: xv). Analysing the 'Arts' used by clergymen to decry their opponents, he points to the 'charge of *Atheism*, which, in their passion or malice, they bully out against any person that presumes to contradict them', and blames the '*priestridden laity*' for imitating the practices of their clerical guides (p. 65).

Toland was well aware of the fact that he was by no means the only victim of this 'conspiracy' of deceit (Toland 1704: 16). Indeed, he was convinced that the force of prejudice always induces men to 'foolishly despise and hate one another for their civil customs' and to 'cruelly persecute and murder one another on the score of their religious ones', especially when the people are 'artfully wrought up' by priests and politicians. According to Toland, 'no people or sect in the world, has had sadder experience of these truths in all times, than the *Jews*'. The Jews provide an exemplary case, as their religious customs differ from all other nations, so that they have had all nations for their enemies. After enumerating the worst of the 'cruelties and barbarities exercis'd against them' by the Christians, Toland accuses the priests of being their 'most inveterate Enemies', 'who devoutly offer'd up those human Sacrifices, not only to share their Goods with the rapacious *Prince*, but also to acquire the reputation of zeal and sanctity among the credulous vulgar'. Several examples of the practices of the deceiving priests led Toland to the conclusion that diverse Emperors, who 'out of their Lay-pity' tried to protect the Jews, were not able to do so, because 'so dangerous and destructive a monster is *Superstition*, when rid by the *Mob*, and driven by the *Priests*' that sometimes it leads to the 'overthrow of those, who let it loose on quite other designs'.[6]

Based on this analysis of the 'monster of superstition', Toland recommends, towards the end of his life, that the philosophers of his own time

---

6. Toland 1965: 26–70. This analysis forms the core of Toland's pamphlet in which he advocated the naturalisation of the Jews in Great Britain and Ireland. For the context of the debates about naturalisation see Champion 2000.

imitate the way in which the ancients escaped persecution. Threatened by
the 'ambitious Priests, supported by their property the Mob', the philosophers were compelled

> to make use of a two-fold doctrine: the one Popular, accommodated
> to the Prejudices of the vulgar, and to the receiv'd Customs or
> Religions; the other Philosophical, conformable to the nature of
> things, and consequently to truth; which with doors fast shut and
> under all other precautions, they communicated onely to friends of
> known probity, prudence, and capacity. These they generally call'd
> the Exoteric and Esoteric, or the External and Internal Doctrines.
>
> (Toland 1718: 65–6)

It is well known that the distinction between public and private goes back
to the *libertins érudits* of the seventeenth century. As Tullio Gregory has stated,
justification by the the *libertins* of the dissociation between the wise and the
populace needs to be seen 'as a response to the Inquisition and censorship'.
As they perceived 'custom', i.e., political and religious institutions as well as
common opinion, as tyrannical authority, they recommended that the wise
escape into solitude and dissimulate truth in public. Stressing the opposition
between the use of reason and the triumph of superstition that characterised
a perverse age, they 'placed themselves outside political and religious struggles where self-interest, force, dissimulation and imposture held sway. The
double roles they found themselves playing represented an extreme form
of split identity' (Gregory 1998: 344–9). Although Toland must have been
familiar with some of the texts of the *libertins érudits* that circulated in the
literary circles in Holland, he employs almost exclusively ancient sources to
explain the meaning of the esoteric–exoteric distinction. His use of these
examples reveals that it applied only to doctrines that concern the nature of
God, the universe, and the soul. In the third *Letter to Serena*, where Toland
mentions the esoteric–exoteric distinction for the first time, he observes that
the theory of stars and planets of the philosophers was very little known, because 'the common People wou'd never endure to hear those things made
subject to a Philosophical Examination, or explain'd by the ordinary Laws of
Nature . . . while they held 'em to be intelligent, eternal, and immortal Gods'
(Toland 1704: 114). In *Clidophorus* he insinuates, quoting Parmenides, that
the Egyptian people believed Isis to be a queen, whereas the philosophers,
who considered the universe to be the highest God, took her for the nature
of all things (Toland 1720: 71). Writing of Pythagoras and his disciples, he
asserts that they never believed in the transmigration of the soul, but that in

their esoteric doctrine 'transmigration' meant 'the incessant flux or motion of all things, and the perpetual change of forms in matter, one never decaying or dying but to begin and take on another' (p. 83). In *Pantheisticon*, Toland presents his own version of materialistic pantheism as the esoteric doctrine of the philosophers. As Lurbe rightly concludes, Toland suggested that from antiquity on, there existed a *philosophia perennis* always known to the philosophers who transmitted it throughout the ages (Lurbe 1995a: 384–5).

The philosophers' strategy of dissimulation was adapted both to the specific nature of truth and to the priests' strategy of deceit. Toland uses the compilation of quotations from the ancients, of which *Clidophorus* consists, to demonstrate that one has to distinguish between two kinds of exoteric doctrines, the one legitimate, the other illegitimate. The former consists of the use of fables, the latter of symbols and metaphors. Establishing a link between fables and mysteries, he attributes the illegitimate use of exoteric doctrines to the Church Fathers (Lurbe 1995a: 390–6). In this way Toland aims to draw a clear distinction between the superstition used by the priests to deceive the people and the popular doctrines used by the philosophers in order to escape persecution.

> For while the Priests industriously conceal'd their Mysteries, lest, being clearly understood, they might by the Philosophers be expos'd to the laughter of the people, as fabulous, false, and useless; the Philosophers, on the other hand, conceal'd their sentiments on the Nature of things, under the veil of divine allegories; lest being accus'd of impiety by the Priests ... they might be expos'd in their turn to the hatred, if not the fury of the Vulgar.   (Toland 1720: 91–2)

The use of divine allegories enables the philosophers to escape persecution and, at the same time, to communicate the truth to those who are not subject to popular prejudices. As this account of dissimulation reveals, Toland did not renounce the public propagation of truth when he recommended accommodation. However, where liberty of thought and expression was oppressed, truth had to be communicated in a secret and cautious way.

In the *Pantheisticon* Toland further elaborated the strategy of subversion thus described. He restricts free discussion to the realm of private societies. Referring to the Socratic societies of the ancients, he conceives of a private society of philosophers – for the most part pantheists – who 'bigotted to no one's Opinion, nor led aside by Education or custom, not subservient to the Religion and Laws of their Country ... freely and impartially, in the Silence of all Prejudices, and with the greatest Sedateness of Mind, discuss and bring to a Scrutiny all things as well as sacred (as the saying is) as prophane' (Toland 1751: 14). The meetings of the society have a ritualistic form. As Cherchi has demonstrated in a detailed examination of the *Pantheisticon*, the liturgy of the society is modelled on heathen rituals and ceremonies. It serves to separate the philosophers from the credulous multitude and to initiate them into the secret doctrine of pantheism. This initiation leads to a rational form of existence that is at the same time peaceable and pleasant (Cherchi 1985). The 'form' or liturgy of the society consists of three different parts, concerning its 'Morals and Axioms', the 'Deity and Philosophy', and its 'Liberty . . . and a Law, neither deceiving, nor to be deceived'. In this way Toland establishes a link between a theoretical conception of God, the soul, and the universe on the one hand, and the practical rules of a brotherly community on the other. He presents the community of pantheists as a model of a free and virtuous society:

> By the extraordinary Form of this Society, now first brought to Light, any one may see plainly that the Manners of the Brethren are not morose, rather, polite and elegant, nay even devoid of all Vice and just Censure. Moreover the Laws of this agreeable Banquet, not less just than prudent, are to be learned; and the attractive Charms of Liberty, far remote from all Licentiousness, are to be thoroughly read, so much the more, as nothing is of prized by the Brotherhood, as not only the cultivating of Modesty, Continence, Justice, and all Kinds of virtues themselves, but also of exciting others, as well by Words as Example, to their Practice.   (Toland 1751: 94)

Although Toland claimed that such societies had been set up in different European cities, it remains unclear whether the model that he described in the *Pantheisticon* was actually related to any of the societies existing at the time. Future research will have to decide whether Toland's allegation that there existed 'in several Places, not a few Pantheists, who . . . have their private Assemblies and societies' was justified or whether his model of a private society was rather, as Toland also insinuates, a fiction (Toland 1751: 109–10). However this question is ultimately resolved,[7] it is important to note that by the publication of the *Pantheisticon* Toland also demonstrates how others are initiated in pantheism through secret communication. Although

---

7. Benítez points to Bonaventure de Fourcroy's description of a society of naturalists. This work as well as Toland's *Pantheisticon* are indebted to a hermetic and magic philosophy. He concludes that it remains unclear whether such naturalist societies existed (Benítez 1996: 191–9). Blanchet establishes a connection between the society of pantheists and the Druid order that was set up in London in 1717 (Blanchet and Danlot 1996: 19).

he declares the religion of the society to be simple, clear and easy to understand, it cannot be presented 'naked and entire, unmasked, and without any tedious Circumstance of words' when it is rendered public. This explains why Toland describes the esoteric doctrine of the pantheists in disguised form. As a published text, the *Pantheisticon* had to be 'adjusted in some measure to the Prejudices of the People, or to Doctrines publickly authorized for true', although it was originally written in Latin and its distribution restricted 'to the Learned and Ingenious Reader' (Toland 1751: 96–7).

VII. Conclusion

As this account of the new strategy of subversion demonstrates, in the *Pantheisticon* Toland did in fact disclose his 'real' beliefs. However, it also suggests that he never intended that the liturgy of the private society of pantheists should replace the ceremonies and ritual of the established church. He was ready to approve of the liturgy and discipline of the Anglican Church, but opposed the ambitious priests who forged superstition and oppressed the liberty of conscience in order to uphold arbitrary power. Although in the *Pantheisticon* Toland revealed his most radical ideas, he at the same time recommended moderation. As he insisted throughout his work, he did not aim at abolishing established religion, but at opposing superstition. All of his political writings about national religion and toleration are accompanied by efforts to justify his own conclusions. In the *Anglia libera* he combines his appeal to liberty with a declaration of his membership in the national church. Recommending Protestantism as the national religion of England, he adds a paragraph on his own behalf, 'both to undeceive the mistaken, and to silence the malitious' (Toland 1717a: 98). In *The Second Part of the State Anatomy* he complains about those critics who suspected him of being either irreligious or a Socinian. He assures the reader that in all the books he ever wrote, there was not one word against religion, and that none of the articles of his creed are 'of that nature, as to hinder me from readily professing my self a member of the National church' (Toland 1717b: 23). To promote the republican project of reform, he adopted two different strategies. As long as he remained optimistic that a Whig government would eventually establish toleration and guarantee the liberty of thought and expression, he insisted on his right to publicly defend liberty and advocate the truth. For instance, in one of his early political pamphlets he declared: 'To employ one's Thoughts on what he pleases, and to speak as freely as he thinks, is the greatest Advantage of living in a free Government.' He even added that 'Life it self should be readily expos'd' to maintain liberty of thought and expression, 'for, without it to live, is, in my Opinion, worse than Death' (Toland 1698b: 5–6; 1701b: 3). As we have seen, the analysis of the 'monster of superstition' made Toland conclude that where philosophers were threatened by persecution, truth had to be communicated in a secret and cautious way. This is why he recommended towards the end of his life that the pantheist 'become wise, or at least possessed of the next Degree to Wisdom'. He 'shall not . . . run counter to the received Theology . . .' and 'shall never run the Risque of his Life, but in Defence of his Country and Friends' (Toland 1751: 107). As a wise man recognises that it is impossible to root out superstition of the mind of all persons, he endeavours to do 'all that can be done, that is, plucking out the Teeth and paring the Nails of this worst and most pernicious of Monsters' (pp. 98–9).

It is obvious that it was extremely difficult for Toland to convince the public of his political moderation. As the contradictions between his political and his philosophical writings demonstrate, in his case the tensions between the professed loyalty to the English monarchy and the advocacy of radical reforms lead again – as at the times of the *libertins érudits* – to a form of split identity. Despite his efforts to disarm suspicions that he was an atheist, it was ultimately impossible for him to reconcile the double roles he played as a political pamphleteer on the one hand and a 'Spinozist' philosopher on the other. For the historian of political thought, the inconsistencies and contradictions in Toland's work are instructive, because they point to the limits of the republican concept of toleration. As we have seen, the formula 'public religion and liberty of conscience' testifies to the 'dilemma' of republican writing after 1689: to advocate the republican ideal without questioning the post-revolutionary régime. As Toland concluded towards the end of his life, the idea of forming an alliance between 'free-thinkers', low churchmen, and dissenters in order to make of England a free government proved to be illusionary. The failure of this attempt helps to explain why the republican concept of toleration, which aimed at combining acceptance of a national religion and liberty of conscience, did not survive in the course of the Enlightenment. In Great Britain as elsewhere, the confrontation between the clergy of the national church and the philosophers who claimed freedom of thought and expression led to the demand to abolish any national establishment. Thus a republican such as Thomas Paine considered the abolition of any religion established and maintained by the state as an essential condition to protect the universal right of conscience. For that reason he advocated the separation of church and state (Paine 1969: 110, 166).

However, the difficulty of combining a national religion and liberty of conscience was ignored by a strand of republican writing that was more concerned with the political function of a public religion. As Moyle had pointed out in his *Essay upon the Constitution of the Roman Government*, Numa – the founder of the religious system of the Romans – 'interwove his moral precepts with his religious doctrine'. For the principle of his morality, justice, was based on the persuasion that 'the gods were the most excellent nature, and the great examples of highest virtue'. According to Moyle, it was from this root that sprung 'that noble branch of their morals, the love of their country, which afterwards grew to be the fundamental article of their ethics, and the standard of all virtue and vice' (Robbins (ed.) 1969: p. 212). This link between public religion and virtue was to be taken up by Rousseau, who conceived of 'civil religion' not as an exclusive national religion, but as a kind of political supplement to Christianity, which for him played the rôle of private religion. As the latter contradicts the political ends of the state, Rousseau introduces civil religion to serve the state's interest in promoting the citizen's virtue, which in turn guarantees the stability of the political order (Rousseau 1762a: 464–9). Adopting Rousseau's concept of civil religion, Gabriel Bonnot de Mably later recommended that the government of the United States introduce a 'moral and political catechism' in order to restrict toleration (Mably 1977g: 412). This seemed necessary for two reasons. First Mably fears that the diversity of religious sects promotes a 'general indifference' in religion and ultimately leads to deism and atheism. The latter endangers the social order, because religion is best suited to making the citizens love the most important virtues (pp. 403–7). Second and more importantly, Mably is convinced that the establishment of unrestricted freedom of thought and expression opens the door to the dissemination of 'errors' and 'lies' that easily dominate men. He thus recommends that the Americans imitate the ancient republics of Sparta and Rome, which prohibited all that could endanger the manners (*mœurs*) (pp. 417–18).

4

The Mechanisation of Virtue: Republican Rituals in Italian Political Thought in the Sixteenth and Seventeenth Centuries

Vittorio Conti

In sixteenth- and seventeenth- century Italy, the word 'republic' was all but a synonym for Venice. When 'republic' was mentioned, Venice was automatically evoked. It is therefore Venice which I shall discuss in this essay. My interests currently focus on demonstrations of the republican spirit in the Venetian world in the sixteenth and seventeenth centuries, and on the ways in which this spirit was disseminated.

The fundamental elements of this are contained, as is well known, in Gasparo Contarini's *De magistratibus et republica venetorum* (1543) and Donato Giannotti's *La republica de' Viniziani* (1540). However, I believe that Contarini's work is much more important than Giannotti's in terms of providing a coherent interpretation of the Venetian world. Contarini was a Venetian aristocrat who tried to propose an image of his homeland which would serve, both at home and abroad, to reinforce the self-awareness of citizens on the one hand, and on the other, to disseminate the image of Venice as a model to be imitated by foreigners. Certainly, Contarini's work was much better known abroad than Giannotti's, thanks to the fact that it was translated into Latin, which meant that the European élite could read it, and thanks also to numerous translations into the main European languages (see Contarini 1599). John Pocock has spoken of 'the mechanisation of virtue' with regard to Contarini's work, and he has defined the description of Venice found therein as that of an 'artificial angel'; this serves to confirm the beliefs of contemporaries, who held that Venice had managed to construct laws which could force Venetians to act in a virtuous manner (Pocock 1975).

Contarini's writings begin with the most obvious of humanist appeals, that of the 'almost eleven hundred years' during which 'the city of Venice survived' and of the 'reason why and form in which it has persisted for so long' (1626: 12–13). Nevertheless, immutability in the form of government

73

of the republic was not considered of great importance in itself, but was in turn founded on an essential element of humanist political thought, that of virtue. The republic had remained unchanged for a very long period of time because its founders had all been of extraordinary virtue, all pursuing the good of the state rather than self-interest (*ibid.*: 13–14). Aristotle's influence had been clearly demonstrated several times in Contarini's works. In this passage it was already evident, even if only implicitly, in the contrast between public and private interests, which was the very factor which Aristotle used to distinguish a good form of government from an evil one (Aristotle, *Politics*, III, 6, 1279a).

The level of abstraction of Contarini's project is evidenced by the opposition between Venice and every other political form described, even the most famous and admired. In other republics the men who remained virtuous and dedicated to the common good constituted the minority, and their actions had been almost entirely stifled by the majority, who lacked virtue. By contrast, it was notable that of those who had founded Venice 'all had devoted themselves to the study of the good of the fatherland' (Contarini 1626: 13). Thus Contarini claimed that Venice was not only exemplary, but unique; it was impossible to compare her with any previous political reality, and she was superior even to the abstract models which the most eminent thinkers had propounded (*ibid.*: 15). Venice was presented as a reality superior even to any Utopia. The author's initial opinion could have no other logical conclusion than that with which the work ends: Venice undoubtedly had divine characteristics.

The virtue of those who founded Venice was translated into the laws, 'the sacred laws', in which virtue had been crystallised, preserving itself from every type of corruption and becoming, in some way, eternal (*ibid.*: 21). The city's founders had even determined the mechanism through which the virtue of its origins could be rendered eternal and objective. It could therefore be claimed that in Venice the sovereignty, the *summa imperii*, did not belong to men, but rather to the law (Silvano 1993: 88). And yet it was men who had to apply the law. The problem was therefore in the form of government proposed by Contarini in the first approximation, that is of the alternation between the rule of a single person and the government of the multitude, the *multitudinis gubernatio*. Of course, the latter solution was to be preferred to the former, especially if the decision was based on examples from history (Contarini 1626: 22). However, pluralist government could provoke public disorder, and for this reason the greatest philosophers had prescribed a due and tempered mixture of the aristocratic and popular state of government, a *temperatio ex optimatum et populari statu* (*ibid.*). The example of Sparta was therefore given, even if a certain form of disgust at it was expressed at the same time ('it is good to discern what cannot be needed under any kind of government')[1] which gave the definitive refutation of the model. This refutation also implicated the model represented by the Roman Republic, and was tied to the fact that Sparta, like Rome, had been created by war, while Venice had been built on peace. The comparison served only to heighten the exaltation of Venice, which (unlike classical models) was oriented towards virtue and the peace by those who had founded her (Contarini 1626: 24).

According to Contarini these values had been consolidated through the use of the mixed state, that is a mixture of good forms of government, of princely sovereignty, of governance by the nobility, *optimatum gubernatio*, and of rule by the citizens, *civile regimen*; these forms had been mixed in such a way 'that the whole appears as balanced as equal weights' (Contarini 1626: 24–5). Commentators have not stressed enough that the theory of mixed government, which was so widespread in the sixteenth century, was not the same as the one which had been handed down by classical tradition. This will be seen in the thought of Gasparo Contarini, who is considered to be one of the main proponents of this doctrine. But this observation could be all but generalised. In the thought of the modern period the three forms of government no longer corresponded to three different social groups, but merely to three different principles relating to the exercise of power. The substance of the classical doctrine of mixed government was no longer used; merely its outward form remained.

Contarini's subsequent statement makes it clear that mixed government was a technical device which was essential to the constitution of the state, rather than a matter of the real involvement of different social groups in its administration. According to him, the supreme authority, the *summa autoritas*, on which the Senate and every Venetian magistrature depended, was to be found in the Maggior Consiglio (Great Council), in which 'all noble citizens come together' and from which the common people were strictly excluded; they had no right of citizenship because, according to Aristotelian philosophy, they carried out servile work (Contarini 1626: 25–7; Aristotle, *Politics*, III, 5). Contarini is considered to be the major theorist of the mixed state in the modern era, but in reality the Venetian example that he set out was none other than that of an aristocratic republic which used complex structures in the exercise of power, structures which were as much of a monarchical nature

---

1. 'bene dignosci nequeat sub quanam gubernation is specie fuerit...collocanda'.

as of a republican one. And nevertheless those who formed part of these structures were always drawn from the same social order, i.e. the aristocracy.

The classical mask of the state was reduced to a delicate artifice of constitutional engineering, which represented an instrument of equilibrium, allowing for the perfect functioning of the machine of state. It was therefore essential to identify the original basis for the recognition of the aristocratic class, which had been the governing class from the very beginning; riches were not the deciding factor, since that would have led to the risk of giving access to government to lowly people who had made money. Those chosen were therefore rather 'men who were distinguished by their nobility, virtues and merits for the good of the republic' (Contarini 1626: 27–8). The descendants of these characters constituted 'the great council, which is in full possession of the highest jurisdiction over the whole republic' (*ibid*.: 28). The Maggior Consiglio was not the expression of the popular state, but it carried out this role, as in a well-constructed play. It was, in sum, a case of form prevailing over substance. The mechanism was more important than the spirit, and guaranteed the immutability of the system.

Popular reason, *ratio popularis*, and aristocratic reason, *ratio optimatum*, also came together in electoral procedure. Voters, who had been chosen by the drawing of lots (*ratio popularis*), freely chose the ablest candidates according to their merits. The former system was characteristic of popular government, the latter of the aristocratic system, but both were reduced to technical principles and provided a harmonious balance between two conflicting impulses (Contarini 1626: 48–9). The themes of the presence of the technical principle of a popular nature and that which concerned aristocratic selection are repeatedly mentioned in the text. On the one hand we find the confirmation that 'in this republic alone proper governance has been entrusted to the citizens as a whole' (*ibid*.: 47) and on the other the concept according to which the equity of numbers, *aequalitas arithmetica*, was combined with the superiority of virtuous men, or better of the fundamental value of the *ratio optimatum*.

Contarini's later chapters were dedicated to the description of Venetian institutions. The Doge, who represented the concept of unity, was the 'governor of the republic', *moderator reipublicae*, whose power was based on law and was regulated both during his life and after his death (Contarini 1626: 50–5). At the same time, great importance was attached to the formalities and rituals of a lay religion of the state.

The Senate constituted the sign of the presence of the aristocratic state of the republic, its *optimatum status*. It embodied the classical Aristotelian principles of the superiority of the old over the young and the centre of harmonious republican equilibrium (Contarini 1626: 81). The Council of Ten (Consiglio de' Dieci) belonged to the same form of government; it was the structure which had prevented tyrannical degeneration in Venice against which 'almost all Italian cities' had fought, whether ruled by popular or aristocratic government (*ibid*.: 94–100; Tenenti 1987). Contarini's image has the fixity of a cinematic frame frozen for ever, whose artificial nature is revealed precisely through the attempt 'to imitate the natural order as much as possible' (Contarini 1626: 171).

This concept of mixed government in relation to Venice was not posited by Gasparo Contarini alone. This is verified in the works of all Venetian authors who wrote about the republic after him. Gasparo's namesake, senator Pier Maria Contarini, wrote a little book entitled *Compendio universal di republica* (1602), in which he exalted his homeland, analysing all forms of government known in its history (Contarini 1990). He held that the 'mixed republic' was the best form of government, and gave the example of Sparta, where the three forms were perfectly mixed (*ibid*.: 41). Venice was also a 'mixed republic', but she was even better than Sparta because she was the result of the mixture of four forms, represented by the Maggior Consiglio, the Senate, the Cabinet (Collegio) and the Doge (*ibid*.: 41–2). Giannotti's influence is clear in this passage (*ibid*.: 54–9), but we are by this point outside the classical doctrine of mixed government. In another section Pier Maria Contarini had defined the Venetian republic as the mixture of five forms of government: the monarchical form represented by the Doge, the aristocratic by the Senate, the oligarchy by the Council of Ten, a fourth element made up of the order of *citizens* (a category of non-nobles halfway between aristocracy and people), and a fifth element, called *mixed democracy*, which was used for the administration of minor offices (*ibid*.: 56). Indeed, he had already claimed that Venice was a 'pure aristocracy' and, at the same time, the best republic in the world (*ibid*.: 36). It was thus confirmed that mixed government was nothing other than a sort of technical artifice designed to provide a better balance for the organisation of the republic.

The rites of the republic were in fact rules, customs, and provisions of the law. The 'most holy law', the constitutional framework which was immutable in terms of its purposes, but often revised in terms of its contents, guaranteed the maintenance of the republican system. Overturning Gasparo Contarini's original premises, according to which the founding fathers of Venice had all been virtuous, a pessimistic view of human nature governed the institutional politics of the republic. Traps, obstacles, and hindrances were necessary in order to force those in power to behave publicly in an objectively virtuous way; otherwise they could act unvirtuously, turning the *res publica* to their own advantage and thereby practising an evil form of government. The traps were the laws and every trap, while it required virtuous behaviour, constituted at the same time the sign of a vice which needed to be controlled (Queller 1987). This was well known even to foreign observers: the English ambassador, H. Wotton, wrote at the beginning of the seventeenth century: 'The state is peaceful thanks more to its wise laws than because of good intentions' (Muir 1984: 303). If republican rites multiplied with the passing of time, as was the case during the sixteenth century, it was indeed a sign of the increase in internal dangers which threatened the republic.

The limits set out by the law began at the personal level, with the aim of avoiding both concentration of power in the hands of a few individuals and foreign influence. In fact, public office was barred to those who were part of the ecclesiastical hierarchy; more than one member of the same family could not be elected to a single institution. There was a rapid rotation of offices (usually annual) and it was forbidden for any individual to hold a plurality of offices. Nevertheless, someone who was elected to an office was obliged to carry out the service for which he had been elected, unless he had valid reasons which allowed him to refuse. The exercise of public virtue, that is the service of the republic, was obligatory. Minor restrictions on this existed at the level of institutional bodies. Even the Maggior Consiglio, the official seat of sovereignty, and therefore also the body best qualified to issue laws, would encounter obstacles to this function: certain fundamental rules governing the Venetian constitutional framework could not in fact be modified even by the simple will of the Consiglio, unless by qualified majority and with the agreement of the other bodies of the council (Maranini 1974: 81–3). Despite this, however, the Maggior Consiglio remained the arbiter of disputes between the other organs of the state, very many of which could have recourse to it.

The Senate was the institution in which the element of continuity in the exercise of Venetian political power was concentrated. Its importance had grown with the passing of the centuries; at the same time, in the fifteenth and sixteenth centuries, the number of those who had the right to participate in its activities, because of the office that they held, had grown; this was in addition to the sixty elected members (Maranini 1974: 139–62). Practically every important magistrature had access to the Senate, which thus became the chamber where the internal disputes of the governing aristocracy were settled: channelled and formalised in one place specifically appointed for this purpose, these disputes lost their potentially destructive impact and became an element which was constructive in the better functioning of the machinery of state. The importance attached to electoral procedures was indicative of the attention which was turned to the forms, mechanisms and exterior instruments which protected the immutability of the republic and conserved it, as if embalmed, to the admiration of observers and the satisfaction of citizens.

But beyond the balances of a government which defined itself as 'mixed', there was also the network of Venetian institutions, a real spider's web which served to guarantee stability and the conservation of *aequalitas* among citizens. It is said that the vast majority of offices put into place in the republic of Venice served to give position and involvement to the majority of the aristocracy, and also to provide supplementary earnings to the many impoverished nobles who lived in the city (Queller 1987: 68–9). This observation underlines a real problem, but we must be careful not to use our modern mentality to interpret the behaviour of men of the sixteenth and seventeenth centuries. For these men the most important factor in the increase in the number of public offices was the idea that a great number of these were necessary to keep the peace between members of the governing group, and also to stabilise the government thanks to a mechanism that could be defined as 'checks and balances'. Each office served to counterbalance another power and prevent its malfeasance. The creation of the Council of Ten had been one of the most important manifestations of this attitude of control. Another form of guarantee was provided by the principle of collegiality: 'it was always the custom that no one magistrate held supreme authority; rather they preferred to vest supreme jurisdiction in the college and council' (Contarini 1626: 192).[2]

As has been noted above, there were general principles which upheld this organisation of power: the rotation of offices, which gave everyone the chance to take part in the government of the republic; the ban on members of a single family forming part of the same magistrature at the same time, in order to avoid the concentration of power; strictly secret ballots in order to guarantee freedom of judgment and choice; the obligation on all to accept the outcome of the election. Only members of certain eminent magistratures, such as the Doge and the Procurators of San Marco, were elected for life in order to ensure the continuity of the state. They were, however, surrounded – especially the Doge – by such a large number of precautions that it could be said that he was a prince in quality and style, a senator in

2. 'Mos semper fuit ne quisquam magistratus ... summam authoritatem habeat: sed summum jus collegiorum et consiliorum esse voluerunt.'

council and a citizen in public, *in habitu princeps, in senatu senator, in foro civis* (Muir 1984: 288).

The position of the Doge was exemplary from the point of view of the rules of checks at the heart of the Venetian constitutional system. The Doge was at the official summit of the republic, and was elected for life to contrast, in terms of continuity, with the rapid changes in the office holders of the magistratures. He presided over all the political assemblies. He was, however, debarred from any autonomous initiative by a body of legislation which had become ever more stringent with the passing of the centuries, in defence of the republican form of government. Thus the fear that had preoccupied the Venetian aristocracy throughout the medieval period was perpetuated into the modern period: that of becoming a *signoria*, a council without real powers, as had happened in the majority of the main communes in north and central Italy. As late as the middle of the sixteenth century, when Jacopo and Domenico Tintoretto painted the portraits of Doges from the high Middle Ages to their own times in the hall of the Maggior Consiglio in the Doge's Palace, a black cloth stood out in the middle of the paintings, with the words: 'Hic est locus Marini Faletri decapitati pro criminibus.'[3] This was a reminder, to the reigning Doge as much as anyone else, of what became of Marin Faliero, condemned and decapitated during his reign, in the middle of the fourteenth century, because of his attempt to make himself lord of Venice.

Beyond this menacing iconography, all the obligations and limitations which concerned the Doge were contained in the coronation oath (*promissione ducale*), which was continually revised, amplified and made more demanding by the 'correctors' who were elected expressly for this purpose. The Doge could not receive foreign envoys nor Venetian ambassadors who had returned home, unless he was in the presence of a certain number of Councillors who surrounded him at all times (the Cabinet) and the Capi della Quarantia (the supreme judicial magistrature). He could not act freely in the management of his own property; he was subject to a whole series of obligations and limitations. And finally, while he could not give up his mandate without the agreement of six members of the Cabinet and the majority of the Maggior Consiglio, he could on the other hand be deposed. A deposition was, in fact, carried out – although in a quite irregular manner – in the case of Francesco Foscari in the middle of the fifteenth century. Even after the Doge's death the three Inquisitors of the deceased Doge held his property in sequestration,

3. 'This is the place of Marin Faliero who was beheaded because of his crimes.'

until such time as his government's accounts had been examined (Maranini 1974: 273–82).

Another very important factor in the operation of the 'mechanisation of virtue' was made up by the Venetian electoral systems, in which drawing lots was mixed with the secret ballot. Each election had its own rules. If we look at the election of the Doge we shall see the complexity of the system, which aimed to produce the greatest possible impartiality, as well as to provide the conditions by which the candidate whom the majority judged the best could be chosen. The election was held in the Maggior Consiglio, but only aristocrats over the age of thirty could take part. A number of balls, which corresponded to the number of people present, were put into a container, as well as thirty golden balls. Those who took out the golden balls were separated from the others and continued with the electoral processes; inside another ballot box thirty white and nine golden balls were placed. Those who took out the nine golden balls elected forty people. These forty people selected twelve aristocrats from their number who, in their turn, elected twenty-five people. From these twenty-five lots were drawn to pick nine who elected another forty-five. From the forty-five elected eleven were taken who voted for the forty-one electors of the Doge.

Contemporaries admired this system; its principles were used for all elections, although in a simplified form. Francesco Sansovino saw fit to provide a detailed account of the procedure for electing the Doge in his guide to Venice, as if this were one of the marvels of the city (Sansovino 1581, XI, fo. 180ᵛ). These methods also attracted a great deal of attention from foreigners and were a source of profound fascination to them, because they thought that the institutional mechanisms in place in Venice were all but perfect and that the Venetians had thereby written virtue into the law, guaranteeing incomparable balance and stability to the republic. Contemporaries considered this series of measures to be a body of legislation that should be studied and imitated.

In 1619 a Flemish writer, Ioannes Cotovicus, published in Antwerp a work entitled *Itinerarium hyerosolymutanum et syriacum*, the tale of a journey to the East which he had undertaken in 1598; the last chapter of the work was dedicated to Venice. He added a *Synopsis reipublicae venetae* as a conclusion to his work; this was an effective synopsis, because it included complete information about the Venetian magistratures on a single large page folded several times. The reader was thus able to grasp the full variety and subdivision of the magistratures at a glance. It was a demonstration of the need to have, in synthetic and complete form, a general table showing the complex mechanisms which were used to regulate political life in Venice.

Even the ballot boxes and balls used for ballots had precise characteristics which reflected the need to guarantee secrecy and impartiality. And even these technical elements were minutely studied by foreigners, because they saw in them the best methods that human wisdom had been able to invent to help or compel men to be virtuous.

In the collection of the Elzevier 'Petites Républiques', published in Leiden in the first half of the seventeenth century, there is a text which includes the political work of Gasparo Contarini. In the second edition of this volume a short treatise was added to complete Contarini's work (1628: 248–58). It was by Baldassare Bonifacio, a Venetian man of letters, and concerned electoral procedures, the form of the ballot boxes and the characteristics of the balls used in the votes: 'The balls are covered with linen so that they do not reveal by the sound they make as they fall into the ballot box who has been elected' (*ibid.*: 251). All this was reported for the information and imitation of foreigners.[4] The edition of the work of Giannotti, published in the same collection, contained a certain number of prints which depicted the arrangement of the patricians during the sittings of the Maggior Consiglio, voting procedures and ballot boxes (Giannotti 1631).

We should not conclude that all this was the result of a particular extravagance on the part of the Elzevier editor, because the same print of the Maggior Consiglio was also published, with an explanatory caption, in Johan and/or Pieter de la Court's *Political Balance* (1662b), and it is the same engraving which appears on the cover of the book by Haitsma Mulier about the myth of Venice in Dutch political thought of the seventeenth century (1980).

Alongside these theoretical methods and expedients which constituted the form of institutional mechanisation, there were the images provided by republican architecture and iconography, which served to reproduce the rituals of the republic in a plastic or iconic manner, which was therefore immediately interpretable by the people. Edward Muir has written a very interesting book about the civic rituals of Venice in the sixteenth century. These rituals served to give visible expression to the ideology of the republic. The ducal procession was the most important ritual demonstration of this ideology. The order of the procession had been established very strictly, and symbolised the constitutional idea of the republic. It had a structure which

---

4. Contarini 1628: 258: 'The most beautiful principles on which our fatherland is built ought to be transferred to the foreign nations outside of Italy; those educated in these principles will then be able to consider and make some use of them in their public affairs.'

converged towards the centre of the procession, which was identified with the centre of power. In the first part, civil officials took their place, in order of importance. They belonged to the class of citizen. In the second section was the Doge, preceded by the signs of his authority, that is the throne and the golden cushion, and covered by the golden canopy, which symbolised his position between the sovereigns, similar to that of the Pope and the emperor. For this reason the Doge was indeed flanked by two ambassadors, papal and imperial, who represented their respective sovereigns. In the third section the great magistrates of the republic followed, the most important first (Muir 1984: 221–6). All this expressed both republican hierarchy and the independence of Venice from the major sovereigns of the Earth, and it manifested likewise the social peace which reigned in the republic. This internal tranquillity constituted one of the greatest sources of pride which Venetians had in themselves and their state and in the image which they wanted to project to foreigners.

About 1530 the great artist Iacopo Sansovino, father of the prolific author Francesco, rebuilt the Loggetta of St Mark's Square for the Doge Andrea Gritti. In a work of 1562, Francesco Sansovino has left us an interpretation of the allegorical figures in this monument, which symbolised Venice. There was the statue of Minerva, the image of the wisdom of the authors of the laws of Venice. Beside Minerva stood Mercury, who symbolised the eloquence of Venetian magistrates and ambassadors. Apollo was the sun, a unique reality, as Venice was unique; but Apollo was also the god of music and harmony, which expressed the harmonious union of the magistrates, which made Venice immortal. Lastly, there was the statue of Peace, that is of the concord which reigned between the orders of Venice (Sansovino 1562, fos. 20^v–21^v).

Thus the 'mechanisation of virtue' could act at different levels of influence: that of elevated literature, where Venetian republicanism was theorised; that of popular literature, in which the ideas developed in the first level were disseminated; that of artistic or ceremonial image, which inculcated in the people an image which was consistent with the theory.

5

From Virtue to Politeness

IAIN HAMPSHER-MONK

I

Whilst republicanism can be thought of in largely institutional terms, recent Anglophone historical scholarship has stressed a republican preoccupation with more extensive concerns, with what might be called the moral economy of a society. So understood, its scope included the military, legal and economic arrangements of a society and the dynamic interaction of these through time as they shaped the moral personalities of its citizens. Moreover, this view suggested, republicanism was a political *language*. It could – for those using it – become broadly constitutive of attempts to understand the dynamic of political phenomena. Aspects of its analysis could therefore be applied by writers who accepted the monarchical institutions of modern European states (e.g. Montesquieu 1748, and, surprisingly, Burke 1991: 248). The language of republicanism largely contributed to our understanding of the complexity of the historical causes operating on the political. Conceiving of the state as an essentially human response to secular change forced engagement with issues of causality in a way that thinking of the state in terms of the languages of covenant, jurisprudence, custom, grace or providence – to mention the main early-modern contenders – did not (Pocock 1971a, 1972).

The language of republicanism thus became important in articulating and responding to the complex political processes affecting the early modern state. These were traditionally anathematised by thinkers with a republican programme – the rapid increase in commercial activity, the growth in the powers of the executive and the acquisition of empire. Both commercial activity and imperial expansion undermined equality and independence and – by bringing in luxuries and affluence to the metropolis – softened the *mores* and weakened the austerity required for the maintenance of *virtù*. Such developments therefore threatened traditional republican political programmes. The cultivation of the polite arts was often implicated with commerce and the riches of empire: together they formed a polarity opposed to republican plainness, material austerity, and a rule which was both politically and geographically limited.[1] Yet, as David Armitage shows (see Chapter 2 in this volume), despite an awareness of this destructive potential, many early-eighteenth-century thinkers were reluctant to forgo commercial and imperial expansion. Within the language of republicanism a debate took place about the possibility of accommodating these changes within a state which remained under the control of rational, free citizens, and central to this debate was the role and status of polite manners, which, amongst many British thinkers, displaced virtue as the central quality of political personality (Pocock 1985a, ch. 2).

Part of the story here relates the success or failure of this enterprise. Yet in what follows we may wish to consider the possibility that the linguistic adaptation of republicanism to the effects of modernity – particularly in its relationship with politeness – involved the effective abandonment of it as a project.

To many republicans, the polite arts, which flourished with material opulence, produced a manner and an aesthetic which delighted in form over content and which, in celebrating wit in manners above all, valued insincerity and flattery. The difference could be epitomised in the juxtaposition between the sophisticated yet limited rhetorical opportunities provided by a court and the plainer yet unconstrained conditions of the open forum. The constraint required by the polite court context is a well-established *topos* by the time of Castiglione, who devotes the second half of Book II of *The Courtier* to a discussion of the acceptable forms of eloquence and wit (Castiglione 1967: 151–201). As modern commentators note, courtly wit was confined to politically 'safe' objects. Derision of rustics, the politically unsophisticated or the religiously naïve was safe sport, but the courtier must learn not to mock 'those who are universally favoured ... and powerful ... nor again those of such exalted rank that their slightest anger can do one great harm' (*ibid*.: 156). Courtly wit was ultimately incompatible with that independent pursuit of distinction in the service of the public good so closely tied to the *virtù* of the free citizen. Courtiers had 'lost the freedom of the

---

1. The *political rule* of empire, required, as Montesquieu and Rousseau observed, greater concentration of power in the centre, a larger administrative apparatus; and the *culture* of empire commonly involved citizens in the experience of absolute rule in the provinces, both in America (Burke 1887: 31) and in India (Burke 1981: 402–3), which undermined respect for free institutions at home.

open square, the only place where man can practise civic virtues, as earlier humanists like Leon Battista Alberti repeatedly said' (Grafton 1996: 30). The court was a segregated and privileged social space, operating within stylised and prescribed limits precluding open political confrontation. Indeed the artificiality of courtly culture was retrospectively stigmatised as a culture of deceit, linking an aesthetic preoccupation with style to moral deviousness. In the courts of the Italian Renaissance, noted Adam Smith, in his *Lectures on Rhetoric*, 'nothing could be of greater reproach to a man of genius than that he was of an open and undesigning character' (Smith 1983: 114).

In early modern Europe this antithesis between courtly and republican manners was typically explored through reflections on the transition from republican to imperial Rome, and a stance on the conflicting aesthetics of that transition was a prominent feature of the debate. In England this happened at least twice. During the personal rule of Charles I, poets such as Thomas May, Sir Richard Fanshawe and Edmund Waller turned to an Augustan poetics in both form and politics to support Charles's stance against the forces of disorder evident in the overthrow of Buckingham.[2] Horace and Virgil eventually became, for opposition writers such as Pope, the epitome of courtly dishonesty, deploying their art to conceal the destruction of their country's liberty. For one representative anonymous author they were:

> flattering, soothing Tools,
> Fit to *praise Tyrants* and *gull fools*
> (Anon. 1740: 13, cited in Weinbrot
> 1978: 131)

The role of the polite arts in the loss of republican liberty emerges as a clear concern, even for those who wished to distinguish between the Hanoverian and Augustan world. Once the usurping emperor Augustus had 'grasp'd the Helm of State' his 'infant tyranny' needed the assistance of artists:

> Their Harps with flattering Sounds repay'd
> Th' imperial Patron's skilful Cost:
> But whilst th' applauded Artist play'd
> The *Roman* Liberty was lost.
> (Wicksted 1717: 2–3, in Weinbrot 1978: 126)

2. Peltonen 1995: 287–9; Norbrook 1999: 66 ff. One specific stylistic device identified with the royalism of Waller and Denham was the celebration 'of political concord in predominantly closed couplets' with a caesura dividing and balancing each line (Norbrook 1999: 71 n. 29). This bears a striking resemblance to the form from which the radical young Coleridge celebrated his emancipation after 1789, seeking instead '. . . lines running into each other instead of closing at each couplet, and of natural language, neither bookish nor vulgar', cited in Holmes 1990: 35.

At work was a process not of mere exculpation, but of deep moral subversion. The writings of Augustus's apologists not merely concealed vice but undermined the very sense of it. Such artful 'management' (a clear reference to Walpole) eased the path from virtue to shamelessness:

> His sly, polite, insinuating style
> Could please at court and make Augustus smile
> An artful manager that crept between
> His friend and Shame, and was a kind of screen.

There is a widespread republican distrust of polish, wit and the showy intellect, a sense, even, that they are incompatible with moral seriousness. Pope's imaginary speaker chiding the poetic recluse who refuses to trim to the prevailing political winds says:

> You grow correct, that once with rapture writ,
> And are besides *too moral for a wit*.
> (Pope 1738, ll. 19-22, 3-4; emphasis added)

Could wit and polish subsist with moral seriousness? Despite the persistence of this (well-theorised) antipathy between politeness and *virtù* in republican conceptions of politics, the eighteenth century saw several attempts to incorporate politeness into politics deeply imbued with republican values. These were often driven by the perceived need to theorise the effects of an increasingly commercial economy on the manners and mental habits of people. Although the culture of politeness and its conversational ideals thus escaped the confines of the court, it brought with it many of its old associations and problems. Amongst these were the issues of moral sincerity, the relationship of politeness to religion, and the role and scope of public and private, including issues of gender.

II

In a series of important books and articles Nicholas Phillipson, Lawrence Klein and others have explored the origins and aspirations of an early-eighteenth-century language of social analysis which emphasised the political role of polite manners (Phillipson 1987, 1993a, 1993b, 1993c; Klein, 1984, 1989, 1993a, 1993b, 1994; Phillipson and Skinner (eds.) 1993; also Burtt 1992). This can be seen as part of the 'embourgeoisement' of British political culture. It involved the reconceptualisation of man's nature as sociable rather than political – 'men knit together by a love of society, not a spirit of faction'

(Addison and Steele 1710/11, no. 9; Bloom and Bloom 1971: 4–5). Indeed the adaptation of Cicero – an iconic figure in the movement – involved locating the central role given by Cicero to rhetoric and the generation of a *sensus communis*, not in public life but within the more private, and bourgeois sphere of the coffee- and tea-room, conversation, company, and polite literature. The creation of a 'polite' sphere undoubtedly defined a political role for a social group distinct from the 'country' landed interest on the one hand and courtly culture – which in any case declined drastically under the early Hanoverians – on the other.

Politeness was not however simply an economic epiphenomenon. In offering an analysis and persuasive redefinition of that which was 'public', it was a self-conscious political programme (Klein 1989: 588–9) As a programme it aspired to realise the very phenomena it defined and described. The proponents of politeness actively sought, that is, to create a politically significant arena out of these hitherto sociable and still only emergent 'conversible' pursuits.

Authors, whether philosophers or journalists, shared a common concern to formulate philosophically a view of morality, religion, and increasingly politics, grounded in human sociability, and to promote that view to 'society'. The programme was initiated on a range of levels – from high philosophy to the essay and popular periodical – a literary form which itself emerges as part of the movement. But because the formulation of the end was so intimately bound up with the means to its achievement, because sociability was at once a cognitive condition of the values being elaborated, and the means of their promulgation, the vehicle increasingly became the essay and the periodical, in which was portrayed, and which sometimes even constituted, the sociable space which its authors sought to create.

Addison declared his ambition 'to have it said of me that I have brought philosophy out of the closets and libraries, schools and colleges, to dwell in clubs and assemblies, at tea tables and in coffee houses' (Addison and Steele 1710/11, no. 10). Hume, whose still-born *Treatises* (1739–40) had clearly operated at the level of high philosophy, thought 'the separation of the learned from the conversible world . . . to have been the great defect of the last age' and presented himself in his *Essays* (1742) as an 'ambassador from the dominions of learning to those of conversation' (Hume 1985a: 367–70).

Despite such disclaimers, neither Addison nor Hume were mere messengers from the Academy to the Forum. In each case they sought to create as much as to convey, and in seeking to locate the development of new moral and political institutions in the conditions of human sociability, they undoubtedly assisted in the central role attributed to polite manners, and to social, familial and domestic values in the debate over revolutionary France at the end of the century. Like all languages, however, the discourse of polite sociability was open-textured and capable of being evaluated and exploited in diverse ways.

Two quite separate arguments about and in favour of politeness converged in the eighteenth century. One emerged in the England of Anne, associated with the 3rd earl of Shaftesbury and the *Spectator* of Addison and Steele; the other, slightly later, in the mid-century Scotland of Hume and Smith. Each, in different ways, were responses to an oppositionist, anti-court, country, republican ideology with an austere conception of political virtue – independent, simple, frugal, ultimately martial, and public-minded – which might be called 'Catonic' after the eponymous Roman censor. Each sought to fill the syntactic space occupied by the concept of political *virtù* with a contrasting constellation of qualities – sociable, conversible, urbane, decorous (Klein 1989: 586–7). The very structure of civic republican discourse left open the possibility of doing this, for 'manners' had long played a role in the civic understanding of the interplay between institutions, liberty and individual action. The list of qualities outlined by Klein is by no means complete. One increasingly contested dimension is, as will be shown, that along the axis denoting sincerity–irony.

The political thrusts of the two programmes were different. Shaftesbury sought to steal the courtier's clothes by adopting politeness as an opposition programme which could evade the narrowness of country ideology. Hume, conversely, wrote to defuse 'vulgar' political oppositions by showing how polite sociability, far from being an adventitious accomplishment or party tool, was a skill upon which depended the emergence, appreciation and hence maintenance of justice and the social order (Phillipson 1993c).

Both, inasmuch as they sought to recruit constituencies with a mentality informed by a republican oppositionist ideology, had to counter a conviction that a citizen body preoccupied with niceties of taste and fashion tended to the exclusion of any wider or deeper public purpose. Self-absorbed, sensual, effeminate and irresolute citizens were identified with the absolutist court cultures of France, the epitome of decadent luxurious corruption.

Each agreed that progress in the arts and sciences need not, as Rousseau was to claim, be identified with moral equivocation and political corruption. The arts and sciences could be essentially civic adornments, a source of public pride and a resource for political and military greatness. Whilst all this would result in the refinement of republican manners, it need not undermine virtue, in the sense of the disposition to pursue the public over the private good. Conversely, the manners of a court culture such as that of (imperial) Rome did indeed undermine true civility. Whilst we may find there wit and ability, Shaftesbury noted, we cannot find humanity, the sense of the public good or the common interest of mankind. Amongst courtiers there is no true community, 'And where Absolute Power is, there is no Publick' (Shaftesbury 1711: I, 103–7).

There are strong parallels between Shaftesbury and Hume in their moral naturalism, their arguments about refinement and their case for sociability. Both Hume and Shaftesbury note the greater strength of more proximate social relations that results from refined sociability (Shaftesbury 1711: I, 112), the propensity to form parties on frivolous grounds (*ibid.*: 114) and the role of women in the development of sociability (*ibid.*: II, 186). But there was an important difference between Shaftesbury's and the later, Scottish, story. The Scottish account of sociability becomes inextricably bound up with an account of economic process and change which showed ancient societies to be fundamentally different from modern. This made it impossible for the Scots to recommend isolated aspects of ancient policy for contemporary application. Furthermore *all* ancient states are presented as inferior to the possibilities held out by the modern commercial society (Hume 1985a: 383 ff.; Smith 1978: 19–99). Shaftesbury lacks this sense of the historical embedded-ness of culture and this makes isolated aspects of antiquity available to him. However, as Klein has pointed out, within antiquity, Shaftesbury selects Athens as the paradigm of liberty. For Athens, taste, refinement and the arts in general are not simply a product – let alone a morally equivocal one – of the success of civic liberty, rather they are integral to the process of developing and securing liberty.[3] Shaftesbury sees this process not as one which interacts with the economy or military life as in the Scottish and Machiavellian sto-ries, but as internal to the development of culture itself. For it was oratorical competition in a free society that engendered in citizens a refinement and critical judgment which then spread out to embrace other forms of cultural performance and production. A diverse capacity for critical appreciation was both a product of and a medium of public liberty. As Klein felicitously puts it: 'the polishing of forms reflected a reforming of sensibility: politeness was a deep structure of temper' (Klein 1989: 598). Instead of liberty depending

---

3. Shaftesbury enjoyed a huge vogue in Germany, where the project of establishing a political culture through aesthetic education came, partly for political reasons, to be widely pursued. Walter, in *Die Meistersinger*, epitomises this – as Hans Sachs makes explicit – winning full civic status (and his bride) through aesthetic pre-eminence.

on quite other institutions – property-holding, military service and laws as for instance in civic republicanism – liberty was now identified with a public world of critical discussion and debate which sustained both a public sphere and the public values identified with it. The wide-spread and social pervasiveness of this sphere of cultivation itself provided the political support and guarantee of political liberty.

What Shaftesbury was seeking to do was to move the locus of politeness and refinement from the Court to the opposition in the Forum, whilst at the same time showing its values (once deployed there) to be functional for, rather than threatening of, a free society. Such a move reflected the shift of both his own political status and that of his grandfather from court insider to outsider (Klein 1994: 14–20).

Shaftesbury explains his enterprise to the reader, as Hume was to do later, as the remarkable one of introducing philosophy to a polite and fashionable world deeply out of humour with it (Shaftesbury 1711: II, 181 ff.). In doing so he is as careful to exclude that philosophy which is 'immured in Colleges and Cells' as he is to criticise a certain kind of fashionable company which regards any intrusion of philosophy into conversation as pedantry, and morality as preaching. Such a conversational culture is falsely justified as favouring women but would rightly be ridiculed by them and 'is in truth more a Disfigurement than any real Refinement of Discourse' (*ibid.*: 184–6). Such condescension is linked to courtly gallantry and is exploitative rather than respectful of women. It derives from a Gothic culture 'sprung from the mere Dregs of *Chivalry* and *Knight-Errantry*', a culture too (a dig at Catholicism here) where '*She-Saints* are worshipped by . . . Authority from Religion' (*ibid.*: 195).

The mechanism of this conversational culture in sustaining liberty broadly parallels the mechanism which renaissance republicans claimed to have exposed in their study of the ancient societies depicted by classical authors. In Machiavelli's famous formulation, it is exposure to *necessità* in the form of the harsh physical conditions of political founding, severe laws and military service which engenders *virtù*. The advent of luxury and refinement threatens this benign relationship. In Shaftesbury's analysis of Athens, however, the development of polite discourse replaces exposure to *necessità* as a source and support of political liberty. 'All Politeness is owing to Liberty. We polish one another, and rub off our Corners and rough Sides by a kind of *amicable Collision*. To restrain this, is inevitably to bring a kind of Rust upon Mens Understandings. 'Tis a destroying of Civility, Good Breeding, and even Charity it-self, under pretence of maintaining it' (Shaftesbury 1711: I, 64–5).

The process of polishing both required liberty of discourse and opinion, and sustained it by engendering a taste for and appreciation of public debate.

One vital condition obtaining in classical Athens which Shaftesbury iden-tified as necessary to this process was a freedom in the use of humour and satire so that 'Everything which might be imposing, by a false Gravity or Solemnity, was forced to endure the Trial of this Touchstone.' Reviewing the progress of both poetry and philosophy in ancient Greece as a trial between the sublime and the increasingly sophisticated comic culminating in the genius of Menander, Shaftesbury concludes that whatever form criticism takes 'it can become none besides the grosly superstitious, or ignorant, to be alarmed at this *Spirit*'. For Shaftesbury not only was this liberty of 'amicable collision' a vital source of 'Wit, Learning and good Sense', the converse was also true. That is, the attempt to exclude certain areas of life from the reach of wit and raillery was the conversible equivalent of tyranny. This was especially true of religion. Shaftesbury shared the anti-clericalism of many a radical whig.[4] The articulation of his anti-clericalism deployed his new analysis of the role of wit and criticism in the growth of a polite and free society (Shaftesbury 1711: I, 9–13; Klein 1993a: 296–300). The zealot used – or tried to use – his solemnity and *gravitas* to pre-empt conversational approaches in which wit might be used to expose imposture. Institutionalised, corporate zealotry – a standing church – was the conversational equivalent of a standing army, a source of real tyranny and not merely an analogue. In 'Miscellaneous Reflec-tions' Shaftesbury described how the ancient Egyptian priesthood, imposing on a people who lacked the critical resources of conversational scrutiny, had eventually grown so large that it is no surprise to find 'the *Property* and Power of the *Egyptian* Priesthood . . . arrived to such a height, as in a manner to have swallow'd up the State and Monarchy' (Shaftesbury 1711: III, 45–50).

In the *Characteristics* Shaftesbury insinuated a connection between the ancient Egyptians and the Hebrews, and thence into Catholic Christianity (and by extension High-Church Anglicanism), so initiating an extensive eighteenth-century historical debate which was not fired by the scholarly pursuit of truth. Avoiding the Egyptians' fate required a religion as sociable and undogmatic as polite society itself, open to critical and even humorous comment, and which did not try to hide behind an imposing (and possibly imposturing) façade. Exposure to polished wit and ridicule was thus an es-sential test in rendering all parts of human life sociable and fit for liberty. Shaftesbury's insistence on extending this test to religion was persistently

---

4. On the origins see Goldie 1993 and Champion 1992.

opposed by his theological adversaries such as the Revd John Balguy. Stylish as he conceded the *Characteristics* were, yet 'to make raillery the test of right reason and ridicule the touchstone of truth is to maintain something that far exceeds the bounds of a paradox', he complained (Balguy 1726: 4–5).

Shaftesbury's insistence on irreverence in assessing the claims of religion undoubtedly offended Christians, but his substantive position went further, threatening the whole orthodox Christian conviction that value and morality derive deontologically from God. The central purpose of the *Characteristics*, reflected Shaftesbury, was

> to recommend MORALS on the same foot, with what in a lower sense is called *Manners*; and to advance PHILOSOPHY ... ON THE VERY Foundation of what is call'd *agreeable* and *polite* ... to assert the Reality of a BEAUTY and CHARM in *moral* as well as in *Natural* Subjects; and to demonstrate the Reasonableness of *a proportionate* TASTE, and *determinate* CHOICE, [as a standard] in *Life* and *Manners*.
>
> (Shaftesbury 1711: III, 163, 303)

In short, Shaftesbury's design, if successful, entailed the independence of morality from God and religion. In this Shaftesbury was rightly seen in the deist camp. His work gave rise to a century-long polemic centred round precisely this issue.[5] Contemporaries were acutely aware of this issue and no one read Shaftesbury under the illusion that his aesthetic could be considered apart from its moral and religious implications. The language and programme of politeness was furthered in terms less contentious to religious sensibilities by the famous essayists Addison and Steele in their journal *The Spectator*. Yet even such attempts to curb the acerbity of political conflict provoked high-Tory charges of insincerity and hypocrisy (Phillipson 1993c: 307–8).

Although the English and the later Scottish programmes of politeness have been seen as distinct enterprises, influences and persons mingled for a while in the Dublin of the 1720s where Adam Smith's eminent predecessor in the Glasgow chair of Moral Philosophy, Francis Hutcheson, participated in a lively salon surrounding Viscount Molesworth, the celebrated Whig commonwealthsman (Stewart 1987; Stewart (ed.) 1990). Hutcheson joined the circle in 1722 or 1723 (Scott 1900: 26). Molesworth, a correspondent of Locke and a friend of Shaftesbury, provided a haven for John Toland, the notorious deist and freethinker, biographer and editor of the works of the prominent republican James Harrington (1737).

---

5. See the path-breaking Aldridge 1951: 371–85, and now Champion 1992.

Molesworth himself has a part to play in the story of politeness. His celebrated *Account of Denmark . . . in the year 1692* (1694), intended as a warning to the British public about the dangers of tyranny (and complained of as a libel on his country by the Danish Ambassador), had stressed the inverse relationship between politeness and liberty, both in ancient Rome and in modern Europe (Molesworth 1694, sig. A3^v, C2^v–C3^v; Klein 1989). Yet Molesworth seems to have moderated his opposition to politeness. Although he published no work of theory himself,[6] he was an enthusiastic patron: the Molesworth circle was, according to Hutcheson's biographer, engaged in 'systematising Shaftesbury's disconnected opinions, and freeing them from their apparent direct opposition to Christianity' (Scott 1900: 30, 29; see also Moore 1990: 45–7). In this the group followed Addison and Steele's attempts to defend a moderate commercial polity by replacing an essentially Augustinian Christianity with a neo-Ciceronian one (Phillipson 1993c: 308).

Hibernicus's Letters were the major product of the Molesworth circle and dedicated to him. The title page claimed their intention 'to promote the cause of Liberty and Virtue'. Hutcheson's two contributions explored the moral paradoxes of a luxurious economy exposed by Mandeville, and laughter, in which polite boundaries are drawn around both the permissible subject matter and the audience before which wit and raillery should be deployed. This was clearly a limited defence of Shaftesbury against contemporary complaints of 'scoffing'. Hutcheson conceded that the growth of cultivated society could seem to foster an irresponsible and indiscriminate levity but certain precautions could limit this. Following Aristotle, he urged that actions, or events which were truly great, should not be subjected to ridicule, or juxtaposed to mean ideas so as to provoke laughter. Hutcheson stressed the importance of social context in rendering raillery responsible. If you must make fun of what is great, he advised 'let it not be in weak company, who have not a just discernment of true Grandeur'. And in objects of ambiguous status, never ridicule their weaknesses without acknowledging their strengths (Hutcheson 1729: 104–5).

Within the programme of politeness, as we have seen, laughter raised important issues concerning its scope and proper object. Implicit in these were issues of social control. The development of taste and sensibility promised new and secular ways of shaping and restraining the passions of men to render them fit for society. It did so in ways which engaged promisingly, both with the increasingly pervasive Lockean philosophical psychology, and

---

6. But see his introduction to his translation of Hotman's *Franco-Gallia* (1721) – obviously itself an editorial labour of some significance.

with observations of the psychological effects of the new commercial society. Emancipated from puritan and civic mistrust of ease or wealth, Hume could celebrate the way the growth of commerce provided escape from the rude barbarity of rustic life, and how the increasingly specialised character of warfare could spare the average citizen its brutalising arts and heroic ethic. The nimble and opportunistic qualities of mind required (and elicited) by the growth of commerce would sit nicely with the development of taste and discrimination in turn required from the consumer (Hume 1985a, esp. pp. 256 ff., 270–1). Yet such benign interaction was neither guaranteed nor entire: indeed a destructive outcome seemed to some inescapable. There was almost universal agreement amongst the high-Tory Anglican clergy, that, at least amongst the vast majority of men, the fear of God was necessary to overcome wickedness, and to sustain society. Once again Balguy's reflection on both Shaftesbury and Hutcheson was characteristic: 'How then can it be imagined, that in respect of the generality of the world, it [discriminating taste or aesthetic sense] should be sufficient for the support and maintenance of virtue?... what slight hold would such intellectual Beauties take on the understanding of the vulgar; and how feebly would they operate upon them'. Basing a moral order on an aesthetic is to expect 'the greatest part of mankind should become philosophers'. The wrongdoer needs to 'be told that... he is incurring endless misery... [only] this may probably work on him' (Balguy 1726: 17, 19). To make a Shaftesburian programme plausible two issues had to be met. It had to be shown, firstly, that moral or aesthetic senses were, or could be made, as widespread as that political opinion on which, it was increasingly recognised, political society depended, and secondly, that refined taste, manners and wit could combine with and reinforce moral sincerity, rather than oppose it through degenerating into cynicism and 'scoffing'. If the first claim was not vindicated, the socialising and moralising role of taste and cultivation must be restricted to a few, leaving the majority of the populace subject to the violent and misguided passions typical of fallen men; the failure of the second would render politeness unsustainable even at the level of a social élite.

Bernard Mandeville had provocatively suggested that the health of the new commercial society positively required individuals to pursue what had hitherto been thought of as the vices of acquisitiveness and luxurious consumption. In tackling Mandeville's maxims Hutcheson, in his other identified contribution to *Hibernicus' Letters*, is at least as concerned to dispose of the (Augustinian) view of virtue as austere moral necessity, as he is to deny that the unrestrained pursuit of material luxury is necessary to support economic health. In doing this he refuses to meet the dilemma as Mandeville posed it. Men do not have to live as hypocrites or choose between a virtuous austerity and an acknowledgedly corrupt material progress. Instead, by allowing *moderated*, identifiably natural desires, we can support an economic progress and a refinement consistent with virtue. This treatment of Mandeville thus also broaches themes concerning the emergence of polite and commercial society but from a different angle. Indeed Hutcheson's two essays, although starting from such diverse topics in psychology and in moral economy, might each have been chosen to illuminate, as it were from different peripheral points, the intervening area of the structure of polite sociability.

Despite Hutcheson's trimming of Shaftesbury's programme it continued to be seen as a threat to traditional deontology. As late as the publication of Bolingbroke's philosophical works (1754) bishop Warburton complained of the prevailing standards which made him (Warburton) appear to be in bad taste in seeking to tie down and deal seriously with the ironic and evasive insinuations of Bolingbroke's deism. Not to respond to Bolingbroke with horror or ridicule 'for fear of transgressing the civil maxims of politeness, would be like the *Dean* the poet speaks of, who scrupled to mention Hell before his audience at Court... We are now become so delicate and fastidious, that it is the *manner of doing*, even things of the highest importance, which carries all the praise.' Yet this propriety of manners, he claimed, had no foundation in nature: ''tis the creature of fashion and as shifting and fantastic as its parent... nothing else than conformity to our present passions or sentiments; our prejudices, or dispositions' (Warburton 1977, Letter 3, pp. xii, liv–lv).

This presentation of politeness as superficial or subversive froth was the established tactic of the traditional republican opponent of courts. Yet by the mid-century the context of its use had become exceedingly complex – it is here being used by a Whig cleric in defence of his established church and dogma against a Tory politician's deism, a politician who, moreover, had himself adopted a radical Whig stance on matters of historiography, political independence and evasive raillery.

Bishop Berkeley too attacked the moral integrity of both Shaftesbury's and Hutcheson's moral naturalism and decorous politeness in his *Alciphron* dialogues. Berkeley also stressed their motivational inefficacy: 'the beauty of virtue... is not a sufficient principle or ground to engage sensual or worldly-minded men in the practice of it'. The supposed uniformity of human judgments which the irreligious 'minute philosophers' suppose can only be explained by an innate moral and aesthetic sense '[m]ay... be sufficiently accounted for by conscience, affection, passion, education, reason, custom, religion; which principles and habits, for aught I know, may be what you meta-phorically call a moral sense?' (Berkeley 1950: 119, 121). Berkeley summed up his objections by pointing out that a naturalistic ethic was flawed precisely because it decoupled morals from a religious deontology and supernatural sanctions, which alone could ground, and exact, obligation:

> So long as we admit no principle of good actions but natural
> affections . . . so long as we apprehend no judgement, harbour no
> fears and cherish no hopes of a future state, but laugh at these with
> the author of the *Characteristics* and those whom he esteems to be
> the liberal and polished part of mankind, how can we said to be
> religious in any sense?
>
> (Berkeley 1948: 253)

'Talk of moral sense or moral beauty' was essentially frivolous, 'at bottom mere bubble and pretence.' Worse: it was false and hypocritical. Exponents of this view are necessarily committed to the view that love of country is 'mere prejudice', that 'mankind are rogues and hypocrites', self-sacrifice is folly, and that 'charity begins at home' (Berkeley 1950: 131). Thus in a move of exquisite rhetorical symmetry, just as the opposition had adopted aspects of politeness as a critique, established religion took over the traditional repub-lican objections to the now redeployed discourse of polite court wit.

However there was another move available to the defender of religious establishment in the turbulent ideological atmosphere of the mid-eighteenth century. Rather than rehearse traditional arguments against the moral insin-cerity of refined politeness, the controversialist could accept its importance whilst seeking to capture its application for his own religious position and deny it to the radical critic.[7]

We can already identify one example of this move in Berkeley himself. For as well as rehearsing the conventional objections to politeness Berkeley also engaged in a rhetorical re-description of some of the qualities of Shaftesbury's programme of politeness. His 'good writing' was tinsel, his 'wit' was affectation, his politeness pedantry, his 'depth' obscurity (Berkeley 1950: 136). This sounds conventional, but Berkeley's stratagem here is to discriminate within, not to reject, politeness. He accepts polite manners but rejects their *counterfeit* in Shaftesbury. It is Christianity, itself, not the polite wits' campaign against it, 'which, to omit higher considerations, hath so vis-ibly softened, polished and embellished our manners' (*ibid.*: 186). This is a

---

7. The notion of controversialists engaged in rhetorical moves of this kind derives from the
   analysis in Skinner 1988a and 1988b.

significant move in our story. It is one made possible by the well-documented, if gradual, complimentary movement of Christian theology itself away from Augustinian and Calvinist austerities (Moore 1990).

Amongst the emerging common-sense school who sought to mitigate the impact of philosophical scepticism on conventional morality and religion, the valencies attaching to politeness could also be reversed. Although Hume had announced his aspiration to render philosophy acceptable to the world of taste and refinement, as religion itself became 'polite' his theological equivocation impeded this aim. James Beattie, the socially and politically most conventional member of the school, criticised the barbarity and *tastelessness* of Hume's, and indeed any, secular moral vision:

> The Views, and expectations of the infidel and sceptic are so full of horror, that, to a man of taste, that is of sensibility and imagination, they are insupportable . . . what true religion and true philosophy dictate . . . is so charming, so consonant with all the finer and nobler feelings in human nature, that every man of taste who hears of it must wish it to be true.

Anyone who sought to 'obtrude [a secular morality] on the weak and unwary, must have something in his disposition, which, to a man of good heart, or good taste can never be the object of envy' (Beattie 1770: 458–9).

This strategy, of seeking to capture the positive associations of politeness for a political culture and establishment which was both Christian and emphatically monarchical, was assisted by another tactic which undercut the critique of politeness as super- or arti- ficial. For, in a phrase of that influential aesthetician James Harris, which Burke was to epigrammatise: 'the only nature to which art belongs is human'.[8] Art and taste were thus relevant to man's religion too. It was, as Beattie maintained, atheism and the secular vision which was barbaric and tasteless and lacking in refinement.

Such considerations made possible Burke's appropriation of taste and politeness in his later anti-Jacobinism. For by the 1790s he could plausibly claim to be defending a polite, refined, and Christian society from rude, barbaric atheists, who were, moreover, rude and barbaric, because they were atheists. The Christian religion was 'one great source of civilisation amongst us . . . we are apprehensive that some uncouth pernicious and degrading superstition might take its place' (Burke 1987: 80). The revolution in France was indeed 'a revolution in ideas of politeness' (*ibid.*: 61), for by a paradoxical process

---

8. Harris 1744: 12; cf. Burke's famous epigram (in his *Appeal*; Burke 1887: 86), 'Art is man's Nature.' On Harris see Probyn 1991.

the French had 'Subtilised [them]selves into savages'. It was the *Philosophes*, claimed Burke, not wholly disingenuously, who had appropriated the language of politeness by 'endeavouring to confine the reputation of sense, learning and taste to themselves and their followers . . . a narrow and exclusive spirit' which has been 'no less prejudicial to literature and taste than to morals and true philosophy' (*ibid.*: 97). But they had failed; their product – the revolution – was 'destitute of all taste and elegance'; the French Assembly exhibited 'a coarseness and vulgarity in all the proceedings' (*ibid.*: 68, 70).[9]

As the language of taste and polite cultivation became identified with, rather than a threat to, an enduring Christian civilisation, and as civilisation itself came increasingly to be seen as an historical and cumulative product, taste and cultivation could be attached to old establishments and traditions rather than opposing them.

History, however, was now philosophical. The Scots historians of civil society had brought to history a sense of social process. Hume and Smith had tried to show that the interactions which had given rise to and comprised commercial society could also give rise to the manners and beliefs necessary to sustain it. Such harmony was not, of course, guaranteed, and towards the end of his life Hume saw signs of its being threatened by unscrupulous politicians willing to mortgage the nation's future for their own popularity (Pocock 1985a, ch. 7).

There were, though, more alarming versions of the historical process. According to these, the necessary belief systems were not produced by the age that required them. Instead use was made of pre-existing moral dispositions inherited from earlier ages. The 'antient manners' of nobility and religion, thought Burke, provided the refinement and civility, the 'shade', under which both modern learning and a modern economy flourished and depended (Burke 1987: 70). In Robertson's . . . *Progress of Society in Europe* (1769), and in Millar's *Origin of the Distinction of Ranks* (1771), as Pocock has pointed out, Burke could have read accounts of the origin of polite and commercial society in which it was the survival of the chivalric value system produced in feudal society that played a major part (Burke 1987; Pocock 1985a: 197 ff.). Burke may indeed have read them, although neither book was to be found in his library. A book which was, however, was Richard Hurd's *Letters on Chivalry and Romance*. Hurd (1720–1808) was bishop of Lichfield, then of Worcester. The *Letters* were a substantial and popular work, going through four editions between 1759 and 1778. Like the Scots, Hurd also traced the influence and

---

9. The Revolutionaries had continued and would continue to concern themselves with politeness in the sense of forms of address, procedure, and dignity. See France 1992, ch. 8 and refs. therein.

importance of what he called the 'mighty river' of chivalry into the modern world of manners. He too regarded its influence as benign and enduring: the spirit of romance kindled by chivalry had long outlived its demise; and 'continued its light and heat even to the politer ages'. He saw the influence of and relationship between Homeric and classical Greece as analogous to that obtaining between the age of chivalry and modern, commercial society (Hurd 1762: 5, 3, 26).

Hurd contrasted this story with the programme of neo-classical politeness championed, he claimed, by the French, whose language, manners 'and some worse things' were taken up in England after the restoration 'by our Frenchified King and his royalists'. They were perpetuated by Hobbes, Davenant and Shaftesbury ('for whom the "Gothic manner" ... is the object of his raillery'), whilst 'it was ultimately Addison who gave the law here' (Hurd 1759: 80–5). However, given the inspiration he sees the spirit of chivalry providing for Spenser, Milton and Shakespeare, Hurd urges his readers to ask themselves whether 'the philosophic moderns have gone too far, in their perpetual ridicule and contempt of it?' (Hurd 1759: 4).

Hurd presages Burke more extensively, and more precisely, than Robertson or Millar; he also completes the ideological circle we have been tracing concerning the political role of politeness. He construes politeness in defence of the established order and in such a way as to oppose it to radical programmes. He re-interprets Shaftesbury's account of the origins of politeness in classical Athens claiming instead its origins in the degenerate French monarchy and assigns different values from Shaftesbury to the origins of different politenesses. Hurd, as would Burke, asserts the pre-eminence of (romantic) politeness – a product of heroic cultures – as a *condition for*, rather than as a *product of*, the commercial economy. Finally, he explicitly seeks to decouple the origins of *his* politeness from both its embarrassingly courtly and its sceptical sources whilst seeking to link Shaftesbury to both.

The successful polite defence of establishments allowed – or forced – radicals to reassert virtuous simplicity – at least of style – in opposition to polished and mannered prose. It becomes a preoccupation of the delegates to the French National Convention. Delegate Manuel's proposal to lodge the President in the Tuileries as required by the 'dignité et grandeur' of their enterprise was ridiculed by Chabot, who denied they needed 'autre dignité que de vous mêler avec les sans-culottes qui composent la majorité de la nation'. The opportunity was eagerly seized by Tom Paine, who added a new twist to the simple–artful polarity suggesting that Burke's support for the ancient régime was not merely collusion with a court culture, but a

collusion grounded in linguistic artifice – Burke 'degenerates into a composition of art' and 'lived within the bastille of a word' (Paine 1969: 51, 80) – and
which could be dissolved through ridicule or plain speaking. The argument
about politeness comes to focus on linguistic propriety and reform, and
scholars have increasingly echoed participants in noting the rhetorical
and linguistic dimension of the clash between Burke and his protagonists
(Boulton 1963; Smith 1984; Lock 1985; Hampsher-Monk 1988). Reformers
increasingly sought through the reform of language to *dismantle* the mannered politeness, which was used as a means of class exclusion (Spence 1775;
Tooke 1786–1805), or pursued programmes of education for effective speaking (Burgh 1761; Priestley 1762; Thelwall 1808; Cobbett 1819, letter 1).

This contribution has shown that although the language of manners was
originally deployed by Shaftesbury against an Anglican monarchichal establishment, for recognisably civic republican ends, by the end of the century it
was being used to *defend* the established alliance between church and state
against republican opponents. This should not surprise us. The conception
of political theories as languages enables us to conceive of them as flexible
entities within which not only a range of locutions but politically quite different strategic moves were possible (Pocock 1985a, ch. 1; Skinner 1988c:
passim).

However the rhetorical exploitation of one area of a language for political
purposes produces stresses or enables counter-claims to be made in others.
The emphasis on manners, politeness and socialisation politicised wide areas
of social life, ranging from the propriety of humour to the proper limits of
economic consumption. In an important sense too it politicised the domestic
sphere. This is not to say that it empowered women but it made possible a
new range of claims in which might be framed arguments for that end.

Women had long been linked with discussions of wit and the development
of polite manners. In Castiglione's *Courtier*, Giuliano makes the scholastic
point that since gender is a difference in *material*, *bodily* form, the minds
of women are (at least) equal in understanding to those of men. In the
ensuing playful discussion the puckish claim is advanced (surely a daring
play on Aquinas's famous dictum) that 'woman does not receive her being
from man but rather perfects him' (Castiglione 1967: 218, 225). It is women
moreover who intervene to remind speakers of the boundaries of propriety
(*ibid.*: 176, 221). Addison and Steele stressed that Spectatorial conversation
was to be found at the tea-table as much as in the coffee house (1710/11, no. 4),
and a crucial stage in the development of French polite conversation took

place under the aegis of female *salonières*. 'Women', agreed Hume, were 'Sovereigns of the Empire of Conversation'. It was requisite that their alliance be sought against the 'enemies of reason and beauty', for they were 'much better judges of all polite writing than men of the same degree of understanding' (Hume 1985a: 535–6). For the severer defendant of austere virtue, of course, such claims only reinforced suspicions about the fickle and unsubstantial quality of refined politeness as a substitute for *virtù* – the eponymously male quality.

The role of women in eliciting and sustaining the manners appropriate to a polite and free society eventually became salient in the family and in child-rearing. A focus on the domestic sources of character- and belief-formation, given the dominant role of women in this sphere, could lead a writer like Mary Wollstonecraft not only to excoriate the cold, unnatural and property-oriented aristocratic family, but to call for a recognition of the rights and political contribution of women in this sphere, and, had she lived, in the sphere of politics conventionally understood too. Paine and Wollstonecraft each denounced what they saw as Burke's meretricious identification of the natural family with the artificial institutions of primogeniture and hereditary property. These, in fact, violated natural familial affection, sacrificing the younger children to the oldest – 'Aristocracy never has more than *one* child; the rest are begotten to be devoured' (Paine 1969: 82; Wollstonecraft 1995: 21). Concern to concentrate the descent of property, thought Wollstonecraft, inhibited early marriage, the ensuing repressed desires encouraging libertinage and coquetry (Wollstonecraft 1995: 22).

Her argument contributed to a growing debate about the political implications of the family and domestic character formation. In her *Vindication of the Rights of Woman* (1792) Wollstonecraft exploited the increasingly acknowledged political salience of manners to stress the political character of the domestic arena and the distorting consequences of women's confined roles there. The structure of the home reflected, she claimed, the flawed – because unequal – relations of the parents and so influenced their children. The prevailing model of femininity – weakness and vulnerability – prevented women from fulfilling an equal role or even eliciting respect from their husbands (Wollstonecraft 1975b: 158).

However, this issue was captured by the anti-Jacobins and radical apostates who, whilst agreeing that the family was the school of those natural sentiments on which morality and refined manners relied, stressed the role of deferential and submissive femininity as an essential basis of it. The pre-revolutionary sexual laxity and post-revolutionary easy divorce of the French (reinforced for many by Wollstonecraft's own sexual career) was even held responsible – through undermining the family – for the excesses of the revolution (Montluzin 1988: 13). Looking back, Burke's old protagonist and vindicator of revolutionary France, (now Sir) James Mackintosh, reflected that 'Purity is the sole school of domestic fidelity and domestic fidelity is the only nursery of the affections between parents and children, from children towards each other, and through these affections, of all the kindness that renders the world habitable' (Mackintosh 1851: 119; Deane 1988: 53 ff.).

It is perhaps perverse to see William Godwin as an outcome of the programme of politeness.[10] For Godwin's criterion of both political justice and private virtue was 'the greatest sum of pleasure or happiness' (Godwin 1985: 76, 185). To this end he supported a strict act utilitarianism to which all obligations arising from promises, familial duty and conventional institutions such as marriage and political society were immediately vulnerable. Nevertheless this principle was accompanied by, and frequently in tension with, two others which owed much to his dissenting background. One was the absolute obligation of sincerity and truth-telling, and the other that the 'conviction of a man's understanding is the only legitimate principle imposing on him the duty of adopting any species of conduct' (*ibid.*: 208, 311 ff.). Godwin consistently held that principles cannot be enforced. A 'revolution of opinions is the only means of attaining to this inestimable benefit' (*ibid.*: 716). Formal associations, let alone political parties, were 'of a highly dangerous nature' (*ibid.*: 288); indeed, Godwin criticised all collective activity not resulting from conscious and continuing individual conviction, expressing serious reservations even about theatrical productions and orchestral playing (*ibid.*: 760). His utilitarian utopia was to be brought about through discharging a duty laid on each of us to inform each other where they had failed to pursue the happiness of all (*ibid.*: 311 ff.). This might well seem to overstep the bounds of politeness; indeed it did if by politeness we mean that which stands 'between the feelings of the heart and external behaviour' and if it means there is 'vastly too much politeness in the world'. Yet Godwin fought for the term, insisting – with a reference back to Shaftesbury – that politeness, 'properly considered, is no enemy to admonition' and 'seldom or never at variance with sincerity' (Godwin 1993: 221, 229, 231). Moreover, psychologically, the very ability to act virtuously was conditional on our ability to situate ourselves 'in the place of an impartial spectator . . . uninfluenced by our prejudices . . . [but by] the intrinsic circumstances of our neighbour' (Godwin 1985: 174).

10. But see the important suggestion to this effect by Gregory Claeys (Claeys 1993: 189), on whose title I have drawn.

In this, and in his programme of sincerity and conversational confrontation of error, Godwin philosophically encodes many of the features of spectatorial politeness, and indeed seems not unaware that he is doing so.

The move from *virtù* to politeness began as an attempt to defend liberty through defining the *fora* in which it was to be created and sustained as so unbounded and independent as to escape the control of political establishments. In this way the argument paralleled classical claims that liberty could only be established and sustained by placing it in the hands of economically, and so militarily and politically, self-subsistent individuals. However, with this move, two other possibilities emerged. One was that in the struggle over its definition and content, politeness, whilst retaining its positive evaluation as a source of liberty, would be captured by the defenders of – and so come to endorse – a monarchical, Anglican and patriarchalist *ancien régime*. The other was that the ultimate logic of the argument about polite manners would be to diffuse politics not only from the court to the forum but from thence into every corner of social and domestic life, a condition to which Godwin looked forward (Godwin 1985: 248, 552), but which every republican must dread, as the euthanasia, not only of government but possibly even of politics itself.

6

From Civism to Civility: D'Holbach's Critique of Republican Virtue

Jean Fabien Spitz

Eighteenth-century French political theory is replete with paeans to the virtue of the ancients; numerous are the encomia on the cities of antiquity and particularly on the prodigious feats they were able to achieve in giving the world examples of virtue and liberty that no later epoch could equal. From the pen of Rousseau, of Mably, even of writers not as likely to be suspected of adoration of Sparta and republican enthusiasm – Helvétius for example – we find time and again the same astonishment when confronted with a body of austere and egalitarian legislation that obliged men to raise themselves above the common level and, in every case, to furnish examples of greatness, disinterestedness, independence and generosity which the modern age seemed incapable of imitating. On several occasions we find – in Montesquieu, among others – the idea that man seems to have shrunk, as it were, since that heroic age, to such an extent that what ancient writers and historians tell us about it seems mythical and barely credible: people's ability to sacrifice personal advantage to the common interest – the very definition of ancient virtue – seemed at any rate highly paradoxical and alien to modern minds.

The praise of ancient liberty was less universal because very early on – in any event well before Benjamin Constant's famous speech (Constant 1819) – doubts began to be expressed about its possible drawbacks, in particular about the subjugation of the individual, in his every action and even in his thoughts and most intimate activities, to what Constant was to call social authority. But the fact remains that many eighteenth-century thinkers were attracted by the political state of the ancients because of its ability to harness individuals' energy, civic and military commitment, active interest in the service of the common weal, concern for the public good and, above all, their quasi-divine rejection of all forms of dependence and servitude. People often found disquieting, yet endlessly fascinating, this passionate devotion to liberty expressed in terms of independence. Classical education was after all the only kind on offer in the eighteenth century, so, owing to the fact that they had been nurtured on the works of the Greek and Latin historians and political philosophers,[1] even those least susceptible to the charms of ancient republicanism continued to feel an ambivalent admiration for its model of heroic humanity.

This aspect of the eighteenth-century myth of antiquity is well known (see *inter alia* Rawson 1966; Leduc-Lafayette 1974; Hartog 1993; Vidal-Naquet 1990; Guerci 1979; Raskolnikoff 1990; Parker 1937), but the effect so far as we are concerned is to obscure the efforts of those who were trying to undermine it and propose a redefinition of man's humanity which was to culminate in an at least partial inversion of the normative postulates. For what is found in certain eighteenth-century authors – particularly in d'Holbach, but also in Borde (1753), de Pauw (1788), Vauvilliers[2] and Goguet (1758) – is an explicit critique of the ancient definitions of 'liberty' and 'virtue' as perpetuated by classical education and by repeated contact with ancient authors, and in parallel with that a re-evaluation of the categories of self-interest, ulterior motive and self-love in the construction of a positive model of human action.

1. Ancients and Moderns

The thesis of the superiority of the ancients was for d'Holbach[3] mere prejudice. In his view all talk about modern corruption and depravity was groundless because real corruption and real depravity consisted not of over-indulgence in idle pleasures or the constant pursuit of self-interest, but lay rather in showing cruelty and injustice by favouring the rights of one's own country to the exclusion of those of humanity as a whole:

> The nations were originally mere savage hordes, and savages are neither happy, nor wise, nor truly sociable. If they have been free of a thousand needs since engendered by luxury and the vices which it begets, they have also been ferocious, cruel, unjust, unruly, and strangers entirely to all feelings of equity and humanity. If the early history of Rome offers us examples of frugality in the shape of a Cincinnatus or a Curius, it also reveals in every Roman an unjust,

1. And on the abbé Lhomond's *De viris illustribus*, first published in 1779.
2. Vauvilliers 1769; on Vauvilliers and his debate with Mably, see Dockès-Lallement 1996a and 1996b.
3. On d'Holbach's social and political thought, see Tega 1978; di Lasio 1993; and Wickwar 1968.

> treacherous and inhuman ambition that can hardly predispose anyone
> in favour of their morality. In the republic of Sparta, whose virtues are
> vaunted so frequently, all that a man of probity can see is a highly
> austere and extremely vicious band of brigands.   (d'Holbach 1820: xxv)

Further on d'Holbach ponders the qualities of the good citizen and concludes, against the Romans and Spartans, that the best citizen is one who,
free of all taint of injustice or treachery, is able through self-interest and
ulterior motive to behave with mildness and benevolence towards others;
indeed, he wonders, what morality and what real virtues could possibly be
found among the Romans,

> to whom everything from earliest childhood instilled an exclusive love
> of the fatherland calculated to make them unjust towards every other
> population on earth . . . A truly sensitive, fair-minded and virtuous man
> would have passed in Rome for a very bad citizen.   (d'Holbach 1820: xxvi)

By 'a truly sensitive, fair-minded and virtuous man' d'Holbach meant a man
who did not restrict his feelings of benevolence and his quest for fruitful
exchange to members of his own nation and fatherland, but extended them
to the whole of humanity without division or limit. The citizen of antiquity,
on the other hand, separated arbitrarily and without good grounds – since
all men are endowed with one and the same nature – his compatriots from
the rest of humanity, reserving for the former his most elevated feelings
(d'Holbach 1820: 96–7).

Rousseau had attempted to persuade people that one cannot really love
all men, that the love of humanity was merely a discourse to which love of
country – less extensive, perhaps, but more real – ought properly to be substituted. Seeing in the modern age, unlike antiquity, much fine talk but few
good actions, Rousseau considered the intervention of the human universal
a pretext for loving no one in particular and for standing aloof from people
belonging to one's own city, and accused the moderns of corruption and real
inhumanity cloaked by the most generous oratory.

D'Holbach countered with the argument that it was the classical citizen
who was inhuman because his sensibility and his ability to foster fruitful
exchanges did not extend beyond the walls of his city; it was he who was
depraved and corrupt because natural feeling was stifled in him by favouritism
and division, and it was he who was a bad citizen because he was driven by
unjust feelings that lacked all objective basis where the vast majority of his
fellow-men were concerned.

The attempt to turn things on their head is patently obvious here. D'Holbach inverts the positive and the negative: nobility of soul, magnanimity, patriotism, courage, heroism, indifference to death, appetite for glory, concern for the public good; these all characterise a basically very inhuman individual because at the same time a very insensitive, very unsociable and very dangerous one. On the other hand self-seeking, ulterior motive, self-interested benevolence, gentleness, indulgence, the spirit of compromise, deference to the wishes of others, all characteristics despised by the classical citizen as worthy only of women, lie at the heart of truly modern humanity, sensitive, humane, peaceable, regular in its conduct, mellow and civilised. It is hard to get modern man to do anything, but his behaviour is predictable and always grounded in reasons of self-interest and ulterior motive that can be both understood and anticipated. He is cold but a seamless and rational structure provides a framework for his conduct that diminishes its erratic character. He is not impulsive but firmly inserted into the web of temporality; he takes past experience and the future consequences of his own actions into account, and this too gives his behaviour a predictable form which makes association with him possible.

Nothing indeed is more unsociable or more awkward than touchiness in the hero: odd, exceptional, espousing no common form, unpredictable, fickle, alternately indolent by reason of his rejection of any industrious occupation and hyperactive with heroic frenzy, refusing to learn from past experience and indifferent to the consequences of his actions, sudden and impulsive, the classical hero shows himself in his conduct to be a model of unsociability, a capricious character in the grip of the imagination. If modern man is reassuring by reason of the ordinariness and consistency of his purposes – even being mildly despised sometimes for the paltriness of his ideals and the coldness of his affections – the classical hero provokes fear and anxiety, his instability, impulsiveness and contempt for the most natural and widely shared feelings setting him apart from other men and striking terror in their hearts: how, they wonder, can one get on with a man who agrees so readily to sacrifice his children to his country? How can one live with such cruelty, inhumanity and insensitivity? How can one associate with a man who cares so little about the consequences of his actions, who in order to save his honour would see the entire world perish, who manages to learn nothing from his experiences, whose behaviour is so utterly unpredictable, whose aggressive instincts are tempered by no regular activity, who refuses to be bound by any progressive rule of conduct, who is quite incapable of investing patiently in order to reap dividends later on, and who is ignorant of the art of deferring gratification in order to enhance it? How, in a word, can one coexist with a being so artificial and so little in tune with natural feelings and impulses?

D'Holbach points out the downside of shining virtue: those who show it are set apart from ordinary mortals and provoke in them not only envy and resentment but fear and suspicion as well; republics, he argues, are especially prone to jealousy of this kind because they extol the principle of equality, which results in people strongly resenting the fact that certain individuals are able to rise so high through their merits. In this respect classical virtue is certainly divisive, making it harder for individuals to get on with each other (d'Holbach 1773: 69). Modern man, with his cold and calculating outlook,[4] is able to make long-term investments, conduct his affairs in a progressive manner and fit comfortably into an environment that is forward-looking and characterised by deferred objectives. Such a man is not as great, nor is he as charismatic, but he is certainly a lot easier to get on with.

The reproach levelled by d'Holbach at the classical citizen is that of believing himself more than a man, indeed superior to the average level of humanity, of taking himself for a god, and of being impervious to doubt or argument, entrenched in the smug assurance of his rights. In this he is just like a cleric. His country is for him the sole locus of the realisation of value: he is simply unaware of the relativity inherent in his convictions and personal history, unaware too of the fallibility of his judgments and of the need to give and take, to share and share alike. Just like the priest, the citizen is sectarian and fanatical: instead of striving for an idea of humanity viewed as a uniform whole made up of individuals all enjoying the same rights, he separates it into opposing factions, feuding groups and walled cities, and instead of accepting the fact of plurality and divergence, he aspires to the homogeneous unity of the closed *polis*. Attacking initially the fanaticism of the priest, d'Holbach writes:

> Should the principles of all the revealed religions in this world be examined, it will be found that they tend to erect barriers between nations, turn men into unsociable creatures, and make of each sect a separate entity whose arrogant members are so firmly persuaded of enjoying heaven's exclusive preference that they look upon the advocates of other creeds with hatred and contempt. How could a devout person, consistent with his principles, like, admire or consort with anyone whom he considers to be the enemy of his God? From this

---

4. D'Holbach 1820: 76–9 'Virtue in general is a disposition or a habitual or permanent willingness to contribute to the constant felicity of the beings with whom we live in society.'

> it obviously follows that every particular revelation tends to a
> narrowing of men's hearts, making them enemies and banishing from
> between them the universal benevolence designed to unite beings of
> their kind. The spirit of religion was and always will be incompatible
> with moderation, kindness, justice and humanity.
>
> (d'Holbach 1994: I, 3, p. 47)

The parallel with the classical city becomes explicit when d'Holbach shows that the republican spirit taught its citizens 'to banish from their hearts all benevolence and all humanity, to cast out natural feelings of kindness and compassion, and artificially to save their energy and their devotion for those they lived with'. Love of the fatherland, he says, is but another name for the attitude which consists in 'feeling intense hatred for all other nations and sacrificing everything to an unfair and unreasonable idol' (d'Holbach 1994: I, 4, p. 57). In common with fanaticised religion, therefore, the classical city is unnatural, unjust and irrational. Firstly, it is unnatural because it compels people to stifle, in favour of the artificial representation of the city as an exclusive group, those feelings which connect men naturally with their kith and kin and with all other members of the human race. Next, it is unjust because it denies what is their due to the great majority of human beings: women, slaves and foreigners. Lastly, it is against reason because it introduces divisions where there ought to be unity, and exclusion where, in a network of mutually advantageous dealings, inclusion should always prevail (*ibid.*: I, 8, p. 125).

The fatherland can thus be described as an idol, that is an image without substance, a phantasmagorical representation, in pursuit of the worship of which men abandon the reality of human relationships and spurn what reason and experience should be teaching them about the beneficial nature of exchange and communication with all other members of the species. In this sense, sectarian patriotism is a form of superstition: 'The ancients erroneously gave the name of virtue to a disordered passion for the fatherland, a variety of fanaticism which often made the Greek and Roman heroes very bad citizens of the world, that is men who were very cruel, very unjust and very inhuman toward the other nations, and therefore guilty of an offence against reason' (d'Holbach 1994: I, 8, p. 98).

War and exaggerated patriotism, which result in a refusal to put up with the smallest admixture and with the slightest interference from foreigners, are forms of intolerance and fanaticism characterised by the same spirit of division and insulation against uncertainty which leads the priest to excommunicate, to cut himself off from those who do not think exactly as he does or who do not hold precisely the same beliefs. In d'Holbach's eyes fanaticism and patriotism represent the total inversion of the feelings which give humanity its value: besides justice, which assumes an aptitude to recognise the universal humanity residing in each of our fellow creatures, there is the capacity to make allowances, the willing acceptance of difference, mildness in our dealings with others, an accommodating attitude where their wishes are concerned, deference toward superiors (d'Holbach 1994: 1, 12, p. 153), politeness to everyone and, in a nutshell, 'the desire to please and to acquire talents and qualities fit to add amenity in the commerce of life' (*ibid*.: 1, 8, p. 130). There is nothing the classical citizen is more ignorant of than this last sentiment.

11. Eulogy of Dependence

A striking example of this attempt to invert values revolves around the notions of freedom or independence. It is well known that the spirit of independence and fierce determination to eschew all vulnerability in respect of the wishes of third parties, if necessary through the breaking off of all dealings and exchanges with others, appears as one of the keys to the ancient definition of liberty, in clear opposition to the condition of the slave, characterised as it is precisely by vulnerability to the whim and arbitrary will of other people (see Pettit 1997). Now it is in a completely explicit manner that d'Holbach, among others, questions the ideal of independence in relation to the will of others. 'A being independent of others', he says, 'necessarily sinks into indifference or malice: it is the feeling we have of our dependence with respect to others that inclines us to kindness instead' (d'Holbach 1773: 9), adding that it is only because each of us knows that he needs to gain the benevolence of others that he displays friendly and sociable feelings towards them. Mutual dependence is thus the foundation of all social and human qualities, and the more entangled the web of reciprocal relationships of interdependence becomes the more civilisation and humanity will progress, because men will be made kind and benevolent through the necessity which makes them depend on the co-operation of third parties for the satisfaction of their own needs (d'Holbach 1994: 1, 12, p. 153).

So the social art is the art of making men dependent on each other to develop between them a mutual benevolence which would not manifest itself if that mutual dependence did not exist. Exposure to the will of others, both in individual contacts and in the relationships between states, thus becomes a factor of civilisation and humanisation: 'The solid foundation of men's duties is the need they have of each other; our happy dependence on our fellow-creatures is the true basis of all morality' (d'Holbach 1773: 145–6).

Mutual fear is itself a restraining factor, a limitation on pride and arrogance; refuting the argument that a government is well constituted if its citizens feel invulnerable and afraid of nobody, d'Holbach shows that a certain amount of anxiety, fear and uncertainty fosters sociability, and that anyone who has nothing to be frightened of, indeed is in a position to make others tremble, 'will scarcely bother with meriting their esteem and affection or take the trouble to please people whom he despises and is able to oppress' (*ibid.*). D'Holbach even goes so far as to call into question the desire to elude all dependence, characterising it as puerile and simplistic; the prickly, inflexible hero who cannot abide the least hint of servitude thereby conveys much less his greatness of soul and the excellence of his humanity than the flight from the risk of interaction, the fear of competition and the wish to duck all responsibility. Unthinking adoration of a jealously guarded independence – the xenelasia which, according to de Pauw, results primarily from overweening pride (de Pauw 1788: II, 270) – is characteristic of mankind in its infancy and not in its adult years, since mature people are well aware of the fact that it is impossible to make progress and to enjoy life (the twin aims of a proper human existence) without engaging in exchanges with others and exposing oneself through this circumstance alone to their will. The spirit of independence expresses a wish for security which is poles apart from maturity, the latter representing on the contrary acceptance of 'trade' and of its consequences as the instrument of progress and self-realisation. For his part, the citizen of antiquity is in search of the anchor of stability, security and the ethical absolute, whereas modern man accepts instability and exposure to risk as factors in human self-realisation. Who is the more adult of the two, he who seeks protection from all dangers, or he who knows how to turn them to account as so many opportunities to make progress and perfect himself?

So true liberty does not consist in making ourselves as little dependent and as invulnerable as possible to the will of others, but rather in exposing ourselves to it in a system of exchanges and interdependencies which civilise us and allow us to satisfy our desires.[5] For d'Holbach it is of course the modern age – the epoch of trading and civilised societies – which has succeeded in deploying the art of freeing men from need, and, by making them benevolent towards one another by reason of the very complexity of the relationships of

5. D'Holbach 1820: 107: 'All is exchange among men.'

interdependence that it has managed to weave between them, has empowered them to satisfy their appetite for enjoyment.

True liberty is a modern phenomenon, therefore, and d'Holbach defines it as the 'faculty for taking any route deemed conducive to personal happiness without prejudice to that of others' (1773: 38); putting it another way, he establishes an even clearer link between liberty and the absence of obstacles when he says that 'the essence of being free is to encounter no obstacles on our road to happiness' (1994: I, 12, p. 158). This concept of liberty as empowerment is increased and not diminished by dependence on third parties, since it is with their help that we benefit from added strength to satisfy our passion for enjoyment (1773: 8). Whereas the city of antiquity accepted a diminution in effectiveness in return for an increase in independence, the modern state opts on the contrary to 'sacrifice' independence in exchange for greater utility.[6] (This sacrifice, though, is not really such, since independence has ceased to be a positive value.)

So ethics is the art of pleasing other people (d'Holbach 1820: 147, 151, 153–4), of showing oneself accommodating towards them, of contributing to the satisfaction of their desires so that they in turn accede to ours. This mutual deference lies at the heart of the social system, consisting as it does of exchange and interconnected forms of reciprocity.[7] To depend on someone, d'Holbach says, 'is to need them in order to preserve oneself and make oneself happy'; thus the need for others is the principle of social life, for 'we depend on those who procure for us goods which we would be incapable of obtaining by ourselves' (1820: 87), so it is just and equitable that we should, each one of us, show deference towards those who are in a position to secure for us the advantages we seek, just too that we should show ourselves all the more respectful towards those who are able to do us more good than we are capable of returning. Thus rank distinguishes itself naturally and hierarchies become established of their own accord, raising to the pinnacle of society those who by virtue of their talents are able to be useful to all (*ibid.*; d'Holbach 1773: 20; see also *ibid.*: 174–7).

If it is permissible to have a true evaluation of oneself, one must also know how to take one's proper place in society and how to show respect, courtesy and forbearance to all and deference, consideration and respect to those who enjoy superiority over us by virtue of the benefits they bestow on society: being grateful to those from whom we receive these advantages and

---

6. D'Holbach 1773: 11: 'Virtue is the utility, vice the damage to human beings.'
7. D'Holbach 1820: 36: 'The fear of displeasing others is the bond of every society and the principle of all virtue.'

doing good to other people in order to deserve their love is therefore merely common justice (d'Holbach 1820: 95). At the opposite end of the spectrum the rabid egalitarianism of republics fails to recognise the simple reality that energy and talents are not equally distributed among members of the human race and that each individual's capacity to serve and to render himself useful to his fellow-men cannot always be everywhere the same (1773: 20). Thus the entire 'republican' conceptual system which sought to associate liberty and independence is discarded in favour of another, rooted in the assumption of interdependence, which establishes a link between liberty and the production of the useful.

III. The Redefinition of Virtue

Far from virtue being the art of forgetting oneself in favour of the *polis*, it is, for d'Holbach, merely the art of getting the *polis* to serve our own interests and of establishing a firm link between the individual and the common inter-est. Private virtue, that is the art of pursuing effectively one's self-interest, is identical with public virtue: the one can never be in contradiction with the other, and the notion that in order to be virtuous one has to give up cultivating one's own interests is an absurdity.

So d'Holbach is putting forward a definition of virtue in terms of people being sociable and not in terms of their disdaining self-interest in favour of the general good. He admits that the virtuous man acts also for his fellow-creatures but denies that in so doing he neglects private interest:

> Society cannot only be of advantage to man by making it possible for him enjoy the goods which nature makes him desire. The more society ensures their supply, the more perfect and the dearer to him it will be, and the more necessary to him it will become. In loving his congeners it is but himself he loves; in helping them he helps himself; and in making sacrifices, he does so to his own happiness. In a word, self-interest or enlightened self-love is the foundation of the social virtues and the true motive for everything man does for his fellow-creatures. *Virtue is but the utility of men living in society.* To be virtuous is to be sociable and to contribute to the happiness of those with whom we are linked by fate in order to make them eager in their turn to contribute to our felicity.
>
> (d'Holbach 1773: 10)

It is in these terms that d'Holbach affirms the existence on the one hand of a close link between ethics and politics and on the other of a rigorous continuum between the virtue of the private individual and that of the public person.

Of these themes the former is explicitly anti-Machiavellian and implies the repudiation of two ideas: the first, that it is sometimes necessary to deceive people in order to govern them; the second, that the preservation of the state occasionally requires things to be done which are condemned by ordinary morality. For d'Holbach the task of government is to enlighten men and guide them permanently on the path of the optimal satisfaction of their passions by showing them the truth, namely that kindness towards others and respect for the laws are always the best means of maximising our own private enjoyment. As for *raison d'état*, it is always injurious, for secrecy and *coups d'état* spread division among men, maintain a climate of fear and suspicion, undermine relationships of confidence, paralyse trade, and in particular scare off investors, who are timid creatures frightened by the least display of authority and the slightest departure by governments from the basic ground rules of social life (see Hirschmann 1980). So in d'Holbach's eyes governments never function more effectively than when they themselves respect the decrees which they have enacted for their own subjects. In this regard truth is the best method of government, whilst secrets and lies should always be banned (d'Holbach 1776: 4).

This leads on naturally to the second theme: there is no virtue specific to the public person, since the preservation of the state is none other than the art of protecting and increasing the interests of individuals. So there can never be anything but a single form of virtue: that which allows men to get closer together, to engage in the process of exchange, to maintain relations of kindness and harmony amongst themselves, and above all to increase their respective usefulness by benefiting from the services they can render each other. Virtue takes but one shape: the art of uniting men, of linking them and binding them together, of making them dependent upon each other. The effect of all forms of violence, secrecy and cruelty, and even of all forms of exceptional heroism and courage, is to engender distrust, division and the breaking of ties. If virtue is to be found above all in sociability, in gentleness and in predictability of behaviour, all forms of disorder, including that which could arise from citizens' excessive involvement in affairs of state, runs counter to the harmony and smooth running of government (d'Holbach 1776: 1).

In this respect, the exceptional is always threatening; heroism and singularity are always factors of division and not of union. So the whole conceptual entity elaborated by Machiavelli – who linked secrecy to the great passions and to a meditation on the virtue of singularity, of the hero and of the exceptional individual – is here rejected: the art of government rests on transparency, regularity and 'mediocrity', that is on the qualities which are alone capable of engendering confidence in a nation's governors, such confidence being the key to the happiness of peoples (d'Holbach 1776: 3).

The passion for a transparent form of politics founded on reason (d'Holbach 1773: 231) is carried so far that d'Holbach criticises all secret devices even if their effect is to maintain a balanced and protective system of government; thus in dealing for example with English corruption, that is with the combination of invisible and unofficial mechanisms by which the English monarchy offset the purely nominal power of Parliament, d'Holbach bluntly asserts that it is harmful by reason of its occult nature and that it ought to be replaced by the principle of ministerial responsibility. The key word in a well-constituted government is security, a concept which has nothing particularly republican about it and which, if it resides above all in rendering it impossible for government to assail arbitrarily the person and goods of the citizen, consists essentially of transparency, regularity and the predictability of procedures. Security of this sort is less the guarantee of balanced practice in the art of government than the exercise of power through clear and precise laws which set out its guiding principles and the limits within which it operates. The English, who rely on custom and practice rather than on the clarity of a written constitution, have thus understood nothing about the true principles of liberty (*ibid.*: 22).

Being opposed to all notion that jurisprudence should be the basis of law, d'Holbach wants clear and rational rules, and he accuses the magistrates of the Paris *parlement* of being conservative obscurantists clinging to ancient forms and outdated customs (1773: 77; see also p. 85). So 'a more reasonable body of legislation' needs to be built up, putting an end to the habit of relying on more or less obscure and more or less unofficial practices. The aim of a good government is the creation of a space of anticipation and predictability in which citizens can indulge in the calculation of their interests in full knowledge of the rules of the game, free of all anxiety about being robbed of the fruits of their efforts and legitimate expectations. Guile, secrecy, legal vagueness and mutability, the passions of the mob, civic involvement, enthusiasm and generosity are all antagonistic to the harmonious social system to which d'Holbach aspires.

So republican virtue, based as it is on commitment to public service and on heroic dedication, is suspect because it cannot be controlled (d'Holbach 1773: 9), while modern virtue is made of different stuff: kindness, benevolence, willingness to compromise, deference to the wishes of third parties, but above all regularity and predictability of conduct and conformity to what is both common and prescribed. Such are the keys to virtue,[8] and so virtue is none other than the corpus of attitudes by which one can win over those with whom one is called on to live, and the aim of education is to teach men to practise them in as lucid and enlightened a manner as possible (*ibid.*: 174–5).

The redefinition of virtue put forward here by d'Holbach is obviously the hook on which he hangs the refutation of the thesis (accepted by Montesquieu among others) of the absence of – or at least the considerable diminution of – that quality in the modern world. Far from it being true that the subjects of the great moderate kingdoms have replaced virtue with honour, a dubious quality closer to vanity than to any socially useful character trait, it is they who, of all known individuals, offer the highest manifestation of virtue in its purest sense: mild, regular sociability (d'Holbach 1773: 13). Virtue is what forges links between men and unites them according to their natural identity;[9] everything is virtuous which presupposes mutual confidence and creates relationships of trade and exchange, thereby demonstrating to all that it is in their interest to serve others in order to be served by them. Everything, on the other hand, which contributes towards separating and dividing men by breaking the natural bonds of interest uniting them with their fellows will be termed vicious. The priest, as we have seen, divides and disunites men by splitting them into sects and inducing them to adopt beliefs rooted in separation and exclusion; the same goes for the politics of republicanism, which denies human universality and creates artificial divisions that are in no way justified by nature.

For it is nature itself which forges the links, binding us by gentle feelings to our blood relations, by self-interest to those at a further remove from us who can be of direct use to us through the relationships of dependence and exchange which we maintain with them, and finally to those yet more distant from us by the sense of a universal natural community and the idea that should the need arise such individuals might well become useful to us. In the name of utopian prejudices and perfectly vacuous ideas the citizen of antiquity and the priest artificially break these bonds – bonds which underlie our relationships with all men and incline us live in peace with them – and they replace them without the slightest reason or justice by exclusion, by

---

8. D'Holbach 1773: 12: 'Justice, goodness and unity of interest between all the citizens and their leaders: that is the only way to protect states.'
9. D'Holbach 1994: I, 8, p. 133: 'Virtue is but sociability.'

intolerance, by fanaticism, by sectarian division planted artificially in the heart of humankind, and the rest (d'Holbach 1994: I, 8, p. 139). Nothing is more at variance with true human virtue, says d'Holbach, than 'exhorting man to isolate himself, to detach himself from the beings on whom virtue must be exercised', because 'true morality, like true politics, is that which seeks to bring men together so as to make them strive by their combined efforts for their mutual happiness' (*ibid.*: 104); elsewhere he writes that 'the unjust man breaks the social ties binding himself to others; in becoming the enemy of all men he grants them the right to do him mischief' (*ibid.*: 122).

These are the headings under which d'Holbach sets out his analysis of the faults and vices tending to separate us from our associates and to make us more or less unsociable.

Firstly, injustice, which causes us to hurt the people with whom we live and to deny others the assistance that we demand of them. Every unjust man establishes a clear distinction between his interests and those of society; thus *extra muros* the cities of antiquity treated unjustly their allies and the peoples whom they were trying to subjugate, and *intra muros* they meted out harsh treatment to entire sections of their own population, particularly slaves and heavily indebted citizens living in poverty.

Next, insensitivity, for social life requires compassion and indulgence (d'Holbach 1820: 294) and condemns the severity and inflexibility that makes us unfeeling towards others.

Then, anger, that is to say the irregularity of character (d'Holbach 1994: I, 8, p. 141) which underrates dangers and suffers from a poor assessment of reality. Because of his rages, of the suddenness of his gestures and actions, and of his unpredictability, the irascible man is feared by others. He sacrifices everything to a concept, to a representation of what is his due: this idea, devoid as it is of all spirit of compromise and of any possibility for negotiation, results from a hierarchisation of values totally lacking in flexibility and marked by a moral absolutism which in its turn is the sign of a rigid and fiercely self-contained character. Modern man, on the contrary, knows that values are contextualised and that it behoves him to weigh them carefully against each other, to enter into the art of negotiation and compromise, and to take account of the wishes and reflections of others; the attitude, for example, that would see the world go hang, so long as honour is satisfied, is quite alien to him.

To these negative character traits should be added, as we have seen, exclusive self-love, a fanatical disposition to favour our own judgments, and an inaccurate and often false opinion of our own value and of the truth of our self-representations. This excessive self-esteem and this self-confidence born of the feeling of mastery are frequently accompanied by contempt for others; they constitute pride and make us at once offensive, disagreeable and thoroughly unsociable. The same is true of excessive candour, since dissimulation is indispensable to the smooth functioning of society: a world in which everyone presented themselves exactly as they are would rapidly become so uncomfortable as inevitably to self-destruct (d'Holbach 1994: I, 8, p. 144).

D'Holbach also attacks the lack of that necessary prudence which reveals to us the consequences of our actions both for ourselves and for others: the truly sociable man is made to observe himself, reflect upon his conduct and carry out his actions in concert with those of the people around him. He refuses to act under the influence of images; he is cold, calculating and does nothing without taking past experience duly into consideration. A certain kind of petty-bourgeois mercantile spirit is therefore indispensable to modern civilised society: *homo sociabilis* must think deeply about his conduct, introspect frequently, weigh the consequences of every one of his actions, and never act as if all that matters is the present moment.

Finally, d'Holbach rejects the fad for equality because, he says, the most useful members of society are justified in claiming the greatest advantages for themselves (d'Holbach 1994: I, 12, p. 153).

Just as modern man is truly free because, unlike the ancients, he is liberated from want of the most pressing kind, he is also truly virtuous because, unlike the citizen of classical antiquity, he is humane, gentle, benevolent and kind towards others; the fact that where he is concerned these qualities are the fruit of enlightened self-interest makes him none the less virtuous on that account.

These two aspects (the critique of the notion of independence and of the role it might play in the definition of liberty on the one hand, and on the other the critique of the idea that virtue ought to be defined by contrast with personal interest) are but twin elements in a much wider critique of the spirit of republican politics. This critique in turn makes it possible to paint the portrait of the ideal modern man, standing as he does at the opposite extreme from the citizen of classical antiquity: mild, peaceable, predictable, regular in his conduct, bound to others by bonds of self-interest and rational calculation, shielded from the influence of sudden passions, engaged in a quest that assigns him a place in the temporal continuum and keeps him away from sudden and unreasoning actions. Modern man is also lenient, ready to forgive offences against him and far removed from all spirit of revenge, not because he is endowed with particular nobility of soul, but because he knows that it runs counter to his enlightened self-interest to inflame society by endless dissensions and interminable vendettas (d'Holbach 1820: 290). If vengeance is the pleasure of the gods – of those who consider themselves justified in punishing without mercy people who offend against them – leniency is the form of gratification preferred instead by simple, humane, sensitive and truly great souls, because greatness of that kind is not a matter of impressing others by striking or extraordinary actions generally encountered only out-side the normal run of mutual services which men are called upon to render each other, but simply of maintaining those processes of trade and exchange and of refraining from undermining them for futile reasons having merely to do with honour and the appetite for glory.[10]

Translated from the French by John Fletcher

10. D'Holbach 1994: I, 8, p.142; on the metaphor of a chain of mutual services, see 1773: 173.

Part II

The Place of Women in the Republic

7

Rights or Virtues: Women and the Republic

CHRISTINE FAURÉ

In October 1789 Antonio Capello, the Venetian ambassador to France, wrote to the Doge about the events in Paris, describing the participation of women in the revolutionary movement in the following terms: 'even this sex wishes to participate actively in the capital in the rebellion so as not to appear inferior to the other . . . crueller still than the men, the women have insisted on marching side by side with them armed with swords. In their ignorance and brutality, the common people remain distrustful' (Fontana *et al.* (eds.) 1997, dispatch no. 201, 5 October 1789). He added: 'I write after the uprising of those women whom we would call *rivendigole*, which began on the morning of Monday 5 October and in the course of which they incited the men to revolt' (*ibid.*, dispatch no. 202, 12 October 1789).

It was in such terms that one of the members of an exemplary and long-established diplomatic corps, representing a moribund republic that was to stagger on until 1797, commented upon the Paris days of the Revolution. The unlikely entry on the scene of women, and the actions of the people with whom they were to some extent identified, appeared to make no political sense. The ambassador also disapproved – in the name of the balance of powers – of the constitutional activities of the Assembly: 'the National Assembly began by seizing all powers and amalgamating within itself all the delegations of sovereignty, usurping the executive's administrative functions and the judiciary's jurisdiction over criminal matters' (Fontana *et al.* (eds.) 1997, Capello's account, 2 December 1790).

Confusion, fanaticism, usurpation: these events shook the foundations of republican culture as it had developed in Venice and Florence over the centuries. Where women were concerned, for want of an institutional framework for their activities within the body politic, it was through civic humanism that republican thinking about women's abilities developed, and civic humanism

125

handled this theme through the reception of historic texts from Greek and Latin antiquity. The aim of this chapter is to enquire into the formation of the notions of virtue and right which took on a different meaning once they related to women.

1. The Invention of the Concept of 'Women's Rights'

The notion of women's rights was not a natural extension of vocabulary developed by natural law, but rather the result of a form of hybridisation. It arose in the wake of the French Revolution of 1789 and was taken up in Europe and America in the course of the nineteenth century, until it was replaced by the concept of 'feminism' (which refers to an organisational function). 'Women's rights' – a term that comes naturally to the lips of a twenty-first-century person – enjoyed exceptional linguistic success. The 'rights of man' had already started to re-model French society, making it less stratified and compartmentalised than the *ancien régime* with its myriads of privileges that had been granted to individuals, guilds, towns and provinces. France could now appear as one, regaining its integrity and homogeneity. For some it was still a fantasy, but at least it was an illusion that made a new departure conceivable, as was shown by the abbé Sieyès's 'Essay on Privileges'.[1]

During August 1791 the phrase 'women's rights' was used for the first time by Olympe de Gouges in a now famous text, the 'Declaration of the Rights of Woman' (de Gouges 1791; also in Levy *et al.* (eds.) 1979), in which she sought to draw the attention of the members of the Constituent Assembly to the condition of women who, she argued, ought not be excluded from the process of social regeneration. Using the most radical contemporary general statement, one which has acquired the quasi-religious force of a new gospel, Olympe de Gouges merely substituted the word 'woman' for the word 'man'. She was thereby suggesting a symmetry between the two sexes which occasionally gave rise to some surprising conclusions: in the Preamble to the 'Declaration' the acts of the legislative power and those of the executive power were replaced by the acts of women's power and those of men's power, as if executive authority were something that could not be exercised by women. In Article XI, departing from her model, she introduced into her declaration of rights remarks in direct speech, putting into the mouth of the woman citizen the words: 'I am the mother of a child which belongs

---

1. 'Ce qui constitue le privilège est d'être hors du droit commun': 'Essai sur les privilèges' (Sieyès 1788).

to you', thereby referring, beyond the similarity of the terms used, to the declarations of pregnancy which used to be imposed on unmarried women by the monarchical *State*. Olympe de Gouges's itinerary therefore took her from the Declaration of the Rights of Man to the Declaration of the Rights of Women through the pregnancy declaration, a potent source of suffering and humiliation for women (Phan 1980, 1975).

This text, which enjoyed great favour in the twentieth century, went almost unnoticed on its publication, for reasons clearly having to do with the often disconcerting aspects of the behaviour of its author, who after the flight to Varennes addressed herself to the *Queen* as the self-appointed spokesperson of an approach which the *King* himself realised constituted an attack on royalty: the *King* had signed the Declaration of the Rights of Man under the pressure of events, whereas the Declaration of the Rights of Women was presented as an act of loyalty towards the monarchy. Such inconsistencies undermined her credibility, and the rights of women seemed a pleasant joke or at least a sort of parodic imitation. At the same time, the *Journal des droits de l'homme*, published by a certain Labenette,[2] declared in an article written in a mock-gallant style: 'without question the finest work to have emerged from the brain of our legislators is the Declaration of the Rights of Man, but they should have created its counterpart; they should, I say, have decreed the Rights of Woman'.

The next use of the expression 'women's rights' to constitute a histor-ical milestone and make the term famous was of course the *Vindication of the Rights of Woman* by the English writer Mary Wollstonecraft, published between 1791 and 1792, and immediately translated into French. A teacher by profession and an occasional journalist, Mary Wollstonecraft rooted her argument in a subject that she was familiar with, education, and reacted in particular to Charles-Maurice Talleyrand-Périgord's questionable com-ments in 1791 about the education of girls, in which he praised the universal character of education only to recommend domestic instruction for women. Although Wollstonecraft was an Anglican, she was close to the Rational Dissenters who opposed the Church of England on the grounds of their democratic ideals; these centred on the equal distribution to both sexes of the gifts lavished by God (especially the 'gift of reason'). She carried off a ver-itable conceptual revolution in attributing to a single population, women, rights that were universally shared, something it was practically impossible for French jurists to understand then and still even today is barely understood

2. 1791; Labenette was the author of the *Journal du diable*.

at the top levels of government administration. Was Wollstonecraft aware of the revolution? Her intellectual and emotional espousal of the views of an oppositionist minority had made her intervention possible. At no time did she mention Olympe de Gouges's text, and indeed was probably unaware of its existence.

Be that as it may, the success of her *Vindication of the Rights of Woman* was such that the work became an inescapable point of reference; in her *Promenades dans Londres* (1840), her London journal, Flora Tristan wrote that it was an 'imperishable work'. What is more, in her iconoclastic approach Mary Wollstonecraft broke with the classic subject-matter of women famed for their virtue by citing in her reference list, perhaps with a smile, the names of Sappho, Heloise, Mrs Macaulay, the empress of Russia and Madame d'Eon, a transvestite diplomat better known under the name of the *Chevalier* d'Eon.

II. Virtuous Women

In Greek[3] and Roman antiquity women had no officially recognised role in the political and administrative life of a republic, any more than they did for that matter in a monarchy or an empire (Gaudemet 1959). In an article on the division of the sexes in Roman law, Yan Thomas, an expert in the field, goes beyond fact and discerns the same logic at work in both public and private law. Through the example of the will in ancient Roman law – 'women could not draw up a will because such a document took on a comitial form and therefore presupposed membership of the political assemblies' – he stresses the unitary nature of a jurisprudence in which the distinction between public and private law is often overdone (Thomas 1990: 156).

On the European scale, the history of ideas has noted the existence of a discourse on feminine virtues, both Greek and Latin, alongside an even more copious literature on famous men, the principal vehicle for which in the sixteenth and seventeenth centuries was the translation of Plutarch[4] for both sexes: the principal but not the sole vehicle, because where this theme is concerned account must be taken of Boccaccio's Latin work, the *De mulieribus claris*,[5] written around 1361 after his meeting with Petrarch. This text had a big following throughout Europe, in Italy (particularly in Venice), in France,

---

3. 'There was not and never had been a feminine form of the term "Athenian": political practice did not recognise the existence of a female citizen and the language had no word to designate the woman of Athens': Loraux 1984: 14.

4. Stadter 1965. Stadter provides a commentary on the twenty-seven histories of the virtues which Plutarch wrote for his friend Clea, priestess of Delphi.

5. On the genesis of the work and the possible dates of its composition, see Boccaccio 1967. On the subsequent publishing history of Boccaccio's text, see Consoli 1992.

in England and in Spain. It owed nothing to Plutarch, as one might believe, because apart from medieval sources the list drawn up by Vittore Branca includes such prose writers of antiquity as Justin, Orosius, Florus, Lactantius, Servius, Macrobius and Solinus as well as Varro, Pliny, Pompeius Mela, Aulus Gellius, Vitruvius, Tacitus, Livy and Valerius Maximus. But even if no recognisably direct link existed between Boccaccio's work and Plutarch's – Plutarch was known to neither Petrarch nor Boccaccio and was not to be translated into Latin until about 1470 – the *Facta et dicta memorabilia* by Valerius Maximus[6] and Livy's *History of Rome* provided the transition between Boccaccio's literary aspirations and a common fund of stories circulating in the ancient world on which Plutarch too had drawn. The *De mulieribus claris* is an original work, a genuine recomposition of the legacy of the ancient world and not a simple compilation job; among the works it influenced were *La Cité des Dames* by Christine de Pisan (1405), which owes as much to *De mulieribus claris* (Jeanroy 1922) as it does to the *Decameron* (Bozzolo 1967). Boccaccio had introduced into his narrative the actions of women known for their excesses of every kind and not just for their virtue whereas Christine de Pisan's book (1986, 1982) gives considerable attention to sacred history and women saints; nevertheless she makes no mystery about this famous precedent since she quotes Boccaccio several times in her text, apropos of the noble Cornificia who had abandoned women's work to devote herself to her studies (1.28), or of Bernardo of Genoa's wife (2.52), or again of Sigismonda, the prince of Salerno's daughter (2.59). This Boccaccio influence was to last until the sixteenth century, because in 1547 trace is found of a *Mirouer des femmes vertueuses*[7] made up of two texts, one on Joan of Arc (in 1429 Christine de Pisan had written the *Ditié* of Joan) and the other on the life of Griselda, the heroine of the tenth day's tenth story in the *Decameron*. Whatever sources of inspiration can be found merging here, the literature on virtuous women reached its climax in the sixteenth century with the translation of Plutarch's great work (1538), as is shown by the dedication of the French version to Marguerite de Navarre.

Montaigne, a great reader of Plutarch, is of particular interest in this connection by virtue of his emotional and intellectual closeness to Mademoiselle de Gournay, his 'fille d'alliance' (daughter by election), as he himself said, who among other things wrote *L'Egalité des hommes et des femmes* (1622),

---

6. Boccaccio 2, *De Semiramide, regina Assyriorum*; Valerius Maximus, *Facta et dicta memorabilia*, Book IX, 3, extension 4. Boccaccio 31, *De coniugibus meniarum*; Valerius Maximus, Book IV, 6. Boccaccio 52, *De Cloelia romana virgine*; Valerius Maximus, Book III, 2, Livy, *History of Rome*, II, 13. Boccaccio 73, *De coniuge orgigontis gallogreci*; Valerius Maximus, Book VI, 1, extension 2. In Plutarch the name given is that of Chiomara (XXII), in Plutarch 1968.

7. A second edition was published in Lyon at the end of the century.

and who after his death corresponded with the Flemish philosopher Justus Lipsius – she became his 'fille d'alliance' also.[8] Montaigne devotes a chapter in his *Essays* 'Of Three Good Women' (Book II, ch. 35), by which we are to understand three women whose virtue – indeed heroism – is revealed in the framework of the 'duties of marriages' surrounding the death of their husband: the anonymous wife of a neighbour of Pliny the Younger, Cecinna Paetus's wife Arria, and Seneca's young wife Pompeia Paulina all steer their husband who, with the exception of Seneca, are wavering in their resolve, firmly in the direction in which valour points. In willingly choosing to die – an example of stoical love which manifests itself in extreme situations – these women embody a form of egalitarian exchange between love and death which of course wipes out gender differences understood as a hierarchical system, and by their acts they are raised to the level of the most virtuous men such as Seneca. We remain nevertheless within the framework of an attitude in the domain of private life which, through intransigence, attains to glory in the public arena. Furthermore this claim to a more or less voluntary death, inspired by stoic philosophy, was often associated with the principle of gender equality; in this connection Olympe de Gouges's maximalist formula springs to mind: 'women have the right to mount the scaffold', she wrote with tragic premonition, 'so they must equally have the right to mount the rostrum'. As for Montaigne, 'the three excellent men' whom he chose in the chapter following that of the 'good women' were Homer, Alexander the Great and the Boeotian general Epaminondas, whose talents stood four square in history.

Up till the eighteenth century the development of the discourse on the feminine virtues knew varying degrees of success. It was neither refuted nor circumscribed by an analysis of the functioning of political authority such as Machiavelli undertook in relation to masculine virtue, unable by itself to justify a governing role in politics (Skinner 1981). No test of reality ever occurred to upset the applecart, and the profoundly repetitive character of the humanist attitude culminated in neoclassical tragedy, especially in France with the creation of Racinian heroines (Racine was also an avid reader of Plutarch). Except under the monarchy, women did not participate in political institutions: reflection on good governance was firmly out of bounds so far as they were concerned.

So how does Machiavelli in his *Discourses on the First Decade of Titus Livius* interpret the way in which the many heroines who appear in the

---

8. On the relationship between Mademoiselle de Gournay and the Stoic philosopher see Schiff 1978.

History of Rome are presented? His position is unequivocal. He acknowledges that the death of the Horatii's sister was a crime perpetrated by the one who had brought down the Curiatii: 'Well organised republics establish rewards and penalties for their citizens and do not cancel one with the other' (Machiavelli 1989, Book I, ch. 24). But he notes 'how a state falls because of women' (Book III, ch. 26) insofar as they are a source of division:

> First, it appears that women have caused much destruction, have done great harm to those who govern cities, and have occasioned many divisions in them; for, as we see in this 'History of ours', the outrage to Lucrece took their position from the Tarquins. That other outrage, to Virginia [Virginia was murdered by her father to save her from slavery and dishonour], deprived the Ten of their authority. So Aristotle gives among the first causes for the falls of tyrants some injury in a matter of women, either by whoring them, or raping them, or by breaking off marriages.

In Chapter 5 of Book III Machiavelli had, however, relativised the importance of the rape of Lucretia in the Tarquins' loss of power: 'For if Tarquin had lived like the other kings, and Sextus his son had committed that crime, Brutus and Collatinus would have appealed to Tarquin for vengeance against Sextus, and not to the Roman people.' Among the reasons for conspiracies that threaten the security of the state 'attacks on a woman's honour are the most common'. Nowhere does Machiavelli express a view on the question of women as active citizens or in government since it did not feature in the Latin example, but he mentions in his *Florentine Histories* some allusions to queens.

III. The Sumptuary Laws

In the transmission from antiquity of republican themes about women, the debate surrounding the sumptuary laws was perhaps the most pervasive; lasting from the sixteenth to the eighteenth centuries, it was pursued with ever-renewed vigour on the advent of industrial societies and the resulting acceleration in the production and circulation of goods. From Livy on, it has been a tradition to ponder the necessity for putting limits on luxury, and many linked the need for restrictions in this area with women, whose vanity and taste for ostentation were well known. An early example of the connection that presented itself took the shape of a translation of Book XXXIV of Livy's *History of Rome* (1957) on the repeal of the Oppian Law. It was translated by an English specialist of Italian history and connoisseur of Machiavelli, William Thomas,[9] and it was published in 1551 under the title *An Argument, Wherein the Apparaile of Women is Both Reproved and Defended* (the only extant copy is in the library at Harvard). Inspired by Castiglione's *Courtier*, it takes the form of a dialogue between an anonymous lady of quality and a critic of women's inordinate taste for luxury; evoking the authority of Cato, Thomas takes the opportunity to recall the account Livy gives in Book XXXIV of the circumstances surrounding the debate on luxury and the repeal of the Oppian Law.

This legislation, passed in 215 BC, was repealed by the Republic twenty years later on the proposition of the Tribunes of the People Marcus Fundanius and Lucius Valerius, and against which Cato the Censor delivered an impassioned speech in the name of public order: 'It was the wish of our ancestors that women engage in no business, be it purely private, without a guardian as guarantor; we now even allow them to take part in public affairs' (Book XXXIV, ch. 3, 11–12). Cato's speech was followed by that of Valerius, in which he pointed out the public acts of generosity performed by women:

> Once the city was taken by the Gauls was not the gold that redeemed
> it brought by women publicly and to universal acclaim?... During the
> last war, was it not true that when money was needed widows came
> to the aid of the Treasury with funds of their own?
>
> (Book XXXIV, ch. 6, 9 and 10)

The Oppian Law,[10] Valerius declared, was a piece of wartime legislation, passed after the disaster of the battle of Cannae, and women as well as men and boys who wore purple on their togas had to benefit from public prosperity (Book XXXIV, ch. 7, 2). For the Romans the wearing of purple indicated 'that it was forbidden to violate the integrity of this body, from magistrates down to freeborn children... purple and gold were the emblems of power' (Dupont 1989: 293). It was within the framework of such a symbolic system that the debate on the Roman sumptuary laws was appraised and evaluated.

William Thomas declares himself on the side of women and against the sumptuary laws, and the question arises as to whether, as Carlson suggests (1993), an allusion to contemporary events can be discerned here: was

---

9. William Thomas, author *inter alia* of *Historie of Italy* (London, 1549) and of *Rules of Italian Grammar with a Dictionarie* (London, 1550).

10. *Paulys Realencyclopädie* 1931. Under the Oppian Law women were forbidden to wear clothes of several colours and more than half an ounce of gold.

Thomas's intention to express an opinion, through the medium of his translation of Livy, on Edward VI's policy with regard to the issuing of new coinage
and the sumptuary draft bill 'For Restraint in Apparel' aimed at putting the
treasury on a sound financial footing again? In his editorial commentary
Thomas informs us that much the same discourse on sumptuary laws – with
its inevitable corollary, the debate on women's virtues and their ability to
contribute materially to the public good – continued from antiquity to the
sixteenth century, transcending the specific nature of the economic measures
taken in each period. Right up to the French Revolution, indeed, it was to remain the framework within which the discussion of the condition of women
took place: the philosophers of the Age of Enlightenment kept the debate
alive with as much assiduity as the humanists of the sixteenth century, the
development of luxury industries making them particularly eloquent on the
subject.[11]

Starting from a common viewpoint – that the state of women was to
be and remain outside any institutional set-up – the *philosophes* spoke with
the same voice as the authors of antiquity. Let us not forget the amazing
cynicism with which Montesquieu characterised each political régime by
the particular situation of its women: enjoying freedom under monarchy,
suffering enslavement under despotism, while 'in republics women are free
by the laws and captured by the mores' (*The Spirit of Laws*, Book VII, ch. 9).
Later on Montesquieu writes: 'One could constrain its women, make laws
to correct their mores and limit their luxury, but who knows whether one
would not lose a certain taste that would be the source of the nation's wealth
and a politeness that attracts foreigners to it?' (*The Spirit of Laws*, Book XIX,
ch. 5). This waning of confidence in the merits of the law was part of a general
movement of which *The Fable of the Bees, or Private Vices, Publick Benefits* by
Bernard de Mandeville (1714) represents the most radical position.

At the other extreme Rousseau anathematised industrial and commercial
society, thereby placing himself with unfailing steadfastness, whenever that
issue was brought up, between Lycurgus and Cato. Despite the craze for
his educational writings among women readers, and female members of the
aristocracy in particular, with Madame de Genlis, a prolific and immensely
successful author, taking the lead, his position was not without ambiguity: if,
as he proclaims in his letter to D'Alembert (Rousseau 1967: 168), simplicity
is for him the most charming finery, he is thinking of course of seductiveness

---

11. Montesquieu 1989. See Catherine Larrère's chapter in this volume.

and not of virtue. Such ambiguity was clearly perceived and denounced by his female commentators. Madame de Staël pleaded for indulgence for him in 1788: 'Although Rousseau has endeavoured to prevent women from interfering with public affairs, and acting a brilliant part in the theater of politics; yet in speaking of them how much has he done it to their satisfaction ... to conclude, he admits the passion of love: his pardon is granted' (Letter I).[12]

The uncompromising and puritanical Mary Wollstonecraft gave free rein to her republican eloquence when she likened Rousseau's position – particularly his rather dubious love for uneducated girls – to an effect of worldly corruption specific to France under the *ancien régime*. The beginnings of the French Revolution did not change the paradigm of the discourse on female virtues: the women of the Revolution, not having been permitted either to sit in the Estates-General nor to take up executive office, had no other means of breaking into the public arena which was barred to them than satisfying the expectations of those in power. The chief finance minister Jacques Necker, who on 29 September 1789 had put forward a proposal for taxation which 'neglected neither men nor women', was preceded in this by the patriotic offer of the artists' wives on 7 September; the speech written by them for the occasion and read out by Constituent Assembly member Bouche was eloquent on the point:

> When the women of Rome gave the tribute of their jewellery to the Senate their purpose was to make available to that body the gold required to fulfil the vow made by Camillus to Apollo before the capture of Veii ... It is with this in mind that the artists' wives have come to offer the august National Assembly gems which they would blush to wear when patriotism bids that they be sacrificed.
>
> ([*Moniteur*] 1847: 445)

The patriotic gift, in keeping with the future definition of revolutionary fiscality – a fiscality freely consented to and based not on inquisitorial activity but on citizens' goodwill (see Fauré 1997) – was inspired by antiquity, by actions that were held to constitute virtue in women. The meaning of these gifts did not escape contemporaries: in Chantreau's *Dictionnaire national et anecdotique*, in the article 'Patriotic Gift', we read: 'various gifts of plate can however be seen as patriotic restitution showing resolution of purpose in becoming a citizen' (1790: 63). As far as women were concerned this aspiration was short-lived. As the historian Catherine Duprat has pointed out in an article on the donation of Year II (Duprat 1994), the discourse that

---

12. Madame de Staël 1788, cited in English edition of 1814.

accompanied the offering was almost invariably masculine, as if the act of making a statement could damage the hierarchical relationship established between women and the Republic and even, on the occasion of a gift, subvert it. This form of protest discourse was both rare and belated; grievances, complaints, denunciations, petitions, demands, all such language acts called for their individual or collective authors to be involved clearly.

iv. On the Equality of the Sexes

In *L'Egalité des hommes et des femmes*, a text of fundamental importance where this topic is concerned, the learned Mademoiselle de Gournay (who knew her classics well) invoked the patronage of Plato and Socrates because they attributed to women 'the same rights, faculties and functions in their Republic and everywhere else' (de Gournay 1993: 42). The authority of Aristotle was also called upon in a manner more surprising to the modern reader than to the reader of Plutarch who saw no contradiction here. Mademoiselle de Gournay's aim was to break with a discourse on feminine virtues which attempted to prove excellence and thus superiority: 'I who shun all extremes am happy to make them equal to men, nature in this regard being opposed as much to superiority as to inferiority.' This struggle for gender equality was far from common, being upheld only very rarely before the French Revolution and then mainly in a work by the French Cartesian Poulain de la Barre, *De l'égalité des deux sexes* (1673), translated into English as early as 1677 under the title *The Woman as Good as the Man*. In both cases the discourse was justified by the concept of the lack of differentiation between the sexes, that is to say, for Mademoiselle de Gournay 'in man and woman virtue is the same thing...humankind was created male and female', while for Poulain de la Barre gender difference ought not to entail a specific social destiny, so he repudiated both the systematic downgrading of women as perpetrated by jurists and the celebration of femininity as understood by the *Précieuses* (*De l'éducation des dames* (1671)). In the second part of *De L'égalité des deux sexes* he also rejected any idea of sociological determinism:

> It is pointless therefore to rely upon the constitution of the body in order to explain the visible difference between the two sexes in relation to the mind...the mind is of no less capacity in women than in men.

For Descartes, gender difference had no ontological value: it was a matter of modes of diversification of extended matter. Poulain de la Barre's position derived in part from the philosophy of Descartes, but without doubt also from the egalitarian attitude put forward by the French philosopher in his correspondence with Christina of Sweden and Elizabeth of Bohemia: whatever its theoretical justification, equality stems from similarity. Montaigne, whose stance on this issue was similar to Mademoiselle de Gournay's, wrote:

> I say that males and females are cast in the same mould, and that, education and custom excepted, the difference between them is not great – Plato indifferently invites both the one and the other to the society of all studies, exercises, commands and occupations, military and civil, in his commonwealth; and the philosopher Antisthenes took away all distinction between their virtue and ours.
>
> (Montaigne 1842, Book III, ch. 5)

This lack of differentiation would have remained a purely philosophical position had Mademoiselle de Gournay not made it the basis of a protest pamphlet, *Le Grief des dames*:

> Blessed are you, reader, if you are not a member of that sex to which freedom and all forms of property are denied in order to make sure that its sole felicity, its unique and sovereign virtue, resides in being ignorant, acting stupid, and serving others. And I speak as a woman!

This mobilisation of the self was necessary in order to subvert, within the order of the discourse, the exclusion to which women were subject in the republic according to both the ancients and the moderns; but this instituting discourse could never suffice to make gender equality the symbol of republican equality in the sense of a similarity of abilities and role.

In outlining the stages which the discourse on the virtues of women went through I have tried to point out its comparative stability in relation to the humanist reception of historical works that had survived from Antiquity. It was a discourse that continued over the centuries with no dissent and no upset in its problematics comparable to that which Machiavelli's work was able to bring about in relation to the virtues of men, virtues which when it came to the exercise of government were quite inadequate. Despite the existence of reigning queens, this humanist reading served to perpetuate ancient societies' prejudices about the place of women in the organisation of the *polis*, so the question arises as to whether phrases or terms like 'women's rights', 'grievances', 'complaints', and so on, brought the discourse of women's virtues to an end. Was it a question of pitting rights against virtues? What we do see is that the expression of rights as climax of a then institutionalised discourse brings all consideration of virtues to a close. In Mademoiselle de Gournay's *Le Grief des dames* the discussion moves explicitly from praise of women's virtues – straight out of Plutarch – to a clearly expressed wish to put an end to it: 'Should I deign to make the effort to defend ladies, I would very soon find support in Socrates, Plato, Plutarch, Seneca and Antisthenes'. In her *Vindication of the Rights of Woman* Mary Wollstonecraft was seeking the authenticity of a virtue that she claimed should always be personified on an individual basis and not seen as the symbolic representation of the female condition. It was the end of the discourse on famous women and of the opportunity for access to public life and renown that was, for them, what the heroic act represented.

Translated from the French by John Fletcher

8

Women, Republicanism and the Growth of Commerce

CATHERINE LARRÈRE

In 1790 Condorcet published an article 'On the Granting of Civil Rights to Women'. This set out with rigorous clarity the argument for sexual equality and the need for women to enjoy the same rights as men, especially voting rights, and it advocated the strict application of the human rights principle of legal individuality and of 'equal liberty': whatever is valid for one person is necessarily valid for all, or, as he put it, 'either no individual member of the human race has any true rights, or everybody enjoys them'. But when he submitted his draft constitution to the National Convention on 15 and 16 February 1793 Condorcet did not even mention votes for women, thereby giving up all attempts to put into practice what he had previously supported. There was thus something oddly shocking about a policy aimed at the political and legal exclusion of women from modern democracy; it contradicted so flagrantly the very principles of the Declaration of the Rights of Man that various explanations have been put forward to account for it. The usual reason given is that people gave up in the face of the 'traditional view' – some would say the 'patriarchal' image – of the relations between the sexes (Rosanvallon 1992: 130–48).

In Condorcet's case there are however certain clues indicating less straightforward conclusions to be drawn. In 1790 he was still inveighing against the fact that 'until 1776 [the year the *jurandes*, or guild-masterships, were abolished] no woman could run a milliner's shop in Paris'. When Turgot, Louis XVI's finance minister, was striving to put into effect the principles of free trade expounded earlier in the century by his mentor Gournay, Condorcet was engaged as his secretary to help launch the campaign for a genuinely commercial society in France. The freedom Condorcet called for was not merely legal, it was also economic, linked to developments in commercial theory. Another clue is to be found in the *Lettres d'un bourgeois de New Haven*

('Letters from a Burger of New Haven', 1788), in which where women were concerned Condorcet was already speaking the language of equal rights, but without much conviction; hence his remark 'now that Rousseau has earned their approbation . . . I cannot expect them to pronounce in my favour' (Condorcet 1986: 217).

Was it a case, then, of Rousseau versus commercial society, of virtue against trade? One begins to suspect that republican notions lay at the root of this debate on the legal, economic and political status of women. The question why women sided with Rousseau, choosing exclusion over participation in political life, remains a puzzling one, but a possible interpretation of the surprising exercise of this option could be this: there were indeed two competing political models in the frame. The first formulation of this political duality was to be found in *The Spirit of Laws*, where Montesquieu showed how 'the condition of women' was linked to the difference in forms of government: in the face of the complete unacceptability of despotism, there were two possible alternative models, one republican and the other monarchical (Montesquieu 1748: VII, 9).

All that one need then do is follow the debate which proceeded to elaborate, develop and modify the way the choice of models was presented. At the outset the monarchical variety was seen to have a general egalitarian potential; this occurred as a result of equality, the key contribution made by commercial society, being conjoined with liberty, which characterised the condition of women in a monarchy. This was the model still being defended by Condorcet at the start of the French Revolution; but in the meantime it had undergone a dual critique. The first was formulated by Rousseau, who thereby breathed new life into the republican model, but the second came from economists: both Quesnay and Smith had shown that the economy tended to exclude women from the public sphere as soon as it impinged upon it.

Had this fairly surprising convergence between the economic discourse of a commercial society transformed by its own growth and the political discourse of Rousseau not occurred, his model – that of the exclusion of women – would probably not have triumphed. But that raises the question of the exact nature of the model which came out on top in this way and of the precise connections between women, republicanism and commercial society.

1. Montesquieu: The Condition of Women, Republic and Monarchy

So the 'condition of women' varied according to the system of government: women were free in monarchies, and 'extremely enslaved' in despotic states, whereas 'in republics, women were free in the eyes of the law but prisoners according to the customs of society'. The question of women, then, was highlighted by Montesquieu's cardinal distinction between law and custom: the condition of women was bound up with the latter (Larrère 1994). The liberty enjoyed by women under a monarchical system ('they are drawn by the opportunity of embracing there that spirit of freedom which is just about the only one rulers will tolerate') had of course nothing to do with power-sharing, to which male subjects of monarchs were also denied access; nor was it the same thing as that form of liberty guaranteed by the law, namely security (Montesquieu 1748: XI, 6), but was a kind of freedom, specific to women, that related to custom and so was distinct from democracy, in which women were 'held captive' by custom. By way of symmetry Montesquieu argued that since despotism was a régime in which there was no such thing as protection afforded by the law, women endured a double slavery: in addition to political servitude, a condition shared by all the subjects of a despot, they suffered (XVI, 1) a particularly onerous form of domestic servitude (characterised by polygamy, XVI, and sexual abuse, XV, 12).

So once again the condition of women reflected the general structure of the typology of governments: despotic institutions constituted the negative pole, while the positive was shared by the two moderate forms of political régime, republican and monarchical (Larrère 1979). But while Montesquieu prided himself on not betraying any preference in respect of either republic or monarchy, he did not maintain the balance quite as strictly when he turned from laws and political institutions to customs and to women.

Under a republican constitution the distinction between law and custom is closely calibrated to that between the sexes, opening up to men the public space of political and judicial institutions and confining women to the domain of custom, of the family, of enclosure, and of separation from the political space. Thus what corresponded to political virtue in men ('love of the laws and of one's country', Montesquieu 1748: IV, 5) was domestic virtue in women ('simplicity' and 'chastity', VII, 9), and that was the factor which proved decisive, because at the heart of the republican arrangement was the 'purity' of conjugal relations in a régime which gave every appearance of being one of law but was in fact held together by custom alone. Indeed when customary morals were corrupted the fall of the régime was the inevitable consequence: 'women, children and slaves will no longer submit to anyone: there will no longer be any morality, any love of order, in a word all virtue will have been destroyed' (VIII, 2). Where women were unchaste, there could be no political virtue. But the sleight-of-hand in the shift from law to custom also involved a departure from the government of equals – the essence of republicanism – to a restrictive social hierarchy: what 'maintained customary morality' was the 'extreme subordination of the young to the old', 'paternal authority' and the close supervision of women (v, 7). The importance of customary morality in republics was a hallmark of their social conservatism: people's preference was for Sparta and the *mos maiorum*.

This régime, that of the 'purity' of women – Montesquieu does not tell us what *they* thought about it – was not exactly calculated to please men either, the scope of whose power did not coincide with that of their pleasure. The harsh austerity of domestic life had perverse consequences: the separation of the sexes encouraged homosexuality (something which Montesquieu deplored) and kept misogyny alive: it was in the mouth of a Roman that Montesquieu put the words 'if it were possible not to take a wife, we would deliver ourselves from this evil' (XXIII, 21). This sour, corrupt view was not confined to ancient republics; in contemporary England, whose customs were republican, Montesquieu recognised the same characteristics: women, kept apart from men, were 'shy' and virtuous, and the men were 'unchivalrous' and given up to 'debauchery' (XIX, 27).

On the other hand the monarchical system was that of freedom where custom and morality were concerned: women lived 'in close proximity to men', and both sexes seemed well satisfied with the arrangement. Montesquieu expressed not only his own opinion but also what he took to be the view of his contemporaries when he asserted: 'it is a great felicity to live in those climes where people are allowed to communicate with each other; where the sex endowed with the greater abundance of charms seems called upon to adorn society; and where women, saving themselves for the sexual gratification of one man, still manage to give innocent pleasure to all' (XVI, 11). In other words, if monarchical freedom tended to encourage licentiousness, that was by no means the whole story, unlike the situation with despotism, a negative régime in which sex, being the only reason for having dealings with women, led to every excess: the enslavement of women and immorality among men. Under monarchy the relationship between the sexes kept its chief usefulness, namely its social function in facilitating reproduction and the propagation of the species. It was ultimately from this perspective that Montesquieu noted a natural inequality between women and men which the 'political and civil laws' reflected: 'they have demanded of women a degree of continence and self-restraint not expected of men because the violation of modesty in women implies renunciation of all the virtues; because in transgressing the laws of marriage a woman departs from her state of natural dependency' (XXVI, 8).

There are a number of elements in the way Montesquieu presented the female condition that recurred in the debate surrounding the question of women, between republican virtue and free trade. One of these elements was the duality of models: the austere, restricting, conservative, classically pure, republican version on the one hand, that of the rigorous separation of the sexes with its firm basis in law and custom, set clear limits to the political arena and allowed of no confusion, whereas on the other hand the monarchical system, that of communication making possible (as we shall see) the spread of egalitarianism in line with the development of trade, permitted a degree of freedom where individual behaviour was concerned that was unknown in the republic and tended to give rise to licence and corruption there. Another element in Montesquieu's thinking about the female condition was the distinction between the two functions of the 'commerce of women', debauchery on the one hand and propagation of the species on the other, in which the argument condemning the confusion between trade and women's freedom was rooted.

ii. The Trade Model

According to Montesquieu, the freedom of women in a monarchical system derived from chivalry and was linked to the question of honour, of which, by picking up on the spirit of independence and the wish to assert oneself, it constituted the feminine counterpart, for the very essence of chivalry, the quest for personal distinction, drove rival noble knights to seek female approval as the surest mark of their success. The milieu of the royal court maintained this practice of appealing to the judgment of women. Freed from domesticity, women mixed with men in a courtly society which was based on mutual sexual attraction and which cultivated wit and the art of conversation, thereby replicating, in jousts that henceforth were purely verbal, the spirit of chivalry. By virtue of being 'most enlightened judges of an aspect of those things which constitute personal merit' (Montesquieu 1748: XXVIII, 22), women kept alive in men the will to please and the incentive to achieve distinction. This umpiring role conferred on women a certain amount of power and tended to put them on an equal footing with men, a position reinforced by the development of polite society: no doubt the world of the court did not do away with the *de facto* inequality between men and women or women's 'natural dependency', but 'courtesy, respect and generosity' compensated for it and so resulted in the 'introduction of a kind of equality between the sexes' (XVI, 2).

This equality, like honour, was the preserve of the nobility, whose main features it shared: commonality of lineage overrode difference of gender, making possible what would have been a complete aberration in a republic, women's access to power. But as Hume was later to demonstrate, this aristocratic model could have a wider application; in his essay on 'The Rise and Progress of the Arts and Sciences' he took up the idea of a common link between the form of government, the role of women and the development of the arts, and emphasised the way aristocratic models filtered downwards in monarchies: republics did not give rise to a multiplicity of ways in which consideration found social expression: each citizen remained cocooned within his independence. The social hierarchy so characteristic of monarchies fostered connections, because it sufficed 'to beget in everyone an inclination to please his superiors, and to form himself upon those models which are most acceptable to people of condition and education; politeness of manners, therefore, arises most naturally in monarchies and courts, and where that flourishes, none of the liberal arts will be altogether neglected or despised' (Hume 1963: 128).

So the spread of gender equality in monarchies echoed the civilising effects of courtesy and in that respect was similar to trade. Even before setting out his famous thesis that while the general effect of trade was to 'bring peace' it had debasing repercussions at an individual level (1748: xx, 2), Montesquieu had introduced the idea in Book xix when speaking of women: 'female society harms morals but refines taste' (xix, 8). This was because under monarchy good conduct was less a matter of virtue than of manners: it bore on the exteriority of behaviour and was bound up with personal relationships; the aesthetics of appearance (taste) overrode the ethics of being (virtue). Thus they indicated the 'sociable' humour of the governed. Manners had more a refining or civilising effect than a moral one; they fostered exchange, brought the social model of chivalry closer to home and spread it more widely, and unlike the stability which characterised the republican model, were a force for change: 'the more peoples communicate with each other, the more readily manners change' (xix, 8). In a diffusion of this kind what was lost in terms of virtue was compensated for by a general gain at the societal level, and that was why it was better to let things be: 'women could be restrained and laws passed to improve their morals and curb their extravagance, but who is to know whether a particular form of taste (a potential source of the nation's wealth) and a type of courtesy (a magnet for foreigners) would not thereby be lost?' (xix, 5).

The reference here, of course, is to 'public benefits' and 'private vices'; Montesquieu was clearly thinking of Mandeville when he advanced this as the justification of women's frivolity: 'Fashion is an important industry; by encouraging levity of spirit it enables new commercial possibilities constantly to be opened up' (XIX, 8; 'see "The Fable of the Bees"', he adds in a footnote).

In the 1750s Gournay and his disciples (Turgot among them) were enthusiastic readers of Montesquieu and took up this idea in order to defend free trade, particularly over the calico affair (this related to printed cottons much liked by women but whose manufacture, sale and use were banned in France). Gournay and his friends campaigned to have the ban lifted, and against those who lectured women on the modesty of their sex and its duty of obedience[1] they advocated the merits of frivolity and the commercial importance of fashion.

What is noticeable in this debate (Larrère 1992: 135–72) is that frivolity and luxury were not seen as identical, and that in moving from one issue to the other, the political model engendered by commercial theories changed. In the luxury argument, such as the one that Melon, for example, introduced into France, the classical example of ostentatious expenditure was the carriage, a manifestation of power and rank, a masculine form of outlay *par excellence*. To apply to it the Mandeville schema of private vice and public benefit ('what does the State care if an individual, envious of his neighbour's equipage, is financially ruined by foolish vanity?') was to bring out the reality, ignored by ill-humoured lamentation over the manners of the age, that the luxury of the rich was the engine of industry. The argument about luxury was merely a squabble over words: properly considered, from the point of view of the state, of the commonweal, luxury did not exist; for Melon it was 'an empty term ... conveying only vague and confused notions, which term, if abused', he said, 'is capable of stopping industry in its tracks' (1843: 744). This brought the discussion back from the vanity of individual whim to the serious interest of the state by demonstrating the concrete nature of everything involved in the making of a carriage: consumption of raw materials, employment of workers, a flourishing manufacturing sector, and the sale of goods worldwide. This was not just appearance, it was reality, the strength of human beings.

Gournay did not look for the seriousness which lay hidden behind frivolity; it was frivolity itself that interested him, so where need be he brought in extravagance too: 'when will people in France accept that, trade being founded as much on extravagance as on ever-changing needs, it makes

---

1. Supporters of the maintenance of restrictions scolded women in terms like these: the half of the country 'most given to complaining and captivating' was demanding the unfettered use of printed cottons, but should keep quiet; 'since it had abandoned to the other half the painful task of commanding in affairs of state and of discussing the same; it had reserved for itself only the glory of obedience'. The mothers of those now making such strident demands were truly submissive, and 'their apparel did not cost the poor their tears' (Forbonnais 1755).

no sense to pass laws set in stone to regulate businesses catering for those needs and satisfying that extravagance?'. The notion of need could always be classified hierarchically as the useful, the agreeable and the superfluous, whereas no purchase could be got on extravagance, a mercurial phenomenon that involved constant changes in the caprice of taste and was resistant to any form of regulatory apparatus. In commerce there was only one rule, what pleased the consumer: 'if a fabric which seems bad to us soon disappears off the shelves, it cannot be bad' (Gournay 1983: 253).

If Gournay and his friends accepted without reservation that the required model was the sort of taste to which no rules could be applied, it was because they saw in this lack of significance the longstop of their critique: there was no better foil to the state interest and its desire to fix quality by regulation than futility, frivolity even. So the state could not understand women? It should stop trying. Trade would gain its independence thereby; what some fault-finding people called 'the tyranny of taste' was the ceaseless mobility and continual variation at work within a network of relationships, that of women, of taste, of 'the world of wit'. In the salons of high society serious matters were not discussed as they were in ministries; every topic of conversation was irremediably marked by futility. That was why everything could be talked about completely freely, between equals, with nothing apart from individual talent distinguishing one person from another. Frivolity and its insignificance marked the end of a rationality that was focused on the state and whose absurdity and dangerous inconsistencies were brought out into the open by frivolity in order to effect the introduction to another, that of commerce and its reciprocal relations.

Free trade and women's emancipation were inextricably linked because they derived from a common ontology, that of frivolity. The term, indeed, had a metaphysical meaning: Leibniz dealt with 'frivolous' or identical propositions which shed no light on being, but which could be 'employed' so as to 'make them useful', since they at once presented a web of relations and thereby offered an opportunity for thought (Leibniz 1966, Book IV, ch. 8, pp. 378–82). Condillac, also writing about frivolity, contrasted to the spirit of innovation the multiplicity of copies of it which were being widely diffused and were met with success: 'the number of frivolous, ridiculous, essentially ephemeral works is growing all the time' (1973: II, I, IV). They were indeed, perhaps, ridiculous or ephemeral or both, but commerce thrived on this proliferation of insignificance, on this superabundance of production; the logic of trade – that of the exchange of substitutable goods – was truly that of the frivolous, relation stealing a march here over being.

Disengaging itself from the state, the liberal critique turned towards the multiplicity of individuals whose rights it set out. Against prohibition Gournay and his friends put forward the 'natural right of everyone (a right never to be unreasonably withheld) to dress as they pleased and as cheaply as possible' (Morellet 1758). Linking in this way a theory of trade (which, in terms of content, differed little from mercantilism) to a systematic defence of individual rights was probably the most novel of Gournay's concepts. In his article 'Fondation' in the *Encyclopédie* (1757) Turgot argued in Lockeian terms that natural rights took precedence over social obligations: 'Citizens have rights, rights sacrosanct for the body of society itself, of which they exist independently, but whose necessary elements they are, and which they enter for the sole purpose of placing themselves, with all their rights, under the protection of the same laws as protect their property and liberties' (Turgot 1970: 77). The campaign in favour of free trade gave a particular spin, that of the freedom of the economic subject, to this general, jurisprudential, line of reasoning; it formulated a critique of prohibitions, regulations, corporations, guilds and companies granted monopolistic privileges, and it constituted an attack on anything that could put obstacles in the way of an individual's freedom to choose and pursue a career.

This economic model – Condorcet's – was an egalitarian one: at least that is what it aspired to be. Montesquieu's concept that 'commerce is the profession of equals' (1748: v, 8) was developed further by the advocates of free trade. Thus in *Le Commerce et le gouvernement* Condillac explained that whereas monopolies and privileges led to inequality of wealth, to its polarisation at the extremes, 'completely free trade' had egalitarian effects and reduced the gap between rich and poor, (Condillac 1980, Part II, ch. 1) and Barnave put forward the same ideas at the beginning of the French Revolution (1988); so it can be seen how the development of trade fostered the realisation of a political model in which *de iure* equality went hand in hand with *de facto* equalisation, or a lessening of inequalities.

III. Rousseau's Drive to Rehabilitate the Republican Model

This was precisely what Rousseau contested: the *Discours sur l'origine de l'inégalité* (1755a) showed how the development of society, of property and wealth, far from reducing inequalities, increased them instead, and led to the antagonistic opposition of rich and poor. Rousseau never stopped denouncing *de facto* inequalities which invalidated *de iure* equality: 'Under bad governments this equality is but a snare and a delusion, serving merely to keep the pauper mired in his squalor and the rich man cocooned in the enjoyment of his usurped wealth. In reality the law is always useful to those who own things and harmful to those who have nothing' (Rousseau 1762a, Book I, ch. 9 = 1966: 367). The 'moderation' of wealth necessary to the maintenance of *de iure* equality did not derive from 'completely free trade' but on the contrary from the ability of a 'good government' to resist the integral economisation of society and keep it under political control. He developed this programme in a markedly republican text, the article 'Economie politique': 'it is pretty well only among free nations that people know man's worth' (Rousseau 1755b = 1966: 257); equality was not an effect of trade, it was a republican phenomenon.

The critique of monarchical manners and of the female condition that characterised it was the exact counterpart of this political critique of commerce. Whereas Montesquieu and Hume spoke of the progressive spread throughout society of aristocratic manners, Rousseau, through the mouth of his character Saint-Preux in his epistolary novel *Julie, ou la nouvelle Héloïse* (1761), showed the discriminatory practices adopted by aristocratic women to keep social distinctions alive. Reckoning on the fact that 'notions of decency and modesty are deeply engraved in the mind of ordinary people' they had rejected all modesty and all decency in order to differentiate themselves from the common herd: 'so, ceasing to be women through fear of being confused with other women, they prefer their rank to their sex and ape loose creatures so as not to be aped in their turn' (Rousseau 1761, Book II, ch. 21 = 1964: 267). So here we have noblewomen treated as whores and trollops: the critique was a harsh one, but it was to be taken up again, with even Marie Antoinette (slanderously referred to as the 'Austrian slut'), being vilified (Hunt 1995). Rousseau was trying in this way to mobilise women in the struggle against the aristocracy. They had to choose between rank and gender; ordinary women, and all virtuous women, would opt for the latter. Hence there was a dual appeal: to social equality, but also to the separation of the sexes. In his letter Saint-Preux denounced the practice of allowing men and women to mix freely, since this led, he argued, to the blurring of gender differences: 'the continual indiscreet mingling of the two sexes puts restrictions on both in terms of the language, air and manners of the others', and in her reply Julie called for the separation of spheres of activity entailed by the separation of the sexes, Rousseau backing her argument up in a sarcastic footnote: 'what would become of the world and the state, illustrious authors, brilliant academicians, what would become of you all if women were to quit the government of literature and business in order to take on the running of their households?' (Rousseau 1761; Book II, ch. 27 = 1964: 299n.).

This was to base political equality on gender difference. The sexes were not equal; Rousseau called that natural, and in doing so he took up Montesquieu's argument, 'there is no parity between the sexes where the consequence of sex is concerned' (Rousseau 1762b, Book v = 1969: 697). But like all inequalities, this one was not active in the state of nature, where men and women enjoyed the same independence. So the social state had to exist in order that gender inequality could play within it the role of a principle of internal organisation governing the distribution of public and private spheres. On the man's side, access to the external world, on the woman's the home, marital fidelity and dependency: Sophie's education was not only an education for service but for servitude too. Women were not made *like* men, but *for* men: their vocation was to obey. This separation and submission were the necessary condition of the republican model which they re-established; the result of gender mixing was uniformity, which suited monarchical government: 'A monarch will probably not care much whether he governs men or women so long as he is obeyed', but political freedom had other requirements: 'in a Republic', states the *Lettre à d'Alembert* (1758), 'there must be men'.

It was a matter of the distinction between man and citizen. The equal liberty of modern natural law did not describe individuals, those subjects by right: the condition for the existence of subjective law was precisely that it retained no quality or status ordering or hierarchising individuals, each thus being equal to others and equally responsible for his own preservation. This equality, pushed to extremes, verged on the indiscernible – 'perfect equality has its price: it rules out the very concept of the individual' (Viroli 1988: 71) – as Rousseau showed in his depiction of the state of nature in the *Discours sur l'origine de l'inégalité*. This was not an awkward point; since individuals in the natural state had no common relationship, it did not matter that they had no clear apprehension of their individuality (which is why the sexual relationship in the state of nature is generic; one is attracted by the opposite sex, there being no such thing as choice where a partner is concerned, and thus no discrimination). But in the social state the reverse was true, and the extreme independence that went hand in hand with natural equality was turned on its head in the uniformity of an extreme submission to despotism, where individuals were equal because they were nothing, and the loss of individuality was a loss of liberty. So how could equality and liberty be reconciled, and how could inequalities be abolished without imposing despotism? Modern individualism dissolved the link between all traditional social entities in which individuals were inserted and by which they were described, but it could not dodge the labelling problem. Hence the interest in sexual difference, for this 'inequality is not a human institution, at least it is not the work of prejudice, but of reason'. Moreover the fact of keeping to the difference between the sexes qualified all males for citizenship as well; the inequality of the sexes was the condition of political freedom and equality: there had to be women so that men could be citizens, not just individuals without qualities, subjected indiscriminately to a despotic power.

So back to hearth and home. Julie stays put, viewing with the most intense dislike any possibility of travelling even a few miles from Clarens, whereas the male characters of the *Nouvelle Héloïse* are wanderers: before his marriage M. de Wolmar was a soldier on active service, and Saint-Preux, on leaving Julie, goes round the world accompanied in these peregrinations by Lord Edward. Julie, and Claire who has joined her, attract in turn these footloose men, and tie them down in a place where they find happiness. In the republican model put forward by Rousseau the condition of women changed from being 'captivated' to 'captivating'; his great originality, indeed, was to have demonstrated the compatibility between republican freedom and the private dimension of manners, and to have separated the family and the state even more rigorously than had been done hitherto. The article 'Economie politique' was a critique of the family model of political authority, rehearsing Aristotle's distinction between the domestic and the political spheres. In parallel with this the *Nouvelle Héloïse* demonstrated that there was no political model for family relationships, Claire pointing out that a 'good husband' is not 'a lord and master' (Rousseau 1761, Book VI, ch. 7 = 1964: 638): 'dependency' characterised women's social situation rather than their private condition. So in his attempt to rally women to the joys of femininity Rousseau called upon them to embrace such entirely private, intimate satisfactions, unknown to the public sphere, as bearing children, loving their husbands and keeping them faithful, and enjoying the company of their fellow-women; in sharp contrast to the bitter rivalries of society ladies who could not bear competition Rousseau held up the close, tender friendship of Claire and Julie. At Clarens Julie set up an association which combined, or tried to combine, what none of the social models of the female condition (despotic, monarchical or republican) was really able to reconcile, sexual pleasure and reproduction of the species, love and friendship, for in Julie's opinion 'a gentleman will never have a better friend than his wife' (*ibid.*, Book VI, ch. 6 = 1964: 670).

So the republican model of the female condition was given new life; in the ancient Greek or Roman version put forward by Montesquieu the republic was represented as the régime which gave an enhanced, public dimension to private manners and family life, making them an affair of state: 'in republics private crimes are more public, that is are more of an affront to the constitution of the state than to individuals' (Montesquieu 1748 III, 5). On the basis of the marital and family home, manners exposed to overt scrutiny a public sphere needing control, that of the censors: 'in requiring that any accusation of adultery be made in public, Roman law admirably preserved moral purity; it cowed women, but it also struck awe into those whose job it was to watch over them' (v, 7). Rousseau no doubt preserved the notion that manners had their own public dimension which was the locus of a moral control, of a censorship conducted essentially by women who possessed there their own space, that of a face-to-face society in which they exercised surveillance over each other, for the female virtue of fidelity had not merely to be real but also seen to be real, because here appearances were decisive: Rousseau described the workings of this 'public opinion' in the *Lettre à d'Alembert*, showing that it had its own efficacy, distinct from that of the law. But beyond this public (though not political) space the 'very intimate society' of Clarens, hidden from gaze, was to be found; its symbol was Julie's garden, a place not visible from outside but which, once one was inside, closed in upon itself, without any exterior view (Larrère 1988).

This was because the family, as Rousseau presented it, was the true focus of morality and could act as the basis for the general reform of society set out at the beginning of *Emile*: if women returned to domesticity and breastfed their children, the whole of society would benefit. In this Rousseau was echoing the demographic and public health concerns of his contemporaries.

IV. Economy and Demography

The constant fear in eighteenth-century Europe was not overpopulation but low birth-rates; there was a general feeling that there had been a steady decline in the population since antiquity (Perrot 1992: 162–72). People vied with each other in proclaiming that in a developing economy which was still poorly mechanised, the power of human muscle was truly the primary resource and most precious asset. Depopulation was feared above all else:

regular catastrophes, both natural and social, food shortages, even famine, not to mention epidemics and wars, threatened not only the lives of individuals but that of the population as a whole. The reproduction of the species was a duty that must at all costs not be neglected, and the literature in favour of population growth was particularly abundant, committed *inter alia* to the denunciation of those who evaded the obligations of marriage, especially monks and nuns, to halting the drift from the countryside to the towns, and to encouraging foreign immigration. In general, though, people trusted to nature to maintain 'the inexhaustible abundance of men' (Montchrestien 1889: 24): the bulk of the demographic measures were aimed not so much at stimulating fertility but at the beneficial canalisation of population flows; the authorities sought to attract workers by offering various incentives, including naturalisation (citizenship being granted with a liberality that seems enviably relaxed to us today).

In the course of the century this approach changed, however, with the development of a medical and public health discourse aimed at encouraging reproduction: its best-known form was the praise heaped on mothers who breastfed their own children. Based on the new psychological and medical discoveries concerning sexuality, reproduction and the role played in them by women, an entire literature on marriage emerged that gave advice on hygiene and good demographic practice. By refocusing on the family in this way secular literature took over from earlier religious literature and caused it to change direction: where marriage was concerned Catholicism concentrated on the couple, whose morals had to be safeguarded, particularly in protecting the man from debauchery; the advice given to the nursing mother who asked her confessor whether she could refuse her husband's advances was to put the child out to a wet-nurse so as to hang on to her husband. The approach advocated by public-health literature was the exact opposite: its propaganda in favour of women breastfeeding their babies insisted that the duty of a mother came before that of a wife. So women's social relationships were of less importance than the successful accomplishment of their natural reproductive function.

The publication intensified of works seeking a solution to the depopulation attributable to luxury, celibacy and debauchery and a means of encouraging marriage, alone seen as being capable of providing a solid basis for demographic growth in civilised nations. The moralists were thus to have the last word in the debate about luxury, which by this time meant frivolity, when they put forward an argument its defenders could understand: the luxury of women perhaps paid the wages of the poor, but it depopulated

France. Whether the effect was intended or not, and whether or not they set out to do so deliberately, women who chased after fashion, it was argued, had fewer children.

Simultaneously with the shift from the frivolity of fashion to the serious business of motherhood, women's work began to be viewed in a different light. In 1778, in his *Recherches et considérations sur la population de la France*, Jean-Baptiste Moheau expressed surprise at the way work was allocated according to gender, and attacked the 'ridiculous and heinous' way in which social functions were shared out, because it allowed men to corner the jobs requiring 'taste' and 'delicacy' (such as writing, painting, engraving, and the making of clocks, watches and spectacles), whereas women were confined to work involving heavy labour; they were to be found, he claimed, 'harnessed to ploughs alongside animals', 'tilling vineyards by hand', and 'carrying burdens not meant for them, and yet they are barely able to earn their daily bread' (Book II, Part II, Chapter 15). What Moheau found most shocking was not just the inappropriate use of the two sexes' skills but also its impact on demography: women employed in exhausting jobs had difficulty conceiving and bore fewer children. That was the chief argument: it was in the name of the needs of population growth that women were going to be considered not as workers, not even as consumers, but as reproducers of the species.

This division between production and reproduction was by no means self-evident. In *ancien régime* France the gulf separating the leisured classes from the working population was a social, not a gender, matter: men and women worked side by side. In the early part of the century Melon had no objection to this, believing indeed that making men and women work together would spur them on to greater efforts (1843, ch. 8). This was not Quesnay's view a little later on: following Gournay's lead he introduced the notion of individual rights into economic theory, and it led him to consider men as economic agents, acting freely and rationally, rather than as labour to be used. In Quesnay's view work was not the chief anthropological characteristic: he saw it as an expenditure of physical effort better undertaken by animals and machines than by men, so he criticised generalised and undifferentiated employment, opting instead for the rational use of specialisation. It was in this context that he ruled out female work as a stopgap solution to be avoided: 'men work, otherwise women and children do it in their place, and do it very poorly' (Quesnay 1958: 514).

In the wake of Quesnay Adam Smith linked gender differentiation of tasks to progress in the division of labour, whose historical development he traced, within the succession of social stages connected to changes in the main method of subsistence. Savage societies, consisting of hunter-gatherers, travelled in undifferentiated hordes: men, women and children were all mixed together, and women could even take part in combat. Barbaric societies, consisting of nomadic herdsmen, embarked on a process of settlement linked to the development of certain forms of agriculture: when the men went to war the women stayed at home and farmed the land, but the latter activity was looked down upon. Complete agricultural settlement revalued such tasks, which became the business of men, and it was only in their absence (usually through war) that women and old men were permitted to take their place. In agricultural societies, nonetheless, the family remained the work unit, and domestic labour met most needs. That is what commercial society put an end to: what Adam Smith reproached factory work with was that it preserved the domestic character of work, which was generally assigned to women, and that it let many products slip through the net of the market's public channels. Such domestic work was for Smith insufficiently specialised, 'gross'.[2] The generalisation of the market brought all products into the domain of exchange, and that included men: 'independent workers' were those who were able to provide for their families by selling their labour, which acquired a public dimension. Such workers were chiefly men: women's involvement in childcare denied them full access to the labour market.

When the economy gained the upper hand over trade this was accompanied by a dissociation of the functions of production and reproduction, economy and demography. Political economy meant raising to the level of the public sphere some of domestic activity's indispensable tasks that henceforth constituted occupations which put individuals in touch with one another and which were appreciated and socially measured. The economic sphere had become a public place governed by the rule of law and legal relationships between independent individuals, but the functions of reproduction still belonged to the private sphere, to that of the intimacy of the family, a secret place where the conduct of individuals, far from seeing its value enhanced, was instead considered a tactic to evade the collective duty of propagation of the species. This explained Moheau's indignation over attempts at birth control: ('these baneful secrets, known in the animal kingdom to man alone, have spread to the countryside; nature is cheated in every village, however remote'), and his call for the 'restoration of morals', that is to say a holistic ethics as opposed to juridical individualism (Moheau 1778: 102).

2. He also talks of the domestic and gross manufactures that necessarily accompany the progress of agriculture and that in each family are the work of women and children (Smith 1976a, Book II, ch. 5 and Book V, ch. 1).

The separation of law and morality mirrored the dissociation of the domestic between the economic, on the one hand, and the familial, on the other.

v. Conclusion: What Convergence?

It was the convergence between this dissociation and Rousseau's republican model which explains why the latter was adopted at the very start of the French Revolution: in the various constitutions 'women, free by law but captive by custom' (Montesquieu 1973: VII, 9) were excluded from the suffrage. The distinction (first put forward by Sieyès) between active and passive citizens mirrored that of law and morality: on the one hand there were independent men with access as economic subjects to the public sphere, and on the other all those – women, children, servants – who depended on the master of the house and were deemed to have no will of their own.

But it was only a convergence: the two models were fundamentally different. Rousseau's stance was that of classical republicanism, of the direct exercise of authority: political virtue consisted in not delegating one's power, in not handing over one's freedom as one might part with an appropriated possession. Sieyès, on the other hand, considered political representation as a form of the division of labour, the application of a general model of delegation which, far from threatening people's independence, encouraged the development of liberty; in rejecting the democracy of the ancients he tried, with representative government, to define modern republicanism as something suited to commercial society and to what he called 'the political systems founded on work' (Sieyès 1985a: 236; Larrère 1992).

How was it possible for these two models to coexist? The likely reason was that Sieyès's approach, like Condorcet's, had no way of describing women: their rights were recognised as individuals without distinction, not as women. Everything that made possible the understanding of their particularities, everything that was included in the study of their condition, fell outside the scope of such an approach. At the same time as he was affirming that women 'must not exercise an active influence on the state' Sieyès was putting his finger on what he had just ruled out (though the sidelining of 'half the human race' did not go entirely unnoticed).[3] But once the exclusion had been decreed, he could offer no valid reason for it: it was, he said, in the

3. Sieyès 198b: 199. Condorcet pointed out that the great scandal of the denial of civil rights to women was not just that it had happened but that it had passed unnoticed, that there had been no need to justify it, nor even to mention it, whereas the legislators had but recently declared the rights of man and the citizen, i.e. those of the whole human race (Condorcet 1790).

'present state' that it operated; at any other time he would have attributed it to 'prejudice'. Condorcet argued similarly that 'usage' and 'custom' explained the exclusion of women. When Pierre Guyomar, one of Condorcet's friends, first defended the decision to grant women civil rights and then agreed that such rights should be restricted, he declared that the 'rigour of the law' had to bow to the 'proprieties derived from manners'.[4]

As it happens Rousseau can shed light on the meaning and substance of the 'manners' here referred to, and that helps explain his success in a situation in which the convergence of points of view more or less completely barred women's access to the public sphere. Madame de Staël certainly had no ideological or intellectual leanings towards Rousseau's position; her sympathies lay more with Sieyès or Condorcet. She did not however share the latter's conception of women's rights and 'did not lay as much stress on the common "reasonable" nature of men and women as on women's specific contribution to civilisation': in her study of the female condition across the Channel she vaunted the 'happiness brought about by the forms of domestic affection' which Englishwomen enjoyed (Raynaud 1989).

To side with Rousseau was to reject the frivolity of trade and to choose republican virtue which, however, did not rule out either pleasure or liberty. In her willing acceptance of a marriage that made of an imposed choice a freely assumed decision, and in her subsequent married life, Julie remained a free subject who (as Jean Ehrard has shown) claimed, even unto death, the rights of the heart – 'the right to love you without sin' – and the rights of the body, 'a revolutionary morality that contrasted sharply with Rousseau's ideological conservatism and contradicted – but did not of course invalidate – the sanctimonious and spiritualistic discourse that runs through the entire novel' (Ehrard 1997). Julie's garden, that densely planted spot which shuts in anyone entering it, thus becomes the symbol of a woman's enjoyment, a private, intimate place where her autonomy can be asserted: something which Virginia Woolf, more than a century and a half later, was to call 'a room of one's own'.

Translated from the French by John Fletcher

4. Guyomar 1793, quoted in Rosanvallon 1992: 140.

9

Feminist Republicanism and the Political Perception of Gender

JUDITH A. VEGA

What relationship could present-day feminist theory build with the tradition of republican thought? What value could a theory developed from the context of the ancient city-states possibly have for a feminism confronted with the infinitely complex interactions between politics, the social, and gender in modernity? In the past decades, feminist theory has in manifold ways explored the utility as well as the impediments of the various conceptualisations of modern society by Marxism, liberalism, communitarianism and post-structuralism. It has allowed these idioms to reverberate in its proper assessments of male dominance and female subjectivities. The respective involvements, meanwhile, instead of accommodating feminism's need for a theory of politics that extended to and suited its proper concerns, rather resulted in exposing the (sexual) politics of theory. The recurring exasperation all idioms caused probably converge on this one specific ground: the various theoretical angles on modernity share a deficient attention to the range of politics in modern life. In one way or another, they suffer from an insufficient or one-sided attention with respect to the specific political quality of the social as an agonistic as well as gendered terrain of both agency and construction of subjectivity.

Also republicanism has been subjected to an exasperated exposition of its sexual politics. The feminist reception of classical republican thought has testified to a profound pessimism with regard to the possibility of employing republican idiom as a resource for feminist theory or practice. Feminist historiography and political theory have shown republican idiom to repress or neglect private and bodily experience, evoking unembodied, literally 'self-denying' images of the good citizen. They have furthermore pointed out that the Aristotelian heritage leads, in a radical reversal of liberalism, to an excessive dedication to public action, guided, moreover, by imperatives of action representing macho values. Finally, they have investigated how, in the tradition of classical republicanism, life's contingencies have been approached through the allegory of fickle Fortune, resulting in a political symbolics which has women personify the frustration of attempts at control. Republicanism thus seems to epitomise the quintessence of a disciplining and masculinist modernity: the obsession with the omnipotent, engineering powers politics ought to possess, and the validation of an egocentric, competing, controlling political and epistemological subject, both steeped in an undisguised fear of and contempt for women.

Only in recent years did feminist interest in republican theory take a different road as a novel reception appeared of the work of Hannah Arendt. The volume compiled by Bonnie Honig represents a marked turning point, a project which sets out to exchange the issue of 'the Woman Question in Arendt' for 'the Arendt Question in Feminism'. The contributions are presented as transforming former receptions of Arendt's hostility to feminism, which concentrated on locating 'the women in the theory', by focusing on the ways 'she theorizes a democratic politics built not on already existing identities or shared experiences but on contingent sites of principled coalescence and shared practices of citizenship' (Honig (ed.) 1995: 3). While this new engagement with Arendt's work is said to be propelled by a set of questions allegedly pressed by post-modern conditions of identity, I would suggest that it may equally guide a reorientation on the very tradition of civic humanist thought. In this article, I will discuss republican conceptions in the feminist history of ideas from the eighteenth century. My argument endorses the systematical thrust of the revaluation of Arendt's thought while rendering it more generally applicable to the tradition she associates with. It also subscribes to keeping both questions on the agenda of feminist inquiry, although it traces this agenda to feminism's original modernity, pursuing an explicit receptivity to what I would call the ironic simultaneity of such questions in modernity. To bring out the broader systematical issue, the historical argument presented below intends to balance the 'res publica Question' in feminism and what should be termed a simultaneous questioning of 'woman' and of 'male dominance'. Newly focusing on historical feminist receptions of republicanism at the break of the conception of modernity can reveal the susceptibility of this quintessential political theory to such a double-tracked feminist programme.

Republican thought can in systematical respect be characterised as differing from the above-mentioned bodies of theory precisely in centring attention on the political constitution of human association and on the practices of fulfilling desires for freedom and equal public presence. It consistently takes the question of politics to be preliminary to questions of the market, labour, community, or aesthetics, and hence directs a heuristics for countering tendencies to naturalise these empirical contexts of action as final sources of identity.

I want to survey two central republican tenets which enabled challenges to the diagnosed masculine modern imaginary. First, eighteenth-century feminist discourse vitally engaged with the consistent public perspective from the civic humanist tradition that acclaimed public virtues and civic participation. It is the perspective from which identities and activities legitimated purely in terms of either market or labour were countered by insisting on the precedence of *homo politicus*, and from which politics was severed from the dictates of the market. Whereas republicanism is sometimes rashly assimilated to communitarianism for its high appraisal of the political bond, and a dominant conviction moreover exists in social and political philosophy that the republican (Rousseauvian) devotion to politics prepared for totalitarian conclusions and closed societies in later eras, a very different reception emerges from eighteenth-century feminist republican discourse. Republicanism's political approach of human nature and its insistence on political solutions over and against economical ones turn out to hold an important intuition with respect to the relationship between social diversity and political union. This is the intuition, not of the communal embeddedness of individual life, but, on the contrary, of the necessity to transcend one's – particularist – social position, in order to reach some sort of political association over and against the modern proliferation of social diversity. Feminist republicans appear to have been acutely aware of the potential here for reflection on and critique of gender identity.

Various feminist studies have established how the republican public approach allowed for designing a female sphere of action, a *vita activa* for women, of which the best-known example is probably the infamous 'republican mother'. This 'sociological' or 'topographical' angle, however, is to be supplemented or perhaps superseded by a more radical theoretical one, precisely where republicanism is no longer identified as one more branch of communitarianism, and the focus is shifted to the deep-seated passion in republicanism for a politically understood life. Republicanism's idiomatic and conceptual peculiarities provided, first, handles on arguing a feminist version of democratic public life, the styling of which was not dependent on some prior 'privatised' femininity, and second, a theoretical potential to 'politicise' gender.

A second republican tenet exists that allows for engaging republican narrative for a feminist modern imaginary. Instead of defining politics exhaustively as concerning the activities of steering, engineering, and controlling society, the tradition of civic humanism can be seen to have conceived of politics as action, not control, and hence to enable recognising the contingent factors always confronting politics. The theme of contingency is, far from being denied, explicitly present within the republican tradition. It is recognised as part and parcel of life – political or otherwise. The classical hero struggles with and is crushed by fate – quite unlike his liberal, and present-day, counterpart who triumphs over difficulties. The question, then, is how this classical heritage was dealt with in eighteenth-century civic humanism. The answer should discount the fact that eighteenth-century civic humanism has, so to say, internalised the *querelle* between the ancients and the moderns: it wavers between two impulses, one directed backward, the other forward. On the one hand there is a Renaissance humanist impulse which relied on the authority of the classical examples, on the other a 'modern' republican impulse which could not but see human beings as destined to live active, as contrary to pre-modern ordained and traditionally grounded, lives. The ancient civic humanist attention to insecure and contingent action gets entangled in this 'modern impulse' to intuit a 'destination to act' within a genuinely modern condition of contingent existence. Both impulses are similarly present in feminist republicanism: the first provided it in imitative fashion with authoritative role models, the second provided it with a notion that 'gender' belonged to political, not ordained existence. I will return to these themes below.

In short: the thoroughly political perspective on human existence of republicanism provided its feminist adherents with an heuristic device that enabled them to carry politics to private and personal experience, and judge the private from a public, the personal from a political perspective, instead of *vice versa* as in liberalism. In what is probably the most drastic deflection from its present-day image, republicanism could be, and was, seen as a reservoir for conceptualising a feminist 'politics of the personal'.

1. A feminist political passion and *mulier politica*

An important lead exists in civic humanist thought which allies with feminist concerns: its awareness of the precarious relationship between social diversity and political union, and the subsequent appraisal of *homo politicus*.

Its contrast with liberal humanism here proves crucial. In the liberal version of the separation of economy, or the social, and politics, political equality should abstract from social differences. These are legitimate in themselves, representing pre-political individuality, political equality being a mere corrective complement to them. Genuine human activity takes place in the innocently pluralist social, not the political domain. Republicans ascribe to politics the task of establishing concord among those who consider themselves free and equal. In its modern context, this amounts to insisting that politics cannot sever itself from social differences as these become the complication to realising the politically charged desire for free and equal life. Taking the place of hierarchical social ranking during the *ancien régime*, the market once again generates and legitimates inequality. Hannah Arendt captured the notion when she dejectedly diagnosed 'the invasion of the public realm by society' in the eighteenth century. Politics is to generate a type of action that supersedes market principles.

As I already mentioned, one feminist reception of classical republicanism perceives an obsessive focus on the distinction political life bestows on its devotees, by which private, bodily, vulnerable and uncompetitive existence is denied a political life. Bonnie Honig has claimed rather different virtues for the – at least the Arendtian – insistence on the priority of politics. Behind it she conjectures an aversion to pre-political identities and redefines this potential as that of a 'performative politics'. 'On Arendt's account, identity is the performative production, not the expressive condition or essence of action' (Honig 1992: 216). To Arendt, conceiving of an acting self implies seeing it as the site of an agonistic struggle which she '(sometimes) calls politics' (*ibid.*: 220). The acting self produces itself, instead of presupposing its proper identity. As mentioned above, Arendt's approach is here recruited for a theoretical and political complex allegedly marked by a specifically postmodern condition. I suggest that it can be shown to be operative in the very conception of modernity – at least in the then feminist imagination of modernity. Honig's assessment of the insistence on the priority of the political can be transposed to republican discourse during the transitional period that the eighteenth-century Atlantic revolutionary era was. Revolutionary politics aimed at producing identities which could relieve monarchy's symbolic representation in the single body politic of the king and establish inter-subjective relations in a political realm. Established social identities, whether from the *ancien régime* or the practices of commerce, were thoroughly distrusted. Antiquity, but also other historical periods, were searched for models for genuine political, or rather public, activity which could relieve monarchical publicity and constitute a genuine bonding of a humanity which was conceived of as egalitarian. While on the one hand the masculinist features of these identifications have been amply documented, on the other hand republicanism's recourse to history and example to find access to a substantially experienced citizenship provided an open and contested source for gender identifications. In this particular historical period mimetic orientation, rather than an essentialist authenticity or expressive identity, guided one's sense of an acting self. The admonition 'let us imitate the Roman ladies' by the republican activist Etta Palm-Aelders (1743–99), whom I will discuss below, illustrates this contemporary mode of performative identity.

There is the further issue of the precise embodiment of the political subject and its relation to feminist politics. Dorinda Outram has explored the theme of the unembodied political man. She observes the 'disappearance of the body' from the history of modern public space and restores the theme to her study of eighteenth-century French revolutionary discourse. She traces republican accounts of public virtue and discipline of the passions to sixteenth-century accounts of Stoicism. The classical Stoic discussions of the relative merits of involvement with and withdrawal from public affairs were in the sixteenth century narrowed and bent towards an exclusive orientation on action, involvement, and a stern self-control. This neo-Stoicism could legitimate the central role of force and discipline in the state, as well as create an ideology of the self-disciplined individual. Neo-Stoic notions of the self joined other ideologies of the individual in a 'cult of the self' in which the urge to achieve self-sovereignty was fed through identification with heroes – whether the great men of antiquity or contemporary cultural and literary models.

> [T]he main object was not antiquarian recreation of the Roman republic . . . but the ability to personify virtue continuously and publicly . . . Solemn demeanour, courageous words, and reserve were . . . the signs of the successful ability to play out a role which compelled attention, created an audience, and validated the authority of the player.   (Outram 1989: 78)

In the revolutionary struggle for autonomy, physical and psychic self-control, and heroic dignity, Outram sees prefigured *homo clausus* who eventually re-emerges as the self-image of the nineteenth-century middle class. She points out how this new Stoic ideal was applied to and used by men rather than women. While the mythological canon did include many female heroes, it produced very different types of heroism for men and women: women reacted, rather than acted.

> *Homo clausus* was not accompanied by *mulier clausa*. Whereas the male
> heroes emphasize their non-reactivity, their remorseless control over
> body and emotion, women, on the contrary perform heroic acts
> precisely because of their reactivity. They react with warm and
> generous outrage . . . they were held to be less concerned about the
> maintenance of dignity . . . In other words, in the Revolutionary
> mythology, women react, relate, perceive, involve; men cling to the
> heroic *moments* and *postures* of personification.   (Outram 1989: 84)

Being defined in terms of reactivity instead of activity, and heteronomy instead of autonomy, female action was deprived of public weight and dignity
as defined by revolutionary heroic idiom. Eventually, 'the middle-class revolutionary creation of political culture was to validate the political participation of men and culpabilize that of women' (Outram 1989: 156).

However cogent Outram's depiction of revolutionary imagery is, it surveys one side of the republican story – the masculine perspective on the
republic – leaving out the active contributions to and uses made of the potential of republican public imagery and idiom by feminists, employing these
for their own goals. Can the oppositions between activity and reactivity, reserve and passionate involvement, 'male controllers and personifiers' versus
'female feelers and doers' (Outram 1989: 85) also be recognised in their discourses? Or did feminist authors rather contribute to the construction of a
new political individual in terms comparable to those outlined by Outram
as accounting for heroic, Stoic manhood? Some of them indeed did. Mary
Wollstonecraft (1759–97), in *A Vindication of the Rights of Woman* (1792),
champions the very republican ideal of contained, distant composure as an
ideal of female dignity. It is the gist of her impatience with women's culture,
with female practices of involved, physical, intimate mutual relationships,
that these conflict with the republican ideal of fellowship. It repels her that
women 'should be more familiar with each other than men are': it is 'a solecism
in manners . . . an insult to the majesty of human nature' (1792: 205).

> To say the truth, women are too familiar with each other . . . Why in the
> name of decency are sisters, female intimates, or ladies and their
> waiting-women, to be so grossly familiar as to forget the respect which
> one human creature owes to another? . . . Secrets are told – where
> silence ought to reign . . .   (1792: 205)

> In short, with respect to both mind and body, they are too intimate.
> That decent personal reserve which is the foundation of dignity of
> character, must be kept up between woman and woman . . . (1792: 206)

Dignified, controlled, reserved behaviour is wished for women, and this is conceived of as an application of republican ideals. The personal and political subjectivity of women conceived of by this feminist author is modelled on *mulier clausa*. Let us direct attention to another feminist author.

Etta Palm-Aelders similarly drafted a feminist republicanism which can neither be subsumed under the idiom of republican motherhood, nor be seen as conforming to the republican image of a reactive and non-public female heroism.[1] Her application of republican public ethos to women and to personal relations, and her evocations of classical and contemporary female heroes tread different paths – not to a disciplining state and self-disciplined subjects, but to a republican society disciplining masculine behaviour in public as well as private contexts, and supplying women with the very public weight Outram sees being reserved for men.

In several instances, Palm-Aelders points out how male morality constitutes the problem for the republic: 'you kept for yourselves all the conveniences of vice ... you have given us all the difficulty of virtue as our share' (1791: 3). She summons men to take responsibility for their own virtues, with respect to their public as well as to their private lives. In general, her republicanism appears to be about a public ethos, rather than a public domain. She uses the vocabularies of rights and virtue alongside each other, combining them in a feminist version of democratic public life. To her, the pursuit of republican freedom is not to show patience with the chance arrangement of societal spheres. Her feminist criticisms of contemporary law testify to her intuition that entering familial life cannot be the criterion by which the citizen stops being a *persona*, a legal personality, and becomes a natural (that is unpolitical) human being, a *homo*. Her work breathes an awareness that the applicability of the concept of politics ought to be broadened, and that a specific relevance exists to women of such a 'broad concept'. The terrain of male–female relationships induces a widened range or a different kind of politics women might foster and engage in. In referring to the specific female struggle of coping with male power and arrogance, it reveals the notion of a politics not simply structured around the demands of the state or the social. Women, meanwhile, are not its sole subjects or agents. Both men and women are to obey the precepts of the republican ethos regardless of the 'space' of action.

1. See for extensive discussions of Palm-Aelders's republicanism Vega 1989a, 1989b, 1991. Information on the Dutch context of thinking on gender can be found in Vega 1996; Vega and Dekker 2002. For the English citations from her texts I have largely copied the translations in Levy, Applewhite and Johnson (eds.) 1979. Page numbers, however, refer to the locations in the French original.

On 26 November 1790, she appeared on the tribune of the Parisian *Cercle Social* in defence of feminist notions, addressing her fellow-women with the words: 'now that the French have become like the Romans, let us imitate the virtues and the patriotism of the Roman ladies' (Villiers 1910: 20). She continued to cite such diverse examples of classic female heroism as the daughter of Cato, the mother of Coriolanus, the warriors at Salamis, Cornelia ('mother of the Gracchi'), the wife of Petus, the Maid of Orleans, and the reigns of Elizabeth in England and Catherine in Russia. She proposed to establish civic associations exclusively run by women – organisations which would secure the republic by translating women's civic responsibility into vigilance against the 'enemies of liberty' and profiteers in its midst. Women were to be *citoyennes* – she never addresses them as mothers. Palm-Aelders's rhetorical use of classical and contemporary female heroes did draw on the image of *homo clausus*, or rather *mulier clausa*. Her linguistic style in addressing her fellow-citizens and in evoking female heroines from antiquity as well as historical and contemporary France is similar to that of the male revolutionaries. Its appeal appears to be lying exactly in its power to command attention, respect, solemnity and dignified courage. Palm-Aelders wants to show that the priority with the public realm a republican outlook implied was not conditioned by a heroic identification dependent on male examples. Her disparate examples of heroines cannot yield one specific directive for women's public performance; they rather evoke an imaginary of female public practices. Republicanism provides her with a legitimation of female authority from historical and literary example, in contrast to an abstract, systematical legitimation from democratic–juristic humanism. Literary and historical female models inject opportunities for personal identification into liberal humanism's call to enter a transcendent, abstract humanity.

Palm-Aelders's notions urge the contesting of an 'original gender' of public identities, illustrating the gist of 'performative politics'; they furthermore accommodate republicanism to a conception of a modern politics beyond the state, testifying to an intuition of the sexual–political productivity featuring the social dimension of modern life.

II. Contingency: From Fickle Fortune to Reactivating Gender

While liberal modernity has in our post-modern era been castigated for underplaying the contingent features of human existence, the presence of the theme of contingency in civic humanist thought is more readily agreed upon.

As has already been touched upon above, this presence is not confined to contorted images of women representing the corruption of free political action. It has been argued that within the civic humanist tradition, in texts of the ancients as well as e.g. the work of Machiavelli, reflection on political community and order involved reflection on ambiguity, difference, and the insecurities of social, political, and historical life (Pitkin 1984; Saxonhouse 1985; Nussbaum 1986). How does this classical heritage of reflection on the problematics of politics and difference figure in eighteenth-century republicanism?

To answer this question, we have to discriminate between two meanings of contingency: impairing versus enabling contingency. In the first sense, it stands for irrational obstructions of deliberated action, for the frustration of preconceived, carefully devised plans. To eighteenth-century republicanism, contingency in this impairing sense is thought to exist in two main circumstances: decadence and corruption. These were attributed mainly, but not exclusively, to female vice. When it comes to the fear of threats to a stable republic, we actually find two recurring gender themes: effeminate posture, and male unruly practices. In feminist discourses both themes were explored, now as frustrations of the possibility of a responsible and purposeful life conducted by women.

In its second sense, contingency – as opposed to destination – provides the very possibility of action. As – or as far as – modernity assumes human beings to be free, their acts determined neither by God nor fixed social order, it has assumed the contingent onset of social life, allowing for a new, unlimited capacity for action. This enabling contingency is of course a vital ingredient of modernity's republicanism, its *homo politicus* being dependent on the acknowledgement and laudation of the human potential for action. The civic humanist accent here lies in the intuition of the (public) world as a human artefact – made by human beings, although not necessarily controlled by them. While control is often presumed to be implicated by a modern attitude towards life's contingencies, acting might well be considered an equally suitable response. Contrary to control, it indicates an open process of production of the political, that is shared, world. It is precisely this insistence on a simultaneously undetermined and active subjectivity which feminist republicanism adopts. The result is not just the promotion of an active woman, a public female identity. What also transpires is an intuition that gender is part of the same conceptual context, the same contingent setting, as the establishment of political association. Alongside the general republican notion that the public realm and public identities are amenable to political, performative production, feminist republicanism entertains the intuition that the categories of femininity and masculinity are subject to performative action by either *homo politicus* or *mulier politica*. Contingency here surfaces not as mere fickle chance – gendered identity accordingly being an arbitrary and un-amenable lot – but as the condition for an agonistic approach of gendered existence and identities.

This is not to suggest fully fledged post-modern insights of eighteenth-century minds. There is, however, more to the republican handling of social identities than Rousseau's monolithic conception of 'the people' would suggest. Eighteenth-century republicanism, in fact, was about addressing the relationship between social identities and politics. Republican feminist discourse illustrates this in a special way. The works of Wollstonecraft are a case in point.

First of all, the Atlantic revolutions were, of course, a giant deconstructionist operation. The opponents of the revolution attack precisely the undermining of familiar social identities by the revolutionaries. It is most instructive to see Edmund Burke (1729–97) enumerate the issues: property, gender and political authorship. The French revolutionaries want to diffuse proprietorial claims among the masses whereas '[t]he characteristic essence of property . . . is to be *unequal*' (Burke 1987: 44, italics in original). He has famously stipulated that '[o]n this scheme of things, a king is but a man; a queen is but a woman; a woman is but an animal; and an animal not of the highest order' (*ibid*.: 67). The revolutionary landscape forms a 'profane burlesque' rising from the 'mixed mob of ferocious men, and of women lost to shame', who 'have a power to subvert and destroy; but none to construct' (*ibid*.: 60). The revolutionaries support a political representation based on popular election, that is, election by anybody. They call into existence a society void of distinction. The revolution erases what is socially and mentally engraved, utterly neglecting to fill in the ensuing amorphous blank. It unleashes a representational activity which is in fact incapable of re-presenting, lacking any solid knowledge about who or what one acts for. One cannot represent what as yet has no firm ground, what has not been rooted in social or political experience.

Those who endorse the revolution, on the other hand, of course point out the arbitrariness of the very identities under attack. The revolution wants to rewrite social and mental scripts, in order to give authority to what is hitherto denied the possibility of being represented. 'Probably you mean women who gained a livelihood by selling vegetables or fish' (1790: 29),

Wollstonecraft retorts against Burke's remark on the women lost to shame. It is precisely 'hereditary distinctions' that obstruct civilisation's grand task of 'humanizing every description of men' (1794: 355). The revolution does not leave a void, but is a project of redefinitions; it fights, in its turn, the political void that arises from the mere representation of vested interests, whether economical, political, or sexual. It will alert to social difference by realising a political association through publicity of government and consultation of the citizens (1794; see Book v, ch. 3), in the hope of having republican government 'be more than a shadow of representation' (1790: 61).

In *A Vindication of the Rights of Woman*, all representatives of the *ancien régime* pose as women: the aristocracy, kings, the soldiers and officers of the standing armies, the clergy and their hierarchically organised colleges, sailors even. Femininity is but a political code-word, and Wollstonecraft is exasperated by a society in which every conceivable human capacity is sexed. Not nature, but society, academic treatises on instruction, and philosophy have given 'a sex to mind' (1792c: 110), 'a sex to virtue' (pp. 46, 75), to souls (p. 130), as well as to body – as we may infer from her discussion of the physical discipline, and enslavement to their bodies, of women (1792c, ch. 3). The meanings of masculinity as well as femininity are constantly and explicitly addressed and juggled with in Wollstonecraft's texts. Contrary to her reputation in many histories of ideas, she does not simply represent 'equality feminism', or humanism's trap in which women have no choice but to conform to men. She is not that enamoured with men or with what they represent.[2] Speaking of the historian and publisher Catherine Macaulay (1731–91), she remonstrates against Rousseau:

> In her style of writing, indeed, no sex appears, for it is like the sense it conveys, strong and clear. I will not call hers a masculine understanding, because I admit not of such an arrogant assumption of reason . . .
> (1792c: 180)

> Indeed the word masculine is only a bugbear . . .
> (1792c: 75)

She does reproduce contemporary idiom in calling the court 'effeminate', but she juxtaposes it to Enlightenment's proper gender metaphorics, its allegories for the new spirit which will organise the body politic: reason, with 'her captivating face', the 'image of God implanted in our nature', and liberty, 'with maternal wing' (1794: 295) – all women (as God seems feminised by

2. For a similar argument see Sapiro 1992.

association) staged immediately after one another. Monarchy's femininity repels; modernity's femininity tempts. Generally, her modernity has no single gender, symbolically or empirically: women and men are both variably complimented and attacked, and neither femininity nor masculinity are that applaudable. In asserting that women should aspire to become like men, while simultaneously jibing at masculinity, her own vocabulary is nothing but an attempt at linguistic resistance. At times, she explicitly revolts against gender identity as such: 'The desire of being always a woman, is the very consciousness that degrades the sex' (1792c: 174). But then again, those gendered beings do exist – and indeed as women: 'I really think that women ought to have representatives' (p. 228). Wollstonecraft appears ready to join Denise Riley's call for 'being "at times a woman"', against 'that unappetising choice between "real women" … or post-women, "no-longer-women", who … prefer evanescence' (Riley 1988: 6).

Wollstonecraft is not a classical republican: she hardly refers to antiquity, and when she does, is sceptical of its culture, social order, and heroism. She is, though, a civic humanist, being a true theoretician of citizenship, and her conception of politics directly belongs to the civic humanist tradition on this point. It is a narrow one: politics has to sober up, expel all stylistic devices alien to its essence. Both 'femininity' and commerce are detrimental to politics; all mere emotional appeal, all seduction, as well as 'negotiations' styled after the market, are contagions in the realm of politics. Politics, like personal relationships, ought to be built upon friendship among – or at least association of – equals.

The way she uses it, femininity becomes indeed a political concept. It is a code-word for slavery, which in its eighteenth-century application to one's proper, European society stands for servile, unenlightened behaviour. But with her, slavery also stands for something more radical: for being conditioned, for the power social identities have over politics. In other words, with her, femininity also denotes the power the social has over political agency.

To her, representation ought to be innovative, ought to uncover new grounds and lend voice to what is either marginalised or 'massified'.[3] There is an Arendtian ring to her ideas: if the social is what determinates human subjects, politics stands for human beings' agency, which can free them from inherited identities and let them express their authenticity. The authenticity she is obsessed with is not some individualistic, 'romantic' one; one should on the contrary express one's authentic humanity, stripped from all particularity,

3. I have borrowed the term from Riley 1988, who speaks of the 'massifications' of 'men' and 'women'.

whether gender or class. Sentiment will be corrupt, unless bared of its particularist, cultural influences in order to express one's humanity. This authenticity is opposed against identity: *coquettes* and virtuous women alike should exert themselves more to 'forget their sex', and quit 'forever trying to make themselves *agreeable*' (Wollstonecraft 1792c: 276). Men likewise never forget women's sex. If representation 'starts from nowhere', if it has to start beyond the already-present, fixed positions of political power, it does have a clearly circumscribed orientation: 'innovative representation' ought not to lead to identity politics, but to a humanist politics cleared of the impairing impacts of identities – where language no longer merely evokes (social identities), but enables (a political, reflective humanity).

Wollstonecraft's republican feminism shows serendipity with respect to the problematic of gender difference and equality. She is a stranger to the idea that one could simply introduce either some original order or blueprint of the future which neglect what is, e.g. simply declare gender equality. This is precisely her problem with the libertines who, with proclaimed egalitarian zeal, abandon women to the established double moral standard, only increasing their objectification, instead of ameliorating their subject status. Libertines have simply denied the reality of minds, virtues, and bodies having been given sexes. She is extremely ambivalent about the engineering possibilities society possesses. Gender is historically and socially produced, but neither to be engineered nor annulled at will. The romantic idea of society (or of gender, for that matter) as a work of art, the aesthetic conception of society, is absent in her thought.

III. Democracy in the Bedroom, or: The Personal is Political

The vital categories for these feminist appropriations of republicanism are not those of the private and the public sphere, but those of responsibility and corruption. The ensuing ethics of political and social life, one which connects the human commitment to acting with responsibility and accountability, is to be matched with an ethics for intimate life. Both Palm-Aelders and Wollstonecraft attempt to address the necessity of an ethics of love as an ingredient of republicanism. In a personal letter to a male friend Palm-Aelders reproaches men for being corrupt in their private utterings of feelings and love. She indicts the defective behaviour of men, who, as men, do not live up to the republican requirement to foster steady and substantive sentiments.

> Many a person desires the liberation of the slaves in America and
> upholds the despotism of the husband . . . You want us to penetrate
> into the very depths of your heart. Oh! How much you thereby in
> general lose! How often do you display feelings you do not possess,
> while more stringent etiquette obliges us to hide the ones that
> consume us. Well? What do your homages mean to us, when they are
> only the fruits of a heated imagination? You court us? Yes, but for your
> own sake; where is the man who knows to love tenderly when he does
> not hope to submit to his will the object of his desire? Ah, sir, there are
> only few people, who know love.   (Cited in Hardenberg 1962: 70; trans. by JV)

The concept of corruption can denote the violation and abuse of relationships of trust. Violence and injustice done to women are thus brought under
the category of political violence. They fall short of the republican ideals: the
indictment of arbitrary violence and inegalitarian human association. The
intimate sphere is obviously not to be excepted from the applicability of political ideals, whether jurisprudential or republican. To republican feminism,
public ideals will guide private practice.

A major characteristic of Wollstonecraft's feminism is to develop a critique
of love-as-ideology, rather than an ethics of love. 'To speak disrespectfully
of love is, I know, high treason against sentiment and fine-feelings; but I
wish . . . rather to address the head than the heart' (1792c: 93). Love seems to
defy dignification on rationalist republican terms, as it is 'in a great degree an
arbitrary passion' (p. 194), where 'chance and sensation take place of choice
and reason' (p. 96). We almost hear Karl Marx criticising alienation, when
she analyses the nature of love: 'And love? . . . To see a mortal adorn an object
with imaginary charms, and then fall down and worship the idol which he had
himself set up – how ridiculous!' (p. 186). She discusses the problems of love
as if they were similes of those of the republic: both imply the struggle for a
secular existence, as neither heaven nor eternity apply; therefore both love
and the republic have to confront problems of temporality as well as dura-
bility. The matter of time, presenting the problem of instability, whether in
the form of unsteady politics or sentiments, occupies a central place in her
reflections. Her works abound with condemnations of temporal pleasures.
The contemporary culture of pleasure, in which one lives 'for temporary grat-
ifications . . . the triumph of an hour' (p. 107), is one of her central worries;
it contradicts reason and the republican ethics of human accountability. He
who 'lives only for the passing day . . . cannot be an accountable creature'
(p. 102).

> Supposing, for a moment... that man was only created for the present
> scene – I think we should have reason to complain that love, infantine
> fondness, ever grew insipid and palled upon the sense. Let us eat,
> drink, and love for tomorrow we die, would be, in fact the language of
> reason, the morality of life.
>
> (1792c: 97)

Making love into an arbitrary, unsteady sensation which dodges accountability, the libertine's régime of pleasure obstructs freedom and turns women, who have anyway not attained equal degrees of freedom compared to men, into mere objects of sense: 'Women ... are degraded by the same propensity to enjoy the present moment' (1792c: 121).

Someone who lives for the moment can be neither citizen nor lover. Love poses problems analogous to those of realising a polity in the civic humanist tradition. The republic has to deal with the secular and therefore time-bound nature of political society, and in the face of this to strive to maintain itself. Likewise, love needs to be withdrawn from on the one hand the celebration of temporality, especially in the pursuit of pleasure, and on the other the promise of timelessness of romantics. And again like politics, love should neither be grounded in inherited tradition (whether the ancient or the aristocratic one), nor rely on temporary allure, but commit itself to reflection and future continuity. Of the present marital state Wollstonecraft is extremely sceptical; legally it has been made 'an absurd unit of a man and his wife' (1792c: 226), and generally, marriages are unhappy alliances which confront women with irresolvable choices between being a happy wife or a good mother. But the alternative to tradition is equally deceitful. Romantic representations of love depict it 'with celestial charms' and suggest the possibility of perfect eternal union where 'the world is to be shut out, and every thought and wish, that do not nurture pure affection and permanent virtue' (p. 146). This kind of happiness, however, is too little material, too little substantial, as to represent a republican passion. '[I]t is not against strong, persevering passions; but romantic wavering feelings that I wish to guard the female heart' (p. 146). If women are to become, and be respected as, subjects in their own right, love will have to respect the distance, the irreducible remoteness, between living individuals. Wollstonecraft is properly confused about the problems social difference poses to a political practice like love. 'A wild wish has just flown from my heart to my head ... I do earnestly wish to see the distinction of sex confounded in society, unless where love animates the behaviour' (p. 126). But simultaneously, she wants to insist on women's humane, instead of sexual, *persona* in love. 'A man, or a woman, of any feeling, must always wish to convince a beloved object that it is the caresses of the individual, not the sex, that are received and returned with pleasure' (p. 174). In this political confusion, however, ethics provide back-up. The ingredients of an enlightened approach to love are to be a recognition of firstly, the ideological dimensions of love, and secondly, of women's subjectivity in love. Her ethics of love is a genuine republican one, requiring a politically experienced life, in whatever 'domain' society has tried to fence off from politics.

It would be a denial of feminism's proper intellectual history to dismiss *mulier clausa*, in her feminist guise of citizen-lover, as somehow a female imitation of masculinity, perhaps inspired even by homophobia – if we remember Wollstonecraft's discomfort with women's culture of mental and bodily intimacy. It should, on the contrary, be appreciated as a position within feminism: one that abhors how '[s]ensibility is the *manie* [*sic*] of the day' (1790: 6); which abhors all would-be authenticity, especially when presented as expression of a definite gender identity; and which distrusts a familiarity, or empathy, that knows no reservations with respect to otherness. Where Wollstonecraft complains that the female world displays less friendship than the male (1792c: 275, 277), that is, has less experience with its requisites of balancing distance and equality, she also again alerts us to the problem of 'massification' which affects the female sex more than the male.

Both Palm-Aelders's and Wollstonecraft's politics of love are motivated and nourished by their love for politics. While adversaries in cultural politics, in a philosophical sense feminist republicanism allies again with – at least Sadean – libertarianism. In their political perception of subjectivity, which results from a process of public performativity, they do not clash with libertarians, but romantics. Feminist republicans are strangers to the idea of individual authenticity. The democracy in the bedroom of Palm-Aelders and Wollstonecraft can be seen as part of the same programme as the philosophy in the bedroom of De Sade (Vega 2000). Both approaches hold that the personal should be investigated, not as the expression of extra-cultural or pre-cultural resources, but as representing public culture. Both, therefore, celebrate reflectivity. Moreover, both dismiss the idea that the bedroom could somehow be a sanctuary from which activities designated as 'public' – like either philosophy or democracy – should, or could for that matter, be dispelled.

The tradition of civic humanism has produced theoretical insights of several types. John Rawls, for example, has characterised the difference between classical republicanism and civic humanism as the difference between presupposing that citizens must possess political virtues in order to take part in public life, and presupposing that participation in public life forms the essence of human existence, the privileged locus of the good life (Rawls 1993). Feminist republicans build upon a third option. Their political perception of gender seizes upon the radical, enabling contingency of modern political life, and presupposes, not so much the priority of a political realm (in whatever weak or strong formulation), but a fundamentally political perspective on human bonding across modernity's societal spheres of life. They are perhaps the most genuine Aristotelian philosophers, as they radically grant political theory a master status with respect to the acquisition of knowledge about human life. 'The sexual distinction which men have so warmly insisted upon, is arbitrary', Wollstonecraft firmly states (1792c: 282). That is, it has been produced within the contingencies of history, which resulted in its ambivalent existence in language. As by the same contingent potential typical of modernity the pre-modern category of chance has been dissolved into human beings' capacity for – voluntary or involuntary – action, these meanings can and will be made into essentially contested ones. To address this contestability as an ingredient of the implementation of an egalitarian society could designate the republican moment in feminism's agenda of principled ambivalence.

Part III

Republicanism and the Rise of Commerce

10

Republicanism and Commercial Society in the Scottish Enlightenment: The Case of Adam Ferguson

MARCO GEUNA

In 1969, in the final pages of his book *Utopia and Reform in the Enlightenment*, Franco Venturi remarked that 'we are still waiting for a comprehensive study of the Scottish Enlightenment' and that this would be 'one of the most necessary pieces of research in the field of eighteenth century European history' (Venturi 1971: 133). Almost thirty years later, Knud Haakonssen, in the introduction to a collection of essays, remarked instead that 'despite the extraordinary variety of fruitful approaches to the Scottish Enlightenment that has emerged in recent years, there seems still to be an unaccountable hankering for *the* total history of the Scottish Enlightenment' (Haakonssen 1996: 8). So, almost thirty years have gone by, and a comprehensive work on the Scottish Enlightenment has yet to be written and, if we take Haakonssen's remark seriously, it may be that this work cannot and should not be written.

During the last few decades, research on the Scottish Enlightenment has certainly developed enormously. Thanks to numerous studies on the eighteenth-century Scottish thinkers and on the most diverse aspects of Scottish culture, it has become clear that the phrase 'Scottish Enlightenment' does not describe a unitary experience, but is merely a convenient expression for a multitude of heterogeneous phenomena. Scholars have recently tended to talk less about the Scottish Enlightenment in general and more about specific aspects of the movement – in Glasgow, Edinburgh, Aberdeen and elsewhere (see Carter and Pittock (eds.) 1987; Hook and Sher (eds.) 1995). Moreover, until a few years ago, the Scottish Enlightenment was thought of as a phenomenon primarily linked to Protestantism, and in particular to Presbyterian culture, whereas more recently a 'Scottish Catholic Enlightenment' (see Goldie 1991 and 1992) has also been brought to light. Still other cleavages could be added to these geographic and religious ones.

It is beyond question that different Scottish authors approached political and philosophical issues in different ways. Consider, for example, the field of analysis which aims to define the scope and limits of human knowledge. We can identify a strong contrast between the sceptical attitude of Hume, who meticulously points out the limits of human reason, and the more ample certitudes which the appeal to 'common sense' allowed to Reid and his school. Consider, similarly, the theoretical framework of the emerging discipline of political economy, in which Adam Smith's stance seems very distant from that of James Steuart. Finally, if we look at the debates over political issues, we find Hume's criticism of factions and parties, together with the importance he places on the rule of law, contrasting sharply with Adam Ferguson's invitation to conflictual political participation. Similarly, and more generally, there is a contrast between theories that focus on the defence of civil rights and those which stress the importance of virtue, public spirit and active engagement in public life.

A number of distinct – and often divergent – analytical frameworks for the study of the Scottish Enlightenment have also been developed of late. As far as the analysis of society and politics is concerned, two opposing paradigms have prevailed in the last two decades. One stresses the importance of 'classical republicanism' or 'civic humanism' in Scottish thought; the other emphasises the role played by the tradition of 'natural law' or, to use the eighteenth-century expression, 'natural jurisprudence'. The first paradigm is particularly associated with John Pocock, who in *The Machiavellian Moment* depicts Scottish thought as a crucial stage in his 'tunnel history' of classical ideas stretching from Italian humanism to the political theories of the American revolution (see Pocock 1975). Pocock's thesis concerning the importance of republican ideas in the understanding of the Scottish Enlightenment – a thesis explicitly opposed to liberal and Marxist historical interpretations – has been elaborated and applied to the Scottish situation by Nicholas Phillipson. Phillipson points out that, after the Union of 1707, virtuous participation in public affairs could no longer take place within a strictly political context, but was forced to take the form of a broader social and cultural involvement in clubs, academies and universities. Eighteenth-century Scots, in other words, are seen as putting into practice elements of an Addisonian morality, trying to preserve and develop the identity and independence of their country in such a way as to make it a true 'republic of letters' (see Phillipson 1981, 1987, 1989).

Within the alternative analytical framework, the research of Duncan Forbes has exerted a decisive influence. In his study of the concepts underlying Hume's 'philosophical politics', Forbes analysed the way in which the seventeenth-century heritage of natural law theories was transmitted and transformed by the Scottish thinkers (see Forbes 1975a, 1982). A large number of scholars, including James Moore (see Moore and Silverthorne 1983, 1984; Moore 1988) and Istvan Hont (see Hont and Ignatieff (eds.) 1983; Hont 1987), have adopted a similar perspective. They have emphasised the crucial role played by Gershom Carmichael, who took up the approach of Samuel Pufendorf and developed it in connection with Locke's ideas. They have also traced the development of natural jurisprudence in the hands of a series of Glasgow professors, especially Francis Hutcheson, Adam Smith and Thomas Reid. Knud Haakonssen has likewise emphasised that the tradition of natural law should not be thought of as a unitary phenomenon, and has stressed that different strands of natural jurisprudence were connected to different kinds of moral philosophy. In particular, he has emphasised the differences between the approaches of Grotius and Pufendorf. Grotius's thought is based on a realistic theory: values are, so to speak, inherent in the structure of the world, and subjective rights, rather than natural law, play a primary role. Pufendorf's thought is based on quite different theological foundations and is built around the concept of will. For Pufendorf, the world is a structure of physical entities without moral attributes; moral values are imposed on this structure by God's will. In this approach, law plays a primary rôle: it is law that, first of all, imposes duties and, only secondly and as a consequence, creates rights which correspond to these duties. In his mapping of the moral, political and juridical thought of the Scottish Enlightenment, Haakonssen points out that some authors, in particular Hume and Smith, draw upon Grotian concepts, while others, such as Carmichael, Hutcheson, Thomas Reid and Dugald Stewart (what he calls 'the mainstream of Scottish moral philosophy'; Haakonssen 1996: 64) took over Pufendorf's framework, developing it in several different ways.

These two paradigms have often been presented as incompatible: the one emphasising the idea of rights, the other the idea of virtue; the one giving priority to the defence of private security, the other asserting the claims of participation in political events and collective self-determination. But this has led to the following historiographical problem: how is it possible that the same thinkers could employ concepts that belonged to the tradition of natural law and, at the same time, to the republican tradition, and could do so not only in different works, but sometimes in the same text?

One answer has been to show that diverse currents existed within both traditions of thought. As a consequence, it has been argued that some developments originating from within these different traditions might well be compatible. For example, it has been shown how certain categories elaborated by Pufendorfian jurisprudence were joined with certain assumptions of Harringtonian republicanism, for example in authors like George Turnbull and Francis Hutcheson (see Haakonssen 1996: 63–99).

A different answer has been given at a more theoretical level. Quentin Skinner, in a series of texts, has shown how the liberty defended by many republican thinkers should not be considered a form of positive freedom but a peculiar form of negative liberty. Moving from an analysis of how Machiavelli understands freedom to studying 'the republican ideal of freedom', he has brought to light how many republicans rejected anthropological assumptions of an Aristotelian kind and instead developed a theory of negative freedom which cannot be assimilated to freedom as non-interference as thematised by Hobbes and appropriated by the liberal tradition (see Skinner 1983, 1984, 1990a). More recently, examining what he calls the neo-Roman theory of freedom, Skinner has shown how many thinkers in Cromwellian England employed concepts of the natural law tradition – in particular the idea that the individual is a bearer of rights – together with typically republican ideas.[1] These investigations have helped to narrow the gulf between the two traditions and to suggest the possibility, even on a theoretical level, of simultaneously employing concepts emanating from both of them.

I have already mentioned that authors like Turnbull and Hutcheson, who appeal to Pufendorfian natural jurisprudence, accepted and reworked some ideas formulated by Harrington. One can add that philosophers like Hume, who seemingly draw on a Grotian approach to natural law, also adopt positions elaborated within the republican tradition on specific questions – for example, on the issues of a militia and of public debt.

At this point it is important to underline that in Scottish thought one can find thinkers who took up the language and concepts of the modern republican tradition without subordinating them to the language and the concepts of other traditions. If in the Edinburgh of the early eighteenth century it was Andrew Fletcher (see Fletcher 1997a) who creatively recovered the ideas of the republican tradition, in the 'Edinburgh of the Age of Reason' it was above all Adam Ferguson who carried out an analogous operation. Ferguson was

---

1. See Skinner 1998: 17–21. Skinner has changed his mind on a crucial point. In his essays of the 1980s, he argued that the disagreement between the two traditions was not 'about the meaning of liberty, but only about the conditions that must be met if liberty is to be secured'. In his last book, taking into account some suggestions made by Philip Pettit, he points out, on the contrary, 'that the two schools of thought disagree about (among other things) the meaning of liberty itself'. See Skinner 1998: 70; see also Pettit 1997: 17–79.

described by George Davie as 'that most Machiavellian of Scottish thinkers' (see Davie 1981: 27). This judgment is shared by John Pocock, who sees in the *Essay on the History of Civil Society* 'perhaps the most Machiavellian of the Scottish disquisitions' on citizenship (see Pocock 1975: 499).

Ferguson admittedly makes use in other texts – for instance, in his political pamphlets and in the edited versions of his university courses (see Ferguson 1773, 1776, 1792) – of conceptual distinctions typical of natural jurisprudence, and has recourse to them to support his arguments. But there is no doubt that his thought, especially in his most important work, the *Essay on the History of Civil Society*, is characterised by a systematic employment of categories belonging to the republican tradition of thought. The question that accordingly needs to be addressed concerns the peculiarity of Ferguson's republicanism: how it differs from the versions elaborated by the Commonwealthmen at the beginning of the century, and how it tackles the problems of a modern commercial society.

To understand and evaluate the transformations that had led to modern civil society, and to identify the possible outcomes of such transformations: this was the nucleus of the investigation carried out by Ferguson in the *Essay on the History of Civil Society*. He discusses the dilemmas of commercial society in the framework provided by an original 'theoretical or conjectural history', to use the expression coined by Dugald Stewart. In elaborating his conjectural history of mankind, Ferguson creatively employs and merges two great paradigms of historical reconstruction and interpretation. On the one hand, in order to trace the development of society 'from rudeness to civilisation', he uses an approach based on historical stages similar to the one developed by other Scottish thinkers on the basis of ethnographic materials and concepts drawn from the natural law tradition.[2] On the other hand, he uses the historical scheme of rise, greatness and decadence, whose paradigm is the history of Rome – a paradigm common to many republicans thinkers from Machiavelli to Montesquieu. In this way, Ferguson manages to formulate a conception of history that is remarkably non-deterministic.[3] The future of the 'polished and commercial societies' can either be freedom or despotism: they contain contradictory tendencies which may lead to radically different outcomes. The problem is to identify the pathologies

---

2. Ferguson singles out three stages in 'the history of mankind'. He does not adopt the so-called 'Four-stages Theory' featured by Adam Smith and taken up by William Robertson, John Millar and others. Among the recent studies on the 'Four-stages Theory', see Berry 1997: 91–119. On the peculiarities of Smith's 'Four-stages Theory', see Pesante 1995.

3. On Ferguson's conception of history, see Forbes 1966 and Kettler 1977; among recent studies, Gautier 1992a, 1992b, Oz-Salzberger 1995b.

of the modern world and see whether, and how, it is possible to provide a remedy.

Ferguson's attitude towards modern civil society is ambivalent: he accepts and yet criticises it at the same time. Overall, Ferguson accepts the new mechanisms for the production of wealth, starting with the division of labour in manufacture. However, he criticises the values and ethos that accompany this 'great transformation'. Above all, he is critical of the politics of modern societies: a politics run by a few professionals that surrenders the defence of freedom to institutional procedures and to professional armies.

Ferguson's interpreters have not always given a balanced account of these contrasting elements in the *Essay*. Some have insisted on presenting him as a critic of modern society in its entirety. These commentators have in turn adopted one of two contrasting perspectives. On the one hand, Ferguson has been seen as a thinker who rejects the transformations in the means of production introduced by the capitalist market economy. He has been thought to advocate a return to pre-capitalistic and pre-mercantile economic and social forms. So he has been presented as an advocate of a 'primitivist romanticism' or an 'agrarian primitivism' close to that of the Commonwealthmen of the early eighteenth century (see Pocock 1975: 499–502; Pocock 1985a: 130). On the other hand, Ferguson has sometimes been transformed into a nineteenth-century thinker, a 'sociologist' critical of the economic developments characteristic of commercial societies, with their unjust, dehumanising and alienating aspects.[4] This latter interpretation has particularly been put forward by scholars influenced by Marx's remarks on Ferguson in *Misère de la philosophie* and in *Das Kapital*.

Both perspectives emphasise Ferguson's criticism of the economic mechanisms of commercial societies; but both miss the sense in which these mechanisms are essentially accepted in his works. Ferguson is indeed a republican thinker, but one marked by his Scottish origins. Since the age of Fletcher and Seton, the Scots had been seeking ways to pull their country out of the condition of underdevelopment and stagnation which had persisted throughout the seventeenth century. With the Union, they decided to surrender their parliamentary institutions to gain free access to English markets. The intellectuals of Edinburgh in the 1720s and 1730s established a 'Society for Improvement in the Knowledge of Agriculture'; and two decades later one of the first official acts of the 'Select Society' – a club established on the initiative of David Hume, Adam Smith and others, to which Ferguson immediately affiliated himself – was the founding of the 'Edinburgh Society

4. Among recent studies, see Brewer 1986 and 1989.

for the Encouragement of Arts, Science, Manufactures and Agriculture' in 1755.

Ferguson's thinking cannot be adequately understood if it is uncoupled from this cultural context. On the whole, he accepts the sort of agricultural and manufacturing development brought on by the advent of 'commercial society' and has no nostalgia for the forms of economic production characteristic of previous ages. There is thus a case for saying that scholars like Pocock, who underline Ferguson's republicanism without taking into account its Scottish matrix, are unable to grasp how the author of the *Essay* appropriates some of the fundamental values and ideas of the republican tradition without adopting the socio-economic solutions championed by the Commonwealthmen fifty years earlier. Conversely, critics who see in Ferguson a 'precursor' of nineteenth-century analyses of 'alienation' and 'exploitation' tend to overlook the fact that his criticism of the dehumanising consequences of the division of labour does not lead him to question its advantages at the economic level, nor to demand that it should be replaced by a different form of economic organisation. Above all, these critics fail properly to appreciate that Ferguson's criticisms are motivated by the values of the republican tradition, within which the concepts of alienation and exploitation had no place.

Ferguson considers the *social* division of labour as a characteristic trait of modern commercial societies. He observes that in these societies men are impelled by a 'sense of utility' to subdivide their occupations endlessly. The modern world is an 'age of separations'. He notes with concern this proliferation of new 'arts' and 'professions, the consequence of which is that each individual specialises in a particular activity. 'Every craft may ingross the whole of a man's attention, and has a mystery which must be studied or learned by a regular apprenticeship. Nations of tradesmen come to consist of members who, beyond their own trade, are ignorant of all human affairs' (Ferguson 1995: 173).

Ferguson's analysis is not limited to these considerations, but proceeds to examine the consequences of the *technical* division of functions in manufacture. His critical remarks on the impoverishment of human faculties among subordinated workers in the great 'machine' of manufacture are well known. But it is worth recalling the most penetrating of these passages – one often cited since the time of Marx:

> Many mechanical arts, indeed, require no capacity; they succeed best under a total suppression of sentiment and reason; and ignorance is the mother of industry as well as of superstition. Reflection and fancy

are subject to err; but a habit of moving the hand, or the foot, is
independent of either. Manufactures, accordingly, prosper most,
where the mind is least consulted, and where the workshop may,
without any great effort of imagination, be considered as an engine
the parts of which are men.   (Ferguson 1995: 174)

These comments, however, should not obscure the fact that Ferguson judges
this process of 'Separation of Arts and Professions' to be a positive one, and
regards it as irreversible. In the same section of the *Essay*, he clearly accepts
that the subdivision of labour in the productive sphere should be considered
a beneficial change: 'By the separation of arts and professions, the sources of
wealth are laid open; every species of material is wrought up to the greatest
perfection, and every commodity is produced in the greatest abundance'
(Ferguson 1995: 173; see Séris 1994). This recognition of the importance
of the division of labour is a constant of Ferguson's thought: we encounter
it not only in the *Essay*, but also in works preceding and following it, such
as the *Analysis of Pneumatics and Moral Philosophy* and the *Institutes of Moral
Philosophy*.[5]

Ferguson clearly regards this *technical* division of labour in manufacture
as an indispensable innovation. The separation of functions at once allows the
employer to increase his profits, and at the same time provides the consumer
with technically improved objects. Ferguson seems to suggest that the economic development of his time – 'the progress of commerce' – finds its main
propulsion precisely in manufacture, in which this separation of functions is
most advanced. He accordingly proposes that this technical division of labour
should be accepted, notwithstanding its high human cost. What remains is
to compensate for the damage thereby caused, in particular by strengthening
the political and military virtue of citizens through the creation or consoli-
dation of appropriate institutions, such as a territorial militia.[6]

Ferguson appreciates the importance of the economic transformations
which had occurred in the modern world and describes them with the aid of
concepts developed by writers who, in many cases, were very distant from the
republican tradition.[7] He also inserts into his reflections certain *laissez faire*

---

5. See Ferguson 1766: 47; Ferguson 1773: 31–2. The first edition of the *Institutes* was published in
   1769.
6. Ferguson does not envisage education as a remedy to the impoverishment caused by the division
   of labour; he does not insist on the duties of the legislator in this field, as Adam Smith does in the
   fifth book of the *Wealth of Nations*.
7. Ferguson, for example, does not share the criticism of the mechanism of public debt, one of the
   leading themes of republican writings from the beginning of the eighteenth century, until the
   1760s. See Ferguson 1995: 221–3; Ferguson 1792: II, 447–56.

theses (to use an anachronism) cherished by the supporters of the 'natural' development of modern societies. In particular, he argues that statesmen should not intervene in the spheres of demographic reproduction or economic production: 'When the refined politician would lend an active hand, he only multiplies interruptions and grounds of complaint'.[8] However, Ferguson is not interested in investigating the mechanisms of development of the new commercial society in the manner of Adam Smith or Sir James Steuart. His objective is rather to mark the limits of economic relations within social relations as a whole – to determine the correct space that the economy should occupy in a modern society. For Ferguson, the sphere of economic reproduction is important, but it is not everything. The political sphere is far more crucial – the sphere which allows citizens to take part in collective affairs and to determine the destiny of the *res publica*. Ferguson is very explicit on this point. 'Speculations on commerce and wealth have been delivered by the ablest writers, who have left nothing so important to be offered on the subject, as the general caution, not to consider these articles as making the sum of national felicity, or the principal object of any state' (Ferguson 1995: 140). Wealth and commerce are not the principal factors in 'national felicity'. Ferguson expresses the claim most pointedly in an earlier section of the *Essay*:

> Wealth, commerce, extent of the territory and the knowledge of the arts, are, when properly employed, the means of preservation, and the foundation of power ... Their tendency is to maintain numbers of men, not to constitute happiness. They will accordingly maintain the wretched, as well as the happy. They answer one purpose, but are not sufficient for all; and are of little significance, when only employed to maintain a timid, dejected, and servile people.   (Ferguson 1995: 60)

As this passages suggests, it is of prime importance to understand how a people, according to Ferguson, can become 'timid, dejected and servile', and how he interprets 'the Corruption incident to Polished Nations'.

The answer is that corruption is not portrayed by Ferguson as a necessary consequence of the economic transformations of modern societies, but rather as the result of concurrent transformations in the political domain. Ferguson's criticism is directed, in the first place, against the form of *social* division of labour that separates the citizen from the soldier and gives the soldier the status of a distinct profession. Owing to this division of labour, 'the keeping and the enjoyment of liberty' are committed 'to different hands'

---

8. Ferguson 1995: 139. See also p. 143: 'The statesman in this, as in the case of population itself, can do little more than avoid doing mischief.'

(Ferguson 1995: 256; see also p. 146). Ferguson sees the separation 'between the soldier and the pacific citizen' as marking the origins of modern commercial society, as the starting point of an ever-widening gulf between the economic and the political sphere, between society and state. In the second place, Ferguson's criticism is directed against the division of labour in the state apparatus, between those who hold political and military power. Lastly, he criticises the division of labour which places the direction of the state in the hands of clerks and accountants who follow routine procedures while losing sight of the political meaning of their acts. For similar reasons, he protests against the division of labour that transforms the army into a body of professional soldiers, who are perfectly disciplined but no longer aware of the reasons why they are fighting, and with very little military virtue (see Ferguson 1995: 173, 213, 216). Putting this in contemporary terms, what Ferguson criticises is the parallel establishment of a professional army and a bureaucratic state apparatus. It is clear that this kind of criticism is rooted in the republican ideal of the soldier-citizen, the citizen who participates in public life and, sometimes – via the rotation of posts – assumes responsibility for its direction.

This criticism of standing armies and professional politicians forms a constant theme in Ferguson's thought. It is introduced for the first time in his *Reflections previous to the Establishment of a Militia*, a pamphlet pleading for the establishment of a popular militia in Scotland,[9] and it is amply debated in various passages of the *Essay*. It likewise stands out as one of the leading themes of the *History of the Progress and Termination of the Roman Republic*, published in 1783, in which Ferguson argues that the specialisation which divided citizens from soldiers and caused the separation between political and military responsibilities was a prime cause of the Republic's collapse (see Ferguson 1783; also Gabba 1995). Criticism of standing armies and support for the militia and for a participative concept of politics are again prominent in the lectures on moral philosophy given by Ferguson in the 1770s and 1780s (see Sher 1989), as well as in other essays from the 1790s which remained unpublished for a long time (see Ferguson 1996b: 26–38, 141–51).

When politics is placed in the hands of professionals, and when bureaucracy prevails, freedom is at risk from both outside and inside. Such states can be easily invaded, while a state apparatus made up of professionals can readily become an instrument of despotic policies. 'Such a State, like that of China, by throwing affairs into separate offices, where conduct consists in detail, and the observance of forms, by superseding all the exertion of a

9. See Ferguson 1756. On the militia issue, see Robertson 1985.

great and liberal mind, is more akin to despotism than we are apt to think'
(Ferguson 1995: 255).

Strictly speaking, Ferguson did not see corruption as solely the result of
the institutional and political transformations that led to the establishment
of standing armies and bureaucratic states. He also saw it as the result of
the political ideologies which, from Defoe to Smith, had accompanied and
supported such transformations by emphasising the superiority of standing
armies over militias, and by championing the private sphere as the primary
field for individual self-fulfilment. Ferguson accordingly became a strenuous
opponent of these ideologies. He writes, for example, that 'the care of mere
fortune is supposed to constitute wisdom: retirement from public affairs and
real indifference to mankind receive the applauses of moderation and virtue'.
And he severely adds:

> our considering mere retirement, therefore, as a symptom of
> moderation, and of virtue ... proceeds from an habit of thinking
> which appears fraught with moral corruption, from our considering
> public life as a scene for the gratification of mere vanity, avarice and
> ambition; never as furnishing the best opportunity for a just and
> happy engagement of the mind and the heart.   (Ferguson 1995: 243–4)

As will by now be obvious, what Ferguson values is participation in public
affairs and devotion to public life, even though this participation will necessarily be conflictual in character. There are plenty of passages in the *Essay* and
Principles in which he truly sings the praises of conflict,[10] of political emula-
tion and even of war (see Ferguson 1995: 28–9). Freedom can only emerge
from conflict between virtuous citizens; political order is defined as that
which allows the emergence of these differences and dissonances and then
synthesises them at a higher level. What stifles freedom is the 'tranquillity'
and the 'unanimity' that prevail in modern societies, where citizens neglect
public affairs and entrust the safeguard of their freedom to professional politicians and the institutional mechanism of the 'rule of law'. 'When we seek
in society for the order of mere inaction and tranquillity, we forget the nature of our subject, and we find the order of slaves, not that of free men'
(*ibid.*: 254 (footnote 97)).

We next need to investigate the reasons that induced Ferguson to praise
such conflicts and animosities. It is Ferguson's belief that freedom cannot
be preserved in modern commercial nations by mere recourse to laws or

---

10. See Ferguson 1995: 62–3, 242, 245; Ferguson 1792: II, 508–12. On the rôle of conflict in
    Ferguson's thought, among recent studies see Hill 1996: 215–20, Kalyvas and Katznelson 1998:
    182–5.

institutional mechanisms. Neither 'the government of laws' nor the separation of powers are sufficient. Ferguson insists that what is necessary is the 'influence of men resolved to be free', the firm determination of each citizen not to entrust his destiny to anyone else. The participation of citizens is needed not merely when laws are being formulated but above all when they are being enforced. 'If forms of proceedings, written statutes, or rather constituents of law, cease to be enforced by the very spirit from which they arose, they serve only to cover, not to restrain, the iniquities of power' (Ferguson 1995: 249). This is one of Ferguson's fundamental beliefs, and he comes back to it repeatedly in the *Essay*, particularly in the passage in which he reminds us that 'the most equitable laws on paper are consistent with the utmost despotism in administration' (*ibid.*: 160).

Ferguson's approach is thus very different from that of Hume or Smith. As Donald Winch has pointed out, Hume's and Smith's politics 'relied more on machinery, than men . . . government [was] seen largely as a matter of balancing, checking and harnessing interests rather than calling forth public spirit and virtue' (Winch 1983: 166). Ferguson's contrasting emphasis distinguishes his approach not only from Hume's and Smith's, but also from that of various other republican thinkers, among whom Harrington is the most important.

If we try to probe precisely what Ferguson considered to be the meaning of political participation, we cannot be said to receive a univocal answer. On the one hand, he frequently claims that we need to participate in collective affairs because only in this way can we prevent corruption and despotism from taking over the nations of modern Europe. On the other hand, he also argues that the value of participation stems from the fact that virtuous engagement in politics is the highest form of human self-realisation. Political participation is not a means to other ends but an end in itself.

This brings us to a difficult question: who, according to Ferguson, deserves the status of citizen? Is this status reserved for the higher ranks of society, or is it open to all the inhabitants of commercial societies, even those engaged in the most humanly degrading occupations? Clearly, the virtue to which he refers – political and military at the same time – rules out participation by women. Beyond this point, however, it is again difficult to find a univocal answer. Ferguson points out that 'men whose dispositions are sordid, and whose ordinary applications are illiberal' are 'unfit to command'. He rhetorically asks: 'How can he who has confined his views to his own subsistence or preservation be intrusted with the conduct of nations?' (Ferguson 1995: 178). But he does not elaborate further, and he gives no definite specifications. His call for virtue seems to be addressed mainly to the higher ranks of society, yet he does not seem to believe that individuals engaged in commerce and manufacturing are *per se* incapable of showing true public spirit.

James Harrington had identified as a precondition for virtue that citizens should also be landowners. Only an *oikos* based on landownership could guarantee a citizen's independence and thereby allow him to practise his political and military virtues. This material precondition for independence, which Fletcher still takes as necessary, seems to be abandoned by Ferguson, who suggests that merchants, manufacturers and even some type of workers in modern societies can and ought to exercise the full range of civic virtues. They must recover their military virtue by taking part in militias organised on a territorial basis. And they must not devote themselves solely to private matters, but must take an interest in public life by using whatever institutional opportunities are made available by their government.[11]

At this juncture we need to ask what, according to Ferguson, are the prerequisites of the individual's independence. Ferguson believed that man could remain substantially uninfluenced by external circumstances, and hence that independence must be based not on material but on spiritual premises. Ferguson had read the ancient Stoics and in particular Epictetus and Marcus Aurelius thoroughly.[12] He believed that modern men can likewise avoid being dominated by their passions and living at the mercy of the forces which seem to govern the external world. They do not have to submit to the dictates of personal interest and can resist being moulded by the forces that rule the modern market economy. Thus Ferguson emphasised the role played by the will, by the capacity for choice present in every man, even those who happen to live in the 'polished and commercial nations'. Such a capacity for choice represents the basis of their capacity for resistance and virtuous conduct.

Ferguson's republicanism, therefore, cannot be reduced to the civic humanism developed by neo-Harringtonian thinkers, as Pocock has implied.

11. Ferguson certainly does not want to challenge the constitutional equilibrium that emerged from the Glorious Revolution. He holds what to the eyes of some of his contemporaries, or from the perspective of seventeenth-century republicanism, may have appeared as a 'constitutional paradox'. That is, the idea that the experience of virtue and freedom is possible even in a monarchical régime. The limits of his republicanism fully emerged in the years of the American revolution. Ferguson published a pamphlet against Price in which he criticised the use of violence by the colonists and denounced the 'extravagant plans of Continental Republic'. On the last issue, see Sher 1985: 262–76; Amoh 1990.
12. See Ferguson 1792: I, 7. On Ferguson and the Stoic legacy, see Kettler 1965; among recent studies, Oz-Salzberger 1995a: 106–21, Hill 1997.

Nor can it adequately be understood in terms of the interpretative model proposed by Nicholas Phillipson, with its emphasis on the pre-political dimensions of culture and manners. We have seen that Ferguson repeatedly criticised the tendency for individuals to enclose themselves within the private sphere. There are passages in the *Essay* where he criticises a lack of interest in public affairs caused not merely by an unrestrained desire for enrichment, but also by the retirement and withdrawal required by reflection and study (see Ferguson 1995: 33–4, 170–1). Studying is, after all, less important than devotion to the *res publica*.

If we look at Ferguson's theoretical proposal from a distance, he seems to have wanted to reconcile commerce and virtue (see Kettler 1977; Gellner 1994 and 1996; Kalyvas and Katznelson 1998), to bring together the new mode of production centred on the division of labour with a politics based on some cardinal values of the republican tradition. Commerce does not appear as a principle that necessarily dissolves political and military virtue. Virtue can still be practised in the age of separations, in the commercial societies of the modern world.

Ferguson not only accepts the new forms of economic production, but also the modern individual who chooses his own ends and pursues them in the sphere of private liberty. Precisely by insisting on the importance of conflict, Ferguson highlights the idea that individuals pursue different ends, all of which may be important and legitimate. Ferguson does not want to replace the liberty and security of the modern individual with the ancient form of politics. Rather, he wants to integrate liberty as non-interference in the private sphere with the self-determination given by participation in public affairs.

In a letter to Karl Jaspers, Hannah Arendt wrote 'You must know that quote from Cato . . . *Victrix causa diis placuit, sed victa Catoni*. That is the spirit of republicanism.'[13] The citation – actually from Lucan's *Pharsalia* – had been used, indeed, by republican thinkers such as John Toland.[14] While Hannah Arendt may have been sure that it expresses the spirit of republicanism, however, I have more doubts. I do not know if there is such a thing as a 'spirit' of republicanism, and I doubt whether it is appropriate to talk in terms of one single tradition of republican thought. In the remarks that follow, I take some aspects of Ferguson's thought as a starting point for a discussion of some basic features of the republican tradition and the differences existing within it.

13. Arendt and Jaspers 1985: 281. The letter was written on 24 July 1954.
14. See Lucan, *Pharsalia*, I, line 128; see Toland 1698a.

'The rivalship of separate communities, and the agitations of a free people, are the principles of political life, and the school of men' (Ferguson 1995: 62–3). I have already stressed that Ferguson believed that conflict has a positive role in social and political life. He was so convinced of this that he made conflict into a constant of human nature. In the *Essay* he writes 'Mankind not only find in their condition the sources of variance and dissension; they appear to have in their minds the seeds of animosity, and to embrace the occasions of mutual opposition, with alacrity and pleasure' (*ibid.*: 25).

Here Ferguson was probably re-working a theme prominent in the republican tradition – the eulogy of conflict contained in the fourth chapter of Machiavelli's *Discorsi* ('the discord between people and senate made that republic free and powerful' – Machiavelli 1960: 136). As is well known, Machiavelli argued that Rome succeeded in maintaining its freedom because of the conflict between patricians and plebeians – a conflict institutionalised in the constitutional form of a mixed government. He radically distanced himself from the praise of 'concord' which up until that time had been traditional within civic humanism, and argued that 'tumults', and those divisions 'which maintain themselves without sects and partisans' were necessary conditions for freedom in a republic.

Not all English or Scottish Commonwealthmen in the seventeenth and eighteenth centuries agreed with Machiavelli's position, which had shocked Guicciardini and others in Florence at the time (see Guicciardini 1983: 528–30). Harrington distanced himself from it explicitly. He saw nothing positive in social and political conflict, and put forward Venice rather than Rome as a political model precisely because of the stability of Venetian institutions, and above all because of the absence of tensions and struggles to which he attributed the fall of Rome (see Harrington 1992: 33, 218–20).

After the Restoration, however, Algernon Sidney reformulated Machiavelli's thesis in his *Discourses concerning Government*, and asserted that 'no sedition was harmful to Rome' (Sidney 1990: 153). Walter Moyle took up a similar position, and in his *Essay upon the Constitution of the Roman Government* even argued that 'the popular seditions under the commonwealth... reformed and perfected the Roman government' (Moyle 1969: 242–3). In the early eighteenth century, Machiavelli's theses were directly evoked and discussed by Thomas Gordon. For example, in a little work on a crucial period of Roman history – *The Conspirators, or the Case of Catilina* – he declared 'and yet I shall not scruple to maintain, tho' it may startle some men at first view, that all these virtue, order and good discipline proceded from the tumults and civil broils that arose in the city of Rome' (Gordon 1972: 84–5). This positive assessment of conflict appears again in some of *Cato's Letters*. The letter for 17 March 1721, for instance, asserts the following general position: 'these opposite views and interests will be causing a perpetual struggle: but by this struggle liberty is preserved, as water is kept sweet by motion' (Trenchard and Gordon 1995: II, 504).

If we now move to the French Enlightenment, we find a number of similar ideas in Montesquieu, the author of whom Ferguson declared himself an admirer and follower. Although Montesquieu cannot formally be considered a republican thinker, he must be recognised as a fundamental link transmitting republican ideas (see Lefort 1992: 181–91). In the *Considérations sur les causes de la grandeur des Romains et de leur décadence*, he had also used Roman history to draw more general conclusions:

> As a general rule, every time we see everyone quiet and peaceful in a state which calls itself a republic, we can be sure that liberty is not present. In a political body, what is usually called union is an extremely ambiguous affair ... There may be union in a state where it is generally believed there is nothing but discord.
>
> (Montesquieu 1949–51: II, 119)

The same idea recurs in the *Esprit des lois* in the passages where England is discussed. Earlier, in the *Lettres persanes*, Montesquieu had remarked that in England 'one is constantly seeing liberty arise out of the fire of discord and sedition' (Montesquieu 1949–51: I, 336). In his major work, he described England 'as a nation where republic hides under the form of monarchy', and above all, as 'a continually heated nation ... more easily led by its passions than by reason' (*ibid.*: II, 304, 577).

In the light of these remarks, we may ask ourselves whether it is not possible to see two groups of republican theories in the political thought of the seventeenth and eighteenth centuries. There seems to be one group which, for convenience's sake, we may call Harringtonian, and another which we may call Machiavellian. The first tends to exclude political conflict from the physiology of the political body; the second sees political conflicts, confined within certain institutional limits, as positive. The first holds that there should be an idea of the common good shared by all citizens, the second puts forward no substantial notion of the common good. The first outlines a political order which – being without conflict – is in a sense fixed for all time. The second sees political order as emerging out of conflict. The first takes Venice as its mythical model, the second Rome with its fruitful discord between senate and plebs.

My aim is not to introduce a rigid dichotomy between families of theories, but rather to underline these differences in emphasis within a shared heritage. But if these distinctions[15] have some basis, they may help us to rethink a number of problems regarding continuities and discontinuities in the republican tradition. It has often been stressed that the tradition has one of its classic sources in Aristotle: the virtuous citizen of early modern republicans is taken to be a re-elaboration of the *zoon politikon*. However, if we think of the writers I have called Machiavellians, the political order they imagined can hardly be seen as a straightforward reformulation of Aristotle's. Aristotle's political order was given by nature, not by convention. Good political life left no room for conflict. In the *agora* there was supposed to be rivalry towards excellence, but no differences between citizens so fundamental as to give rise to genuine conflicts. If this is true, the individual imagined by Machiavellian thinkers is no longer a citizen of an Athenian *polis*, but participates in a new form of republican life.

As I have already mentioned, Ferguson often expresses a certain scepticism about the importance of institutional arrangements – some might say, a tendency to underestimate their importance:

> Even political establishments, though they appear to be independent of the will and arbitration of men, cannot be relied on for the preservation of freedom; they may nourish, but should not supersede that firm and resolute spirit, with which the liberal mind is always prepared to resist indignities and to refer its safety to itself.
>
> (Ferguson 1966: 251)

Laws and institutions are not enough to ensure liberty; without public spirit and constant civic alertness, despotism would raise its head in modern nations. As he adds in another passage from the *Essay*, 'it is not in mere laws, after all, that we are to look for the securities to justice, but in the powers by which those laws have been obtained, and without whose constant support they must fall to disuse' (*ibid.*: 160).

These observations lead me to ask about the tension between virtue and institutions, or virtue and laws, in the republican tradition of thought. To start the reasoning off, we may consider the way in which Harrington presents Machiavelli. Machiavelli, 'the only politician of later ages', is described as a 'learned disciple' of the ancients. The theorists of 'ancient prudence' (Harrington is thinking especially of Aristotle and Livy) conceived of government as 'the empire of laws and not of men' (Harrington 1992: 8–9). It

15. I have already suggested these distinctions in Geuna 1998: 117–22.

is interesting that Machiavelli should be presented as a theorist who considers government as 'the empire of laws'.[16] It is true that he gives great importance to legal arrangements. We need only think of the first book of the *Discorsi*, where he declares that 'it is hunger and poverty that make men industrious, and it is the laws that make them good' (Machiavelli 1960: 136). However, he often appears to give priority to the concept of virtue rather than to that of law. I am thinking here not only of the virtue of the prince and of the great legislator, but also of the civil and military virtues of citizens. This would imply that there are two ways of reading Machiavelli and, more generally, of interpreting republicanism: one that sees the *res publica* as the embodiment of the rule of law, while the other sees virtue as crucial to the survival of any form of republic and of free government.

It might seem that law and virtue are simply two different levels of discourse, and that both are present with equal dignity in all republican thinkers. So we might argue that, when writers emphasise the role of 'the government of laws' they are discussing the functioning of the republic once this has been established. When, by contrast, they stress the role of virtue, they are focusing on the creation of the republic, or on the risk that it may break up – on the moment when virtue loses its hold and corruption takes root. But is it really true that the two dimensions have equal value for every republican thinker? Some writers appear to restate the civic humanist heritage based on virtue, whereas others place a greater emphasis on the importance of institutions and laws. And this appears in turn to shape republican theories which are significantly different from each other. An emphasis on the rule of law goes with a more static view of politics and, in some cases, with a belief that it is possible to identify the institutional framework of a perfect republic. An emphasis on virtue, in contrast, is more associated with a dynamic vision, with an acute awareness of the role of chance in human affairs, and of the impossibility of escaping the pressures of history.

This tentative distinction leads to a number of further thoughts to round off this account. First of all, in order to avoid impoverishing simplifications, we may recall that those republican thinkers who give prominence to institutions and law also need to come to grips with the problem of virtue. For when they explain the genesis of republican institutions, they need to refer

16. It can be recalled that the emphasis on the 'government of law', on the 'rule of law', is not specific to the republican tradition. Emphasis on the rule of law was more or less common coin in early modern thought – it was a theme present in both the Aristotelian and the natural law traditions, and also in those tendencies which we would today call constitutionalist. See Larrère 1997.

to figures like legislators, whose virtue must be assumed. Secondly, the emphasis on virtue contains more problems than might appear at first sight. On the one hand, it gives prominence to factors that may seem appealing and even relevant to us today. Giving importance to virtue means giving priority to innovation, to the founding of institutions, the *novus nascitur ordo*. Alternatively (if the institutions in question are already founded) it may mean stressing – as Ferguson does – the need for constant civic alertness if liberty is to be maintained. On the other hand, other aspects of this approach seem more problematic from the point of view of the modern conscience. First of all, there is the question of who are the virtuous; and secondly, the issue of how virtue is to be kept alive and transmitted. The question arises as to whether there are individuals or ranks in society who incarnate virtue *par excellence* – whether virtue is a privilege of the upper ranks, for example, or of moralising intellectuals, and whether these ranks and individuals have a particular rôle *vis-à-vis* other citizens. A final question is what measures should be taken when virtue becomes corrupt or disappears. This brings us to Machiavelli's problem of *ridurre ai principii*, the exceptional means that may be necessary to bring a halt to the corruption of the republic. This is yet another aspect of the republican heritage that cannot fail to attract the attention of the disenchanted historian of the present day.

11

Scots, Germans, Republic and Commerce

Fania Oz-Salzberger

1. Introduction

During the second half of the eighteenth century, the major texts of the
Scottish Enlightenment made their most significant Continental debut in
the cultural and scholarly centres of the Holy Roman Empire. Scottish books
met with an alert and admiring German reading public, and affected many
aspects of German intellectual life. German philosophy, especially epistemol-
ogy, ethics and aesthetics, and *belles-lettres* and literary theory were inspired
by the writings of David Hume, William Robertson, Adam Ferguson and
Thomas Reid. By interesting contrast, Scottish political thought was one
of the fields that least affected German readers. More specifically, Scottish
ideas of the modern polity, seen as a full-fledged commercial society, and
the Scottish fascination with the possibility of retaining republican virtue
therein, mostly remained beyond the discursive scope of German political
thinkers. Consequently, as I will argue, it is possible to discern two, at the
very least two, very different 'republicanisms' in Europe prior to the outbreak
of the French Revolution.

If we focus our gaze mainly on the history of books and reading, this omis-
sion is difficult to explain. The published works of many Scottish authors
arrived in Germany between 1760 and 1800, either in their original English
versions, or in English-language reprints, or, most often, in rapidly produced
and fairly accurate German translations. Scottish authors were avidly read.
Most highly regarded, alongside the fascinating but questionable Hume,
were Smith and Ferguson, less questionable and no less fascinating (Maurer
1987; Gawlick and Kreimendahl 1987; Waszek 1985; Oz-Salzberger 1995a).

Both these thinkers offered in their major books a powerful reassessment of republican ideas. While Smith discussed commerce as a mainstay of

197

modern economy and modern society, Ferguson proposed a critique of the modern interplay between economic and moral aspects of political society. Smith and Ferguson thus represent two Scottish solutions, at times over-lapping and at times openly rival, to the crucial new question of wealth and virtue: how, if at all, should civic virtue survive alongside the new ethos of self-serving acquisition and deployment of wealth?

The German reception of this corpus of ideas reflects a profound dif-ference between German and Scottish republican traditions. German and Swiss authors in the late eighteenth century, among them Immanuel Kant, Moses Mendelssohn, Friedrich Schiller and Isaak Iselin, had their own ideas of republicanism and of commercial society. These ideas, I submit, differed substantially from contemporaneous Scottish thinking. In consequence, readers of Ferguson and of Smith found their political and their political-economic statements at times difficult to digest, and at other times highly objectionable.

In this essay I propose to examine Scottish and German ideas of republic and commerce, partly by way of direct comparison, and partly by tracing the reception of Ferguson, and in some cases of Smith, by German readers and authors. The limits of this reception, I suggest, delineate the deep di-vergence between late-eighteenth-century Scottish and German republican thought.

Scottish republicanism was at that juncture in the process of moderni-sation and adaptation to new ideas of political economy and the modern state. German republicanism, during the same period, was not being mod-ernised. When German political economy eventually came to draw on Adam Smith's theories, in the early nineteenth century, the task was conducted outside the sphere of republican discourse and devoid of republican props. Consequently, the Scottish dilemma, the need to accommodate wealth and virtue, remained hornless in German political thinking: ideas of commercial modernity were developed without a theoretical framework for addressing the questions of civic participation and republican virtue.

II. Scottish Republicanism and the Uses of Commerce

Adam Ferguson's *Essay on the History of Civil Society* (1767) is one of the major, and also one of the last, Scottish attempts at retaining and rethink-ing the Scottish republican tradition. Two generations earlier, Andrew Fletcher of Saltoun had created a republican theory for pre-union Scotland that rested on agrarian, patriarchal assumptions. Some four decades later,

David Hume dispensed with the republican imperative by pointing at the relative advantages of well-governed monarchies in the modern age, and extending 'the perfect commonwealth' into a theoretical dimension where active civic virtue no longer played a crucial role (Robertson 1985).

While several other Scottish writers insisted that an element of active civic participation is still indispensable for the modern polity,[1] Adam Smith developed Hume's line of argument and brought the main stream of Scottish political economy to 'the limits of the civic tradition', as John Robertson has put it.[2] According to Smith, the social mechanisms at work in modern states and in free markets made active civic virtue obsolete. Communal well-being was created and maintained as an unintended product of economic exchange, complemented and balanced by careful governmental input in certain areas and buttressed by the psychological benefits of polite human interaction.[3]

Ferguson's approach was substantially different. Witnessing the birth pangs of political economy at first hand, he was in a position to launch the first effort to reclaim the Aristotelian–Machiavellian idea of civic virtue for the modern state, where, he insisted, it was still indispensable. From the mid-1760s, when the *Essay* was written, through to the early 1790s, when the *Principles of Moral and Political Science* (1792) was assembled from decades of university lectures, Ferguson conducted a spirited, ironic and sometimes angry *Auseinandersetzung* with the languages of sociability and natural law as used by his friends David Hume and Adam Smith. At the same time, he endeavoured to bring his own variant of the discourse of civic humanism into line with the more innovative and fruitful of their insights. This was not often brought out as a full-fledged debate, and Ferguson's gusto varies according to mood or intended audience. It is nevertheless possible to show a consistent attempt by Ferguson to question the foundations of Hume's and Smith's trust in the political and moral mechanisms of modern commercial society. His writings are spiced with linguistic skirmishes with his philosophical rivals, many of them encoded by using the key terminology of the relevant discourse with no names named, and thus mostly overlooked by skimming or quotation-seeking readers. Yet these interplays – Ferguson would have

1. An overview of this discursive setting is provided in Pocock 1983.
2. Smith is understood primarily as a developer of political economy from the tradition of natural jurisprudence by Duncan Forbes, Donald Winch, Knud Haakonssen, Istvan Hont and Michael Ignatieff. Smith's position as a civic moralist is defended by Nicholas Phillipson. For a general view of the two interpretations see Robertson 1983a.
3. In 'a civilized and commercial society', with its advanced division of labour, Smith conceded that 'some attention of government is necessary in order to prevent the almost entire corruption and degeneracy of the great body of the people': Smith 1976a: v, ch. 1, Part III, art.2.

appreciated the term – amount to an original philosophical statement about citizenship, legalism and the role of individual moral participation in large political systems.

By pointing to the sophistication of his engagement with the political languages of his day, it is possible to show that Ferguson was neither an invisible-hand theorist, nor a die-hard classical republican. While making use of the theory of unintended consequences in describing the emergence of social and political institutions, Ferguson never applied it to his theory of the polity and of citizenship. He consistently refused to accept that politics was solely, or even chiefly, the science of institutions and of laws mechanically regulating individual self-interests for the collective benefit. This was the crux of his disagreement with Hume and Smith. Without becoming an all-out battle, this disagreement cut deep into the Scottish Enlightenment, which was not, as it is sometimes portrayed, an ensemble of friendly soloists playing variations on one theme.

Adam Smith's stance as a civic moralist has been contested in recent scholarship, and in the present context it would be well to repeat the important observation that he was not the full-blown 'unintentionalist' some writers have taken him for. As Book v of *the Wealth of Nations* spells out, moral refinement cannot be left to blind mechanisms alone, and government intervention is necessary for some types of public works, notably education. As Book III concedes, the invisible hand does not always get it absolutely right; some complex spontaneous orders, for example the early commercial growth of towns in Europe, can in fact be 'contrary to the natural course of things' (Smith 1976a: III, ch. 4) and slow the pace of economic progress. As for man's moral behaviour, the final version of the *Theory of Moral Sentiments* (1790) reveals enhanced concern about corruption and a reinforcement of the Stoic belief in moral self-control.[4] Nevertheless, as one scholar put it, Smith's politics, 'like Hume's . . . was a politics that relied more on machinery than men . . . government is seen largely as a matter of balancing, checking and harnessing interests rather than calling forth public spirit and virtue' (Winch 1983: 266). The gist of Smith's political economy is that irreversible economic and social progress can come about through unintentional processes comprised of multiple self-interested (though not necessarily selfish) actions, and defended by legal-institutional mechanisms. Ferguson's rejection of all these claims is the crux of his own theory of civil society.

---

4. See the editors' introduction in Smith 1976b: 5–10. The integrity of Smith's moral philosophy and political economy is defended, most recently, in Winch 1992.

That 'property is a matter of progress' Ferguson was happy to concede (1995: 82). His idea of material progress, however, was more cautious than that of many of his contemporaries. As Duncan Forbes has emphasised, Ferguson was far from progressivism in its crude, one-way, 'Whig' form. He denied, and indeed denounced, the view of mankind as unintentionally and/or irreversibly progressing along any moral, social or political course. This did not deter him from conceding that the advance of technology, the arts, commerce and political institutions can often be successfully described in terms of unintended consequences. Ferguson was anxious to emphasise that human advance has been uniform and cumulative, that 'the beginning of our story was nearly of a piece with the sequel' (Ferguson 1995: 5; cf. Forbes 1966), primarily in order to fill in that unfortunate abyss dug by Rousseau between the natural and the artificial chapter in the history of mankind. There is, Ferguson retorted, an unconscious drive for self-improvement, and its products accumulate over long stretches of time.

Political participation is the punch line of Ferguson's idea of intended consequences. His statements of civic activism are interesting both in the British context, where they were considered potentially radical on at least one occasion,[5] and in the continental context, especially in Germany, where Ferguson's benign image as a solid Stoic *Moralphilosoph* was marred by the untranslatability of his concept of public spirit and by the unacceptability of his ideas of civic self-assertion (Oz-Salzberger 1995a, chs. 7–8).

When read with an eye for the Scottish Enlightenment's competing political languages, especially the keywords 'property', 'justice' and 'refinement', many passages in Ferguson's works acquire a polemic colour. Consider the following criticism of Locke's political language, incorporating some of the cornerstones of the Whiggism shared by Ferguson's Scottish colleagues:

> If to any people it be the avowed object of policy, in all its internal refinements, to secure the person and the property of the subject, without any regard to his political character, the constitution indeed may be free, but its members may likewise become unworthy of the freedom they possess, and unfit to preserve it . . . If this be the end of political struggles, the design, when executed, in securing to the individual his estate, and the means of subsistence, may put an end to the exercise of those very virtues that were required in conducting its execution.
> (Ferguson 1995: 221–2)

---

5. The leader of the Yorkshire reform movement, Christopher Wyvill, appealed for Ferguson's support; see Sher 1985: 274–5; Kettler 1965: 86–8.

The concepts of personal freedom, secured property and individual rights are thus branded insufficient if divorced from the civic concept of active virtue and political struggle. In a later defence of his classical mentors, the Stoics, whose name had become 'in the gentility of modern times proverbial for stupidity', Ferguson reminds his jurisprudential-minded readers that from the Stoics 'the better part of the Roman Law was derived; and, to such decided distinction of right and wrong, jurisprudence must ever recure [*sic*]' (1792: I, 8).

Ferguson left no doubt that his whole critique of polished society rests on the problem of political passivity, for which the doctrine of unintended consequences could provide an impressive philosophical justification. This was spelt out even in the university textbook, *Institutes of Moral Philosophy* (1769), where the complacency of the Stoic slave Epictetus ('I am in the station which God has assigned me': Ferguson 1769: 169) is qualified by the seldom-quoted reservation that 'the circumstances in which men are placed; the policy or government of their country; their education, knowledge and habits, – have great influence in forming their characters' (*ibid.*: 170). The book asserts that 'Where-ever the state confines political consideration to a few, who sacrifice the rights of others to their own interest or fancy, it cannot be loved', and that 'The reason and the heart of man are best cultivated in the exercise of social duties, and in the conduct of public affairs' (*ibid.*: 289–91).

Unlike David Hume, Ferguson did not find much merit in the contemporary European monarchies. He insisted that all the existing European forms of government which were not thoroughly despotic ought to be able to accommodate the political participation of many of their members, not just in a dim future, after educational goals are achieved, but at the present, as an urgent moral requirement and a basic truth of civil society as such. Insofar as civic activism exists in a monarchy, however, it is fed by the wrong causes and may almost count as an unintended consequence of feudal social stratification: 'Intangled together by the reciprocal ties of dependence and protection, though not combined by the sense of a common interest, the subjects of monarchy, like those of republics, find themselves occupied as the members of an active society, and engaged to treat with their fellow-creatures on a liberal footing' (Ferguson 1995: 71). But their lack of the republican mental equipment, a 'sense of equality, that will bear no incroachment on the personal rights of the meanest citizen', an 'indignant spirit', a selfless 'public affection'; and the lack of republican institutions, 'national councils, and public assemblies', leaves such pseudo-citizens on very shaky grounds. Quoting Montesquieu's 'principle' of monarchy, Ferguson highlights the

insufficiency of the political language of commerce and refinement used by
Hume and Smith:

> If those principles of honour which save the individual from servility in
> his own person, or from becoming an engine of oppression in the
> hands of another, should fail; if they should give way to the maxims of
> commerce, to the refinements of a supposed philosophy, or to the
> misplaced ardours of a republican spirit; if they are betrayed by the
> cowardice of subjects, or subdued by the ambition of princes; what
> must become of the nations of Europe?   (Ferguson 1995: 71)

The answer is that the nations of Europe are in need of a moderate republican
approach, encouraging public spirit and allowing some degree of political
participation by a broad-based, if unequal, citizenry. Not only Ferguson's
outspoken *Essay* but also his mature, toned-down *Principles*, asserts that

> the most important objects of human concern, and the most improving
> exercises of ability, are furnished to the members of a free state: And
> we may now also assume that forms of government may be estimated,
> not only by the actual wisdom or goodness of their administration, but
> likewise by the numbers who are made to participate in the service
> or government of their country, and by the diffusion of political
> deliberation and function to the greatest extent that is consistent with
> the wisdom of its administration.   (Ferguson 1792: II, 508–9)

Ferguson's theory of conflict, and his (long neglected) idea of play, were
constructed with the same two-tier structure as the rest of his political
philosophy. Conflict and play contribute to social cohesion as a matter of
unintended consequences in childhood and in the early times of civil society.
Even in advanced stages of the history of civil society, 'Liberty is maintained by the continued differences and oppositions of numbers, not by their
concurring zeal in behalf of equitable government' (Ferguson 1995: 128;
cf. p. 125). However, especially in political societies whose self-image is
polished and 'civilised', conflict and play must be carried on as essential
parts of self-conscious civic participation. '[T]he rivalship of separate communities, and the agitations of a free people, are the principles of political
life, and the school of men'; the love of peace must not be confused with
misplaced quietism, for 'Nothing . . . but corruption or slavery can suppress
the debates that subsist among men of integrity, who bear an equal part
in the administration of state' (*ibid*.: 61–2). Even those epitomes of refinement, scholars, must beware of losing their creativity and 'animated spirit' if,

awed by full libraries, they become 'students and admirers, instead of rivals' (*ibid.*: 217). Ferguson's idea of conflict as a dynamic maintenance procedure for civil society – an inherently imperfect and contingent civil society – can be compared, but must not be confused, with Kant's and Hegel's concepts of social conflict as the unintended accelerator of a historical process leading to a meta-historical end-state.

Ferguson's notion of play merits particular attention, because it conveys a particular version of modernised republicanism which harks back to classical sources yet tellingly points at future sociological theory. Play, a subtle and highly enjoyable type of conflict, also belongs to both 'physical' and 'moral' aspects of life: animals can play, especially the 'nobler animals', whose 'active exertion', 'ardour' and defiance of death lends them an almost civic posture in Ferguson's *Principles of Moral and Political Science* (1792: I, 14 ff.). Play is a central tenet in boys' nature (1995: 46; 1792: II, 88); yet there is also a truly moral playground for men, as the Stoics noted, in the most noble of human endeavours, the facing of danger and war (1792: I, 7). In 'civilised times' it is particularly the theatre where men can play, and the stage can provide a moral public entertainment resonant of the ancient republican scene, showing that 'Whatever our peculiar occupations are, virtue is the business of all' (1757: 18). Play is, indeed, the clearest opposite of labour, and particularly of 'divided' labour. It is the integral, purposeless, wasteful, counter-productive exertion of human powers and application of human choice. Play is un-economical. As such, it is valuable for the good polity.

In the last paragraph of the *Essay* the various themes of deliberate moral action in the polity converge in a call for individual responsibility. This is an open attack on those surrendering to 'fatality' in its religious or secular forms. Politically active men, Ferguson says tongue in cheek,

> are the happy instrument of providence employed for the good of mankind; or if we must change this language, they show, that while they are destined to live, the states they compose are likewise doomed by the fates to survive, and to prosper.   (1995: 264)

The *Essay on the History of Civil Society*, then, is a book teeming with the idea of voluntary civic action, not just of great individuals, but of all members of a polity. Ferguson clearly worried about the deterministic elements underlying the application of the theory of unintended consequences to modern history and politics. Unaware as he was of the forthcoming Kantian solution, the *verborgene Plan der Natur* which would retain both individual freedom and an unintended process of human advance (Kant 1784, Eighth Proposition), Ferguson would in all probability have rejected it had he known and grasped it. Kant, like Mandeville and Smith, accepted individual selfishness as a catalyst for progress; Ferguson, a modern Aristotelian, did not.

It would be misleadingly easy to register the famous episodes of tension between Ferguson and Hume (upon the publication of the *Essay* in 1767) and between Ferguson and Smith (probably in the early 1780s) as the results of a philosophical quarrel turned sour. In neither case is there sufficient evidence for a clear-cut explanation for the causes of tension. Hume, we know, was unhappy with the final version of Ferguson's *Essay*, although he had praised an earlier work which might have been a preliminary version of the book. Hugh Blair and William Robertson thought that Hume disliked the *Essay* for its moralism, its 'Rousing and animating Spirit' (Sher 1985: 197); Hume may have been averse to the all-important place of moral action in Ferguson's theory of government and politics. It is likely that Hume was disappointed with Ferguson's denunciation of the jurisprudential model of the modern state – incorporating the theory of unintended consequences – as methodologically insufficient for the history of civil society.

There was, nevertheless, one clear and open disagreement. As John Robertson has shown, Ferguson and his Edinburgh circle were well aware that both Hume and Smith did not share their enthusiasm for a Scottish citizens' militia (Robertson 1985: 238–43). He was also aware, to some degree, that this gap signalled a deep philosophical chasm. Hume and Smith were the perpetrators of a new political philosophy which to classical republican eyes was highly legalistic, a philosophy based on 'the ethical attitude that holds moral conduct to be a matter of rule following, and moral relationships to consist of duties and rights determined by rules'.[6] Smith's 'science of a legislator', as Knud Haakonssen has demonstrated, is a development of Hume's original theory of justice, which included an account of the origins of justice in terms of unintended consequences and slow historical evolution (Haakonssen 1981, esp. pp. 12–21).

In the language of natural jurisprudence, a modern commercial state is the realm of 'strict justice', 'the guardian of contrasts and promises', regulating a society made up of profit-seeking individuals who may or may not be privately virtuous, but are never collectively so.[7] In Hume's words, 'we are, therefore, to look upon all the vast apparatus of our government, as having ultimately no other object or purpose but the distribution of justice' (Hume 1985b: 37). As Smith puts it, 'the first and chief design of every system of government is to maintain justice; to prevent the members of a society from

6. This is Judith Shklar's apt definition in *Legalism* (1964: 1).
7. Hont and Ignatieff 1983: 43, quoting John Millar, 'Political consequences of the Revolution' (1812).

incroaching on one anothers property, or seizing what is not their own'
(Smith 1978: I, 1; cf. 1976a, Book v, ch. 1, b, 12).

The natural jurists' government, a system of political and juridical institutions run by magistrates who administer justice, is blatantly opposed to
the civic vision of a citizens' polity. 'Order in society, we find', says Hume,
'is much better maintained by means of government; and our duty to the
magistrate is more strictly guarded by the principles of human nature, than
our duty to our fellow-citizens' (Hume 1985b: 38–9). Most kinds of individual intervention in this spontaneously generated and self-perpetuating
system, particularly those professing some moral motivation, are unnecessary or damaging. Hume modified the civic tradition by inserting into it the
individualist–jurisprudential notions of universal liberty and universal citizenship. The future, he thought, belonged to large commercial states, where
all would be citizens, but only watered-down citizens by the exacting standards of the classical republicans. The way to this future might well pass
through 'civilised' monarchies, including absolute governments of the Continental brand (Forbes 1975a: 152–72, 224–30).

Smith, in his *Wealth of Nations*, broke further with republican tradition by
abandoning the notions of political community and citizen militia. Instead,
he developed a natural–jurisprudential theory of political economy, where
individual wealth-pursuit can be made to fit into a great natural course,
politically safeguarded by the British doctrine of parliamentary sovereignty
(cf. Robertson 1983).

Ferguson was well aware of this legalist turn in Scottish thought, and his
concern is summed up in the *Essay*'s contention that 'the influence of laws,
where they have any real effect in the preservation of liberty, is not any magic
power descending from shelves that are loaded with books, but, is, in reality,
the influence of men resolved to be free' (Ferguson 1995: 263–4). With a
degree of political realism unusual in eighteenth-century discourse Ferguson
points out that 'In every society there is a casual subordination, independent of its formal establishment, and frequently adverse to its constitution'
(*ibid.*: 133). Like other passages in the *Essay*, this reflects a new imperative
to defend, and perhaps redefine, the civic ideas against the legalist concepts
of government that Hume had put forward and Smith was in the process of
developing. In practice, Ferguson was fighting against Hume's and Smith's
sanguine attitude to national defence, a chore they were happy to allot to
the state, dispensing with the seminal civic concept of a citizens' militia,
Ferguson's cherished political cause (Robertson 1985: 201–9).

Ferguson endorsed Hume's and Smith's denunciation of the fictions
of social contract and ancient legislators, but he did this in order to shift

the balance of intentional effective intervention in history from heroes to citizens, not in order to diminish the role of individual intention in history. The crucial difference between the (unintended and cumulative) generation of political structures and the deliberate action vital for their preservation is proclaimed in the *Essay*, sharply distancing Ferguson from Hume and Smith: 'Although free constitutions of government seldom or never take their rise from the scheme of any single projector, yet are they often preserved by the vigilance, activity, and zeal, of single men' (Ferguson 1995: 134). Such were Cato and Brutus, and such, too, were Nero's opponents Thrasea and Helvidius, men whose spirit was 'late and ineffectual' in times of overbearing corruption, but still illustrious for 'The pursuit, and the love of it' (*ibid.*: 135). Civic virtue cannot always salvage a deteriorating polity; but it must nevertheless be upheld. 'Men certainly act from opinion as well as instinct or habit and correct opinion is desirable in itself whatever be the measure of its influence in the general affairs of men' (Ferguson 1996a: 144).

Hume's and Smith's sense of 'arriving' at a mature free state is alien to Ferguson's sense of an ever-transient political community: liberty, in its English sense, may provide a community-fortifying goal, but it can also prove a community-stifling achievement.[8] Ferguson could not accept that an economic civil society, prospering in an advanced stage of the spontaneous order, is morally self-sustaining. In the section 'Of National Felicity' in the *Essay* Ferguson engages with the language of wealth, commerce and refinement, restricting its subject matter to the realm of physical subsistence.

> Wealth, commerce, extent of territory, and the knowledge of arts, are, when properly employed, the means of preservation, and the foundations of power. If they fail in part, the nation is weakened; if they were entirely with-held, the race would perish: their tendency is to maintain numbers of men, but not to constitute happiness . . .
>
> Great and powerful states are able to overcome and subdue the weak; polished and commercial nations have more wealth, and practise a greater variety of arts, than the rude: but the happiness of men, in all cases alike, consists in the blessings of a candid, an active, and strenuous mind.
> (Ferguson 1995: 60)

This is not meant merely as a premise for the token republican proposition that nations should remain independent and small. Ferguson in fact acknowledges that in modern Europe small republics 'are like shrubs, under the shade of a taller wood'; he accepts the pragmatic rationale for the United Kingdom

---

8. Ferguson 1792: II, 124 f. See Kettler's analysis of Ferguson's relationship with Hume and Smith in terms of 'the contrast between the worlds of spectator and actor': Kettler 1977.

as seen in a European perspective: 'When the kingdoms of Spain were united, when the great fiefs in France were annexed to the crown, it was no longer expedient for the nations of Great Britain to continue disjoined.' What he does wish to see is the preservation of the equal dignity of these constituent nations, 'In order that they may possess that independence in which the political life of a nation consists' (*ibid.*).

In his philosophical writings Ferguson launches few, if any, direct assaults on contemporary writers other than Rousseau. We nevertheless find many instances of dissent from the political languages whole-heartedly adopted by fellow Scots, most significantly by Hume and Smith. The section 'Of the Separation of Arts and Professions' in the *Essay*, where Ferguson provides a memorable phrasing for both the blessings and the harms of the division of labour, contains tacit reproaches against both Hume and Smith for putting far too much trust in the process of unintended, amoral advance. Against the political economists' ideal of the commercial state Ferguson brings his dismal 'Nations of tradesmen', whose members, 'beyond their own particular trade, are ignorant of all human affairs, and . . . may contribute to the preservation and enlargement of their commonwealth, without making its interest an object of their regard or attention'. He sees these tradesmen as inferior to 'The savage, who knows no distinction but that of his merit, of his sex, or of his species, and to whom his community is the sovereign object of affection' (Ferguson 1995: 181). In an unpublished essay, 'Of the Separation of Departments, Profesions [*sic*] and Tasks Resulting from the Progress of Arts in Society', Ferguson bluntly observes that 'the mind of a tradesman, in many instances, is less practised in thought then [*sic*] that of a savage' (1996a: 144).

The ancient Roman 'union of departments' is Ferguson's ideal answer to the modern 'separation of departments':

> In the Roman commonwealth, in many respects the model of felicity to nations, the departments of state and of war were not only strictly allied and known to each other but for the most actively filled and conducted by the same person . . . This union of departments was early provided for in the very first elements of the Roman constitution. It was provided that every citizen should state himself as part of his country's strength and to qualify him for any civil or political advance by having actually served a certain term in the wars of his country.
>
> (1996a: 148–9)

This ideal must, of course, be subjected to adjustments in the modern state: since not every citizen can be a statesman-warrior, at least as many citizens as possible must have some experience in both fields, and 'professional' statesmen and warriors should be skilled to some degree in each other's tasks.

This modernised civic stance underlies the *Essay*'s attack on the interpretation of national strength in terms of population and revenue, an attack whose unnamed addressee was probably Hume: 'The state may estimate its profits and its revenues by the number of its people. It may procure, by its treasure, that national consideration and power, which the savage maintains at the expence of his blood' (Ferguson 1995: 173). However, such an approach can only be supported by the unintended consequences and division of labour model of the state, in which

> The soldier is relieved from every care but that of his service; statesmen divide the business of civil government into shares . . . They are made, like the parts of an engine, to concur to a purpose, without any concert of their own: and, equally blind with the trader to any general combination, they unite with him, in furnishing to the state its resources, its conduct, and its force.   *(ibid.)*

Both levels of specialization, in manufacture and in politics, can thus inflict a degree of depravity overruling their economic advantages. Smith is the obvious target of the remark,

> it has been observed that by the separation of tasks and professions the work is improved and obtained at a smaller cost. The artist also is sometimes improved in his designation of intelligent and manhood: but if neither is always the case; it is no doubt of moment to distinguish the instances in which the separation of arts and profession[s] is unfavourable in the result whether in respect to the character of the artist or the value of his work.   (1996a: 144)

Ferguson is thus offering a more complex model for calculating the rentability of the division of labour, a model incorporating what we might call 'psychological factors'.

Significantly, 'Of the Separation of Departments' ends with an explicit attempt to reclaim Adam Smith for the republican stance and to play down his endorsement of a standing army instead of a citizens' militia. Ferguson launches this attempt with the remark that 'The occasions and the manners of human society are transient and successive . . . And no age can with advantage legislate unalterably for the ages that follow' (1996a: 150). This essentially civic stance is ventured, somewhat misleadingly, as the rationale for Smith's discussion of the government's role in education in the fifth part of the *Wealth of Nations*.

> On this account a late writer of eminence on the wealth and other concerns of nations places education on the same foot with trade and other concerns most safely entrusted to the part concerned and reprobates fixed institutions or intervention of government. From this general rule however he excepts every case in which defence or publick safety is at stake and of course should except education so far as the publick safety is concerned. A committee of parliament or other publick authority might no doubt with great advantage be interposed to report from age to age what regulations might be requird [*sic*] in publick schools to prepare the rising generation for that part which necessity might impose on every individual for the safety of his country. He who cannot defend himself is not a man and he who cannot take part in the defence of his country is not a citizen nor worthy of the protection which the laws of country bestow. Other cares may be delegated and become matter of separate profession to a part of the people: but to set valour apart as the characteristic of a few were to change virtue and happiness itself as matter of profession and study peculiar to a devision of the community.   (Ferguson 1996a)

This explicit response to the *Wealth of Nations* provides us with an accurate yardstick for the length Ferguson was willing to go in his open disagreement with Smith. Ignoring Smith's abandonment of the cause of citizens' militia, Ferguson seems to argue that government-supervised military education for a mass of the citizens is a necessary conclusion from Smith's own premises. Whether Ferguson was trying to affirm Smith's civic loyalty, or, rather, to reproach his betrayal of the civic ideal, remains an open question; Ferguson evidently preferred to play the disagreement down rather than up. It is nevertheless clear that the error of abandoning civic-military education in favour of a market education is embedded, in Ferguson's view, in the ruthless application of the division of labour theory to the sphere of public life, the misapprehension of politics and war as professions ripe for separation. It is also clear that citizens, in his mind, must earn the legal protection administered by the state through active virtue. The rift with Smith, though couched in gentle phrasing, could hardly have been greater.

The foremost message of the *Essay* is thus its call for self-conscious political participation and civic alertness, a refusal to rely blindly on either natural or man-made laws. In the history of political thought Ferguson was one of the theorists most distrustful of the 'legalist' frame of mind. This aversion includes not only systems of thought which elevate laws and legislators to the position of fountainheads of political stability, but also the highly individualistic Kantian legalism which aspires to a point where each man shall be his own supreme law-giver. It is not man the legislator, let alone man the subject, but man the player of games, the opinionated polity-member, which is the central *persona* in Ferguson's ethics.

While accepting the economic and political realities of a modern state, Ferguson refused to abandon the essentially voluntary, activist, citizen-dependent and historically non-determinist dimensions of the classical republic. As his texts amply demonstrate, he relished an interplay of discourses – be it a blend or a conflict – in which the essence of older traditions of thought need not be eradicated by the innovations of the new ones.

The Scottish debate between modernised republicanism and political economy did not, however, succeed in crossing the linguistic and cultural borders into German political and economic discourse. As a perusal of Ferguson's reception in Germany may demonstrate, the issues at stake were not taken up by German readers and authors. This does not imply a lack of German republican tradition or an absence of new responses to challenges coming from Switzerland, Britain, America and France. It does suggest, however, that the kind of debate involving the feasibility of a new sort of republicanism for modern European states, Smith's and Ferguson's debate on the viability of civic values in commercial society, was irrelevant in the German context, where political discussion did not involve the modernising of a republican tradition.

III. German Republicanism in the Late Eighteenth Century

The 1770s mark a transition from early modern German political thinking, which seldom drew on republican sources and did not regard the remaining independent imperial towns as viable models for political theorising, to a new phase in which challenges from north America and France – and, by further reflection, from Switzerland and Britain – led to an intensive and short-lived reconsideration of the idea of a republic.

Early modern German political theory mostly drew on a history of unqualified subordination of the subjects to the territorial rulers (Vierhaus 1987a; Möller 1989). The vast majority of theoretical political texts centred on the prince and the principality: this was the focus of both 'utopian' and 'reason of state' analytical orientation (cf. Nitschke 1995). The republican alternative, the contexts in which republican terminology used, was employed either as a means to describe the federal structure of the Holy Roman Empire – and such republicanism was metaphorical, in the sense that the participating *personae* were states rather than citizens – or, more relevantly, to address the governments of the free imperial cities. By the mid-eighteenth century there were about seventy 'free' cities, subordinated directly to the emperor, including Lübeck, Hamburg and Bremen in the north and Augsburg and Nuremberg in the south. The early sixteenth century had been a turning point in their political fortunes: while several southern cities joined the Swiss Confederation, many others remained in the Empire and became embroiled in the confrontations and alliances triggered by the Reformation.

Protestant political thought revived the civic ideal, in a sacral form, by invoking the Augustinian concept of the *civitas dei* and applying it to communities of believers. As religious corporations, cities such as Augsburg, Nuremberg, Strasbourg and Magdeburg were ready to defy the imperial army and its allies. Lutheran and Calvinist jurists used the example of the ancient Greek *polis* and the classical idea of civic freedom to support their claim for a right of resistance against tyrannical oppression. This doctrine, predominantly in its Calvinist form, derived from classical sources the right of 'popular magistrates' to offer resistance to (anti-Protestant) 'tyranny' (Mackenney 1989: 32–4).

The Reformation, however, also caused the destruction of civic liberties and the paralysis of civic discourse. Luther's negative response to the Peasant War of 1525 helped to reinforce the powers of the princes against opposition from below. The earlier alliance of towns and emperor to curb the ambitions of territorial princes gave way to Protestant leagues which facilitated princely interference with civic liberties. The Calvinist doctrine of resistance, which was effective in the history of Scottish political thought through Knox's teachings, did not yield similar results in Germany. The German adherents of the Reformed Church were more influenced by Calvin's later emphasis on the 'godly polity' ruled by a 'two-fold government', where spiritual and civil authorities and duties coexist in full harmony (Höpfl 1982). The dominant political theory in Protestant Germany remained the Lutheran acknowledgment of the superiority of princely power – Luther's preferred type of secular rule – in all temporal matters. This legacy was reinforced by the Augsburg Settlement (1555). After a century of religious polarisation and war, the Peace of Westphalia (1648) further released the territorial rulers from political control from above, making the Empire even more 'symbolic' than it had been. In the meantime bloodshed, exhaustion and traditions of obedience kept popular pressures from below at bay. The good state, for most political theorists after the Thirty Years War, approximated the ideal set by Veit Ludwig von Seckendorff in his *Teutsche Fürstenstaat* (1656): a well-governed principality with obedient subjects, an authoritative and fatherly ruler, and a sound administration dispensing order, stability and common welfare – the German concept of *Polizei* (Raeff 1983; Hughes 1992, chs. 5–6).

Civic life in Germany did not cease. In the seventeenth century there were some 4000 German 'home towns', as Mack Walker has called them, and their inhabitants were about a quarter of the entire German population. After the Thirty Years War imperial free towns were protected by the imperial aulic council, the *Reichshofrat*, which also intervened in several disputes between rulers and their Estates. It was instrumental in the creation of a new constitution for the city of Hamburg in 1712, resolved religious conflicts, and in a few cases – notably those of Nassau-Siegen and Mecklenburg-Schwerin – deposed tyrannical rulers. The dwindling economic prowess of Frankfurt and Hamburg did not erase their civic independence, although other city-states, such as Königsberg and Strasbourg, were taken over by ambitious neighbouring rulers in the late seventeenth century. However, as the cases of Hamburg and Frankfurt best demonstrate, many civic issues remained unresolved and bitterly disputed. Hamburg was a hotbed of religious friction, and the political participation of citizens was marred by perpetual struggles with magistrates. Frankfurt's aristocratic oligarchy, the *Geschlechter*, kept the burghers away from political power, and both groups resisted large-scale increase of manufacture (Walker 1971; Whaley 1985; Mackenney 1989: 37–9).

The persistence of civic particularism in eighteenth-century Germany is an important reminder that territorial absolutism never held full sway. Yet the towns, like the imperial structure itself, were too weak to provide inspiration for a viable modern *theory* of government which could compete with the prevailing concepts of state. The republican legacy of the German towns, including its federal aspects, no longer supported a living and adaptable political discourse. The civic issues discussed in the towns were limited to the traditional organisations of guilds and other corporations, concerned with the economic well-being (*Nahrung*) of their members and with the regulation of crafts and trade, or, in the larger communities of Hamburg and Frankfurt, with ruling oligarchies and religious coexistence (Mackenney 1989: 38–40). This could not serve as an alternative to the rising political discourse of centralised princely rule. Thus the leading political theorists of the early and middle eighteenth century, those concerned with the imperial scope like Christian Thomasius and Friedrich Carl von Moser, as well as patriots of their territorial state like Justus Möser, shared an essentially monarchical outlook. No major thinker before the last quarter of the eighteenth century made a sustained attempt to revive the German republican tradition in the context of a modern political theory.

During the 1770s, even before external political affairs inspired different political thinking, there were new literary impulses at work which affected received notions of government. The relationship between ruler and subject was sentimentalised. The personalities of rulers like Frederick the Great of Brandenburg-Prussia and duke Karl-Eugen of Württemberg aroused powerful feelings, often negative, at times more complicated than that, among the younger generation of German *literati*. The results were at times passionately monarchist, as in the case of Christoph Martin Wieland. His celebrated novel of 1772, *Das goldene Spiegel*, extolled absolute monarchy. By contrast – and the contrast was thematical rather than emotional – Friedrich Schiller's early play, *Die Räuber* (1780), touched its audience with vague phrasings of republican feeling.

Yet the *Sturm und Drang* notions of freedom did not draw on a political reassessment of prevalent forms of government. Political theory prior to the French Revolution almost invariably defined liberty in terms of the well-governed princely state. It is significant that Locke's two *Treatises of Government* (1790), as well as Mandeville's *Fable of the Bees* (1714), had very little impact in eighteenth-century Germany. Locke's greatest political work was translated into German only once during the eighteenth century, and aroused little attention. By contrast, his *Some Thoughts concerning the Education of Children* (1793) went through at least five German translations during the century after its initial publication (Price and Price 1934: 113–14).

The reception of English and Scottish texts by German readers in this period, intensive and attentive as it was, did not allow many of the themes and subtleties of the British debate to cross the linguistic and cultural border. Most crucially, the theoretical tension between a law-based state and a virtue-based polity, which permeates the debates of the Scottish Enlightenment, went unrecognised. The economic idea of a free market subject to a benign spontaneous order did eventually find its way to German discourse through the writings of the Physiocrats and Adam Smith, but that was a late and limited reception, which was promptly incorporated into the much stronger idea of a state-controlled economy (Treue 1951; Tribe 1988: 133–48).

The German reading of Montesquieu, as Rudolf Vierhaus has shown, was strikingly selective. *De l'esprit des lois* (1748) was first translated into German in 1753, and quickly achieved fame; but, as Vierhaus shows, this 'immortal work' was criticised by its German readers from the outset. Initially it was reproached for being 'too political', and subsequently for its inadequate political premises, especially for being 'general and superficial'. Justus Möser and Friedrich Carl von Moser attacked the doctrine's inapplicability to specific cases, and Herder joined them in excluding Germany from Montesquieu's over-simplified climatology. The quest for a 'spirit', however, appealed to German readers, and led the way to many other concepts of *Geist*. The basic principle that laws determine and represent a form of government was well received, because it was deeply rooted in the absolutist definition of the ruler as law-giver. Yet there was no consensus as to the location of the 'German national spirit': the Swiss republicans found it in their republic, the Prussian Thomas Abbt argued against Montesquieu that virtue, and not just honour, can be the foundation of 'a well-ordered monarchy', and F. C. von Moser anchored it in the Holy Roman Empire. Abbt and Moser, like many of their contemporaries, took 'German freedom' for a unique form of freedom which substantially differed from Montesquieu's chief model of a free state, England (Vierhaus 1987b).

The most crucial fact about the German reception of Montesquieu was that his ideas on the separation of powers and the checks on monarchic authority were not taken up by his German followers. The abstract distinction between executive and legislative powers was often acknowledged, but it seldom implied any limitation on the absolute ruler. The political theorist Johann Heinrich Gottlob von Justi spoke of a 'third way', in which the king will be given all powers, but will be taught to rule wisely and benevolently. Indeed, Montesquieu's rejection of despotism was eagerly echoed in Germany; but his 'pouvoirs intermédiaires' were understood (and here one might say misunderstood) to refer to the old, powerless Estates, *Zwischengewalten* with no real *Gewalt*. Until the French Revolution, and to some extent even later, the German Enlightenment continued to rely on 'the good prince', ruling by laws and improving his citizens, as the best governmental form for German lands and the best guarantee for German freedom. This 'rejection of the separation of powers' was formed by polemicising against Montesquieu, but, as Vierhaus shows, its advocates often regarded themselves as his followers. Such selective reading of Montesquieu could enable Ewald Friedrich Graf von Hertzberg, the minister of Frederick the Great, to claim that Prussia was a 'free monarchy', because its provincial Estates took part in the executive (Vierhaus 1987b: 24–9).

As far as political liberty was concerned, two major ideas of freedom can be traced in German thought prior to the French Revolution. One was articulated by the defenders of the ancient rights of the Estates, who demanded that traditional corporate freedoms be upheld, either on the imperial level (Johann Jakob Moser) or on the local principality level (Justus Möser). The moral *persona* on which this idea of liberty was centred was the *Bürger*, not a classical citizen, but the traditional town-dweller, craftsman, member of a guild, whose rights and duties are perfectly delineated by his social place and his corporate identity. This was Möser's idea of freedom, which he contrasted with the new-fangled meaning of the word in the eighteenth century (Möser 1964: 33–4; cf. Sheehan 1989: 11). This, too, was the core of Herder's encomium of a long-lost medieval bliss. The figure of the traditional master-craftsman is celebrated in Schiller's poem *The Lay of the Bell* (*Das Lied von der Glocke*), where the old town society is a 'divine order', a godly artefact allowing industrious *Bürger* to cohabit in 'sweet accord' and time-honoured social hierarchy.

The other idea of freedom belonged to the theory of the strong centralised state, often conceived as absolutism or enlightened absolutism. The meaning it gave political liberty referred to the subjects' personal freedom from tyranny and oppression, guaranteed by laws and by the ruler's benevolence. Justi was representative of this approach when he defined citizens' freedom in terms of their obedience to good laws, laws which promote the common welfare. The influential Austrian cameralist Josef von Sonnenfels was especially adamant about the state's duty in leading the way to material and, especially, moral progress. The groundwork for this theory of state had been prepared by the *Aufklärer*'s teacher Christian Wolff, who enshrined the all-binding power of the state over its subjects in the idea of rationality: as long as the state is rational, it is by definition moral and its laws promote welfare and security. It is thus entitled to unerring obedience. And obeying laws created by Reason is, as Kant defined it, the very essence of freedom (cf. Sheehan 1989: 194–5).

It is important to note that both the corporate and the absolutist ideas of freedom were similar in one crucial sense: despite their appeal to such historical mechanisms as tradition, custom, or law, both depended on an ideal of non-individual virtue – either the virtuous community where the *Bürger* fulfil their traditional role in the social scheme of things, or the virtuous ruler, taught and advised by wise men and promoting his subjects' welfare in the light of Reason. In the 1790s some German thinkers articulated a broader range of concepts of political freedom such that included notions of civil rights and democracy;[9] but these concepts were tempered by the demand

---

9. Krieger 1957; Schlumbohm 1973; for a recent critical revision see Klippel 1990.

for an evolutionist approach, for long-term education and cautious political gradualism. Revolution, like freedom, was largely banished to the intellectual sphere (Vierhaus 1990).

If we borrow the distinction, articulated by Benjamin Constant in the nineteenth century and redeployed by Isaiah Berlin in the twentieth century, between 'freedom from' and 'freedom to', we may find that the Scots and the Germans had very differing meanings for both these concepts. In Scotland, 'freedom from' was primarily the jurisprudential guarantee for personal freedom enabling economic self-promotion, and it could be rephrased in the language of rights; 'freedom to' was the civic freedom to participate in the political game and assert one's humanity by exercising one's citizenship. In Germany the situation was subtly different: political freedom was primarily 'freedom from' the undue intervention of the ruler in the subject's private life and intellectual autonomy; but the *Aufklärung* saw this political arrangement mainly as a necessary support for its strong moral (but not political) notion of 'freedom to'. This freedom was neither about participation in government nor about social mobility; it was the freedom to think and express one's thoughts, to practise one's form of Christianity, and (largely in Protestant terms) to find and follow an individual path to spiritual perfection. This, for many of the thinkers discussed in our study, was the freedom that really mattered. The state, as Kant thought, could reform itself in the course of its evolution, and individual 'intervention' was therefore useless and meaningless. In Fichte's view, no other freedom but the freedom of thought was requisite for the metaphysical–historical process that he called 'the progress of the human spirit' into a future state of perfection (Vierhaus 1990: 569–70).

In this discursive world, the term 'republic' could be understood in three possible ways: (1) as a strictly historical term for a 'pure' form of government, understood in the contexts of ancient Rome, present-day Venice, and a small number of other examples; (2) as a term denoting German imperial cities, *Reichsstädte*, regardless of the particular oligarchic arrangements controlling them; or (3) as any small state.

During the last quarter of the eighteenth century, however, new energy was instilled into the term 'republic' in German political discourse. The two Atlantic revolutions, which triggered reconsiderations of Britain and Switzerland alongside America and France, aroused a plethora of retrospective, often agonised discussion. Gottfried August Bürger wrote of 'Die Republik England' (1905: 160–3) and C. F. D. Schubart of the free American colonists (1776). Laments of 'German slavery' abounded, often in the context of the notorious forced conscription during the American war. From 1789 till 1795 these voices rose to a chorus of enthralment with the

French revolutionaries, filtering into a spirited discussion of the German republican attempt in Mainz. Most pieces written in these context during the
early 1790s were formed as reports, journalistic or personal, rather than theoretical analyses (cf. Eberle and Stammen (eds.) 1989). Analytical discussions,
however, can be gleaned from the works of Herder, Friedrich Schiller, A. G. F.
Rebmann, and others. Although these authors were occupied with questions of pluralism, federalism, the combat against despotism, and the clash
of government types and individual temperaments, they did not develop a
whole republican scheme. Immanuel Kant and, later, Friedrich Schlegel, who
did put forward proposals for republics, did not apply them to present-day
Germany. Kant's republic in *Perpetual Peace* (1795), and Schlegel's critique
of Kant's work, 'Versuch über den Begriff des Republikanismus' (1797), emphatically pointed towards a blissful far future and a global harmonisation of
federated, republicanised states.[10]

Schlegel, indeed, used the term 'republic' plentifully, but almost always
metaphorically, to convey his vision of unified art and elevated, aestheticised
human existence in a future state of beauty and harmony (Schlegel 1797b).
His friend and fellow-Romantic, Friedrich von Hardenberg (Novalis), was far
less enamoured with the republican metaphor, and openly embraced aristocracy as a metaphor and as a viable political mainstay.[11] Strikingly, Schlegel's
'republic' and Novalis's 'aristocracy' are similar in the sense that they are both
metaphors, using political and social concepts to denote higher human and
poetic orders that are yet to come.

More mundane was the attitude of the Swiss thinker Isaak Iselin, one of
the few participants in the German Enlightenment who had first-hand experience of republican politics in his native city of Basle. Iselin did not adhere to
a participatory republicanism; as his writings show, Iselin's political outlook
was marked by an increasing disillusionment with short-term involvement
in public affairs. He had an interesting reflection on the relativity of all government forms, following his re-reading of 'the whole of Montesquieu' in
1765 (Im Hof 1967: 312). Years of frustrating petty politics in Basle, and
his newly acquired Physiocratic notions, led Iselin in the direction of 'legal
despotism'; he even inserted pro-monarchic remarks into the second edition
of his renowned universal history, *Geschichte der Menschheit* (1764).[12]

10. Kant 1795; Schlegel 1797a. Cf. Beiser 1992: 250–2. Beiser stresses Schlegel's early 'radicalism',
    but also points at his nascent 'conservatism'. The observed difference between Schlegel's
    'democratic' republicanism and Kant's is overshadowed by the sense of distance both authors
    convey when viewing their aspired goal.
11. See especially Novalis *ca.* 1795–6.
12. He removed most of them, however, from the fourth edition (1779); Im Hof 1967: 313.

Iselin was deeply impressed by Scottish works, including those by Hume, Smith and Ferguson. Ultimately, however, he was more interested in their vision of modern commercial society than in their political philosophy. In his physiocratic tract *Versuch über die gesellige Ordnung* (1772), Iselin signalled a resignation from state affairs and political speculation which typified his last years (Im Hof 1967: 123–7). The 'harmonious' civil order described in the *Versuch* included an idea of freedom which focused on each person's unhindered self-perfection within his place in the civil order, namely his social class (Iselin 1772: 70–1). Personal rights for security and property are part of this freedom, but political participation is merely an external feature of the republican form of government (cf. Im Hof 1967: 128–30). Human well-being is not, as Ferguson would have it, action-dependent, but law-dependent. Subjects (*Untertanen*) can be happy only in a state ruled according to 'the eternal laws of justice and order'; this is itself an 'unbreakable law of nature.[13]

To several of the thinkers mentioned here, the role of commerce in modern states was understood in terms of individual freedom and a new sense of order and rational dissemination of communal well-being. Notably, the philosopher Moses Mendelssohn was a proud and vociferous advocate of commerce, which he pointedly classed as dignified gainful employment. He upheld this position in the face of contrasting opinions, both within the German Enlightenment and the Jewish Haskalah, which considered artisanry and agriculture as favourable for the amelioration of members of marginal groups, and in particular of Jews (cf. Sorkin 1996: 17). Mendelssohn, himself a prosperous Berlin merchant, would not add his voice to any social theory demeaning the moral value of trade. Discussing the issues pursued in Christian Dohm's treatise *On the Civil Amelioration of the Jews* (1781), Mendelssohn was happy to recognise the modernising and civilising effects of commerce (*ibid.*: 111–15). He did not, however, place commerce in a republican context, nor was he obliged to follow his Scottish contemporaries in their debate over the relationship of economic activity and civic participation.

Discussions of political economy in the German Enlightenment tended to incorporate a newly acquired appreciation of commerce within the contours of monarchic government. Iselin was one of the earliest adherents to physiocratic theory, and represents several other thinkers of his generation who hailed this theoretical departure from German cameralism, without envisaging a parallel political alternative to the princely state. Around 1769–70

---

13. Iselin 1772: 110. This statement is part of a discussion of the duties of princes.

he fell under the spell of the French physiocrats, especially Quesnay, and his *Versuch* was one of the first German formulations of their doctrine. Order is the basic concept: *bürgerliche Ordnung* is but part of a larger harmony of economic, moral and political orders underpinning the stratified social order. Civil society is a natural, non-contractual institution, obeying the laws of nature and subject to divine justice: 'not human beings, but God and Nature themselves are the founders of civil society' (Iselin 1772: 108). The laws of nature regulate economic life – for instance, free competition (*ibid.*: 68) – but also the 'higher' moral destination of man (*ibid.*: 88 ff.). Iselin saw economic prosperity as a necessary condition for a virtuous society, while virtue was a necessary condition for sustaining economic bliss. The economic and the moral orders develop interdependently, but in Iselin's conclusion they melt into a simple, all-embracing 'Order'. The civil order is perhaps the least perfect, since God and Nature left its details to men's own devices under the eternal laws (*ibid.*; see also Becher 1978: 25). As a moralist, Iselin felt grateful to the political economist who had spelled out this divine harmony; he expressed it in his approving review of Smith's *Wealth of Nations* in 1777 (Iselin 1777, esp. 587; Iselin 1779).

Iselin easily incorporated the wealth-and-virtue equation into a spiritual vocabulary of human amelioration: 'Only under the beneficent influences of economic well-being does the human soul (*Seele*) rise to great and publicly useful institutions and to the higher truths, through which it becomes acquainted with its dignity and its destination (*Bestimmung*)' (Iselin 1772: 92–3). Iselin's application of the language of civic virtue and the imperative of political activism to a framework of non-participationist monarchism was the gist of his and Moser's *patriotisch* vocabulary. His definition of 'political virtue' was 'that which makes the state flourishing and strong . . . the courage, passion for honour and diligence of the citizens and especially the wisdom and the vigilance of the rulers, who regulate the citizens' virtues as well as their vices and weaknesses in a happy harmony for the general welfare'.[14] He was critical of Montesquieu for making honour rather than virtue the principle of monarchy, and hailed contemporary 'free' European monarchies which seemed to be undergoing enlightened reform: Struensee's Denmark, Sweden of Gustav III, Poniatowski's Poland, and even Catherine's Russia (Im Hof 1967: 134–5; see Iselin 1768: II, 339). The state being the great giver of order for civil society, and laws the chief vehicle of order, monarchy was the natural abode of virtue.

---

14. Iselin 1770a: I, 237–8; quoted by Im Hof 1967: 133.

The legacy of classical republicanism and the new ideas of the physiocrats were subjected by Iselin to this basic structure, serving mainly as indicators of its good working order: virtuous citizens and a 'fermenting' free market became two hallmarks of a well-governed state. True freedom remained for Iselin nothing more than 'the rule of laws and of the great fundamental drive for general welfare' (1768: II, 305), a definition tailored to fit the enlightened autocracy. 'Could it not be possible', the *Geschichte der Menschheit* concludes, 'that the freedom of the republicans is not yet the true freedom, which might bless a civil society in its most beautiful times? Could it not be possible, that it might be contrary to the eternal laws of justice rather than in accordance with them?' (*ibid.*: II, 342). The secretary of the Basel town council thus arrived at a very mitigated view of republican bliss.

Two decades later, Friedrich Schiller, followed by Fichte and Hegel, made use of the basic concepts of contemporary political economy to envisage a new political community which is 'republican' in a particular German sense: that of an everlasting harmony, resting on the elevated historical plain of Hegel's 'ethical life' (*Sittlichkeit*). An analysis of this republic of aestheticised, or moralised, plethora of unified souls is beyond the scope of the present essay. Its roots, however, lie in the same conceptual soil as Iselin's seemingly practical reading of French physiocracy and of Smith's *Wealth of Nations*: free commerce is a vehicle, and it is also a metaphor, for the free exchange of minds which will unite and uplift human society to a state of future spiritual perfection.

IV. The German Reception of Ferguson: Republic Postponed

While Adam Smith was fairly easy to read and accommodate into the pattern of realist monarchism and spiritual republicanism, Adam Ferguson would pose a greater problem to his German readers. It was Ferguson, in ascending opposition to Smith, who demanded active civic life within modern commercial society, and advocated conflict and strife as parameters of a republic in good working order. Yet his wrestling to accommodate civic and economic languages was rejected by his German readers: it was banished from the text and disregarded as a subtext.[15] The linguistic intricacies of Ferguson's writings, especially the *Essay on the History of Civil Society* (1767) and the *Institutes of Moral Philosophy* (1769) were dismantled by the German translators of the two books, C. F. Jünger and Christian Garve respectively. Garve, a renowned

15. For a detailed analysis of Ferguson's German reception see Oz-Salzberger 1995a.

Popularphilosoph, subverted Ferguson's republican intentions in a celebrated commentary he appended to the *Institutes* (Garve 1772). Isaak Iselin, for his part, openly denounced Ferguson's conflictual republicanism in a major review of the *Essay* for the *Allgemeine deutsche Bibliothek* (Iselin 1770b).

For Ferguson, language was a very important tool in conveying the uneasy coexistence of two political traditions. While driving home the point that commerce and specialisation were both the legitimate offspring and the potential banes of civil society, Ferguson was also waging an ingenious linguistic battle over the terms 'politeness', 'polished', 'civility' and 'manners'. Whereas the majority of the Scottish Enlightenment, in the words of John Pocock, 'replaced the *polis* by politeness, the *oikos* by the economy' (Pocock 1983: 242), Ferguson was trying to push these demons back into their bottles by reviving their original meanings. This terminological battle would make a daunting challenge to any translator.

Ferguson made it clear that he did not opt for any obscurantist separation between 'civil' and 'commercial', which he freely conjoined as adjectives for 'arts'; 'polished' and 'commercial' as adjectives for 'nations'; and the nouns 'politeness' and 'civilisation' with one another. At the same time, he tried to bring out the political meaning inherent in the terms 'polite', 'polished', 'civil' and 'civilised', and thus subtly to distance both families from the unrelated and unbeloved 'commerce':

> The term *polished*, if we may judge from its etymology, originally referred to the state of nations in respect to their laws and government [and men civilized were men practised in the duty of citizens]. In its later applications, it refers no less to their proficiency in the liberal and mechanical arts, in literature, and in commerce [and men civilized are scholars, men of fashion and traders].[16]

Ferguson obviously wanted some partial revival of the original values through the original meaning. To some extent, he manages to re-politicise (and from his viewpoint to rescue) some of these terms: 'polished' is used when the active, 'the knowing and the polished', are contrasted with the 'commonly more quiescent' men who are 'ignorant and artless'. Another way of reclaiming terms from the enemy camp is through pseudo-irony: 'The celebrated nations of antiquity made war under their highest attainment of civility, and under their greatest degree of refinement.' Similarly, the recognition of true, active happiness was 'a refinement that was made by Regulus and Cincinnatus

---

16. Ferguson 1995: 195. The text in square brackets was added by Ferguson to the second edition (Edinburgh, 1768). Cf. Ferguson 1995: 271 ('List of Variants').

before the date of philosophy ... a refinement, which every boy knows in his play, and every savage confirms ... ' (Ferguson 1995: 48). The irony is not directed at the term 'refinement' itself, but only at its pretentious misuse: this is made clear through Ferguson's sceptical look at modern European notions of 'civilised' warfare, and his open distrust of 'the supposed conditions of accomplished civility' and 'the boasted refinements ... of the polished age'. Further down the road, corrupted nations 'generally flatter their own imbecility under the name of *politeness*' (*ibid*.: 242). The phrasing implies that there is real civility, real refinement, and real politeness, to be found in a political culture closer to that of the celebrated ancient nations.

'Commerce' was a more difficult term to claim for civic vocabulary, although Ferguson conceded that in most cases 'the commercial and political arts have advanced together'. While prone to present their malicious effects, stifling creativity, Ferguson is forced to admit that corruption 'does not arise from the abuse of commercial arts alone; it requires the aid of political situation'. However, no linguistic tactics are wasted on commerce. There is perhaps one blow in the direction of 'oeconomy', when we are reminded of society's obligation 'to admit numbers, who, in strict oeconomy, may be reckoned superfluous, on the civil, the military, and the political list' (1995: 225). It is possible that the term 'oeconomy' in this context means not merely 'efficiency in resource management', but also a hint at the new political science developed by Ferguson's friends.

Civic language was thus utilised in the *Essay* to appropriate and redefine both jurisprudential terms (civil society, civil liberty) and 'Addisonian' language (politeness, polished, civility, refinement). It may now be useful to reflect on the extent to which a German reader in 1768 could follow the linguistic transactions we have described. How far could a translator preserve, or a reader observe, the clash of paradigms which is recognisable in the English text?

The linguistic obstacles, as the evidence suggests, were enormous. Ferguson's campaign for the lost political meanings of 'polite' or 'polished' fell flat in Germany, where the old Latinism *polit*[17] had been replaced by the German *höflich*. The latter, derived from *Hof* (court), is obviously the wrong end of the stick. Jünger translated both 'polished' and 'polite' as *gesittet*, which was no great help (Ferguson 1768: 87, 104). When Ferguson warns against the corruption of modern monarchy, where the principles of honour might 'give way to the maxims of commerce, [or] to the refinements of a

---

17. August Langen traces the heyday of this term to the late seventeenth century, when *politisch* meant 'gallant' besides 'diplomatic' and 'statesmanly': Langen 1974: 32.

supposed philosophy' (1995: 71), he uses 'commerce' and 'refinements' with deliberate reference to the 'Addisonian' vocabulary; by translating 'refinements' as *Klügeleyen*, Jünger successfully rendered the *prima facie* meaning of the original, but was unable to transmit the commerce-related connotations of 'refinement', which constitute the author's intended irony in this case.

Shifts of connotation went further than that. 'Commerce' became either *Handlung*, or an awkward, somewhat proverbial *Handel und Wandel*. This dimming of clear, acute terminology continued with 'commercial nations' becoming *Handel und Wandel treibende Völker*, while 'civil and commercial arts' were rendered *bürgerliche und zur Handlung gehörige Künste*. 'Commerce' in the sense of social intercourse, was rendered, fairly enough, *Umgang*, but this accepted translation shut out the 'Addisonian' paradigmatic equation of economic and cultural transaction (Pocock 1983: 241). Much of Ferguson's irony and implied criticism were lost when this set of familiar English terms, along with their 'polite' associations, disappeared into newly fitted, unassociated German terminology.

Of course, Ferguson's books were not the only ones posing their German readers problems of conceptual accessibility. The early German translator of Adam Smith's *Wealth of Nations* (1776–8) translated 'civilised and commercial society' into 'civilisirter und handelder Staat' and 'mercantile nation' into 'Handelsvolk' (in Garve's 1795 translation: 'Handelsstaat'). These were all new combinations, the translators were experimenting, and their readers could not be expected to recognise either positive or negative connotations of the term 'commerce' and its variants (Erämetsä 1961: 58, 75).

Language, however, is not the sole issue at stake. The problem was by no means only on the level of creating new German words for old English concepts. For Iselin, Ferguson's republicanism was disconcertingly 'wild', and his doubts about modern civilised society seemed out of place. Iselin found 'a great misunderstanding' in Ferguson's view that civilisation does not positively enhance virtue, but merely checks lower passions and violence:

> Undoubtedly the seeds of tender human feeling, of noble thinking and honourable character, lie in the preliminary structure of the human mind, but we doubt very much whether they can develop for the general utility without the animating light of cultivated reason, and without the beneficent warmth of good government [*Policey*]. – We willingly admit that savage nations such as those Herr Ferguson describes in that point of time can witness the effortless introduction of a Spartan constitution . . . But was the Spartan constitution in principle much better than a systematic barbarity?   (Iselin 1770b: 159–60)

Most crucially, Ferguson's republican vision sadly lacked *Ordnung*. To Iselin, this was a fatal error in the interpretation of virtue. '[T]he way [Ferguson] expresses himself could mislead one to think that political divisions, factions, turmoils, are in his view the only convenient means to keep virtue going.' Iselin hastened to defend Ferguson from such misreading: '[B]ut we believe that he only wants to say that, human opinions being by nature varied, each person should shamelessly express his [opinion] and fearlessly defend it. And he is right [in saying] that when this is no longer the case, then the state had been corrupted and freedom had vanished' (Iselin 1770b: 164). Thus the difficulty is explained away by claiming that it is freedom of expression, not political discord, that Ferguson advocates. Verbal intercourse subtly replaces party politics. Iselin systematically toned down or explained away the more disquieting parts of Ferguson's critique: his analysis of the modern type of corruption from political indifference, and his idea that conflict, and even war, is an essential action in a functioning political society.

The final rejection of the Scottish form of republican virtue is incorporated in Christian Garve's resounding admission that he is unable to translate the English concept of 'public spirit' into German. Garve's remarks on Ferguson's *Institutes* include a fascinating discussion of British political language, which peaks in his treatment of 'public spirit'. Garve was not pleased with the available German equivalents, and, as in the case of other English terms, he candidly shared his difficulties with his readers:

> Public spirit . . . is not patriotism, because that extends itself to any society one is a member of, and at most to mankind; it is not the love of men, because that is applied to individual persons as well, whereas public spirit [*öffentliche Geist*] [applies] only to whole parties; it is the inclination of the soul to see itself always as a part of a whole; it is the capacity of the spirit to conceive this whole vividly; it is the warm participation in everything that we perceive to be occupying a greater number of our fellow men. No virtue, no characteristic is in fact rarer among us [Germans], because it has two qualities, both of which are either less characteristic of the temperament of present-day Germans, or are obstructed owing to their circumstances: a great warmth and extension of the imagination; and a certain firmness and toughness of the mind. [We lack] the one, because we are stirred by nothing that we cannot conceive of: in order to be filled with concern for one's town, for one's fatherland or for the human race, one must somehow carry their picture everywhere; this picture must be immutable and vivid, if any prevailing inclination of the soul is to emerge from it. [We lack]

the other, because whenever we become very occupied with our own joys and sorrows, they always captivate our heart completely, and leave no room for alien feelings and more remote interests. The man of public spirit must forget his own self, and he must be able to put society in his stead . . . He must be able to fire his imagination to a high degree. Therefore the public spirit is solely the virtue of great souls.

(Garve 1772: 330–2)

For one or two generations after Garve, the *Republik* itself remained, in many German discussions, the repository of great souls: in the present, that of writers and artists and other 'beautiful souls', and, in the dim future, a universal frame to encompass a spiritualised humankind.

This conclusion, Republic Postponed, was only temporarily suspended by the short-term German enthusiasm with the American revolution and the French *Republik*. Such enthusiasm did not involve an attempt to rework German republican traditions, or any other republican legacies, either the living ones of the free towns or the theoretical heirlooms of classical and early modern republicanism, into a new paradigm for modern German statehood. The Scottish attempt at such reworking, and its resonances in the United States and in nineteenth-century Britain, thus remained irrelevant to German political thinking.

12

Neo-Roman Republicanism and Commercial Society: The Example of Eighteenth-century Berne

BELA KAPOSSY

1. The Swiss Republics and Machiavelli

What were the life-chances of republics in the modern world of commerce? According to Montesquieu, whose *Esprit des lois* provided one of the most influential analytical frameworks for thinking about republics in the eighteenth century, the chances seemed very slim indeed. Republics, as he described them, were small, compact, highly motivated polities whose capacity to secure and uphold systems of government based upon laws, not men, depended upon maintaining a strict equality among their citizens. They were, he claimed, unable to cope with the socially dislocating effects of a modern economy; nor, in the long run, were they able to shield themselves from the values and ideals of neighbouring (and more splendid) commercial monarchies. The only way they could maintain the public spirit and patriotic self-denial they needed to survive was under conditions of natural poverty and the constant threat of political annihilation. Montesquieu did admit the possibility of commercial republics, but he insisted that for commerce to remain compatible with both the moral and social requirements of republican politics it had to be driven by necessity and be a central part of a people's continuous struggle for survival. This had been the case with the early Dutch and the early Venetians, who, as he put it, were 'constrained to hide in marshes, on islands, on the shoals, and even among dangerous reefs' and who, in order to live, were forced to draw 'their livelihood from the whole universe' (Montesquieu 1989: 341).

For Montesquieu, as indeed for the large majority of his contemporaries, Venice and Holland had clearly lost their role as model republics and were now no more than warnings about how trading republics could degenerate into plutocratic oligarchies. If Venice had become a fossilised, collective tyranny

227

that maintained its rule over both its citizens and the *terra ferma* through a politics of fear, Holland in turn presented the image of a purely commercial and less than virtuous society, where even 'the smallest things, those required by humanity, are done or given for money' (p. 339). But Holland not only confirmed the corrupting effect of commerce on republican solidarity; to many eighteenth-century writers the decline of Holland exemplified above all the risks that emanated from a nation's disproportionate dependence on a volatile trading economy within an increasingly commercialised Europe, a view neatly summarised by Montesquieu's admirer, La Beaumelle, in his *Mes pensées* (1751): 'The Dutch are no longer redoubtable because they are no longer rich once they stopped being the factors of the universe.'[1]

Montesquieu's unusual revival of the old Machiavellian theme linking liberty with poverty quickly became the starting point for a long cycle of debate about the place of virtue in the politics and economics of the modern world. His assessment of the distinctive attributes and capabilities of republics provided a new set of criteria for making judgments about their prospects in a world in which the future appeared to belong to the large territorial states which had grown up in Europe's recent past. In this debate, the Swiss republics had a particular salience. When eighteenth-century writers were looking for contemporary examples in order to better understand the future prospects of classical republican politics within a commercial Europe, they usually pointed to the republics of the Swiss Federation. 'It is in Switzerland', the French political moralist and indefatigable apologist of the republican principles of Sparta and Rome, Gabriel Bonnot de Mably, wrote in his *De l'étude de l'histoire* (1775), 'that the truest and most natural ideas of society have been preserved'. It was here, he claimed, and here alone that it was still possible to practise the noble ideals of true politics, where 'no man should be sacrificed for another man', where property was inviolable and where the magistrates' authority was founded less on force and 'external decorations' than on their moral integrity and total dedication to the common good (Mably 1977f: 145). Mably was not alone in praising the Swiss republics as the last home of virtue and true liberty. Thinkers as different as Rousseau, Raynal, Hume, Ferguson and Smith adopted, adapted or reworked many of the themes scattered throughout Montesquieu's great book in their various assessments and re-assessments of the claim that it was in the landlocked, agrarian, mountainous Swiss republics, rather than in the

---

1. La Beaumelle 1997: 171. 'Le Hollandais n'est plus redoutable, car il n'est plus riche, depuis qu'il a cessé d'être le facteur de l'univers.'

more splendid maritime trading republics of Venice and Holland, that one could still find an image of ancient politics.

In contrast to Holland, the Swiss republics, it was often (and quite mistakenly) argued, had never fully entered the world of international commerce and finance but had instead maintained much of their initial agrarian simplicity and, as a result, an enviably high degree of political stability : 'si l'état des Suisses est moins brillant que celui de la Hollande', the Italian Carlo Antonio Pilati argued in 1777, 'il est certainement plus solide, & de nature à devoir durer beaucoup plus long tems' (Pilati 1777: 186). It was also essentially for these reasons, namely the absence of the excessive riches which, so Pilati claimed, had led the Dutch 'to imitate the luxury of monarchical states', that 'the Swiss are the only modern people that know and practise that virtue commonly called the love of the fatherland, and of which the other nations don't even have a clear idea' (p. 188). What made the Swiss republics stand out among the remaining free states in Europe and assured them a central position in eighteenth-century debates over ancient versus modern liberty was, above all, their continuing conformity to the image of a traditional military republic and their possession of one of the most effective and successful militias in European history.

Switzerland had gained its reputation as a federation of healthy and quasi-Roman military republics during the fifteenth century, and in particular through its military victories over Charles of Burgundy at Grandson, Murten and Nancy in 1476–7, when the Swiss militias had effectively annihilated one of the largest and technologically most advanced armies in Europe. The defeat of Charles of Burgundy had a tremendous impact on the European political imagination and throughout the early-modern period it was often cited as the single most convincing historical argument in favour of republican politics. The charnel house in Murten containing the skulls of the fallen enemies remained one of the sacred sites of European republicanism and a major attraction for foreign (and notably English) visitors right up to the end of the eighteenth century. The symbolic importance of the Swiss struggle for liberty is perhaps reflected most clearly in the writings of the sixteenth-century Italian humanists, especially Machiavelli, for whom the Swiss military exploits were living proof of the continuing superiority of ancient Roman military politics (Reinhardt 1995; Walder 1944). The Swiss, Machiavelli argued in the *Discorsi*, 'are the only people who still live as the ancients did, being uncorrupted in both their religion and their military service' (Machiavelli 1994: 119); they were 'the best of modern soldiers' (p. 178).

Or, as he put it in Chapter 12 of the *Principe*, they were 'armatissimi e liberissimi' (p. 39).

Machiavelli's praise of the Swiss was not limited to their military exploits. He also praised their constitutional arrangements as an ideal of self-government. What made the Swiss the freest people in Europe, even freer than the German cities, was, above all, the absence of the *gentiluomini*, the feudal lords and rentiers who, as Machiavelli explained in the *Discorsi*, 'live in luxury and without working', and who represented a major internal obstacle to a politics of the common good. While the Italian republics were marked by clientelism, factionalism and political indecisiveness, the Swiss military republics, he believed, were meritocratic, united and able to maintain a strict equality amongst the citizens. It was in this sense that Machiavelli claimed, in his *Ritracto delle cose della Magna*, that the Swiss were not only in a state of *libertà*, but in a state of *libera libertà* (Machiavelli 1979: 352).

Machiavelli's idealisation of the Swiss republics, their militias and constitutional arrangements was picked up by many of the English neo-Roman writers, as can be seen from the diplomatic correspondence between the English parliament and the Swiss Protestant cantons. One of the official addresses to the cantons, written by John Milton, reads:

> We rejoice with all our heart, that you, who with the special help of God and through your courage have more than any other people in Europe fought for your liberty, and have maintained it with great wisdom and moderation for so many years, should praise and think so highly of our newly acquired liberty ... While everything around is full of war and conflict, you yourselves continue to live in a state of good and tranquil peace, and for this reason have for everyone become an example and model to strive for the same peace.
>
> (Anon. 1823: 586–7)

The admiration which many of the Commonwealthmen had for the Swiss republics was well captured by Algernon Sidney who, in his *Discourses concerning Government* (1698), claimed that 'their state is as well settled as anything among men can be, and [we] can hardly comprehend what is likely to interrupt it' (Sidney 1990: 207). A similar tone was struck by the Scottish 'neo-machiavellian' author, Andrew Fletcher, in his advocacy of Scottish militias (1697): 'The Swisses at this day are the freest, happiest, and the people of all Europe who can best defend themselves, because they have the best militias' (Fletcher 1997b: 22). Speculations about the actual size of the Swiss militia remained a popular theme throughout seventeenth- and eighteenth-century political literature; the Venetian ambassador Vendra-mino Bianchi estimated (somewhat enthusiastically) that the 'whole Helvetic Body has Men fit to bear Arms, almost Three hundred thousand' (Bianchi 1710: 144); while the English writer, John Campbell, insisted as late as 1753 that the Swiss continued to remain 'the most unconquerable People in Europe' (Campbell 1753: 466).

II. *SPQB*: The Republic of Berne as a New Rome

What most early-modern foreign writers called 'Switzerland', or 'the Swiss republics', was in fact little else than a loose grouping of very distinct political bodies tied together through a highly complex web of mutual treaties and defensive alliances. The core of the Swiss Federation consisted of thirteen independent republics who were entitled to the lion's share of the incoming foreign pensions and who participated in the rule over the commonly held subject territories. These thirteen republics, or *Orte*, were joined by a number of allies, the *Zugewandten Orte*, which greatly varied not only in size but also in their individual political constitutions. While some of them were cities, like St Gallen, Mülhausen, or Biel, two of them, the prince bishopric of St Gallen and the principality of Neuchâtel, were monarchies. The Valais and the Grisons furthermore were considered as independent federate republics and hence on an equal footing with the thirteen *Orte*. The same complicated arrangements could also be found within the republics themselves, especially the larger ones like Berne or Zurich where some of the municipal towns had managed to maintain a considerable degree of local autonomy (Peyer 1978).

Although the Swiss republics gained formal independence (or, more correctly, *exemption*) from the Empire in 1648, this newly acquired status seems to have had comparatively little effect on Swiss political and legal thought of the late seventeenth and early eighteenth century. From the mid-eighteenth century onwards, however, Swiss thinkers were locked in a sustained and lively debate on the possibility of reforming the late-medieval constitutional heritage of their city republics. There was an especially noticeable increase in the volume of Swiss political literature during the period of the Seven Years War (1756–63), when it looked as if it would be increasingly hard to disentangle the fate of Switzerland from dangerous developments elsewhere in Europe. In light of the vast economic problems of Europe caused by the war, Swiss authors also had to face the problem whether their cherished characterisations of what free states might be allowed to do with their economy, without undermining their political character, might have reached its ultimate limits. When dealing with the vicissitudes of Swiss republicanism in the eighteenth century, modern scholarship has often focused on Rousseau's native city of Geneva, and some scholars have even argued that Rousseau's political writings should be read as the essence of Swiss republicanism. This view would have found little support amongst contemporary observers. Geneva was not identical to Switzerland; it was not even a member (strictly speaking) of the Swiss Federation, the core of which consisted of thirteen independent republics, all with their own very distinctive and highly self-conscious republican traditions. For most Swiss and foreign commentators Geneva was not the flag bearer of Swiss military republicanism but rather its opposite, namely a highly unstable commercial republic which managed to maintain its independence only because of the vital role that it played in the French deficit-based system of public finance. As an alternative to Rousseau in German-speaking countries, readers tended to concentrate on the ambitious and recognisably modern vision of how to accommodate the Swiss republics within the modern European world of commerce which could be found in the writings of the secretary of state of the Republic of Basle, Isaak Iselin. From the mid-1750s onwards Iselin rose to prominence as the author at the forefront of formulating a specifically Protestant theory of modern republicanism which spelled out the conditions needed for a market society to fulfil both the republican and Christian requirements of stability and distributive justice expected in a Swiss city-state. He concentrated his attacks on the protectionist policies of Basle's city guilds not only as economically disastrous but as anti-political and amoral. Iselin developed this vision into a broadly based advocacy of an inclusive and economically competitive republic, and created a magnificent edifice of a complete conjectural history of liberty and of the human mind to support it. His *Philosophische Muthmassungen über die Geschichte der Menschheit* of 1764 had a considerable influence within the German-speaking Enlightenment (especially on Herder who in turn considered him as a precursor of Kant) and foreshadowed many of the key ideas of Swiss commercial republicanism that the founding fathers of the Helvetian Republic later used to distinguish their intellectual position from that of revolutionary France.

In what follows, however, I want to focus neither on Geneva nor Basle, the two most commercial of the Swiss city-states, but on yet another variant of Swiss republicanism, that of the military, aristocratic republic of Berne, and wish to highlight the importance of the Bernese debates on economic and political reform in the second half of the eighteenth century. Bernese patrician reform thinkers proposed a fundamentally different solution to the problem of how best to overcome the modern tensions between politics and the economy from that of their fellow republicans in Geneva and Basle. In contrast to Iselin who hoped to curb the monopolistic policies of the Basle guilds, manufacturers, and financiers by means of opening the markets to competition and by a broadly based system of representative democracy, Bernese patrician thinkers argued that the only way to effectively forestall the corrupting influence of commerce was to opt for a strict separation between the economy and politics and to firmly retain the duty of taking care of the common good in the hands of a virtuous, impartial and economically autonomous military aristocracy. Although Berne was not identical to Switzerland either, nonetheless it was generally believed to be the republic which most clearly captured the traditional image of a flourishing Swiss military republic and came closest to fulfilling the classical Machiavellian ideal of a free state. Thus when thinkers like Hume, Smith, Mirabeau, or Turgot wrote about Switzerland, they hardly ever talked about the commercial Geneva but rather about the agrarian and military republic of Berne. This seems to have already been the view of a number of mid-seventeenth-century English republican writers who hailed Berne as the loyal protector of the exiled regicides like Edmund Ludlow, and for its categorical refusal to succumb to the threats of economic pressure voiced by the English crown. It was also essentially for these reasons – Berne's unconditional international republican solidarity as it were – that during the 1760s the English republican ideologue and editor, Thomas Hollis, donated a substantial part of his library to the republic of Berne (Utz 1959: 88 f.).

Berne was the largest city republic north of the Alps and occupied more than a third of the Federation's territory. Through a consistent expansionist politics Berne had managed to set up a local empire which included the Pays de Vaud in the west, the Oberland and the Aargau in the east. Although most Bernese territorial expansion occurred between the fourteenth and sixteenth century, the republic of Berne continued to be seen, rightly or wrongly, as the republic most hungry for further expansion, and for these reasons was often compared to early Rome. In a report of 1715 the French ambassador, Du Luc, described Berne as a military camp; it 'has everything it needs for war, its granaries have been refilled, and the people are being trained by capable officers' (Du Luc 1889: 392). It was also this image that was picked up by Montesquieu in his *Considérations sur les causes et la grandeur des Romains*, when he identified Berne as a potential new Rome: 'There is at present in this world a republic which no one knows and which secretly and in silence increases her strength each and every day' (Montesquieu 1949–51: II, 120). Montesquieu's association of Berne with ancient Rome became a commonplace in eighteenth-century literature on Switzerland, as in Masson de Pezay's *Soirées helvétiennes*, of 1771, where he claims that 'one of the things that most reminded me of ancient Rome in modern Berne are her public baths' (Masson de Pezay 1771: 331). Most travellers detected the similarity between Berne and Rome less in its baths than in the numerous Bernese public institutions, like the new granary, the orphanages, hospitals, the armoury where visitors were shown the booty that came from the defeat of Charles of Burgundy and especially in the recent network of cantonal roads lined by hour-stones indicating the time it would take to reach the city gates of Berne. Foreigners were fascinated particularly by the so-called *Äussere Stand*, a uniquely Bernese institution which presented a shadow state where younger patricians could familiarise themselves with the workings of the Bernese constitution and acquire the rhetorical skills needed for a later career in politics. The *Äussere Stand* was directly modelled on the actual government; its members could thus become the *Schultheiss* or the *Landvogt* of one of the *Äussere Stand*'s subject territories, which consisted of dilapidated castles that had been destroyed during the early phase of Bernese expansion. Although by the middle of the eighteenth century it had lost much of its initial significance as a republican institute of political education and had acquired the reputation of an exclusive drinking club, for many foreign observers the *Äussere Stand* remained one of the most outstanding examples of Berne's classical republican heritage.

The association of Berne with Rome very much corresponded to how many of the leading Bernese thought about themselves and their republic. The building of the cantonal roads during the 1740s for example was promoted on the grounds that,

> of all the means that the Romans deployed in order to conquer
> their own and other empires and peoples, to keep them in a state
> of obedience, to make them happy, to accumulate treasures, and to
> increase the size of their territory, none was more effective, more
> important and more adequate, than the establishment and
> maintenance of their large country-roads.   (de Capitani 1982: 228)

It was also reflected in the inscription that adorned the various new public buildings and which often contained the formula SPQB, or, as in the case of the city gate, read 'Ponte portisque vetustate lebescentibus cura Reipublica restitutis et ornatis A.V.C. MDCCLX'. An even more open reference to Rome could be found in the inscription added to a newly restored Roman bridge in the Pays de Vaud: 'Pontes et vias collapsas olim Roma nunc Berna restituit' (de Capitani 1982: 229).

The allusions to ancient Rome became a distinctive feature of Bernese patrician culture and played a crucial role in the propaganda that the patriciate wrote in defence of its own aristocratic politics. From the end of the seventeenth century the patriciate presented a strictly separate corps within the Bernese citizenry, which maintained a firm control over the sovereign council of two hundred (Steiger 1954). Entry into the Council of Two Hundred constituted, as the Bernese city librarian and reformer J. R. Sinner aptly put it in 1781, nothing less than the 'souverain bonheur'; not merely because it presented the 'honneur de partager la souveraineté', but also, as he explained, because it allowed a patrician to apply for one of the innumerable administrative posts some of which, like the post of *Landvogt* in one of the richer districts, could be highly lucrative (Sinner 1853: 13). Obviously, Berne was not the only Swiss republic with aristocratic tendencies. Between 1680 and 1713 virtually all Swiss city republics underwent constitutional changes, which in most cases led to the further concentration of political power in the Small Councils. The only exceptions were Basel, St Gallen and Biel, where the respective guild-dominated Great Council managed to fully exert its function as the sovereign body. The process of aristocratisation was most noticeable perhaps in the three Catholic city republics, Lucerne, Freiburg and Solothurn; in Lucerne the ancient right of the citizens to be elected to the Great Council was effectively abolished and became the hereditary prerogative of a small number of select families. In Zurich and Schaffhausen, too, the Small Councils managed to consolidate the power they had acquired over the course of the seventeenth century, although here the aspirations of the Small Councils were checked by the political presence of the guilds (Peyer 1978).

Berne differed in several respects from her Protestant sister-republics. For one, in Berne the guilds had little or no bearing on the political life of the city. More importantly, Bernese patricians, unlike the ruling elites of the other Protestant city republics, notably Basle and Zurich, were virtually all landowners and proprietors of large country houses to which they retreated during the summer months. Financial and entrepreneurial activities of any kind were thereby shunned as lowly professions and discarded as fundamentally incompatible with the status of a magistrate. The continuing aristocratisation of Bernese politics meant that by the 1780s sovereign power was concentrated in the hands of no more than eighty families, which earned the Bernese patriciate the reputation of an oligarchy. Montesquieu had already warned the Bernese, in his *Pensées*, of degenerating into a 'multi-headed monarchy' (Montesquieu 1949–51: 1453), while the English ambassador, Abraham Stanyan, had graphically likened Berne's constitutional arrangements to a pyramid which stood on its head (Stanyan 1714: 105). The attractiveness for many patricians of linking Berne to ancient Rome resided in the fact (or so it was argued) that the Roman model provided a framework of thinking about republican politics in a distinctively aristocratic way, where the emphasis was not so much on the origin of political authority but on the quality of political rule. Bernese patricians hence saw themselves foremost as a Roman-style senatorial elite, a republican *noblesse guerrière* which, owing to its frugality and internal discipline, managed to combine the advantages of a republican rule of law with the generosity of a caring and benevolent paternal government. A telling example of this identification with the military aristocratic ideal of ancient Rome is that of the Bernese magistrate and war hero of the Prussian army, Robert Scipio Lentullus, who traced his family back to the Roman general Lentullus and whose coat of arms showed the inscription *SPQR*.

III. The Paternalistic Régime of the Bernese Aristocracy

The principles of Berne's paternalistic republicanism, which formed the mental horizon of people like Lentullus, were outlined by the patrician historian Alexander Ludwig von Wattenwyl in his *Rede eines Eidgenossen von der Glückseligkeit der Unterthanen unter einer freien Regierung*, published in 1765. The principal aim of his speech was to explain why Bernese subjects, despite being excluded from the political life of the capital, were properly speaking in a state of liberty. Wattenwyl started his apology by making the classic Roman legal distinction between living under the rule of law and living under the will of another person.

> Princes, however just one might imagine them to be, and even if they indeed happened to be just: they always consider their authority as their property; power and violence surround them: how often do they not find themselves in a situation where their private interest collides with that of their subjects? . . . Where then is the security, that makes our homes so dear to us, if the arbitrary will of a human being can deprive us of them?
> (Wattenwyl 1765: 15)

None of this applied to the case of Berne, where, as Wattenwyl argued, the guarantee of law was fully maintained, even in the absence of popular sovereignty or participation, through Berne's complex constitutional arrangements: 'There are so many eyes that watch over the well-being of the entire people ... here one is constantly occupied with the maintaining of a certain balance amongst the members of the government, so that peace inside the state is guaranteed at all times, and the most dangerous ambitions of pride and selfishness are always being opposed and destroyed' (Wattenwyl 1765: 19). Nor were Bernese subjects, in contrast to the subjects living in modern commercial monarchies, forced to carry the financial burden of their ruler's military ambitions. Owing to the patricians' politics of peace, their own military frugality, and their willingness to support public expenditure with their own personal means, the Bernese state apparatus hardly depended at all on tax revenue. This meant, Wattenwyl insisted, that Bernese subjects found themselves in a state of maximum liberty; they could have all the benefits of living under the rule of law and still enjoy fully the advantages that came with the entitlements associated with private property. 'Were those not fathers who opened their treasury in order to provide their children with bread and doctors ... Where can one find rulers, who do not harvest their riches on the heads of their subjects? Who can say with better reason, the bread that I have won is mine and that of my children?' (*ibid*.: 24).

The praise of Bernese liberty, as freedom from personal rule as well as taxation, where the requirements of the state and of national security did not clash with the rights of individuals to private property, can be found in a great number of eighteenth-century Bernese patrician writings, most enthusiastically perhaps in a letter that Albrecht von Haller wrote from Göttingen in 1753, shortly before his return to Switzerland: 'No taxes, no unconstrained minister, no standing army and not the faintest sign of any threatening war! Can one find anything like this in any other place on earth? This is how the golden age has been. Ambition and riches have deprived the rest of the world of it' (Oncken 1886: 22). The fascination of Bernese patricians with their own achievements was shared throughout Europe, and prompted one of the most insightful pre-revolutionary debates on the relation between republican rule and public debt finance. In his *Wealth of Nations*, Adam Smith for example held up Berne as a model of ancient republican 'parsimony' (Smith 1976: 901), while the Göttingen professor Christoph Meiners promoted Bernese patrician rule as a healthy and promising alternative to the debt-ridden and militarily aggressive trading monarchies of Europe:

> In all other large states taxes have been increased to an incredible
> degree, and yet all of these states ... have been swamped by
> immeasurable debts. Berne on the other hand continues to ask from
> its citizens and subjects no more than it did two hundred years ago,
> and has even with these same taxes managed to accumulate
> considerable fiscal treasures.   (Meiners 1788: I, 287)

Not all of the Bernese were as confident about the republican qualities of
patrician rule. The most virulent critique of patrician rule and its republican
pretensions came from the local artisans, who had lost most of their influence
in city politics and who accused the patricians of systematically undermining
the rights and privileges that belonged to all members of the city as a whole.
The attack on patrician rule peaked in 1749 during an attempted coup d'état,
which sought to establish the political role of the city guilds and replace the
patrician *governo stretto* with a more democratic constitution similar to the
one which had been forced through in Basle in 1691. Many of the arguments
that the artisans advanced in their own defence were formulated in terms of
constitutional history and aimed at what they claimed to be their historical
right to be part of the sovereign body. Consequently, the artisans were fiercely
opposed to the patrician neo-Roman ideology which they denounced as an
ideological smoke screen that served to legitimate their usurpatory politics.
We can see this from the manifesto that one of the leaders of the revolt,
the Bernese Samuel Henzi, wrote in defence of their attempted coup d'état,
where he repeatedly attacked the import of Roman vocabulary into Bernese
political language: 'In 1722 they changed the inscription of the great seal
of the city of Berne from *Civitas et Communitas* into *Respublica Bernensis*'
(Henzi 1823: 423). The senatorial pretensions of the patrician class were
likewise condemned as fundamentally 'Machiavellian': 'Recently at the Great
Council someone proposed that the mandates should contain the formula:
Our subjects in town and country [*Stadt und Land*], so that they now even want
to refuse us our citizenship.' The reason for this, as Henzi explained, was to
'wipe out all the remains and traces of the sovereign community of Berne,
so that one could finally be forced to honour merely the *Stand*, rather than
the City of Berne itself' (*ibid.*: 415).

    Criticism of a similar kind was also launched from the subject territo-
ries, especially the Pays de Vaud, which accused the Bernese government of
having deprived them of their liberty to engage freely in trade and commerce.
Here, as in the case of the Bernese artisans, the argument was frequently
expressed in terms of historical rights, such as the manifesto of major Davel
of 1723, where he defended his attempt to liberate the Pays de Vaud from

Bernese rule on the grounds that 'the rights and privileges of various towns of the Pays de Vaud have over the course of time gradually been absorbed' (Davel 1970: 67). The call by Vaudois authors for the restitution of ancient privileges was often accompanied by a further critique that aimed not so much at Vaudois independence from Bernese occupation but, on the contrary, demanded a stronger integration of the provinces into the *respublica* through representation of the local elite within the Bernese Council of Two Hundred and the introduction of constitutional measures to counter the arbitrary character of patrician rule. This critique of patrician politics as incompatible with republican liberty was at the heart of Edward Gibbon's youthful but nonetheless quite remarkable essay, *La Lettre sur le gouvernement de Berne*, written most probably in 1758 during his first stay in Lausanne. To be in a state of liberty, Gibbon argued, required more than simply the absence of constraint, that 'one never sees the sovereign' or that 'one only rarely feels his presence' (Gibbon 1952: 125). Nor were the conditions of liberty fulfilled simply through the sovereign's good will. The liberty to be found in free states, in contrast to the liberty that derived from the good will of a prince,

> consists in being subjected only to laws that aim at the common good of society . . . [I]n a despotic state the prince can at times have a good will: but it is only in a free state that he can will nothing else [but the common good]. The real happiness of a citizen and that of a slave are often the same, but with the difference that while the happiness of the latter is uncertain because grounded on the passions of men, that of the former is assured.   (Gibbon 1952: 130)

As Gibbon described it, the liberty and happiness of the Bernese subjects was neither certain nor assured, but, in the absence of a real representative constitution, depended entirely on the will and fancy of the Bernese oligarchy. Nor, as the alarming state of the Vaudois economy seemed to confirm, was there any strong evidence to suggest that the Bernese régime was particularly good-willed; especially if one compared the history of the Pays de Vaud since the time of occupation to that of other European states, notably France, Holland and England, where a politics of economic development had made 'Barbarians become civilised, ignorant men become enlightened, and the poor become rich' (Gibbon 1952: 131). On Gibbon's account, the people of the Pays de Vaud suffered the same fate as did the Roman people under the rule of Titus who, despite the republican propaganda of its leader, had been forced into a state of servitude. Moreover, by failing to set up a modern economy as the basis of a new alignment between commerce and the Christian Enlightenment, Gibbon argued that the Bernese were now repeating the very same mistakes that had led to the downfall of the Roman republic. Even earlier, in his Swiss travel diary of 1755, Gibbon had voiced his perplexity at the Bernese indifference to the lessons of the past: 'The Bernese have studied history, so why have they not noticed that the same causes produce the same effects?' (Gibbon 1952: 53).

IV. The *Economic Society* of Berne and the Critique of the Bernese *Ancien Régime*

I next want to consider a third kind of critique of the Bernese patrician régime, one that emanated neither from the artisan community, nor from the subject territories, but rather from a group of often younger patricians who were deeply anxious about the future prospects of the Bernese aristocracy. Although they were highly sensitive to the oligarchic tendencies of the patriciate, these reformers firmly subscribed to a neo-Roman view of Bernese aristocratic politics and they spent a great deal of energy in refuting Henzi's guild-centred history of the Bernese constitution. A good example of this neo-Roman reading of early Bernese history is Vincent Bernard Tscharner's article 'Bern', first published in 1775, where he argued that Berne had begun as a free aristocratic 'military colony' and was founded with the direct purpose of countering the ambitions of the Burgundian aristocracy:

> From these kinds of colonies, that were constantly engaged in military exercises, one could expect a greater capacity of forestalling the ambitions of the enemies and for expanding their territory at the latter's expense, than is usually the case with merchants and artisans, who think of nothing else but to hide from passing dangers and to make safe their possessions behind the city walls.
>
> (Tscharner 1782: 123; Stoye 1954)

The question that the patrician reformers like Vincent Tscharner most frequently addressed in their writings and speeches was thus less concerned with political reform as such, than with the economic and cultural conditions needed for Berne to fulfil the requirements of its Roman republican heritage.

The commitment of the patrician reformers to the ideals of neo-Roman politics was at the centre of a series of annual lectures that Tscharner initiated in 1757 at the *Äussere Stand* and which specifically aimed to promote the image of early Berne as a model of Roman republicanism. The condition of neo-Roman politics, and especially of the neo-Roman notion of liberty, Tscharner argued in his opening speech, were fully realised under the impending threat of political annihilation, when it became clear that it was 'better to be small under the laws than to be distinguished in a state of slavery' (Walthard (ed.) 1773: 20). It was 'the need of the fatherland that makes all citizens become soldiers. They do not fear any dangers, because they fear slavery more than any other danger' (p. 21). And finally, it was 'the common danger which brings all together into a strict unity' and which convinced the citizens that their individual liberty depended entirely on the fate of the city itself and its capacity to remain free from foreign subjugation (p. 19). Tscharner's insistence on external threat as an ideal condition for Roman republicanism was picked up by many subsequent speakers, most enthusiastically perhaps by the pro-Bernese historian Johannes von Müller, in his influential essay, *Considérations sur le gouvernement de Berne*, of 1781, where he held up the early phase of Bernese history as a model of republican social cohesion. The subjects of Berne, Müller claimed, 'never asked how far the power of the Small Council went, but where the enemy could be found. The government in turn considered the people not as their subjects but as comrades in arms...and the time of true liberty was when no one spoke about it' (Müller 1810–19: XXVII, 68). For the patrician reformers, it was this complete identification of the citizens and subjects with the ideals of the body politics which had allowed the republic to flourish and to pursue a politics of expansion which, as several of the speakers insisted, was more successful than that of the early Roman republic. As the jurist Johann Rudolf Tschiffeli put it, 'Berne has had during its first three hundred years a greater destiny than Rome during the same period, it has produced equally great men, defeated greater enemies, and conquered a larger territory' (Walthard (ed.) 1773: 63). For Tschiffeli, the strong similarity between early Berne and Rome equally served to explain the way in which the city was to relate to its subject territories: 'Wise as Rome, courageous as its citizens, Berne uses the same policies in the same circumstances. Far from destroying the defeated enemy, it becomes one of the first principles of reconciliation that he should become a supporter, a fellow protector, a citizen of the state. His fortresses become comparatively open houses of the republic' (*ibid.*: 77).

One of the central problems that the then Bernese régime had to face, as the patrician reformers discovered during the course of the lecture series, was how to preserve this high degree of public spiritedness and social cohesion, when it looked as if the Bernese republic had lost much of its capacity for

territorial expansion and was no longer under the constant threat of external military aggression. The Bernese reformers were fully aware that they
were asking a crucial question of Enlightenment thinking from within the
republic which many eighteenth-century observers considered as the most
healthy republic in Europe, and during the 1760s and 1770s they were actively
engaged in trying to make Berne become the platform for a European debate on the possibilities and conditions of republican reform. A great effort
in this direction came from the unfortunately short-lived *Patriotic Society*,
founded in 1762 by the jurist Daniel von Fellenberg, which maintained close
and amicable links to such insatiable propagators of Roman republicanism
as Rousseau and Mably and which solicited intellectual support from such
eminent Enlightenment figures as Adam Smith, John Brown, Kames, Herder,
Sulzer, Algarotti and Helvetius, to name but a few (Guggisberg 1951;
Mülinen 1900).

However, the real intellectual centre of the patrician reform debates was
the newly founded *Economic Society*, set up by Tschiffeli in 1759. The leaders
of the society, notably the brothers Niklaus Emanuel and Vincent Bernard
Tscharner, the city librarian and later *Landvogt* Samuel Engel, and Emanuel
von Graffenried, were all holders of relatively minor positions within the
public administration. In the 1760s the *Economic Society*, helped by its republican credentials, acquired a European reputation as one of the leading centres
in Europe for the promotion and dissemination of agrarian thinking. We
can readily see this from the long list of honorary members, correspondents
and contributors to the Society's journal, the *Mémoires et observations recueillies par la Société Oeconomique de Berne*, which included writers like Mirabeau,
Turgot, the marquis Turbilly, count Berndorf, William Bell, Karl Friedrich
margrave of Baden-Durlach, to name but a few, who regularly provided the
Bernese editors with first-hand accounts of new developments at the cutting
edge of the continent's intellectual life and reinforced their confidence in
seeing themselves as spokesmen for the last genuinely republican state in
Europe (Bäschlin 1913: 281 ff.).

v. Neo-Roman Investments: Berne and the Financial Crisis of the Seven Years War

The reform programme of the Bernese 'economic patriots', who wished to
transform Berne into an economically autonomous, agrarian republic, needs
to be understood within the context of the debates on the expected collapse
of the public debt systems of the large European nations, especially those
of France and England, that took place at the outset of the Seven Years War.

Berne itself was proud of not having any debts, and for these reasons was often cited as a paragon of political wisdom and stability. In fact Berne was more than debt-free, it was running a system of fiscal surplus – and it was this surplus which led to the republic's entanglement with the crisis of the war finance of the major belligerent states of Europe. Berne's role in international public debt finance was through its role as a major investor in the debts of other states, notably England, Holland and various German principalities. The republican reformers (with a few exceptions) were highly sceptical about the long-term stability of European public debt finance, and hence one of the major concerns of people like Tschiffeli or the Tscharner brothers was precisely to prepare Berne for the sudden bankruptcy of any one of Berne's debtors and to counteract the disastrous consequences of such an event for the internal stability of the republic. This concern seemed entirely justified, since the revenues from Berne's investments in European state papers amounted to almost a third of the entire public revenue and were thought to play a crucial role in the patrician class's paternalist policy of promoting low taxation and generous public welfare programmes (Landmann 1903: 9). The importance which leading patricians attributed to Berne's policy of investing in European public debts from the point of view of the future prospects of preserving the Bernese aristocratic régime can be seen from a speech that Carl Friedrich Steiger gave at the *Äussere Stand* in 1784 where he, in contrast to the critical stance of the agrarian reformers of the *Economic Society*, praised the policy of foreign investments as the genuine modern equivalent of Machiavellian politics. Thanks to its foreign investments, Steiger argued, virtuous Berne was able to profit 'from the very causes, that in all places bring about nothing but misery and destruction' and thereby to fortify its 'power and liberty' (Steiger 1952: 30). All those Bernese public institutions and alms-houses, and the government's highly expensive policy of maintaining grain reserves which, as Steiger insisted, ensured the loyalty of the subjects, depended entirely on the income from the republic's investments: 'these manifold good deeds of the government ... would have never been realised without the aid of foreign finance ... Perhaps no state draws less advantage from its members [than does Berne]; no subjects enjoy more benefits from the state (*ibid.*: 36, 37).

It is thus important to realise that the critical attitude of the 'economic patriots' towards Berne's policy of foreign investments was not fuelled by moral scruples about the fact that Berne happened to profit from the wars of other states or that the fiscal largesse of the patricians toward Berne's own subjects was financed by ever-increasing taxation in the countries which were Berne's debtors. They fully subscribed to the Machiavellian (and in the case of V. B. Tscharner to the Rousseauvian) understanding of international relations as a state of persistent hostility and to the idea that the source of political and moral values should be sought within rather than outside the republic. Nor did they perceive the patrician policy of generous public welfare programmes as in any way detrimental to the republican requirements of maintaining a strictly impersonal régime of legality. Although the Bernese reform thinkers repeatedly warned of the negative effects that public charity might have on productivity, they considered both the fiscal surplus and the public provision of welfare as necessary measures in a republic that wished to accept, and indeed respect, the principles of private property. This point was neatly summarised by Johannes von Müller in 1774, when he claimed (with explicit reference to Machiavelli) that 'the maintenance of a republic requires a public cash reserve; and to rely on nothing but the hearts of the citizens is a chimera [propagated] by those who don't know men' (Müller 1810–19: xv, 381). If there was a reason to be critical of Berne's European investment policies, it was rather that they prevented the Bernese republic from fulfilling its promise of rising to Rome's greatness by undermining the republic's independence and hence its sovereign capacity to initiate political action when it saw fit. The 'economic patriots', count Zinzendorf noted in his study of the Bernese reform debates, 'wish to argue that the high interest rates were bound to generate luxury and that by investing the state's capital [Berne becomes] too closely aligned with the interest of other states' (Zinzendorf 1936: 306–7).

One of the most frequently voiced fears, as Zinzendorf rightly observed, was that the interest which both the republic of Berne and various of its leading families received from foreign funds served as a vehicle for the import of distinctively non-republican, courtly values of conspicuous consumption, politeness and decoration, and as a result corroded the old Bernese spirit of equality which, as Niklaus Emanuel Tscharner insisted in a letter to Iselin of July 1769, was one of the fundamental conditions of republican rule: 'In a free state a sovereign should not neglect . . . the physical equality amongst the citizens, which can be maintained through sumptuary laws. For the more [equality] we can find in a free state, the more perfect it will be' (Wälchli 1964: 164). Moreover, the dependence on foreign funds placed considerable strain on the citizens' loyalty towards their own polity, transforming the traditional republican social bonds of military fraternalism into an open, commercial society. Patriotism thus understood simply became a matter of profit maximisation, while the old term of 'citizen', as Tscharner complained in another letter to Iselin of October 1777, meant little more than a person who was 'an inhabitant of a city, a member of a public, who has no other connection to the body politic than his self-interest. A political butterfly who, once he has fed himself on one flower, flies off to the next' (*ibid.*: 238).

The investment policies also had a more direct impact on Berne's capacity for political action in that its fortune and, as the reformers feared, even political survival was rendered hostage to the economic and military success or otherwise of its debtor nations. Adam Smith, in his discussion of the Bernese case in Book v of the *Wealth of Nations*, gave a similarly critical assessment of the political risks attached to Berne's public investments policy.

> The security of this revenue must depend, first upon the security
> of the funds in which it is placed, or upon the good faith of the
> government which has the management of them; and secondly, upon
> the certainty or probability of the continuance of peace with the debtor
> nation. In the case of war, the very first act of hostility, on the part of
> the debtor nation, might be the forfeiture of the funds of its creditor.
>
> (Smith 1976a: 820)

For many Bernese reformers it was precisely the republic's subjection to the 'good faith' of a debtor nation that prevented Berne from fulfilling its Roman potential and from acquiring the qualities inscribed in the Roman ideal of a free state. The idea that economic dependence was incompatible with the requirements of a free state for absolute political self-determination had already been strongly promoted in the lectures at the *Äussere Stand*, as for example in the speech of Emanuel von Graffenried, where he urged his listeners to 'despise all these golden chains with which one tries to bind you! live in such a way that you can be content with what you possess! ... Whoever can make us rich or poor has more power over us than we think' (Walthard (ed.) 1773: 76). We can also find it at the heart of the early debates organised by the members of the *Economic Society* where they promoted the necessity of agrarian reforms on the grounds that self-subsistence in matters of primary goods was an elementary prerequisite for Bernese liberty. '[W]e are in a state of dependence with regard to our neighbours', Jean Bertrand argued in his essay of 1760, for 'it cannot be denied that whenever a country is incapable of feeding its inhabitants, it is dependent [*dans la dépendence*] upon the state from whom it is forced to receive its subsistence' (Bertrand 1760: 103). The same point was made by E. von Graffenried: 'Agriculture is the principal foundation of the liberty of a state, and we might well one day be forced to pay the price for our negligence by losing the liberty which our ancestors bought at the price of their blood' (1762: 56). It was also through the encouragement of its agriculture that Berne could best revive the Roman military culture and civic-mindedness that had served the early republic on its path to glory.

vi. The Beginning of the End: The Bernese Aristocracy and the French Revolution

While the editorial activities of the *Economic Society* found an echo throughout Enlightenment Europe, in Berne itself they met with rather little enthusiasm, especially from those patrician families who derived their livelihood from foreign funds and French pensions. In 1766, when the editors published a statistical essay on Berne's population, the government even deemed it necessary to subject the Society to strict supervision. The reformers' highly critical understanding of the tensions between neo-Roman patriotism and foreign investments nevertheless had a great impact on Bernese political discourse, especially during the 1790s, when the foreign investments were seen as perhaps the chief reason for the unexpected sympathy of the local patrician elites towards the French revolutionary cause. No one was surprised that the Genevans were caught up in the fiscal catastrophe of the tottering French monarchy. The events there were well captured by the Göttingen professor, Meiners, in his *Briefe über die Schweiz* of 1788:

> What will happen to all these lethargic millionaires, and what will happen to the city if the credit of the French court was to sink once again? I think it is a terrible situation if the well-being of the entire city, or at least that of the most respected families, depends on the good-will or the fate of a powerful debtor.   (Meiners 1788: ii, 325–6)

The Bernese, whose empire bordered on Geneva, also noticed this and feared its consequences for themselves too. Impending danger was clearly the impression of Karl Victor von Bonstetten, when arguing, in a letter to Frederike Brun of September 1791, that

> the great interest in the fate of the French has its real source in the French funds, especially in the life pensions. I am not saying too much if I claim that the entire wealth of individual families in Geneva and the Pays de Vaud is placed in the French funds. This is how the political ideas of the citizens became attached to their purse, that is to say to their heart. They feared that bankruptcy (a horrible ghost) would return to the throne with royal power and breathe hunger and despair over this land.   (Bonstetten 1997: 513)

Views similar to Bonstetten's criticism of foreign investments as the nemesis of Bernese liberty increasingly became a staple item in a great number of patrician and other pro-Bernese pamphlets and speeches at the time and regularly appear in Bernese correspondence. Even Gibbon, who from his Lausanne perspective had usually nothing good to say about Bernese rule, was reported to have accused the bourgeoisie of the Pays de Vaud of being '*rentocrats* to whom the present [French] system appeals only because they believe that it will secure their revenues' (La Roche 1793: 67). But the devastating effects of this financial patriotism were believed to have been nowhere more visible than in Berne itself, where, as the marquis de Bouillé later recalled, the speculations on the *assignats* and French life annuities effectively split the patriciate into two opposing camps, thereby importing French Genevan corruption into the very heart and political core of the republic of Berne: 'most of the Swiss officers who had served in France and who, like many old families, had received pensions from the king of France, had now become open supporters of the revolution; of course the new government had promised them the continuation of their salaries in the name of the nation' (Bouillé 1822: 364). The catastrophe for Berne was near. The mantle of the new Rome had passed over to France, and in 1798 the Directory intervened militarily in Switzerland. The Corsican general Napoleon Bonaparte had advocated intervention in order to dominate the strategic routes between France and Milan. But the French Republic and its army also desperately needed financing for their republican military ventures, and Napoleon thus desired to seize the treasury of Berne to bankroll his overseas expedition in Egypt. In February 1798 the French invaded Switzerland, crushed initial resistance, occupied Berne, and looted vast sums of money from the city republic's famed treasury, and with the support of a significant minority of the urban population imposed a new constitution upon the Swiss people. The creation of the Helvetian Republic was the end of Berne's dreams of being a new Rome. When liberty and independence returned to Berne after the French occupation the city republic and its wealth rose again from the ashes of the devastation by the new neo-Romans of France, but this liberty was not any more that of the ancients but of the moderns. Berne earned a new reputation, together with Switzerland, as an agent of peace rather than military virtue. The habit of investing in Europe survived and has gone from strength to strength ever since.

13

Republicanism and Commercial Society in Eighteenth-century Italy

ELUGGERO PII[†]

In the eighteenth century, before the treaty of Aix-la-Chapelle was signed in 1748, Italy was made up of states large and small, a kaleidoscope which coalesced and dissolved continually in accordance with the ever-changing alliances between the monarchies of Europe. Whereas those actively engaged in the practice of politics took good care to adapt to the changes, the *literati* showed a tendency to search for common themes with a view to launching a debate in opposition to the armed might of the victorious powers. That explains why, in the context of the highly varied situation that pertained in Italy, they found in the republican tradition an important element of cohesion, based on two factors: the first arising from the palpable existence of concrete realities – in the shape of states like Venice, Lucca, Genoa and San Marino – which offered living proof of the resistance offered by the republican form of government to the monarchical system of the great kingdoms of Europe; and the second, of a cultural nature, deriving from the memory of republican Rome transmitted through the literary genres and styles of the local academies in accordance with the tired gestures of academic life, enlivened from time to time by an occasional burst of energy.

But if republican sentiment had difficulty, understandably, in fulfilling the role of guardian of republican memory whilst striving to accommodate itself to conditions of everyday reality, it did not find it any easier to foster a lively ideological debate, and even less to transform itself into a fully elaborated system. Without ever ceasing to be present, it was driven underground, and it remained fragmentary and for the most part implicit within a discourse that was obliged to conform to realities. On the one hand, it expressed the need to legitimise its own existence which had continually to be reaffirmed if it was to be sustained (Venice carried on doing this for a long time), and on the other it constituted an acknowledgment of the fact that recourse to republicanism was more or less dependent on future political arrangements arising from the wars of succession (first of Spain, then of Poland and finally of Austria) and from events connected with the disappearance of the great princely houses (such as the Medicis and the Estensi). The aim indeed of much of this republican literature was to establish the validity of the Italian states' claim to the authenticity of the origins of their freedom and of their exercise of self-rule which would serve as a bargaining counter in negotiations with their new masters (Spanish or Austrian, under the watchful eye of France and Great Britain) over the latter's proposals for setting up centralised forms of government. But if the characteristic note of opposition to despotism emerges clearly from the texts, the development of the themes of republicanism, liberty and self-rule remains marked by the instrumental nature of the expression, without managing to form an autonomous republican discourse. There was another obstacle too. In Europe at this time reality and the cultural debate were both undergoing radical transformation: the affirmation of forms and styles that contributed to the definition of commercial society had a profound influence on the arguments involved in republican discourse. The basic principles of virtue and liberty were discussed in the light of the qualities that trade demanded. In Italy it was inevitable that the revival of republicanism should maintain a disparity between tradition and a present which for its part was complicated by opaque realities, often on the fringes of the centres of decision-making and production.

If Italian historians agree about the presence of a republican discourse they differ in their evaluation of its intensity and capacity for development.[1] Such a mosaic of facts implies difficult choices for the historian in the search for a suitable perspective with which to represent it. There is no individual situation or particular person capable of summing up the diversity, and yet to take as point of departure an examination of the most significant cases would mean losing sight of the wood for the trees. At the risk of excessive generalisation, therefore, it is preferable to present some points of connection which, although they do not constitute the whole picture, represent important

1. For a rather weak interpretation of the role of republicanism in eighteenth-century Italy, which became a point of reference for an entire strand of Italian historiography see Diaz 1973. Much more fundamental guides to the research on this issue are Procacci 1965 and Rosa 1964. For the general framework see Venturi 1970. Particular attention has been paid to the case of Venetian republicanism, which has often been seen as an 'active presence', as in Venturi 1990. The position of Del Negro 1986 appears to be more lukewarm.

    In this chapter I follow the traces of the 'Machiavellian moment' (see Pocock 1975), taking a domestic trajectory for my research. My point of reference for the study of the significance of republicanism, republican virtue and liberty is the definition found in Skinner 1984, 1986 and 1990a.

aspects of it, providing elements for discussion and laying down markers for future research. With that aim in mind I have divided my paper into four sections, each dealing with one of the following themes: i) The republic of the *literati*; ii) Venice in the looking-glass; iii) Vico's heroic republic; iv) The republic of merchants. Since it is necessary to proceed in this way by snapshots, as it were, I shall review my initial selection at the end.

i. The republic of the *literati*

When the War of Spanish Succession was already well under way, and while the disputes between the European dynasties heralded new arrangements within Italy too, Ludovico Antonio Muratori wrote from Modena to the *literati* scattered among the academies of the peninsula with the proposal that they join together in a 'literary republic' (1704) to represent Italy in the Europe of culture. His proposition-proclamation already contained the outlines of a statute: the members were to elect a senate of archons, from whom the first archon was to be chosen, and he was to be assisted in his turn in the government of the republic by two censors and by a secretary-member deputed to undertake the task of cataloguing errors and abuses in the sciences. The qualities required of people wishing to join such a republic were a 'virtuous desire for glory' and a disinterested love of culture, while its aims were defined as a commitment to expand and perfect the arts and the sciences through communication and regular peer-appraisal. So what was demanded of an ideal member were such virtues as merit, honour, the love of truth and the sacrifice of personal interest on the altar of the common good (Muratori 1964), resulting, in brief, in a virtuous man of letters whose perfect reference was the fact that he belonged to a *republic*.

It is obvious that the very name of such a perceived need echoed other contemporary cultural projects in Europe (one thinks for example of Pierre Bayle's *Nouvelles de la république des lettres*), but Muratori, while going well beyond envisaging merely an 'Italian section', sought to stamp his project with a national character and to create an ideal unity capable of being superimposed on a rather differently structured reality. The discussion which Muratori's project gave rise to encouraged the *literati* to work towards a unity which would, *ipso facto*, be able to afford them a sense of self-identity. This was the climate which fostered scholarly research and attempts at a general historiography from which emerged, in the 1720s and 1730s, images of a 'free Italy' in response to what had progressively been established in various treaties – those of Utrecht, Rastadt, London, Vienna, Turin and so on – and in the realm of the theatre this same climate led to the exploration in tragic drama of the motif of tyrants being put to death and of republican governments being lauded to the skies. The Italian *literati* got the message, and if they kept their activities within the bounds of literary scholarship, they conducted themselves from that point onwards as members of the republic, with literary society modelling itself on an ideal of political society. It was of course not a case of independent individuals; what was involved here was in large part a fiction, but that is not to gainsay the fact that the charade forged a link between the society of men of letters and the new civil society, or as they put it, the '*res publica civile*' (their version of the *res publica* of the Romans), directing scholarly study towards the search for 'useful' themes. Behind Muratori's proposal lay a political need, but it was precisely around this need that ideological uncertainties and an awareness of practical realities tended to focus. In this way the subject of reform of the sciences, of the utility of literature, and of the quest for '*felicità pubblica*' ('public happiness') came to dominate learned discourse, but the practical impact of all this proved to be rather more problematical.

The elements of a republican discourse were present, but so were – and to the same degree – the difficulties hindering their development. The possibilities for republicanism can be measured and observed withering on the vine as soon as a way is sought if not to surpass, at least to consider and calculate the gap between the dimension of the literary project and that of the political schema. When the discourse required some connection with reality, on the eve of the advent of enlightened reformism, in Muratori the very term 'republic' (but the same would have gone for 'monarchy') was being diluted to refer to the entirety of the well-governed subjects of a considerate prince. 'I have used the word "republic"', he wrote, 'and it must be considered that everyone has to understand a truth thereby: that is, that even if a state is governed by its prince, its people do not on that account stop being a society and a republic whose leader is this prince and whose members are its subjects' (Muratori 1964: 1518).

Let us take the case of Tuscany. The anticipated demise of the house of the Medici set in train (between the first decade of the eighteenth century and 1737, when a solution was found) a particularly intense burst of diplomatic activity involving the courts of Europe in which the Tuscans sought to have their say too. As more or less everywhere in Italy, a new way of making history was being worked out. Its intention was quite explicit: it could be said, to put the matter simplistically, that the quality of the product was being extolled in order to make sure that it was treated with respect. In 1721 a professor of law at the university of Pisa, Giuseppe Averani, wrote in Latin and in French a *Mémoire sur la liberté de l'état de Florence*. The text recalled the city's communal origins and its struggles to safeguard its freedom with such conviction that the *Signoria* of the Medici was presented as a choice desired and sanctioned by the popular consensus; Averani then called for this decision-making power to be restored to the people. His *Mémoire* was aimed at diplomats, and through them at the sovereigns of Europe. It would be interesting to find out what were the repercussions of its circulation among the royal courts, but we do know its outcome: that the Grand Duchy would be assigned to a foreign dynasty.

It is probably more interesting to consider the internal reverberations of the *Mémoire*. If what strikes us at first sight is the naïvety, for the period, of its pretensions (it called for the official recognition of the right to autonomy founded on history), we are confronted with the most serious commitment on the part of a group of men, that of the *literati* to which Averani belonged. Some of them were members of the nobility: they included the Buondelomonti, the Niccolini, the Bottari and the Bandini, aristocrats who a few years later played host to Montesquieu during his visit to Italy, and a couple of decades afterwards put on a very short season given over to a republican reading of *The Spirit of the Laws*. As men who, in their discussions about freedom and self-rule, sought to avenge the Florentine republic against the Medici government, they placed once more centre-stage the ideals of republican virtue and liberty, and in laying the foundations of their resistance to the Lorrainers, rapidly took on the role of defenders of an ideal and of representatives of an opposition which, outside the rituals of the cult, stayed always in the shadows. In reality, however, they busied themselves with restoring to favour in their homeland of Italy the name and work of Niccolò Machiavelli: as republicans they looked tacitly towards the *Discorsi* and the *Storie fiorentine*, and contributed material to the oblique interpretation of his writings. A careful search in the family archives (Giuliano de' Ricci's copy of the original manuscript was discovered in 1726) and the conscientious exegesis of the sources made possible the preparation of the reconstitution of a documented biography (to replace the fancifulness of legend) and of the important Tuscan editions which were to follow in the 1760s and 1780s (1760 and 1782). Machiavelli kept alive the cult of republican virtue and provided justification for the condemnation of imperial Rome, while at the same time supplying a model of self-government; above all, though, his name sanctified the relationship between freedom and virtue, a link so nourished in people's consciousness that before they began thinking of it in terms of self-government they were convinced it needed to acquire the weight and depth of a passion.

In its search for concrete outcomes where republican awareness was concerned, however, the next generation was to discover in its impact with reality the full extent to which these feelings were found to be bereft of defences: the Lorrainers had in the meantime set up shop in Tuscany and were looking for people to work with, and the Treaty of Aix-la-Chapelle (1748) having finally stabilised Italian internal arrangements in their entirety, the *literati* of the republic saw themselves once again obliged to confront particular situations which required them to adapt to a general European situation characterised by important changes.

Still within the Tuscan context, in 1756 another law professor at the university of Pisa, Giovanni M. Lampredi, made no secret of the fact that in his view the only régime capable of safeguarding the people's liberty was republican government. He went so far as to seek proof of his assertions in pre-Roman Italy; he found that the reasons for the power and happiness of the ancient Etruscans lay in the form of self-rule which was exercised within each community, and in the fact that these communities, having grouped themselves together in a federal republic for the purpose of defending their individual freedom, were strongly united by their love of independence and by their patriotism, always a key element in republican virtue. Four years later, in 1760, Lampredi produced an edition of the *Opere inedite* by Machiavelli, 'the spirit of an authentic and free republicanism', and included in it a text that had not appeared before, the *Ragionamento sul governo di Firenze*. At the same time he published a new book on the Etruscans, *Del governo civile degli antichi Toscani* (Lampredi 1760). But the accent had shifted in this work from the 'grandeur' to the 'decadence' of the Etruscans. Lampredi's argument presupposed the questions raised by Machiavelli's distinction between the 'republics that wish to stay the way they are' and the 'republics that seek to extend their borders'. He latched in particular on to the fourth chapter of Book II of the *Discorsi* which deals with the decadence of the Etruscans. However, Machiavelli appears to have served merely as a pretext: Lampredi's concern was to focus on the contemporary issue of the preservation of states, and the present influenced the way he envisaged the origin and nature of liberty itself. If Machiavelli was inclined to attribute the cause of the Etruscans' fate to moral laxity verging on complete oblivion where their own identity was concerned, Lampredi offered detailed analyses in pursuance of his denunciation of the limits of self-rule. Equality and liberty, he argued, sustain republican governments, but as soon as 'industry' and 'commerce' make their effects felt on the body social, 'the forces of all the small elements that go to make up ordinary society' start rushing off in all directions (Lampredi 1760). Here Lampredi was getting to the nub of the great eighteenth-century question, that of the relationship between virtue and commerce, and of the balance of power within contemporary European mercantile society.

Could republican sentiment withstand the attack by special interest groups? The breach had after all been opened up by Machiavelli; people who drew their inspiration chiefly from the cult of the Florentine gradually lost sight of his true message and found support in Montesquieu through the medium of Chapter 19 of *The Spirit of the Laws*. Lampredi asserted that republics could not aspire to the power of monarchies. Denouncing the limits of republicanism, he claimed that freedom sprang from adversity and was nourished by it; in that sense, however, liberty was not a concept or acquired condition but rather a natural given, linked to the human situation and thus subject to change. Republics were obliged to stay within the confines of a limited, infertile territory; they had to try and remain in their original state without modification, restricting themselves to the economics of trade, not seeking expansion, and could not, without grave loss, abandon austerity and live in comfort. Whereas beforehand origins constituted an argument in favour of the present, now they represented on the contrary an obstacle which prevented people from subscribing to them. In his conclusion, finally, Lampredi suggested that once a clear differentiation was established between the various components of society they could not be ruled by any form of self-government: the binary of liberty and virtue was broken, ceasing to belong to a civic unity or a social group (the intermediary bodies or the community, in a word the 'numerous forces' of the totality); prosperity was the compensation offered for the loss of freedom, virtue being transferred to the Prince, an enlightened despot, and the man of letters, formerly a member of the literary republic, became a state functionary. With Lampredi republicanism began to look for its own content in the reformism of the Enlightenment, and the reading of Machiavelli provided *despotisme éclairé* with legal arguments legitimised by tradition. The republicanism of the *literati* got bogged down in the present; if, at the beginning of the eighteenth century, its revival had had an anti-despotic function, the role now assigned to it was one of backing the authority of a single individual, that is, a form of legal despotism.

And yet, among the citizens of the republic of the *literati*, one of them – no marginal figure, indeed rather a well-known one – strove for about forty years (from *Vita civile*, published in 1710, to *Il politico moderno*, 1740) to gain acceptance, in the face of contemporary despotism, for a project to draw up the constitution of a 'feasible republic'. Paolo Mattia Doria, a Genoese by birth who took up residence in Naples, was among the first in Italy to grasp the significance of what Machiavelli was proposing, and he devoted himself to putting into practice the teachings of the Florentine statesman who had embarked on a close study of history in order to show how states were constructed. Having found in the history of Rome the reasons for the success and validity of the binary of liberty and virtue, understood as love of personal independence and love of country, Machiavelli proposed in consequence a republican model. Doria saw that day-to-day activities, just like great actions and heroic enterprises, had to be inspired by an ideal that was higher than the very contingencies of the event, both quotidian and heroic. Linking Plato and Machiavelli in this way, Doria introduced the ideal into factual reality, and from the grafting of the one on to the other the project of his 'feasible republic' was born, and it was from this viewpoint that he conducted his analysis of contemporary European history. He made a distinction within political activity between a 'science of the state' on the one hand and a 'politics' on the other; in other words he separated the main thrust of government involving the functioning of the state from the principles that inspired it but did not reside in governmental practice. The science of state normally prevailed over politics; princes and their ministers, who were at that time following a 'science of the state', strained every sinew to regulate a (mercantile) 'politics of commerce', entrusting the 'force' of the state to 'commerce'. But in this depressing picture there was a positive model, that represented by the Dutch republic. The Dutch practised the politics of commerce, but their actions were guided by a love of their free country; such a feeling was civic virtue, which made republican citizens out of the Dutch people; in following the 'science of state' they pursued economic prosperity while holding fast to liberty, which was the effect of 'politics'.

It was rare for the specific character of the forms of republican government to be put forward in the shape of a political project as clearly as they were by Doria, an aspect of whose significance was not lost on Montesquieu. But Doria became increasingly suspicious and critical of the 'natural practical commercial politics' of modern states: that was why during the 1740s he changed his mind about Holland too: as had happened in Venice and Genoa, the rich aspired to suppress popular liberties and transform the democratic republic into an aristocratic one. If anyone undermined the bonds of virtue, freedom was imperilled; republics died and monarchies – in other words tyrannies – took their place. Doria had reached the central question in his research: was the continued existence of virtue and liberty possible when the state of necessity had been left behind? In other words, could virtue and freedom coexist with prosperity, comfort, luxury and a life of leisure? There was, Doria believed, one European country where the benign effects of a commercial politics seemed reconcilable with political freedom, and that was England. Contrary to what might have been expected, it was not the form of English government which was being valued here: Doria confined himself to pointing out that the guarantor of the freedom of the English people was the House of Commons. So although he hinted at an institutional answer to his question, it was not the path that he followed: he showed that the liberty of the English stemmed from a natural disposition, so that they were free 'by nature' and not 'by virtue'. So if England was able to be a free nation, it did not for all that offer a model which could be imitated.

Yet education and human effort were close to 'nature'. Doria's reasoning led him to affirm the superiority of the 'moral discipline' of citizens; philosophers were the guarantors of the linkage between virtue and liberty, and the dangers of modern times were remedied by subordinating 'the practice of trade to the principles of metaphysics'. Doria's proposal was so absolute that when his book *Idea d'una perfetta repubblica* was published posthumously in 1753, the critique of monarchy offered in it was so strong that the volume was ordered to be burnt by the public executioner. If republican sentiment was strong in Doria, it had obvious limitations in practice. His vision of commerce was confined to considering it subject to the 'politics of trade', whose function did not go beyond 'extracting money from the people' in order to enrich the princes or the nobles, indeed some who later backtracked in order to undermine public virtue. On the other hand the philosophers in Doria's *Republic* were separate entities from the people, a few individuals raised above the lumpen masses. The republicanism of the philosophers and the *literati* foundered once again on the rocks of the present, leaving the disturbing question as to whether there could be a possible future for the republic.

II. Venice in the Looking Glass

In pursuing my enquiry into the possibility of the existence of a republican form of government, I shall deal rapidly with two points: they concern Venice and Vico respectively. In Italy republicanism manifested itself in relation to particular situations, and as we have already seen to some extent, its verification came from the impact with 'commercial policies' or 'the developments of trade'. Historiography, even the most recent, has assigned Venice an emblematic function – that of representing the persistence of the republican ideal in a Europe of monarchies – but the fact remains that in Venice the common republican language can only be understood in context, being closely linked to the contingencies of city politics and expressing in consequence a meaning that was strongly conditioned by local factors. Love of republican liberty took on the significance of the cult of its own history, making civic virtue the latter's conscience, and as the situation evolved the persistence of the Venetian model of the republic was transformed into an obligation to survive.

Following the Treaty of Passarowitz (1718) and the loss of the Peloponnese which thenceforth confined the exercise of Venetian power to the Italian peninsula, the restriction was as much psychological as territorial, and gave rise to a long line of works written by members of the nobility reflecting upon the republic of Venice, 'still great' and 'still free' after 1,300 years, but a victim now of 'the ravages of time'. Gianfrancesco Pivati was one of the first of these writers, wondering in 1723 whether the city's decline had not taken place during the long transition from popular democratic administration to aristocratic rule, and concluding that the change had been necessary: 'the refinement of manners' had led to the abandonment of the 'natural instincts' which were the basis of the independence of a government open to all, thereby enabling Venice to begin drawing from prudence and practice its particular precepts, those which constituted the essence of 'political science' and which had led to the formation of a perfect régime in Venice and thus made the greatness of the republic possible (Pivati 1723).

Any doubts that Pivati might have entertained about all this he soon banished in the light of the solidity of the institutions, any prolonged loss of effectiveness among which could, he argued, be remedied rather by a fresh appeal to *virtù*, that is to say to the 'greatest prudence' in the evaluation of facts great and small. During the course of the eighteenth century there were to be several other occasions on which this reference to virtue was to be taken up anew, but the prudence-virtue at issue here implied only minor corrections and adjustments within what existed already. And if Pivati had a fleeting moment of hesitation, the future doge Marco Foscarini painted a robustly confident picture of Venice, stressing the very particular nature of the perfection of the republic's government, going so far as to dispense with the habit of resorting to parallels with classical examples as terms of comparison when illustrating such perfection. The secret lay in the art of reconciling the varied interests of citizens within the pluralism of institutions and of having endowed those institutions with the stability of social relationships, they (the institutions) becoming in their turn the guarantors of liberty because they had maintained their independence in the face of monarchical temptations (Foscarini 1983: 139). What virtue meant for Foscarini was a lively awareness of the stability of institutions, so that the virtuous citizen was one who demonstrated his love of them by respecting their laws. Foscarini concluded his history of the Venetian republic within the patriciate, and closed by celebrating the already well-established myth of stability. And his text ended with a clarion call – not lacking in interest – for fresh vigour to be brought to bear upon the activities of trade, on the grounds that it was they, and not conquest, which constituted the foundations on which 'the republic's grandeur and opulence' had been built (*ibid.*).

Apart from being promoted editorially in some dictionaries and in a few commercial texts, this appeal had no impact, either on the level of a (distinctly improbable) revival of economic policy, or on that of discussion about the society 'of merchants and traders'. The most radical proposals did not go beyond denouncing the concentration of accumulated wealth in the hands of an ever-diminishing number of aristocratic families and the resulting impoverishment of an ever-increasing proportion of members of the nobility. Although there did not lack voices raised in condemnation of a type of 'republican despotism' (a term later popularised by Montesquieu), remedies were sought preferably in improvements to the myth of Venice. An average kind of nobleman like Niccolò Donà made a historical axiom out of the city's origins: 'the very same means which were valid for the construction of a thing should serve also to maintain it' (Donà 1734: 134). That sounds like something worthy of Vico: 'The nature of things is none other than their appearance at a given moment and in clearly defined circumstances, and so long as those conditions persist, things will occur in the same way and in no other' (Vico 1953, *degnità* xiv). What was lacking in Venice, however, was that element by virtue of which communities can be renewed and revitalised: the strongly felt need to understand one's own history.

Reaching in mid-century a final conclusion in his reflections on these matters in *Della letteratura veneziana* (1752), Foscarini defined the meaning of Venetian republicanism in exemplary fashion. In order that the 'civic essence' of the life of the republic could be preserved, he directed his efforts towards a 'civic history' of Venice, writing a new version based on solid documentation and on the results of a juridico-institutional analysis of the past favouring the history of laws. Political and social conflicts could be forgotten, he argued, since they were summed up by the laws: the aim was to develop people's consciousness of belonging to the republic's common civic tradition; all society's movements and aspirations, in other words, were to be directed towards fostering a shared awareness of republican membership. In Venice, as can readily be imagined, law had been, and still was, perceived as operating at a practical level, as a procedural or institutional event directly inferred from the political moment, so it is easy to understand how the republican civic tradition proposed by Foscarini tended to coincide with the whole practical political system of 'particular dictates' which Pivati had talked about: that was the 'essence' of law and republican despotism. Only in the form of myth could Venice put up any resistance: in order to maintain itself as an aristocratic republic, as Vico suggested, it had no need of a virtue which it did not recognise, but rather of prudence, or – to use Foscarini's term – of 'the shrewdest caution', that is, 'the ability to balance deeds great and small'.

III. Vico's Heroic Republic

During the course of the debate on the republic in Venice all reference to Machiavelli was studiously avoided, but he loomed larger than is generally realised in Vico's political thought. I have chosen to concentrate here exclusively on this aspect of the complex personality of the author of the *Scienza nuova*.

   In the *Diritto universale* (*De uno universi iuris principio et fine uno*, 1721–2), Vico argued that the Roman republic achieved the grandeur for which it has since been so greatly admired because it managed to devise the best form of mixed government. It was not his intention to extol the achievement of social harmony or the traditional institutional play of concordance, but he did acknowledge the mixed régime's dynamic ability to regulate the struggle for power and the conflicts between the different sections of society. The 'disunity between senate and people' became a force for progress to the extent that the relationship between power and liberty was governed simultaneously by the senate which held the power and the people who exercised freedom, fostering the mutual exchange of virtue and liberty between the two. Textual comparisons indicate that Vico had assimilated, even appropriated, the fourth chapter of Book 1 of the *Discorsi*. His study of Machiavelli did not merely influence his reading of the history of republican Rome, it extended much further, leaving its mark on his schema of the development of the human race. Not only did the *vis* of conflict help explain the great success story that was the history of Rome, it gave rise also to the forms of law through which the *Summum numen* deployed its design of universal history and which had a direct effect on the history of all other peoples.

In the third edition of the *Scienza nuova* (1744), as is well known, Vico excluded all forms of the mixed state as impure, and classified human governments whose actions were regulated by Providence (the *Summum numen* of the *De uno*) under three headings, axiomatically and in order of succession: heroic or aristocratic republics, free popular régimes, and monarchies. He did not drop all reference to Machiavelli, but he did pursue an adversarial dialogue with him on the subject of what value should be attached to internal conflicts within states. If in Vico's earlier version disputes of that kind led directly to liberty and virtue, the reality stressed in the 1744 edition was that such struggles masked the human desires which first gave rise to them, for the primary object of confrontation was in fact the distribution of wealth (land and capital), followed closely by the desire for honours and, in third place only, the acquisition (because of the freedom they conferred) of aristocratic titles: 'Men begin by aspiring to riches, then they seek honours, and finally they pursue titles of nobility' (Vico 1953: 660, para. 986). The forms of political power succeeded each other in order to overcome conflict; Machiavelli's realism was thus brought into conformity with the plan of Providence.

Vico had a clear notion of the utilitarian nature of political power, and of the fact that it enshrined a paradox: while aspiring to universality, it remained attached to the contingent. Self-interest was the wellspring of all human action, but at the same time man could satisfy his needs only in society; and whenever anything was realised in accordance with the interests of one person, a blow was simultaneously struck against the common interest. The history of power was linked to the possession of land, which first established the distinction between rich and poor, but such tenure constituted authority as well. The succession of the forms of government corresponded to the sequence of ways by which such possession could be enjoyed and of the legal systems flowing from them. Viewed from this perspective it is not the valorisation of conflict that we see but its elimination through its transfer to the realm of law. The duty laid upon political power was to regulate private interest until it was eliminated. The day when individuals in society were made to desist from each comparing his own interests unfavourably with the next man's would be the day when freedom was achieved.

I will now sketch here the broad outlines of Vico's description – which he based on examples drawn from his somewhat idiosyncratic reading of Roman history – of the historical development of human governments. First, heroes defined the boundaries of their estates and settled down as heads of households, welcoming the weak and the landless, granting them protection and offering them employment to enable them to survive. These local chiefs were generous, merciful and anxious to be well thought of, but they would have been savage and cruel in the same measure had Providence not guided their actions in the path of common prudence, the quality which characterised the way they governed. The heroes defended their personal independence in the face of threats from their neighbours and united (in an aristocratic republic) against anyone who sought to outdo them. They paraded the cult of virtue, but their rule was not virtuous, since 'each drew private advantage from the public interest' (Vico 1953: 648, para. 950); they were driven by 'their excessive fondness for their sovereignty' to embark upon magnanimous, but not virtuous, enterprises. Not being very sensible, they never sought to avoid conflict between their personal interests and the common good, thereby provoking the revolt of the plebeians, 'who realised how much vanity lay at the heart of this heroism', and who discovered above all 'that they were the equals of the nobles' (*ibid.*: 698, para. 1102). The hero-nobles were prepared to concede use of the land, but (such being the nature of aristocratic republics: participation in the ownership of wealth but exclusion from the exercise of power), they reserved freedom for themselves.

Struggles for political power dominated the transition from each of the three forms of government to the next, and the move from the first type (the heroic republic) to the second (the free popular republic) was effected in a particularly violent fashion as a result of disputes over the possession of land. In Vico's reconstruction of the historical process, the change to a free popular republic took place in three stages: the census of Servius Tullius allowed the use of land by non-patricians, a concession later enshrined in the Twelve Tables, but it was not until a century later that the rite of solemn marriage, conferring the possibility of making a will, was extended to plebeians. Indeed, despite institutional changes (the creation of the office of tribune of the people, for example) and despite wider social recognition (such as that bestowed by the right to own property), the republic maintained its aristocratic government until the hotly contested law on marriage. Here it was not a case of plebeians wishing to 'marry into the nobility' as was commonly believed, but rather something which the patriciate found more disturbing because it had hitherto been its exclusive preserve: what the plebs demanded was the right to 'contract solemn marriages with each other' (Vico 1953: 661, para. 987) so that they could then make a will. Furthermore, in 'laying claim to membership of the order of citizens' (para. 1101), they signalled their strong desire to accede to the condition of full citizenship. Vico's discourse may well have been of dubious validity from a historiographical standpoint, but what counted were its theoretical consequences. In the course of the transition between the two forms (which saw the resolution of the agrarian conflict between patricians and plebeians, and which lasted in reality about three centuries, from the fall of Tarquin the Proud to the Publilius Laws of 338 BC), Vico ruled out any solution based on the mixed state (elements of which he may have come across, as in the *De uno*) and sanctioned the establishment of the popular republic in the framework of the civil equality achieved between patricians and plebeians. In the new form, scant attention was still being paid to the institution, whereas the connotative element seemed to be citizenship, reserved at first to the hero-nobles and then extended so as to become the common condition. Vico gave the following definition of free popular republics: 'individuals hold in their hands the public interest, broken into as many tiny parts as there are citizens making up the sovereign people' (Vico 1953: 648, para. 951).

A major development – a true model of the open society – occurred at this point: heroism spread widely, everyone participated in heroic virtue, philosophy asserted itself, manners became refined, the image of the great magnanimity of the republican people was born, and heroic enterprises kept on following hard upon the heels of each other. However, from the moment that the popular republic took off to the time when it reached its greatest extent, it bore within itself the principle – the *tarlo eroico* or heroic flaw – of its own destruction. 'Heroic virtue' was not pure, as we have seen, because it remained attached to its particular interests, and the new citizens inherited from the preceding forms of government the same tendency to look after their own. Vico meant to emphasise that the origin of popular republics was dictated by private interests, and moreover that their formation revolved entirely around the possession of land and was never free from a certain 'naturalisation' character. As was his wont, he introduced here one of his teleological processes, a historical force according to which citizens, incapable of governing their own 'private interest', broke up into groups, 'parties sprang up, leading to acts of sedition and to civil wars', and everyone found themselves thrown back 'into a world of solitude' (Vico 1953: 668, para. 1006). In celebrating republican heroism, Vico furnished the countervailing techniques of disenchantment.

Republics tended to slide into monarchies in which 'the subjects needed to take care only of their own interests, leaving the task of looking after the common good to their sovereign prince' (Vico 1953: 648, para. 951). Providence had ordained a 'natural and eternal royal law' thanks to which

humanity ensured its self-preservation. Monarchy developed the jurisprudence which prepared the way for these special mechanisms, making them
capable of transforming private interests into public virtues. I do not wish
to linger over Vico's monarchical discourse, nor over the figure of the jurist-
philosophers who backed it up, but I do want to draw attention to the way
he viewed republics as an imperfect stage in politics, and I am also interested in considering the reasons that led Vico to change his position where
Machiavelli was concerned.

According to Vico, Machiavelli presupposed that the republican citizen
was not necessarily a natural given, but something which could be created;
on the Renaissance model, Machiavellian man could, as Vico put it, construct
himself in the circumstances of history and realise himself as a republican,
just as he could position himself in situations of conflict and resolve them
one way or another. The outline or, if the term can be applied in this instance,
the system elaborated by Vico did not accept this vision of humanity. Man
for him, as we are aware, can only know what he does, and is ignorant of
what he does not do. He therefore knows history and proceeds to deduce
from it the laws of human development, basing an *a priori* knowledge upon
it and deriving from it an understanding of the most hidden movements.
But if he knows what he does, man cannot know himself: there is in him a
part of which he is not the creator. Nevertheless the indivisible unity that is
Vico's man presents itself as an ensemble of separate parts, body and mind,
the attachment to necessity and the aspiration to the universal. It is up to
man himself, thanks to his capacity of cognition, to keep his entity indivisible. Vico knew that the 'modern philosopher kings' (by which he meant the
authors of the concept of natural law, Hobbes and Pufendorf) tended to consider those parts separately and to calculate human nature on the basis of the
relationships between the parts. He also knew that such a vision of mankind
presupposed the division of knowledge according to the various human activities. Politics and economics tended to constitute themselves as autonomous
sciences and to set up separate relationships with the natural world, relationships which it was impossible for man to know. Machiavelli, who inspired
this trend of the moderns, could serve to uphold the separation of branches
of knowledge. Leaving aside Vico's possible personal political sympathies,
we can be sure that his distrust of the republic as an institution was born
of its presumption to set itself up as an autonomous project. This was the
crucial determining factor, given that Vico consciously developed his theory
in relation to a context in which economics and politics were detached from
metaphysics and benefited from their respective independent processes. Not

only did he reject republican discourse, he believed that political language was severely limited if it did not simultaneously embrace both metaphysics and jurisprudence.

iv. The Republic of Merchants?

Up till now we have seen the obstacles facing republican discourse, obstacles which highlighted above all the inadequacy of that discourse to give comprehensive expression to the novel characteristics of the age. We have observed it sliding into the despotism of enlightened princes and even, in the case of Venice, bolstering aristocratic despotism. However, the terms in which these arguments were couched showed little coherence. On the one hand, in Vico, and to a certain extent in Doria, the term 'republic' is attested in the sense of 'democracy'; on the other, the arguments about republican inadequacy in relation to that age revealed a confused grasp of the moment, and even a failure to understand it. When the particular character of the age was located (identified) in trade and consequently in the affirmation of the republic of merchants, it was commerce itself that was interpreted according to categories which either were already discredited or were becoming discredited. What was not recognised – or, in the best-case scenario, what was only hesitantly recognised – was the very novelty of the nature of trade. It was still looked upon as a practical activity aimed at and directed towards the expansion of the state; its development served merely to accentuate its characteristic tendency to corrupt personal relationships, and wealth continued to be seen in relation to the power of the state. This point of view corresponded to the commercial policy of mercantilism denounced by Doria; hence the condemnation of trade and the search for a form of government capable of containing its worst effects, an impossible task for a republican government since it conceded space to its citizens.

When it occurred, the acceptance of trade was achieved through the concept of *felicità pubblica* (public happiness, an expression invented by Muratori), seen as the objective that virtuous governments set themselves, but to which Christian values contributed in large part, or, to repeat what I said earlier, the values of a Machiavelli recycled as confidential adviser to the legal despot. In Italy, at least, the rise of commercial society – and of the society of political economy, which was closely related to it – presupposed a set of favourable conditions, prominent among which was the priority given to a break with the conception of politics according to *raison d'état*. In making a distinction between the 'science of the state' and politics proper,

Doria should no doubt take the credit for having perceived the necessity of such a break, whatever his personal antipathy to trade and strong preference for (Platonic) philosophy. To some extent Vico was to follow in his footsteps, albeit taking a somewhat different route.

Positive impulses were not lacking, but it was hard for them to emerge into the full light of day; it was also true that there was no one to organise them in an exemplary manner. There could in any case be no innovation, where republican discourse was concerned, without a new way of understanding trade, something which, as we know, raised difficulties never before encountered, in so far as issues involving the relationship between similar semantic fields were seen to be opened up and, more importantly, where people began to ask the question whether it mattered if one form of government was adopted rather than another. If the term 'politics' was frequently used in a diluted form, it was because the investigation had to respect intersecting aims and a multiplicity of spaces.

In Italy the first person to bring about, in conformity with the spirit of the age, a re-evaluation – and even a rehabilitation – of trade in the modern sense was the Neapolitan cleric Antonio Genovesi, ex-metaphysician, ex-theologian and first holder (from 1754 to 1769) of a chair in economics. The mechanism of the rehabilitation was not new: trade was connected with forms of *socialitas* as it was presented in the modern doctrine of natural law. Through his training based squarely on the texts of the Neapolitan jurists known as the *culti*, Genovesi was drawing on the same sources as the works of Vico and Doria, and carried out a modification of viewpoint which turned out to be quite extraordinary. In the process of describing a closely knit web of relationships in which trade fulfilled its role as a force for change, reviving and reconnecting the different human activities, he held up the prospect of an opening-up of spaces on the basis of an ideal, uninterrupted comparison with Europe. In short, trade was the exchange of goods, but also communication; the pursuit of trade was not confined to the amassing of wealth but had an impact on manners, culture and life style, typifying the atmosphere and tone of the community. I cannot go into the details of the debate about commerce here, but it is appropriate to indicate the consequences of this mental shift and stress two points relating to the discourse which I am concerned with in this chapter: (a), a new version of the evolution of human history, and (b), the repositioning of the individual at the very core of that history.

(a) Genovesi's conception was a vision of the evolution of humanity fully inserted into the scheme of natural law and an integral part of it. In his description of mankind detaching itself from the state of nature he did not place particular emphasis on the way political power was built up, but he did stress the transition to civil society by noting the changes in the material conditions of life; he investigated the transformation of the means of subsistence and production in order to elaborate a scheme corresponding to a clearly defined theory of the progressive stages of human history. In the process he constantly highlighted the activities of human beings in their relationships with each other and with nature and the environment. The effect of the alternative tension contained in this scheme can well be imagined in a city like Naples, and more generally in the territory of the literary republic, where everyone continued to treat Vico as an isolated case but was fully aware of his providential vision of history based on the theory of cycles.

(b) In Genovesi's scheme, the concept of man as an indivisible entity did not hold up; it gave rise rather to a disintegration of the whole into a number of parts, each of which fell within the purview of either the physical or the moral. These were the two fundamental possibilities. Both were autonomous in their activity, both operated movements in the network of relationships driven by the new motor of commerce. Both individual parts were also connected with each other in the totality that is man, which now was the result of a sum of autonomies, that made up his essence and that conferred on him the central characteristics and functions of humanity. So man was always a controlling unity ('each contains his own world within himself') and his position at the centre of his actions – making up his history – was rooted in his autonomy.[2] His nature therefore consisted in his ability to live relationships, create links and operate within them, and it was these that gave rise to his characteristics as a social and political animal, features not normally thought of as natural givens.

Thus it came about that, viewed in the context of the particular history of the theory of progressive stages in human development, the Aristotelian vision of man as a political animal by nature, a concept adapted by Saint Thomas and extended to refer to man as a social and political animal, found itself severely compromised. It should be pointed out that this arose, probably for the first time, in the context of a narrowly Roman Catholic culture with no recourse to any type of atheist solution or to any form of materialistic rehabilitation. The rehabilitation of the civil/civic element in the Renaissance paradigm, on the other hand, was made possible by such a conception of man as a rational entity.

2. 'Man is a being; the physical laws governing beings are chiefly two: 1) to love existence; 2) to act, because action is the essence of each being . . . Man is a body: the principal law of bodies is the cohesion of their parts, which engenders their unity . . . Man is a spirit united with the body: the physical law of reason is the calculation of the principles, the means and the ends' (Genovesi 1766: 36).

It is obvious that Genovesi was yielding to attempts both at mending fences with the world of Christian values and at making adjustments of a pragmatic nature; for example the matter of the equity of price in the theory of value, and the issue of good faith and of the respect for promises entered into, qualities intrinsic to the concept of 'merchant', were two questions in which the influence of religion and the attempts at defining the virtues of the merchant-citizen in a secular manner interlocked. It is also difficult to reach a conclusion about the success or otherwise of the premises that lay at the heart of his political discourse, but one cannot help but remark the great importance of the intuition of the man-individual at the core of a history that he was the only one to construct (not in the sense in which Vico understood it, as self-comprehension, but as craftsmanship). Individuals, as we have seen, with their ambitions, their desires, their passions and their lonelinesses, represented the weak point of republics, and Genovesi – with what degree of 'republican' consciousness, one can only speculate – addressed the issue of the education and training of these individuals. It was from their functions and within their functions that emerged the intermediate political forms such as civil society, the power of public opinion, and the propensity to create groups and set up associations. The enquiry shifted from the institutions of government to individuals who were later called upon to choose the form of administration which suited them best.

It is hardly surprising that, in order to give added weight to his conception of man, Genovesi should choose from all the writings at his disposal to transcribe in the text of his *Diceosina o sia della filosofia del giusto et dell'onesto* a long passage (minus the closing paragraph) from Chapter 10 of Book I of the *Discorsi*, the Christian name and surname of the author of which – in defiance of the ecclesiastical censors who kept a close eye on him – he spells out unambiguously as Niccolò Machiavelli. The Florentine master's impassioned chapter is constructed according to rhetorical procedures which served to give firm direction to the invective contained in the theoretical discourse. Genovesi's commercial society was an open one in which man had to be free to act; provision was made for the training of new individuals in accordance with the character and needs of that society, but there was a prior requirement for a movement of liberation from, as Genovesi put it, 'the fine and inextricable little chains' that 'bind us to the rules governing the production and conservation of our happiness'.[3] Whilst this liberation will manifest

---

3. 'Such fine and inextricable little chains bind us to the rules governing the production and conservation of our happiness that we do not yet know how to free ourselves from them' (Genovesi 1766: 32).

itself primarily in our mind, it will subsequently need to be translated into practice.[4]

The *Lezioni di commercio o sia di economia civile* (1765–68) described the ways of arriving at this world of freedom: what were required were demands for the transformation of compulsory cultural methods, for the elimination of customs barriers and of the restrictive laws and regulations governing work, and so on. A state's fiscal system must not tax the *industry*, *skill* and *toil* of its citizens; the perennial condemnation of luxury was transformed here into a civil theory of consumption in a reality where 'an equitable distribution of wealth' would exist. When forced to commit himself on the question of the forms of government, Genovesi took refuge in a laconic reply about 'the rule of the best'. Although in his project the best had to be 'as numerous as possible' and drawn from the different social classes, his true answer needs to be sought in his theory of the relationships governing human choices, such as the links between individuals – and between those individuals and the government – founded on a continuous contract (the contract of natural law).

To find a radical formulation of individual autonomy we have to turn to Cesare Beccaria's *Dei delitti e delle pene* (1764), Chapter 26 of which, entitled 'Of the Spirit of Family', seems a digression prompted by the custom of confiscating the property of convicted criminals. Beccaria condemned this practice which, in punishing the guilty individual, also struck at the innocent members of his family, especially the children who had nothing to do with the offences committed by their father. Confiscation was always widely approved of, and practised even in the 'freest republics', because people 'thought of society in terms of a union of families rather than in terms of a union of individuals' (Beccaria 1984: 80). Writers of many different persuasions were in agreement when it came to considering the family the original nucleus of society and the state, and in the course of the eighteenth century reform programmes were much concerned with the family's educational role. But in advance of this educational investment Beccaria turned the traditional point of view on its head: looking at the position not from above (the state), but from below (the individual), he invited his readers to consider that the family was a political unit. The family was either a republic or a monarchy. If a state consisted of twenty thousand families of five members each including the head of the household, that could mean either one hundred thousand free men, or twenty thousand free men and eighty thousand slaves.

---

4. 'It cannot be said that reason exists in a nation which has otherwise reached full maturity when it lies more in the abstract than in people's hearts and hands' (Genovesi 1766: 33).

Political writing about submission to the father, about the duties of children and of fathers to their children, about respect, protection, and so forth,
ended up creating a substantial area of ambiguity and led people to forget
that the family was not the source of a state or of a society, but rather a reflection of the two. According to Beccaria, that was where the birth of the
republican or monarchical spirit was to be sought, and that was where virtue
and submission were exercised:

> Where the republic is made up of men, the family is not an institution
> in which subordination is by command, but by contract, and as soon
> as children reach the age at which they emerge from a state of natural
> dependency, they become free members of the *polis* and submit to the
> head of the household, in order, like free men in societies, to partake
> of the advantages that submission offers.   (Beccaria 1984: 81)

It was before reaching public level that the contract of political formations
had to come into effect, between individuals and within the framework of
the family; there could be no firmer foundation for man's autonomy. To
reinforce the point, the process of acquiring liberty had to be tackled on
the basis of each individual's own origins. By calling family relationships
into question Beccaria was distancing himself even further from Aristotelian
and Thomist man, but at the same time offering a remarkable indication
of the ideal of the family as a republican unit endowed with all the voices
of its own semantic field. This contribution was neither corroborated nor
invalidated by the second part of the chapter. In the face of the likelihood of a
multiplication of interests Beccaria made clear his concern that the 'vain idol,
aptly named as "of family"', would override the autonomy of its constituent
parts and thus weaken the 'republican feeling', to maintain which it would
be very necessary to have recourse to the law, but what was being prepared
was the intervention of a single person who, 'were he to be a philosopher',
would compensate the citizens for the loss of their own authority in return
for guaranteeing their security and well-being. We are once again in the
presence of the characteristic slide from the republic towards despotism,
this time of the enlightened variety, but is what we are reading really what
Beccaria wrote? It is well known that the text of *Dei delitti e delle pene* was
revised by Pietro Verri, who corrected and completed Beccaria's draft, making
for considerable difficulties in the attribution of certain passages. Recent
philological comparisons between the first and subsequent drafts have made
it possible to confirm that this second part of Chapter 26 shows traces of
additions by Verri, although the fact remains that Beccaria accepted them in

the 1766 Haarlem edition (the last he revised in person), and that both he and Genovesi brought out clearly the link between natural law and the autonomy of the individual by indicating in the contract both the fundamental element which led to autonomous government and the principle legitimating the demands of freedom.

The effects of the intuition I have just drawn attention to can, I believe, be traced in Beccaria's economic thought. His lectures on economics, delivered in Milan between 1768 and 1771, illustrated a theory of value not divorced from self-interest. As is well known, he explained the phenomenon of value through self-interest and scarcity, although after Galiani's time that was a commonplace in Italy. The Italians discovered individual utility very early on, probably because attentive observation of reality, in a situation where supply fell well short of demand, highlighted the primacy of the desires of the subject. The interest of Beccaria's theory lay in his description of the mechanism of the hypothetical market in which price was arrived at. The reason for exchange was indeterminate in isolated transactions (such as, for example, between individuals bartering oil for grain), but the arrival of other individuals launched a process of competition and thus determined the price. At the root of this mechanism – at the basis of competition and of ways of arriving at a correct price between 'quantity asked and quantity offered' – Beccaria presupposed the existence of a number of autonomous individuals, that is people free of prejudice, subjection and tyranny, people released from all the bonds that were not the exact expression of the balance between nature and need, as set forth in a measure that was appropriate to the civilisation of which the individual was the bearer. This presupposition expressed the positive sense of commercial sociability, a meaning recognised in so far as Beccaria was not severing the link with the society of natural law. He was appointed to the Austrian administration of the Duchy of Milan from 1771 onwards and turned himself into the scrupulous executant of one of the many programmes of enlightened despotism. Being a civil servant for Beccaria, though, meant opting for silence.

This movement for individual liberties was frequently echoed elsewhere. Among the technical dictionaries a title that should be mentioned is the *Dizionario del cittadino o sia ristretto storico teorico e pratico del commercio* which, in the preface, designated as a true 'citizen' the merchant, because he 'looks after his own country'. In his *D'una riforma d'Italia* (1767) Carlo Antonio Pilati maintained that the first act of revival consisted in 'freeing Italy from the tyranny of prejudice, superstition and ignorance', and went on to denounce the ruin of trade and the abuse of mortmain; obstacles had to be swept away, he said, because 'the citizen must be guided solely by reason, patriotism and a sense of fairness' (Pilati 1767: 48, 35, 58). Many other examples could be given of images of liberated individuals, of free citizens and of fatherland being superimposed on images of commercial society.

Before bringing this discussion to an end, I would like to raise the following question: what form of government would have been best suited to such revitalised, liberated and free men in a hypothetical commercial society, once it had finally been set up, even in Italy? Or, in more concrete terms, to what form of government did the middle classes – those who in other words were the intermediaries between the patricians and the lower orders – actually aspire? If we turn to the answers given by contemporaries to this question, there is only one that emerges clearly: through conviction in the case of some, as a necessary response to the situation prevailing at the time in the case of others, the choice fell, unequivocally, on enlightened despotism. As we have seen, following the 'rediscovery' of Machiavelli at the beginning of the century, which was sustained through the successive re-editions (of 1760, 1768, 1772 and 1782) of the *Opere di Niccolò Machiavelli*, the 'true republican spirit' was recruited to the cause of supporting the legally established enlightened despot. And that happened in Naples as well as in Florence, in Milan as well as in Parma.

That remained however a necessary choice, one which in my view was readily accepted because the link between the liberties of commerce and the *socialitas* of natural law was not cultivated by the majority of the constituent elements of the literary republic, who represented a point of reference for everyone, even for those finding themselves in the role of civil servants, and certainly – with the notable exception of Genovesi and Beccaria – for supporters of the *felicità pubblica*. Cutting the link meant rooting man's freedom in commercial society, that is to say in effective reality. That opened the way to the birth of *homo economicus*: the foundations of the liberties were attached to the forms of the time, in denial of what might be called their projectuality.

Generally speaking, historians in Italy today argue that the quest for liberty and the drive towards republicanism, even when transferred and displaced on to the vision of a commercial society, did not succeed in becoming a republican discourse and did not manage to develop a theory or formulate a set of demands, primarily because of a failure to graft on an encounter with the more advanced forms of European enlightenment thinking such as Toland's atheism or the radicalism of the French *philosophes*. In my view this line of reasoning needs to be corrected: the element in Italy which, in the particular case of the republican discourse, blocked a philosophical development which in general showed notable advances, was – as I have been at pains to stress – the lack of reflection on the concept of *socialitas* in modern natural law. Among the factors holding things back, only one need be mentioned: the extent to which Christian values were rooted in the culture of the literary republic, so much so, in fact, that the values of the natural law of the moderns were assimilable and were assimilated into the entirety of the values of the eternal law of nature of the Roman Catholic Christians.

Here are two further examples: Pietro Verri called for a world of liberties for man. These did not differ from those of Beccaria and Genovesi, but neither of them would have subscribed to a passage to be found in Verri's text entitled *Della economia politica* (1771):

> It is with the introduction of universal merchandise that societies
> come closer together, get to know one another and communicate
> with each other; from this it can clearly be seen how much the human
> race is indebted to the invention of money (perhaps more than has
> been thought), to culture and to the artificial organisation of needs
> and industry; it is by virtue of these developments that civilised
> societies are so remote from and so isolated against the savage races.
>
> (Verri 1964: 133).

These were different freedoms and autonomies from those which derived from *socialitas*.

In Naples in 1779 Galanti wrote a courageous *Elogio* of Machiavelli, but this courage tended to get diluted as praise of the Medici focused attention on the figure of the prince most immediately to hand. In 1772 the same Galanti had written an *Elogio* of Genovesi (Voltaire thought highly of it), in which his subject was celebrated as *nudus sacerdos naturae*. Ten years later, in a new, 'revised and corrected' edition, the former master was reproached with not having given religion its proper place in his description of the development of mankind. Galanti meant something more than a recognition of the historic role of religion: he wished to assume that function as the foundation of values.

There is no doubt, however, that some trace remained of the presence of the republican discourse. It was to be found in a new, vibrant debate which, in the 1780s, returned with a transformed sensibility to the origins of that discourse among the Italic peoples, within those communities which, before the foundation of Rome, had defended their own autonomy and devised forms of self-government. The writers who breathed new life into the old

Italic models were the very same as those who, a few years later, were drafting constitutional instruments. But by then the events which Edmund Burke in October 1789 called with terse understatement 'the late proceedings in France' had turned the world upside down, and nothing was ever the same again.

Translated from the French and the Italian by John Fletcher

14

Republicanism, State Finances and the Emergence of Commercial Society in Eighteenth-century France – or from Royal to Ancient Republicanism and Back

MICHAEL SONENSCHER

I

One reason for the immense popularity of Fénelon's *Telemachus* during the eighteenth century was its clarity about the prospects for Europe's future. As Fénelon presented it, Europe had to find a way to promote trade and prevent war. The problem, from Louis XIV's wars onwards, was that trade had become deeply entangled with war because of the increasing use of public credit to fund the costs of war, turning trade into a source of tax revenue for interest payments and generating a deadly competition between the great powers to acquire, or prevent others from acquiring, the resources needed to fund their debts. As one of the principal agents of the Stuart pretender to the British throne informed the marquis d'Argenson in 1755, on the eve of the Seven Years War, the rivalry between England and France was 'like an affair of grocer to grocer, whose quarrel will come to an end only when they have each discredited one another' (Voyer de Paulmy 1852–67: 59–60). In the British case, d'Argenson noted, this could be achieved by a Jacobite rising accompanied by a Stuart proclamation to cancel all the debts contracted by the house of Hanover. He did not bother to record what the French equivalent might be, but it is not too difficult to imagine. As Arthur Young noted soon after the end of the Seven Years War, the French system of absolute government was a powerful advantage in 'an affair of grocer to grocer'. The Seven Years War, he wrote, had gone well for England only because the French had failed to use their political advantage as lethally as they might have done.

> Had they by the most regular punctuality lulled all Europe into an opinion of their funds, until they had encreased them as much as their utmost possibility would bear, and then spunged the whole into mere life annuities to the then possessors alone, they would have added

infinitely to the strength and power of the state, and lost very little more of their credit than they have done without such a conduct – There is nothing so pernicious to a ministry, and even to a kingdom at large, if under an arbitrary government, as their being knaves by halves.[1]

From this perspective, the eighteenth-century combination of war, trade and public credit amounted to republicanism's nemesis not only because it lay behind the massive increase in the monetary, fiscal and financial resources of the modern state, but also because the peculiar type of property embodied in a public debt represented a profound threat to the decision-making capabilities of a free state.

The growth of government borrowing during the eighteenth century found expression in repeated conflict over how the burden of war-generated debt might be equitably funded from tax revenue – in the United Provinces in 1747, in France at the time of the Brittany affair and the Maupeou coup of 1771, in Sweden in 1772 and in North America at the time of the American revolution. It also cast a new and alarming light over the international balance of power by raising the possibility of a war-induced cycle of debt-defaults, as first one power then the next opted to withhold interest payments on their debts, using all their available tax revenue for a quick push for military supremacy. From the perspective of international power politics and the brutal imperatives of *raison d'état*, opting for a republican system with an inherited public debt – in a world in which the possibility of armed conflict was all too real – raised an awkward question about whether the decision-making procedures of a republic, coupled with the diversity of interests arising from a public debt, could match an absolute monarchy's ability to disregard its engagements to investors in the public funds (or capitalists as they were known in eighteenth-century France) and default on its debts if it was faced with a choice between preserving its debt and preserving itself.

The financial legacy of modern politics thus posed a question about the extent to which a republic might be able to behave with the same 'ruthlessness' or 'willingness to discount the demands of justice and act with

---

1. Young 1769: 418. Young's warning captures the style of eighteenth-century *Realpolitik* thinking remarkably well. For an even more lurid example (verging on the insanity to which he eventually succumbed), see Pellissery 1776: I, 74, 77: 'Je vous ai déjà dit qu'en matière d'état, quand on se met au dessus des formalités ordinaires... il faut se justifier par de plus grands crimes... En système d'état rien n'est crime, dès que l'on peut se justifier par l'utilité publique'. On this basis, he suggested that Britain, during the Seven Years War, should have defaulted on her debt and used the extra revenue to foment revolt in the Spanish colonies, creating a client Mexican monarchy and extending her empire to the whole American continent. On Pellissery's subsequent history, see Pellissery 1792 Labourdette 1990: 144–5.

cruelty and perfidiousness when this is necessary to uphold the common good' as a monarchy (Skinner 1984: 216–17). Advocating a republican form of government meant finding a way to match an absolute monarchy's capacity to preserve its freedom from external subjection while simultaneously maintaining the domestic political liberty associated with a republic. The aim of this essay is to describe two republican ways of thinking about how to trump absolute government's capacity to deal with the debt problem. The first centred on the idea of a patriot king. The second was associated with the idea of a republican debt-reduction scheme. As it transpired, however, finding a way to deal with the ramifications of public credit either by purely political means or by using the economic resources of the modern funding system to underpin a republican system of government stretched prevailing conceptions of a republicanism up to and, perhaps, beyond their limits.

II

The 'patriot king' solution to the debt problem was the product of a recognition, voiced initially in England by Charles Davenant and, more famously, by Henry St John, viscount Bolingbroke, that public credit was a threat to a free constitution because a government which was forced to default on its debts would still have the tax revenue used to fund its interest payments at its disposal. This was why eliminating the debt had to be the work of a patriotic government, committed to creating a balanced, republican-style constitution to neutralise the despotic potential of a bankruptcy. In France this idea of a patriotic programme of political reform was usually associated with the cult of Henri IV and his virtuous minister Sully, a cult which developed in parallel with a certain interest in the ideas of Bolingbroke and the English Commonwealthmen. As Edmund Burke noticed (in his *Letters on a Regicide Peace*), this interest grew up in French military and diplomatic circles in the wake of the humiliations of Louis XV's wars and was particularly pronounced among the assorted diplomats, *faiseurs* and gofers involved in the parallel system of secret diplomacy which Louis XV maintained alongside the official French alliance with the house of Austria. As Burke put it,

> They had continually in their hands the *Observations* of Machiavel on Livy. They had Montesquieu's *Grandeur et Décadence des Romains* as a manual; and they compared, with mortification, the systematic proceedings of a Roman senate with the fluctuations of a monarchy.
>
> (Burke 1899: 367)

Appalled by French loss of power and influence, these 'diplomatic politicians', as Burke described them, began to call the capacity of monarchy itself into question.

> What cure for the radical weakness of the French monarchy, to which all the means which wit could devise, or Nature and fortune could bestow, towards universal empire, was not of force to give life or vigor or consistency, but in a republic? Out the word came: and it never went back.   (Burke 1899: 369)

However much it may have been jaundiced by hindsight, Burke's identification of republicanism with a group of 'diplomatic politicians' horrified by the new direction of French foreign policy in the wake of the Austrian alliance of 1756 was broadly accurate. Burke himself referred to the political opinions of the military engineer, the marquis de Montalembert – a strong advocate of putting the government in 'truly popular hands' in 1789 to restore France to wealth and greatness – and to a pamphlet written by one of the luminaries of Louis XV's secret diplomacy, Jean-Louis Favier, entitled *Conjectures raisonnées sur la situation actuelle de la France dans le systême politique de l'Europe* as examples of the thinking he had in mind.[2] Neither Montalembert, whose patriotism was highly praised by Jean-Paul Marat, nor Favier, who edited Bolingbroke's diplomatic correspondence and whose *Conjectures*, originally written in 1773 at the time of the first partition of Poland were published as a pamphlet by the republican *Cercle social* in 1793, were particularly original thinkers. Most of their ideas echoed the work of the best-known 'diplomatic politician' of the second half of the eighteenth century, the abbé Gabriel Bonnot de Mably, who first came to fame as the author of the *Droit public de l'Europe fondé sur les traités* in 1748.

Mably's most explicit demonstration of the relevance of the political ideas of the English Commonwealthmen in a French context was his privately circulated essay, *The Rights and Duties of Citizens*, probably written in 1758, at the lowest point of French military fortunes in the Seven Years War.[3] In it, he used a character – initially named Harrington and then (in the posthumously published version of the essay) Stanhope – to outline a scenario of how the patriot king formula could be used to reform the French monarchy by way of what he called a 'managed revolution', where the magistracy would force

2. Burke 1899: 366, 368. On Favier, see Flammermont 1899; and for the texts of his memoranda see Ségur (ed.) 1802. On Montalembert, see his (anonymously published) *Première collection de petitions . . . 1789*: 4) and Lecanuet 1895.
3. On Mably, see Wright 1997 and on this essay, see Baker 1990a, ch. 4.

the king, under the pressure of a war-generated funding crisis, to establish a balanced system of republican government, based upon a revised version of the ancient system of representation by estates. The obvious candidate for the role of patriot king was Louis XV's son, the Dauphin of France, known to be hostile to the house of Austria and a great enemy of the duc de Choiseul, the minister most closely identified with the Austrian alliance.

France, however, was not Britain and could not opt out of its European responsibilities in favour of a blue-water foreign policy as readily as, according to Bolingbroke's admirers, was possible for Britain. Although Mably referred enthusiastically to John Brown's *Estimate of the Manners and Principles of the Times* (1756), telling the founders of the American republic that he knew nothing as 'profound in politics', he was unusually unimpressed by the contemporary cult of Henri IV, presenting him in his *Observations on the History of France* as one of the principal architects of absolute monarchy.[4] Instead, Mably's model of a patriot king was Charlemagne. 'It cannot be denied that the more a state is extended, the more easily abuses slip in', he wrote in his *De la législation*, published in 1774 as a reply to the programme of political reform advocated by the French economists.

> But however vast an empire may be, neither the number nor the extent of its provinces amount to insurmountable obstacles to its policies, whether one wants to reform it or simply to maintain good order. Wherever they are, men have the same reason, the same needs, the same social qualities and the same principle underlying the same passions and this amounts to a great point of union. A skilful legislator, by giving different provinces the same laws, the same government and the same interest would be able to form a single state with a regular mechanism and movement. By dint of art, he will be able to oppose the abuses that arise in an extensive society by establishing magistrates as vigilant as those of a small republic. All that is required to succeed in this enterprise is to decompose, so to speak, a state and turn all its provinces into as many federated republics. Their union will be their strength abroad and the small size of their territory will be their security at home.

This, he continued, was what Charlemagne had achieved.

> He began by dividing the lands of his dominions into a hundred different provinces. His secret was to give them individual assemblies open to every order of citizen. They were responsible for overseeing

---

4. Mably, 1977b: 421. On Henri IV, see in his *Observations sur l'histoire de France* (1977c: II, 244–73).

> the needs of their district, for repressing abuses and maintaining
> respect for the laws. By way of this division, each province acquired
> the movement that could be imprinted upon it and the whole Empire
> acquired a new spirit and new manners.   (Mably 1977d: 286–7)

This federal system was the key to the survival of republican government
in a large, territorial state. While, Mably wrote, Henri IV had taken advantage of the political exhaustion produced by civil war to consolidate the
sovereignty of the crown, Charlemagne had used the aftermath of civil war
to destroy the feudal power of the great nobility and revive the Estates-
General (Mably 1977c: II, 266). As he presented it, Charlemagne's empire
was the archetype of an extensive system of republican government, headed
by 'a prince who was simultaneously a philosopher, a legislator, a patriot
and a conqueror' (*ibid.*: I, 221). Its constitutional core was a revived and
more stable version of the ancient republican assemblies of the Francs.
Under Charlemagne's aegis, and as the French people came to 'possess a very
extensive territory', each county of the empire came to depute a dozen representatives every autumn to a closed meeting on the *champ de Mars* followed, in May, by a general assembly of the bishops, abbots, counts, lords
and deputies of the people, sometimes deliberating separately, sometimes
as a single body, so that, as Mably put it, 'there can be no doubt that the
legislative power resided in the body of the nation', with the king as its executive head (*ibid.*: I, 229). All this implied that the task of a patriot king
was rather more considerable than the one that Bolingbroke had outlined,
involving both the establishment of a balanced system of government at
home and the conquest of sufficient power abroad to ensure that the problems of war and paying for war would be swallowed up within an extensive and peaceful reincarnation of the Roman republic. It is well known that
Mably's model of Charlemagne as a patriot king greatly appealed to Napoleon
Bonaparte.[5]

Mably himself did not, however, expect France to play the part of a republican hegemon. His unwavering hostility to both the Austrian alliance and the
political system from which it emerged was an expression of his growing conviction that the corrupting combination of absolute government and public
credit had eliminated the prospects for free government in France and had
come to threaten the very survival of liberty in Europe as a whole. His fear,
echoed in Favier's memoranda to the comte de Broglie (the head of Louis XV's

---

5. Napoleon read and annotated Mably's *Observations sur l'histoire de France* while at Auxonne: see
   Masson 1908: 63, 78. (I owe this reference to Chris Prendergast of King's College.)

parallel diplomatic system), was that the French alliance with Austria, instead of giving France a free hand to deal with Britain, amounted to a blank cheque to underwrite Habsburg ambitions in central, eastern and southern Europe. France would then be even more exposed to the paralysingly divisive domestic effects of the combination of war, debt and taxation and acutely vulnerable to the possibility that the Empire might ditch its French ally and side with an even more heavily indebted and desperate Britain, forced, by the severity of its domestic political dissensions, to solve its debt problem at the expense of the rest of Europe. 'I would tremble for the liberty of Europe', Mably warned in one of the later editions of his *Droit public de l'Europe*

> if, instead of all those exchanges and cessions that can be read in our peace treaties, I was to see a people that was to force its enemies to reimburse its wartime expenditure and pay its debts.
>
> (Mably 1776: III, 383)

Mably pinned his hopes for Europe's future on Prussia – the Sparta of the North – as the only power uncontaminated by the modern funding system still able to defend itself with a patriotic, quasi-feudal, militia system. 'The reign of France, the house of Austria and England is over', he announced soon after France entered the American war. 'For the good of Europe, it is to be desired that Prussian power, which we have seen take form, is able to maintain itself and come to be incontestably recognised (Mably 1977e: 395)'. Prussia would be Europe's only bulwark against despotism if the other states were to succumb to the Armageddon of a general bankruptcy. 'We are nearer than one might think', he warned, 'to the revolution which Asia underwent, and the time may not be too far away when Europe will languish under the splendour and the misery of despotism and slavery.'[6]

Mably was no more confident about the prospects of the American insurgents. 'Love of money necessarily suffocates love of liberty', he warned, 'and the insurgents' bad laws will not be able to preserve their republic from the misfortune menacing it' (Mably 1977e: 474). The best hope for liberty, he argued, would have been to leave the Americans to their own devices, forcing them to fight a long, bloody but ultimately victorious war to establish their independence, while trapping Britain into a protracted military disaster in a distant country was the best way to promote a British revolution. A long-drawn-out war of liberation would serve to instil the military virtues

---

6. Mably 1977e: 396 (and, on the threat of bankruptcy, see p. 390).

in the nascent republic and reinforce the moral and political authority of the Continental Congress over the selfish proclivities of the individual states, thus protecting the vulnerability of their mainly farming and trading populations from ambitious and unscrupulous political leaders. Having achieved liberty too easily, the republic would have to find a surrogate for virtue to neutralise ambition.

> The voice of justice, and above all benign justice, has a great empire over the spirit of citizens who are content with their lot and who are not moved by violent passions. But there are men whose atrocious souls can be contained only by terror.   (Mably 1977e: 459)

This was why, as a short-term expedient, he was prepared to support the bugbear of republics and commonwealths, a 'standing army', arguing that the Congress should arm itself with a 'body of troops' directly under its power, to be assembled and used 'according to the needs of the conjuncture'. 'I do not think', he added,

> that this indispensable establishment will ever become dangerous, for as long as the delegates of the United States to the Congress enjoy this supreme magistracy for a limited and very short time.
> (Mably 1977e: 460)

Mably did not live to see his advice about what the Americans ought to have done come home to roost in France, the country in which he expected it least.

III

In a short notice on one of Mably's last works, his essay *Of the Study of History*, the French republican man of letters Jacques Pierre Brissot described Mably's ideas as one of the 'last embers' of the great vogue for antiquity which had flourished over the past two hundred years (Brissot 1784, no.3, p. 228). He continued his discussion of Mably's works in a review of his *Observations on the Government and the Laws of the United States* along with Richard Price's *Observations on the Importance of the American Revolution* in the *Journal du lycée de Londres* in 1784. He agreed with both Mably and Price that the greatest danger facing the Americans was the 'baneful mania for overly extensive trade' and the risk of entanglement in the European system of luxury that it housed, but argued that neither of them had identified a way to 'restrain trade within such limits as to prevent the alteration of the virtues and simple tastes of these republicans'. Price, he claimed, failed to address the part played by the passions in any political society, while Mably, on the other hand, displayed an unwarranted hostility to the people, overlooking the fact that an aristocracy (even the elected aristocracy provided for by the constitution of Massachusetts which Mably commended) had 'a hundred times stronger passions' than a democracy (Brissot 1784, no. 3, pp. 270, 276, 279, 283).

Brissot was one of the small number of advocates of a straightforwardly republican solution to the French monarchy's financial crisis in 1789, arguing, well before the fall of the Bastille, that the Estates-General should summon a constitutional convention to draft a new republican constitution for subsequent ratification by the French people. This strategy, which he explicitly counterposed to the one laid out in the abbé Sieyès's *What is the Third Estate?*, was coupled with the idea of a republican debt-reduction scheme as an alternative to the patriot-king solution to the debt problem. Its purpose was to create a single, common interest as the basis of a patriotic commitment to the public good. Brissot recognised that this sort of common interest could be something entirely immaterial, like the idea of a social contract, in small communities with strong, stable values, like the Quakers. But in a large populous country like France, adjusting the passions to the rule of law had to entail something more material. This was the point of an overtly republican debt-reduction scheme, modelled on the American continental currency. Its advocates – including Tom Paine as well as Brissot – argued that a genuinely national debt could be accommodated within a unitary republic with a decentralised government, modelled along the lines suggested to the Americans by the former French controller-general of finance A. R. J. Turgot in his famous open letter to Richard Price. Just as the American continental currency had served to secure American liberty, so a territorially based analogue could do the same in France.

In a review of two English works on public credit published in his *Journal du lycée de Londres* in 1784, Brissot had already argued that speculation on the public funds was not necessarily an evil. The facts, he pointed out, showed that England and Holland, two countries in which playing the markets had existed for a long time and had been raised to a high level of technical sophistication, housed 'a great number of political geniuses, citizens distinguished by their public benefactions and all that characterises the soul of a patriot' (Brissot 1784, no. 3, p. 330). There was no reason to be amazed that patriotically playing the markets could be combined with 'pure manners and the public virtues' if one remembered that the reason for doing so was interest. 'The benefactor of humanity is interested and speculates for others; the egoist is interested in himself and speculates for his own benefit' (*ibid.*, no. 3, p. 332).

Combining the funding system with a republican system of government was a way of giving the abstract modern idea of a political body a more immediate salience and making everyone interested in getting rid of the debt. Brissot's starting point, extensively laid out in his only published book, called *De la vérité*, was Rousseau's remark, in his *Julie*, about the need for observation as the prerequisite of finding a way to articulate human passions and the rule of law. As Rousseau put it via his fictional spokesman Wolmar, 'I noticed ... that one cannot see anything simply by looking, and that one has to act oneself in order to see how men act, so I became an actor in order to be a spectator'. By living for a while in every social class, Wolmar concluded that self-interest was not, as he had earlier believed, the sole prime-mover of human actions and that among the mass of prejudices opposed to virtue there were also some that favoured it.

> I realised that man's general character is a self-love (*amour propre*) that is indifferent in itself, good or bad according to the accidents that modify it, and these latter depend on customs, laws, ranks, fortune and all our human police.
>
> (Rousseau 1761, Part IV, Letter 12, p. 475)

Brissot took this insistence upon the need for observation in conjunction with Rousseau's emphasis, in the *Social Contract*, on the need to adapt governments, as executive agents of the sovereign people, to circumstances, to point out, in a review of an anonymous *Essay on the Best Method for Studying Constitutions*, that studying constitutions involved acquiring a knowledge of what he called 'general facts'. Observation, organised under such general rubrics as custom, law, ranks or fortune as Rousseau (following Montesquieu) had indicated, would make it easier to identify the type of government appropriate for given conditions. 'Knowledge of general facts is the science of philosophers', he noted, 'that of particular facts is for narrow minds' (Brissot 1784, no. 2, p. 21, note 1). In a later note, referring a little vaguely to a review of Mably's historical works by Dominique Joseph Garat, the future interior minister of the first French Republic, Brissot signalled that the philosophical way of approaching the relationship between history and the laws, which Montesquieu had initiated, was what Mably had failed to see.[7] As Garat put it in his review,

---

7. Brissot 1784, no. 2, p. 161. It is likely that the reference was to the important major review essay by Garat of Chabrit's *De la monarchie française* (1784).

> When one has been through the abbé de Mably's works with any
> attention, one can see that, out of the whole history of the human race,
> he has been struck by one single thing, the constitutions of empires.
> With every people, whether ancient or modern, he looks for their
> constitution; all the authors he talks of are admired or dismissed in
> terms of what they had to say of constitutions; according to him, there
> is only one sort of genius, the one that conceives of and executes a fine
> constitution; there is only one sort of happiness, which is to live and
> die in a free constitution.[8]

This limited procedure, Garat stated, had been superseded by Montesquieu's recognition, following Gravina, that studying events alone was no way to know what to make of events, just as studying laws by themselves was no way to understand the laws (Garat 1784: 67). According to Garat, the model of the proper way to proceed was to be found in William Robertson's introduction to his *History of the Reign of Charles V*. His aim had been 'to outline [not] a picture of our constitutions, but a double picture of feudal barbarism and civilisation in the whole of Europe', dealing with constitutions solely 'to see how their different forms had contributed to delaying or accelerating civilisation' (Garat 1784: 23–4). As Brissot understood it, this philosophical approach to the study of history was the starting point for what he took 'observation' to mean, offering a guide for devising constitutions and forms of government which had no historical precedent and eliminating the need for a Machiavellian *ricorsi* as the basis of political reform.

IV

The financial crisis that led to the convocation of the Estates-General in 1789 gave Brissot an opportunity to develop this approach to devising a new type of republican constitution in the historically given setting of late-eighteenth-century France. Recognising that defaulting on the debt would place all the existing tax revenue in the hands of an unreformed (and potentially far from patriotic) government, he insisted that public credit itself had to be used as the basis of a debt-reduction system which would also have the effect of setting the relationship between human passions and the rule of law on a more stable footing. Brissot and his two close political associates, Jérome Péthion de Villeneuve and Etienne Clavière, argued for a republican system

8. Garat 1784: 22–3. As another of Mably's critics noted (referring to his *Observations on the Government of the United States*), 'the abbé has the idea that every law is or should be in the state constitutions': Mazzei 1976: 141, note 1.

of representative government based in some measure on the ideas of Brissot's friend, the Anglo-Welsh dissenter and critical admirer of both Rousseau and Thomas Hobbes, David Williams.[9] Brissot was responsible for the French translation of Williams's *Letters on Political Liberty* in 1783 and wrote a long review of the second English edition of the work in his *Journal du lycée de Londres* in 1784, a review quoted extensively early in 1789 by Péthion in his *Avis aux français sur le salut de la patrie* in the context of discussing the specifications and goals of a reformed political system (Dybikowski 1993: 309–10).

Williams's main idea was that it was possible to combine civil and political liberty in a modern commercial society by decentralising the state. 'In every community, where slavery is abolished', he stated in his *Letters on Political Liberty*

> the first order of men, consists of those who occupy or cultivate the soil, and produce food. The second, of those who stimulate the former, whose invention and industry offer such conveniences as heighten the enjoyment of life. The third, of those who convey from one class, or from one nation to another, the produce of all kinds of talents. The fourth, of those employed to contrive and execute public regulations for the peace and prosperity of the state. – The first three classes, constitute the People: the fourth is either a delegation, representing the other classes; or it is a factitious and spurious body, whose principle is diseased blood, and whose component parts, are all the vices which disgrace humanity.   (Williams 1789: 83–4)

To prevent the 'political evils' which arise from the 'operation of the fourth on all the other classes', Williams called for the establishment of a double system of representation: the first to improve the existing system of representation in parliament; the second to house many of the executive functions of government by distributing the activities of the fourth class over a range of decentralised bodies. The system he proposed was a revised version of the ancient Saxon constitution, consisting of a hierarchy of elected bodies – assemblies of ten men (tithings) electing a representative to assemblies of ten tithings (hundreds), and so on through thousands, ten thousands, a hundred thousands and a thousand thousands. The aim of this particular version of an ancient republican organisational idea was to create more than a more equitable electoral system. Its 'immediate object', Williams emphasised, was not 'a representation for the purpose of a legislature; but to form political

---

9. On Williams, see Dybikowski 1993 and his edition of the surviving correspondence between Williams and Brissot (1987–8).

powers in the body of the people, to controul, balance, or give stability to the legislature and crown; and to effect the purposes of defensive and internal police'. It was the 'want of this political power', he explained, that had been felt in the ancient republics of Greece and Rome, neither the ephors nor the tribunes of the people being able to supply it (Williams 1789: 61). This system of representation was, Williams emphasised, designed to complement a representative legislature, uncoupling government from legislation and allowing civil and political liberty to work in tandem because the Leviathan had been dissolved into its constituent parts.

Brissot combined these ideas with the theory of public credit produced by another of his friends, the Genevan exile Etienne Clavière, in a long pamphlet published late in 1788. 'Society', Clavière stated, 'is an individual which has only one birth and one death. Its life is made up of a multitude of lives which, beginning and ending at different moments, do not allow for any break in continuity' (Clavière 1788: 31). To claim that public credit entailed drawing bills upon posterity was, he claimed, meaningless, for the simple reason that 'the word "posterity" has no relationship to the word "nation"' (ibid.: 31, n. 1). When, in this context, he asked, does 'posterity' begin or end? The idea of pre-commitment could not have any relevance to a nation's credit. This was the case, Clavière argued, even when a society has a single head: the sceptre, he pointed out, does not fall for a single instant. 'This is the principle which governs corporations (communautés). Societies are great corporations. All of them alienate the future on behalf of the present, because the present prepares the future and the one is inseparable from the other' (ibid.: 32). A nation which defaulted on its debt would not be a nation. 'It would not form a body, a political association. It would be a monstrous gathering of men, seeking to deceive one another in every relationship designed to establish national security and to follow a common interest' (ibid.: 47). Would Rousseau, Clavière asked rhetorically, have believed that a National Assembly, occupied with a public debt, would dishonour the nation? (ibid.: 76). As a short-term solution to the monarchy's financial crisis he proposed the creation of a temporary, voluntary system of bills payable to the bearer to maintain public credit, encouraging the capitalists to issue such bills on the security of their interest payments and the royal treasury to do the same for anyone prepared to play the traditional republican role and convert their gold and silverware into coin. This injection of an additional circulating medium into the money supply would, he argued, prop up the public funds until the Estates-General was able to reform the fiscal system and place the nation's credit on a more stable footing by reducing its debt.

Turning this proposal into a more ambitious debt-reduction scheme in the wake of the confiscation of the property of the church in November 1789 raised the question of how to ensure that the new funding system, based on the issue of *assignats* entitling their purchasers to buy national property over the following decade, would be used for patriotic rather than self-interested purposes. The answer, Clavière stated, was to make the new monetary medium compulsory. Anything other than a forced currency, he argued in 1790, would fail to solve the double problem of liquidating the debt and promoting prosperity. The inherited legacy of accumulated debt left little room for any other choice than one between a forcibly introduced currency or a forcibly imposed reduction of the debt. The question was which kind of force would do least damage to liberty (Clavière 1790).

V

It is well known that the confiscation of the property of the church and the monetisation of the debt horrified Edmund Burke. As J. G. A. Pocock noted, his attack on the course of events in France in his *Reflections on the Revolution in France* was couched in standardly republican terms.

> All other nations have begun the fabric of a new government, or the reformation of an old, by establishing originally or by enforcing with greater exactness some rites or other of religion. All other peoples have laid the foundations of civil freedom in severer manners and a system of a more austere and masculine morality. France, when she let loose the reins of regal authority, doubled the license of a ferocious dissoluteness . . . as if she were communicating . . . all the unhappy corruptions that usually were the disease of wealth and power.   (Burke 1987: 933)

This, he argued was why it was a mistake to see

> nothing in what has been done in France but a firm and temperate exertion of freedom, so consistent, on the whole, with morals and piety as to make it deserving not only of the secular applause of dashing Machiavellian politicians, but to render it a fit theme for all the devout effusions of sacred eloquence.   (Burke 1987: 9–10)

In Burke's terms, opting for a forced currency, rather than a forcible reduction in the debt, simply amounted to postponing having to face the original question of how a republic might be able to choose between preserving itself and preserving its debt. Opting for modern prudence in economics and ancient prudence in politics was, Burke argued, a formula for catastrophe.

Opting for a forced currency, rather than a forcible reduction of the debt, added a new dimension to the responsibilities of government, replacing the risks associated with a patriot king by those associated with mismanaging the money supply either by issuing too large an amount of money or by failing to collect enough tax revenue. One partial solution was to propose, as Condorcet did in February 1792, the establishment of an elected treasury independent of both the executive and, as far as possible, the legislative power, with responsibility for overseeing the collection and disbursement of tax revenue by France's eighty-three departmental administrations, leaving the legislature responsible simply for setting levels of government expenditure every year. As a measure of its importance, Condorcet proposed that the method of electing treasury officials should be a smaller-scale version of those in existence for choosing a Regent, with a small national electoral college made up of one representative per department, who had to have no connection with the department in question to be eligible for election, forming the electorate of what amounted to a Federal Reserve Board (Condorcet 1847: 53–67).

Two months later, however, France declared war on the Holy Roman Empire and, by the end of 1792, had become a republic. The unexpectedly protracted character of the war served to bring the difficulties associated with combining a republican government and a public debt into sharp relief. The more democratic the republic's government became, the more difficult it was to make a distinction between the public interest and the interests of the republic's creditor-citizens. In a mirror-image of the original republican nightmare of an absolute government's power to choose between preserving its liberty and preserving its debt, Robespierre, in his speech on the principles of revolutionary government, argued that necessity meant sacrificing the republic's free, peace-time constitution in order to preserve its currency for the duration of the war-time emergency.

> For some time past (he stated) our public order has been dependent on the whim of foreigners. It was at their behest that money flowed or disappeared from circulation. It was when they wished it that the people found bread or were compelled to do without it; and crowds gathered at bakers' shops or dispersed at their beck and call ... We know it and see it happen; yet they continue to live in our midst, and the sword of justice eludes them.   (cited in Rudé (ed.) 1967: 64)

VI

The imperatives of public safety meant that the price of preserving the modern funding system was to dispense with political liberty. This reversal of priorities can be taken as an indication of how difficult it was to find a republican solution to the problem of the public debt. The possibility that this might happen was one reason why, in 1789, the abbé Sieyès took up the question of the nation's debt in a rather different way. He did so at the time that the National Assembly was discussing the question of whether to deal with the problem of the deficit by confiscating the property of the church. Sieyès, notoriously, rejected this solution not only because it would entail a massive increase in the powers and responsibilities of government but also because he was not, in principle, opposed to the existence of a public debt. He did not, in fact, think that it was desirable to eliminate the debt at all and, instead, drafted a plan for reducing the debt as a purely expedient measure. 'This plan', he noted, 'is based on the supposition of the political theories recognised up to now ... The true doctrine of taxation, true social theory, does not require either repaying the debt, since it was going to set all production under the hands of the state, or freeing the landowners from their fiscal obligations to the state.'[10] Sieyès's claim that 'true social theory' meant accepting the existence of a public debt also meant that he rejected the republican hope that it might be possible to eliminate the monetary, fiscal and financial entanglements of the modern state. He fully recognised, however, that there might be a moment at which a modern republic might have to face opting for injustice in order to preserve the public good. But in an (undated) note entitled 'Emergency' (*Urgence*) he flatly rejected the idea that deciding what to do in an emergency should be subject to any kind of democratic procedure. 'I have just one question on the subject', he wrote.

> Doesn't a single individual judge things better than any kind of
> gathering of men when one is forced to decide hurriedly without
> being able to hear the interested parties? An individual is never
> deprived of the advantages of reflection and deliberation; a body of
> men is without reflection and deliberation from the moment that it is
> forced to decide in a hurry. In its case, deliberation is verbal and slow
> while with an individual it is purely intellectual and quick. I conclude

10. 'Ce plan est dans la supposition des théories politiques reçues jusqu'à ce jour. La véritable doctrine de l'impôt, la véritable théorie sociale ne demande ni le remboursement de la dette puisqu'elle alloit à mettre toutes les productions entre les mains de l'état, ni l'affranchissement des propriétaires terriens envers l'état': Archives nationales, Paris, 284 AP 4, dossier 9, 'Destination des biens ecclésiastiques'.

> that a body that is forced to make a hurried decision does not
> deliberate, and therefore that its act is not moral. It is a purely
> mechanical action. Is this, then, how to constitute it for the purposes
> of liberty and improvement (*perfectionnement*)? Among the ancients,
> when a decision did not allow for delay, one created a dictator.[11]

From Sieyès's perspective, a permanent representative of the state (a hereditary king or life-president), able, in the last instance, to decide that emergency action was necessary, was a better agent for preserving political and civil liberty than a Committee of Public Safety.

This fundamental concession to the idea of monarchical government (based, however, on a representative republican idea of sovereignty) had the effect of making a republican solution to the debt problem remarkably similar to the royal solution which republicans in late-eighteenth-century France were so determined to avoid. Interestingly, Sieyès's assertion that 'true social theory' entailed accepting the existence of a public debt was similar to the position adopted by Immanuel Kant in his *Perpetual Peace* of 1795. Although Kant stated that one of the preliminary articles of a perpetual peace between states would have to be a clause stipulating that 'no national debt shall be contracted in connection with the external affairs of the state', he did not commend either of the eighteenth-century republican solutions to the debt problem. Since there were national debts, peace would have to come about indirectly, by means of commerce and the mutual interest of states. 'And of all the powers', Kant noted, '(or means) at the disposal of the power of states, financial power can probably be relied on most. Thus states find themselves compelled to promote the noble cause of peace, though not exactly from motives of morality.'

From that perspective, the way to Salentum, the peaceful and prosperous society which Fénelon described in his *Telemachus*, could not come from making a choice between commerce or the financial power of the modern state but, instead, had to come, however erratically, from them both.

11. *Ibid.*, 284 AP 5, dossier 13, 'Urgence'.

15

Commercial Realities, Republican Principles

DONALD WINCH

I

After 1776, especially in the Anglo-American world, practical as well as philosophical understanding of commercial realities increasingly depended on the work of Adam Smith, whether by absorption or reaction. In this respect the wider world came to appreciate what Smith's Scottish friends were the first to welcome when the *Wealth of Nations* was published. William Robertson predicted that the book would 'necessarily become a Political or Commercial Code to all Europe, which must be often consulted both by men of Practice and Speculation', an opinion seconded by Adam Ferguson when he said that Smith was 'surely to reign alone on these subjects, to form the opinions and I hope to govern at least the coming generations' (Smith 1987: 192–3). Smith was not the first member of his generation of Scottish philosophers to analyse the benefits and drawbacks associated with commercial society: David Hume and Ferguson had preceded him in both these respects. Nevertheless, Robertson and Ferguson proved correct: Smith became the premier late-eighteenth-century guide to the science and art of the legislator faced with the problems and possibilities associated with this type of society. This has ensured that Smith remains the validating agent for much that we, in retrospect, wish to say when assessing the moral and political implications of commercial societies, despite the long accumulation of experience of living in such societies since Smith's death.

Which position or positions Smith does in fact validate or even instantiate, however, remains a matter of dispute. Requiring Smith to remain in the

I am grateful to Quentin Skinner for persistent questioning of the earlier version of this paper, though I doubt if the outcome will be entirely to his taste. I should also like to thank Richard Whatmore for his comments on the penultimate draft.

position assigned to him during the nineteenth and twentieth centuries as the pioneering analyst-cum-apologist for liberal capitalist values is no longer obligatory, particularly since the revival of interest in those ideas to which Smith himself referred when he addressed 'men of republican principles' in the *Wealth of Nations*. 'Republican' is, of course, a sophisticated term of political and interpretative art. Uncovering what 'they' meant by it, and deciding how it can best be captured by 'our' interpretative vocabulary – by 'civic humanism' or 'civic moralism', by 'Commonwealthmen', by 'Country' forms of opposition, by 'neo-Harringtonian' or 'neo-Roman' ideology, or more simply by 'classical republicanism' – has been a major preoccupation of historians over the last three decades or more. While opinions may differ on the weight to be attached to the 'civic' dimension of Scottish thinking after the Union of 1707, there can be no doubt that recognition of its pervasive influence has been responsible for some of the most interesting work on eighteenth-century Scottish political and intellectual developments done in recent years. Equally interesting, because more historical, interpretations of Smith's concerns can be arrived at by taking the 'republican' questions seriously.

The resulting readings are less stereotyped than those based on the transhistorical presumption that what became of something is the best guide to what it was. According to such readings, the work of the founder of a separate science of economics must either mark the divorce of the economic from the political, or, worse still, the assimilation of the political to the economic (Cropsey 1957, 1975; Wolin 1960). In either guise this becomes a sign that some important values associated with the classical republican tradition were being bypassed or devalued. Alternatively, Smith must continue to stand as the monument to a particular brand of 'negative' liberalism, according to which self-seeking individuals must be left to pursue their goals within a constitutional framework of legal security that is free from other legislative constraints. Since negative liberty in this sense has been described as *the* classical liberal position, Smith's reputation has remained alive and well in various late-twentieth-century quarters for whom this remains the 'true' version. Of these, the Hayek–Thatcher appeals to Smith's authority were only the most highly publicised, acquiring additional normative purchase from the collapse of the Soviet empire after 1989, when a free market system with an imputed Smithian pedigree emerged triumphant over one based on state planning and public ownership.

The ideological stakes are even higher, perhaps, in the United States because the classical republican readings of the concerns of pre- and post-revolutionary Americans have provoked, in opposition, a revival of interpretations based on competing self-interest between equal and independent citizens as the defining characteristics of American national identity from the outset (Appleby 1984; Nelson 1987; Pangle 1988; Kramnick 1990). We have here an instance of what John Pocock (1987a) has referred to as the *ideologia americana*: liberalism, for good or ill, as the residual category for all things truly American, with Smith continuing to prove almost as essential as John Locke as witness to its qualities. For without Smith, who else could serve the purpose of illustrating, let alone legitimating, a fully articulated, late-eighteenth-century conception of a social and economic order based on competition and the untrammelled pursuit of self-interest?

The tensions between these historical and trans-historical readings of what are often depicted as the diametrically opposed fates of classical republicanism and liberalism have added spice to the modern debate. Testing the accuracy of the labels has been a worthwhile exercise, and one of the best ways of doing this has been to compare the sightings of Smith that can be achieved by viewing his work from various points of view, each representing positions that were genuinely available to him. As Duncan Forbes (1975a, 1975b) was the first to show, Hume, Smith's closest friend and ally in many matters, philosophical, historical, and political, provides the best insight into Smith's position. Francis Hutcheson – one of Hume's starting points as moral philosopher, as well as being Smith's teacher – must also be added to any list of range-finding sightings (Winch 1978; Campbell 1982; Haakonssen 1996). Other Scottish contemporaries within what has been called the 'moderate *literati*', especially Ferguson, are equally natural additions (Sher 1985; Robertson 1985; and contributions above by Oz-Salzburger and Geuna). The part played by Scottish writings in the deliberations of the American founding fathers offers further vantage points connected with James Madison, Thomas Jefferson and Alexander Hamilton (Sher and Smitten (eds.) 1990). Bearing in mind the most significant development in European republicanism after 1789, comparisons can also be made with Jean-Jacques Rousseau, Edmund Burke, John Millar, Thomas Paine and Richard Price. These authors were either known to Smith or showed a detailed acquaintance with his work (Winch 1996: 57–197). With the exception of Burke, they each represent variants of late-eighteenth-century republicanism, albeit so disparate that one can hardly speak of them as forming a single heritage. With the exception of Rousseau, they were all at home with commerce, some of them adopting celebratory positions on its liberating potential.

Taken together, then, these authors ought to provide a comprehensive guide to the ways in which Smith was, or was not, in sympathy with persisting currents of European political thought to which some kind of republican label can be applied – currents that had been given new vigour and direction by those who designed the constitution of the federal republic of the United States of America, upon which Smith maintained a perplexing silence once its constitutional arrangements were settled. That such multiple sightings are necessary reflects the problems of dealing with a figure of Smith's complexity and reputation. It could also be a tribute to the rich, though often ambiguous, qualities of the republican legacy during this period. Any understanding based on one of the sightings risks becoming reductive of Smith as well as of the legacy, as will be illustrated later by comparison of Smith with his more obviously republican-minded contemporary, Ferguson.

II

But do any clear or novel conclusions emerge from these sightings? Those who seek closure in any system of political ideas often do so by enforcing essentialist binary distinctions on historical actors. Employing such methods has led some to question whether it was possible for Smith to find sufficient space to perch on a fence dividing republicanism, often treated as an atavism, from what he is normally taken to represent, namely liberalism (Harpham 1984). Nor will those committed to ideological clarity be impressed by the puritanical argument that while republicanism has a great deal to be said for it as an historical entity, liberalism at the end of the eighteenth century does not. Rather than enter once more into these historiographic waters, however, I shall begin with a binary distinction that has more to be said in its favour from the historian's perspective: between natural jurisprudence and republicanism in one or another of its guises.

   If this is the nature of the choice available, there can be no doubt where Smith must be placed. Following in the footsteps of Gershom Carmichael and Hutcheson at Glasgow, Smith was happy to accept natural law categories and styles of reasoning as the intellectual framework for his own innovations. Granted a longer life he would have made good his promise to develop 'a theory of the general principles which ought to run through and be the foundation of the laws of all nations' (Smith 1976b: 342). Like Hume, he drew a sharp contrast between the strict, though negative, obligations embodied in rules of justice and the voluntary, though positive, calls made on us by codes of beneficence. Justice was confined to commutative rules governing *meum* and *tuum*, those perfect rights which had to be protected from injury in all societies, but where the specific types of injury varied with the dominant form of property relationship. Ideas of distributive justice, based on conceptions of merit or desert, were insufficiently precise to provide the degree of social consensus required for communal coercion by magistrates who, acting on behalf of the promptings of the impartial spectator, register our legitimate resentments when faced with injuries to such rights. Smith rejected Hume's emphasis on utility as the basis for the 'artificial' virtues underlying justice, but he saw the need to supply a history of law and government that would give substance to Hume's argument that rules of justice must be based on a social learning process.

Smith's account of the progress of opulence in Book III of the *Wealth of Nations* endorses Hume's version of the story of how 'commerce and manufactures gradually introduced order and good government, and with them, the liberty and security of individuals' into post-feudal Europe (Smith 1976a: 412). And while he ordered the destruction of manuscripts that contained a fuller treatment 'of the general principles of law and government, and of all the different revolutions which they have undergone in the different ages and periods of society' (1976b: 342), there is enough evidence in the *Wealth of Nations*, now supplemented by the notes on his *Lectures on Jurisprudence*, to show how he would have conducted this inquiry. It would have taken the form of a story involving universal psychological propensities working in conjunction with evolving socio-economic circumstances classified according to four stages or modes of subsistence: hunter-gatherers, pastoral peoples, agricultural or feudal society, and commerce. The purpose of the story would have been to mount a critique of positive law by showing those respects in which, and for what reasons, it had departed from natural principles. By marshalling this evidence Forbes was able to show that liberty for Hume and Smith was essentially that modern form of personal or civil liberty achieved through impartial administration of the rule of law. They saw it as a significant historical achievement, though with some fortuitous elements, and it made the administration of justice, after external defence, the most important of the functions carried out by governments.

Here then surely is the basis for some of the ideas Benjamin Constant (1988) defined as 'modern' liberty when contrasting it with the 'ancient' forms it had replaced. This led to Constant being granted a favoured place in the post-French-revolutionary history of the idea that underlies Isaiah Berlin's (1969) distinction between 'positive' and 'negative' conceptions of liberty. Smith's appeal to the 'invisible hand' and use of unintended consequences as a mode of explaining complex historical and social outcomes within his four-stage framework has become another factor differentiating him from the more active vision often associated with any properly accredited *political* theory, let alone its classical republican variants (Stimson 1989). Employing a convenient pair of anachronisms, it has also been argued that the explanatory style of the proto-social scientist, operating in a proto-positivist manner, is incompatible with the normative moral and political concerns of republicanism (Minowitz 1993; McNamara 1998). In another formulation, the invisible hand leads to interest-group pluralism, but is incompatible with any developed notion of republicanism (Pettit 1997: 203–4, 224–7). At best, such interpretations capture an important 'contemplative' aspect of Smith's writings. They help to explain, for example, why he could arouse the impatience of Ferguson, who was more keen to adopt a committed role when faced with political crises such as the American revolution (Winch 1996: 47–9). In reverse, they may also help to explain why the only references to Ferguson's *Essay on the History of Civil Society* in the Glasgow edition of the *Wealth of Nations* have had to be supplied by Smith's modern editors. As in the case of his economic rival, James Steuart, silent rebuttal could sometimes be Smith's method of response.

Some substantial reasons of a more historical character have been adduced for the incompatibility of a natural jurisprudential approach that grants priority to civil rights with those participatory qualities centring on virtue that are an essential feature of any republican view of human affairs. John Pocock (1983, 1985b) has argued that the jurisprudential interest in the individual as the bearer of rights and the owner of property cannot be easily reconciled with the concern shown by the civic humanist tradition for citizenly participation and self-rule. If this is the case then we have a story in which there was a shift from the civic to the civil in the direction of all those economic, cultural and moral values that now belong to a world covered by the term 'social'. Civility as a code of practice, and civilisation as the process by which it had been established – increasingly in the latest stage in the history of civil society by means of growing commercial interdependency – now appear to provide an alternative way of life and a threat to republicanism. In their disparate ways, Rousseau and Ferguson illustrate the forms that fears of men of republican principles could take when faced with this threat.

But Pocock was surely right to point out that the two languages had long lived side by side; and that there are few signs that Scottish philosophers, from Hutcheson onwards, regarded them as being in conflict with one another. They each found ways of assigning them to their respective roles, with some giving the 'republican' dimension more prominence than others. Quentin Skinner (1984, 1986, 1990a) has also insisted that we ought not to be seduced by the binary distinction between positive and negative conceptions of liberty. He has addressed the problem of reconciling republican ideas of liberty with non-interventionist conceptions of individual freedom by maintaining that negative liberty cannot be achieved without the positive versions associated with republicanism. For if liberty and virtue are mutually supportive, speaking as though rights existed without duties could undermine those rights. One contrasting position for Skinner, historically, is contractarianism of the Hobbes–Locke variety, and in our own times those highly individualistic modern libertarian versions that underlie much of the revival of interest in subjective rights. In the latest statement of his views (Skinner 1998), however, the alternative is represented by late-eighteenth- and nineteenth-century versions of utilitarianism and Berlin's conception of negative liberalism.

An answer to the same problems as they arise in the case of Hume and Smith would begin from the observation that both were opponents of contractarian doctrines, largely because they based their systems of morals and politics on an assumption of basic human sociability that merits the term anti-individualist. They also emphasised the primacy of the passions in a manner that deserves to be treated as a form of anti-rationalism, a position that could bring them into conflict, in their own day, with neo-Lockeans like Price. In a sequence of studies Knud Haakonssen (1981, 1993, 1996) has not only differentiated Hume and Smith from Benthamite versions of utilitarianism, but has shown that the eighteenth-century understanding of natural law was less individualistic than it has often been portrayed. It was always couched in terms of the interdependence of the rights and duties of the various offices we are called upon to perform. Within a scheme of things in which rights cannot be divorced from correlative duties and offices, there is scope for more or less inclusive notions of what duties attach to citizenship. Duties also involve obligations, and since 'virtuous' is a commonplace way of describing those who conscientiously perform the obligations attached to their stations in life, we have a way in which the languages of rights and virtue could live happily side by side. The constitution of the new American republic reveals just how closely rights-based thinking of the natural law variety and republican ideals were originally in harmony, however much later critics have regretted that one or other element has taken over.

III

With the weakening of the jurisprudential/republican divide we are free to pose a republican question based on one of Smith's best-known conclusions: what duties can realistically be expected of citizens who are placed in increasingly specialised socio-economic roles by the system of dividing occupations that is an essential characteristic of commercial society? By so doing we confront one of the dilemmas faced by Ferguson and Rousseau, by some post-revolutionary French republicans troubled by the monarchical legacy of a society of ranks, and by some of the American founding fathers who feared that the new nation was already on the downward-sloping European path towards luxury and inequality. Does equality of condition, sometimes known more perceptively, in Price's terminology, as preserving the 'middle station', have to be added to independence and equality of opportunity as an economic pre-condition for sustaining republican manners and performing the duties of citizenship? Price's warnings to the Americans not to enfeeble republican habits by becoming entangled with foreign trade, and the agrarian preferences expressed in Jefferson's *Notes on Virginia*, contain positive answers to these questions, despite the difficulties later experienced by the new nation in remaining untainted by commercial and manufacturing imperatives.

Smith's agrarian sympathies were not negligible and could sometimes sound positively pastoral. No one who had accorded such scathing treatment to the 'policy of Europe' in giving positive encouragement to manufactures and the colonial trade could be regarded as indifferent to the agrarian foundation for rising opulence. But does this carry with it anything more than a recipe for soundly based economic growth? Are we not hearing the advice of the economic expert rather than the reflections of someone with wider political and moral concerns? Any answer to such questions rests less on Smith's agrarian preferences than on those liberating features both he and Hume associated with the rise of commercial societies in which agriculture itself took commercial forms. For Hume (1994: 112), it was the emergence of that large 'middling rank' associated with commerce that provided a protective bulwark for modern types of liberty. Commerce had bred a new army of supporters which could be counted on to be jealous of encroachments by executive authority and the undue influence exerted by social and political superiors. For Smith, the argument turns on urban commercial and manufacturing activities as forces that have eliminated 'servile dependency' in the countryside (1976a: 412). The initiating impulse could be political as well as economic: Smith's defence of the Anglo-Scottish Union was that it had provided the means by which 'the middling and inferior ranks of people in Scotland gained a compleat deliverance from the power of an aristocracy which had always before oppressed them' (*ibid.*: 944). The story of the rise of opulence in Book III of the *Wealth of Nations* is, in this respect, not merely one in which 'a sort of independent republicks' (*ibid.*: 401), the towns of feudal Europe, play a major role, but a 'republican' story in the larger sense as well.

Under some conditions, then, commerce provides the modern alternative to what the ancients attempted to achieve by means of an agrarian law designed to overcome large concentrations of property and power. The best statement of Smith's position on such matters can now be found in his *Lectures on Jurisprudence*, where he tells his students why, in present circumstances, there is now 'a graduall descent of fortunes' which makes the ancient fear of 'overgrown fortunes' irrelevant (1978: 196). This could serve as an answer to those who sought to revive what Hume had called the 'violent' maxims of the ancient republics, instead of conforming measures to the 'common bent of mankind' (1994: 97). It was probably the reason why Smith, in reviewing Rousseau's second discourse on inequality, spoke of its author as having taken 'the true spirit of a republican a little too far' (1980: 251). Although an admirer of Machiavelli's attempt to seek impartial causal accounts of political events (1983: 114), Smith would probably have endorsed Hume's opinion that Machiavelli's understanding was confined to the 'furious and tyrannical governments of ancient times, or to the little disorderly principalities of Italy' (1994: 51); he had no experience of modern monarchies and the forms of 'free government' associated with the rise of commerce and the arts and sciences to complete the picture. Smith's history of the rise and fall of republics ends with those modern monarchies that 'now set the fashion'; they are better adapted to large states, especially those controlling extensive empires.

The existing European republics receive some attention in Smith's comparative treatment of the wealth of nations, and his remarks on the Dutch republic have been read as an endorsement of republicanism (Cropsey 1957: 65–8, 94; but see Forbes 1975b: 195–7). It is certainly true that Smith was less jealous of Dutch success, but also less of an admirer of Dutch institutions than some of his mercantile predecessors had been at an earlier stage of Anglo-Dutch rivalry. Although he discerned no decay in Dutch trade, he drew attention to the heavy burden of taxation required to support the debt incurred to preserve independence from foreign rule and the encroachments of the North Sea. There is also a suggestion that the 'present grandeur' of the Dutch republic was at risk, depending as it did on the willingness of the mercantile order to accept low rates of return on its capital as the price for the 'respect and authority' they derived from participating in a mixed constitution alongside nobles and soldiers. Should the balance within this mixture shift against them, Smith felt that there could be wholesale capital flight abroad, bringing national ruin in its train (1976a: 108–9, 906). The same could happen in 'landed nations' such as Britain, also bearing a heavy weight of debt and taxation, but the United Provinces were more exposed

to danger through smallness and lack of remunerative agricultural outlets
for their capital. Smith's attack on the 'standing army' of mercantile interest
groups in England might lead one to suspect that he was shedding crocodile
tears here (Stimson 1989: 99), but the more natural interpretation would be
to say that a particular balance involving the mercantile interest was essential
to constitutional stability in Holland.

When faced with the republican habits and manners of the American assemblies, and when predicting what their fate would be when separated from
the British crown, Smith was more forthright. The advantages the thirteen
colonies enjoyed in being free from the laws of primogeniture, an 'oppressive
aristocracy', and an established church were outweighed by the disadvan-
tages associated with 'those rancorous and virulent factions which are inseparable from small democracies, and which have so frequently divided the
affections of their people, and disturbed the tranquillity of their governments, in their form so nearly democratical' (Smith 1976a: 945). That is why
Smith offered his scheme of imperial federation, embodying fiscal harmonisation and representation proportioned to revenues, as a preferable, though
utopian, alternative. What had produced 'infinite Good' (Smith 1987: 68)
in the Scottish case since 1707, and would deliver Ireland from the evils
of religious factionalism if wisdom prevailed in future, could also be made
acceptable to the Americans, as long as their 'leading men' could be granted
the dignity and access to offices, venal or otherwise, which came from membership of the imperial 'states-general'. Like Hume, Smith believed that
'management and persuasion', otherwise known as 'corruption' to men of
Paine and Price's stamp, was essential to the smooth operation of mixed
forms of government.

Although such Machiavellian realism was not allowed to sully the pages of
the *Federalist Papers*, the temporary alliance between Hamilton and Madison
which made their publication possible was based on a similar diagnosis of
the dangers of factionalism. Madison's 'republican remedy for the diseases
most incident to republican government' involved a federal republic of 'wide
extent' that subjected the interests released by its democratical components
to control through competition and mutual dilution. Hence the perplexity
aroused by Smith's failure to leave any record of his views on the constitution.
The results were not available for calm deliberation before Smith's death in
1790, but he might also have been embarrassed by his earlier, though private,
prediction that the loss of 'regal government' (1987: 381–4) would be accompanied by the kind of factional strife he associated with small democratical
republics.

Smith's solution to the American problem reveals that he cannot be enlisted on behalf of the Rousseauvian advantages of smallness, or among those, like Paine, who regarded the very existence of monarchy and hereditary aristocracy as anathema to economic progress and constitutional legitimacy. Commercial realities in the shape of the dynamic forces they released in civil society were, for Paine, the reason why all hereditary forms of government were bound to perish. For a variety of reasons, Smith described Price as a 'factious citizen', one of them probably being his support for the American cause. Another may have been the rationalist approach to morals and natural rights which later made Price the object of Burke's anger, as well as the target of Josiah Tucker's attack on 'neo-Lockeans'. If he had bothered to notice Paine, Price's radical coadjutor in American and French affairs, it seems highly unlikely that Smith would have been favourably disposed towards his brand of republicanism – despite Paine's admiration for Smith's position on a number of crucial matters connected with commerce and the evils of primogeniture.

IV

We appear to have returned to Forbes's twin conclusion: what mattered most to Hume and Smith was 'not the form of government, whether free or absolute, but the degree of civilization'; and that 'one cannot have freedom without commerce and manufactures, but opulence without freedom is the norm rather than the exception' (Forbes 1975b: 198, 201). Hume believed that the benefits associated with commerce could be enjoyed by 'civilized monarchies; where the arts of government, first invented in free states, are preserved to the mutual advantage and security of sovereign and subject'. Francophile sympathies and Anglophobe antipathies could account for Hume's charge of 'high political rant' when the ('scarcely felt') dependence of French subjects for security of their property on the monarch was described as 'tyranny' (Hume 1994: 68–9). By arguing here that 'most of the ends of political society' could be met in the French fashion, Hume was endorsing a decidedly non-republican conclusion concerning the irrelevance of forms of government, always supposing the requirements of legal security were met. At the same time, however, when discoursing more broadly, he could endorse those 'political writers' who in 'fixing the several checks and controuls of the constitution' suppose every man to be a knave. Without such checks, there would be 'no security for our liberties or possessions, except the good-will of our rulers; that is, we shall have no security at all' (1994: 24).

The equivalent evidence in Smith can be found in a number of places, and it bears out Forbes's claim that 'sceptical Whiggism' of the Hume–Smith variety recognises gradations of liberty rather than a sharp republican divide between liberty and slavery. In the lectures on jurisprudence given in the 1760s, Smith sounds more complacent about English constitutional arrangements than Hume managed to be when faced with the problems of public debt and the popular agitation surrounding John Wilkes. The public law concerning limits to the power of sovereigns was less precise than that determined by courts in cases of private law, with the additional complication in England that since it was now the king-in-parliament that constituted the sovereign power 'no one can tell what they can not do' (Smith 1978: 311). The revolution of 1688 had, however, set boundaries to the exercise of royal power. A number of legal and parliamentary safeguards now existed which had created a 'happy mixture of all the different forms of government properly restrained and a perfect security to liberty and property' (*ibid.*: 421-2). The array of safeguards has the standard Whig features: independence of the judiciary, control over the civil list, *habeas corpus*, frequent elections, and parliamentary regulation of the government's conduct. At the same time, again following Hume, Smith distanced himself from contractarian accounts of allegiance and hence from neo-Lockean ideas on rights of resistance. Such rights exist under all governments, but Smith's conclusion was that: 'No government is quite perfect, but it is better to submitt to some inconveniences than make attempts against it' (1978: 321, 435).

Although Smith does not give a connected account of these issues in the *Wealth of Nations*, the same standpoint is adopted. For example, though the discretionary powers embodied in the use of general warrants were judged to be 'an abusive practice', they were not 'likely to occasion any general oppression'. Far worse in this respect was the infringement of 'natural liberty and justice' embodied in the Acts of Settlement which inhibited the freedom of wage-earners to sell their labour in the most advantageous market (1976a: 157). When dealing with the French system of government Smith showed himself to be less Francophile than Hume, while still upholding the idea of gradation: the system was 'arbitrary and violent in comparison with that of Great Britain', yet 'legal and free in comparison with ... Spain and Portugal' (*ibid.*: 586). Although the tax powers of the Intendants were 'severe' and 'oppressive', France – after England – still enjoyed the 'mildest and most indulgent government' (*ibid.*: 731, 905). England was not an exception to the general policy of Europe in economic matters. Indeed, the openness of its parliamentary institutions to pressure from merchants and manufacturers constituted a major threat to the idea of public good Smith was articulating in the *Wealth of Nations*. Nevertheless, only in England were unjust and inexpedient economic policies 'counterbalanced by the general liberty and security of the people' (*ibid.*: 541). This had given rise to an independent yeomanry that might provide a better agrarian foundation for the growth of opulence than any to be found elsewhere in Europe (*ibid.*: 392, 395, 425).

In both the *Lectures on Jurisprudence* and the *Wealth of Nations* Smith recognised that standing armies had, historically, constituted one of the main threats to liberty. On both occasions too he sustained a position that was anathema to men of republican principles, chief among them being Ferguson and other advocates of a Scottish militia within the Edinburgh Poker Club. Although Smith was not 'a war-like philosopher' in Ferguson's mould, he would not have disputed the priority of defence over matters of opulence. The difference of opinion here chiefly turns on the effectiveness of alternative military means. Smith dampened the ardour for militias by maintaining that, as with other features of life in commercial societies, specialisation, through the use of professional armies, was the order of the day, not least for reasons connected with modern military technology. Doubts about the military prowess of militias were reinforced by concern over the higher opportunity costs to commercial societies of withdrawing labour from productive pursuits for the long periods necessary to ensure that militias became as effective as standing armies. The final insult added to injury came from his contention that a nation in which 'the sovereign is himself the general, and the principal nobility and gentry the chief officers of the army', where 'those who have the greatest interest in the support of the civil authority, because they have themselves the greatest share of that authority' – in such a nation 'a standing army can never be dangerous to liberty' (1976a: 706–7). An argument for a Scottish militia aimed at the Scottish gentry, while at the same time soothing English fears of Scottish militarism, was being turned into a case for the existing standing army.

Although this evidence is now well known (Winch 1978, Robertson 1985, Sher 1989), it is not conclusive proof of Smith's anti- or non-republican sympathies. It merely shows that on this issue Smith believed that commercial realities conflicted with an interpretation of republican principles that was no longer relevant to British conditions. In other respects Smith was more optimistic than Ferguson about the educational benefits of militia training in the larger civic sense. Loss of 'martial spirit', along with an inability to appreciate 'the great and extensive interests of his country', was part of the social disease inflicted on all those at the bottom of society's pyramid who were subject to the 'mental mutilation' associated with the division of labour (Smith 1976a: 782). Unlike Ferguson, Smith did not confine his remedies to insulating the political élite from over-immersion in economic life by appealing to their public spirit. If martial spirit in the male populace could be encouraged by means of militia training, not only could the standing army be smaller, but the spirit itself would provide further insurance against any constitutional threat posed by a standing army. Indeed, this espousal of the necessity for standing armies could be given a pre-eminently republican reading: it was a case where self-interested behaviour in commercial societies prevented citizens from appreciating the dangers of neglecting their public duties.

Again in contrast with Ferguson, Smith did not despair of the lower ranks becoming, through militia training, through membership of religious sects, and by means of elementary education, a passive influence for good. They might not be capable of contesting abuses of power directly, but they could form part of an educated public which supported those who did so. The fears of Hume and Smith on factions, especially those based on religion, are brought into play on this subject. Education would make the lower ranks 'less liable . . . to the delusions of enthusiasm and superstition', more respectful of 'lawful superiors', and 'more capable of seeing through the interested complaints of faction and sedition' (Smith 1976a: 788). All this could account for the discomfort of modern libertarians when faced with much they find in Book v of the *Wealth of Nations* on the duties of the sovereign; they are distressed to find that Smith paid so much attention to defence and was in favour of any kind of military conscription (Letwin 1988: 70–1). Presumably, they would be equally uncomfortable with the implications of another of Smith's educational proposals: the idea that nobody from the middle and upper ranks of society should aspire to any 'liberal profession', any 'honourable office of trust or profit', without first achieving a publicly-certified command of 'science and philosophy' (1976a: 796).

Like Hume, Smith must be accounted among those who placed more trust in machinery than men, but a society based solely on private prudence regulated by contractual relationships was 'less happy and agreeable', commanding merely a 'cold esteem' (Smith 1976b: 216). It was better to live in a society that offered scope for public service, even when the complexities of commercial life meant that it would not be the sole or best mechanism for achieving many of its ends. This dimension can best be expressed as a concern with what Smith, Ferguson and others referred to as 'character', often their equivalent of the idea of virtue. Smith accommodated preservation of character as one of the duties of the legislator by means of terminology derived from natural jurisprudence, with Pufendorf and Hutcheson being credited by Smith for the essential move. It belongs to the category of 'imperfect rights', those cases where political agency was called upon to do more than enforce the negative yet perfect rights of commutative justice. It involved establishing 'good discipline', discouraging 'vice and impropriety', and prescribing rules 'which not only prohibit mutual injuries among fellow-citizens, but command mutual good offices to a certain degree'. As the final caveat suggests, however, Smith was conscious that 'Of all the duties of a law-giver...this perhaps is that which requires the greatest delicacy and reserve to execute with propriety and judgment. To neglect it altogether exposes the commonwealth to many gross disorders and shocking enormities, and to push it too far is destructive of all liberty, security and justice' (*ibid.*: 81).

Herein lies the real difference between Smith and Ferguson, for there can be no doubt that Ferguson would have laid more stress on these imperfect rights and legislatorial duties and less on the dangers to liberty, security and justice. As he said: 'If the pretensions to equal justice and freedom should terminate in rendering every class equally servile and mercenary, we make a nation of helots, and have no free citizens' (Ferguson 1995: 177). Echoing Pocock's term, 'commercial humanism', this could serve as a definition of the difference between a 'commercial' and a 'republican' concept of liberty. Like all such binary distinctions, this could have boomerang properties, but it captures another reservation Smith entertained on the subject of republican modes of thinking and acting that further compounded his offence in the eyes of his Poker Club friends. A 'well-regulated standing army', commanded in the British fashion, could be *favourable* to liberty when it allowed the sovereign to dispense with discretionary powers to deal with every manifestation of 'popular discontent' and 'licentious liberty'. Republics were less well placed to exercise such tolerance: 'The security which [a standing army] gives to the sovereign renders unnecessary that troublesome jealousy, which, in some modern republics, seems to watch over the minutest actions, and to be at all times ready to disturb the peace of every citizen' (Smith 1976a: 706–7).

V

While this may seem to be conclusive proof that Smith would have shared Constant's concerns over recent French attempts to implement oppressive 'ancient' forms of liberty, we should pause before casting both men as advocates of *mere* civil liberties in the negative vein. Contrary to some recent interpretations (Pettit 1997: 18, 50) Constant did not contrast ancient (positive) liberties based on democratic participation with modern (negative) civil liberties. Accepting what had been achieved by the revolution, however disastrous its methods, was essential to Constant's position. In its newer representative forms, therefore, political liberty was, for Constant, the bedrock of modern liberty, possessing expressive as well as instrumental qualities (Castiglione 2000). Constant can be counted among Smith's 'liberal' French admirers, alongside those, such as Jean-Baptiste Say, who remained more committed to the inculcation of 'republican' social habits, the absence of which he believed had led to the collapse of earlier experiments to reconcile commercial realities with stable republican institutions (Whatmore 1998). In this respect these two French disciples reveal how one could draw a mixture of liberal and/or republican conclusions from their reading of the *Wealth of Nations*, where neither corresponds precisely with our attempts to recruit them into our categories.

It is an ambivalence with which historians, as opposed to modern political theorists, must respect by exercising caution in not confusing *werden* with *sein*. What is often seen only as evidence for Smith's free-trading and *laissez faire* credentials can be given a 'republican' reading, provided we are not too strongly attached to those versions the relevance of which Smith himself had questioned under modern conditions. Enough has been said here to show that one of Smith's chief interests in tracing the political impact of commerce was its effect in dissolving feudal relations of dependency. This interest also underlies his distinction between dependence and deference, as well as his argument that political power of an arbitrary kind was no longer the *necessary* concomitant of economic power (Winch 1978: 79, 91). The historical processes that had brought this about, however, had hardly begun to operate in many parts of Europe and were incomplete even in England, as the laws of primogeniture showed. As far as the future was concerned, what attracted Smith to the system of natural liberty was its ability to undermine the corporatist powers and privileges of those producer-based interest groups brought into being by the mercantile-inspired policy of Europe. How else to explain Smith's 'very violent attack' on these policies and the unusual tone of anger noted by Dugald Stewart when commenting on this attack (Smith 1987: 251; 1980: 316)? Such policies had created within commercial societies new forms of oppression and injustice, with wage-earners, consumers and tax-payers, the clear majority in any consequentialist account of their results, being the chief victims. Smith's antagonism to monopoly privilege and its lack of accountability, whether exercised by merchants, bureaucrats or academics, is an assault on institutions and practices resulting in dominance over the legitimate rights and ambitions of the excluded, the marginalised and the less well-organised. The claims of modern libertarians that *le marché peut tout* should not prevent us from appreciating that markets characterised by free entry and persistent rivalry were a liberating force in a world pervaded by monopoly, unchallengeable authority, and unequal bargaining power. We can even call Smith's conception of public good 'democratical', though his credentials as a spokesman for an extension of political representation are slim (see, however, Robertson 1990).

Smith's language, being closer than ours to both dead and living forms of republicanism, lends itself to 'our' republican interpretations as well, though it is useful to ask how much such interpretations add to our understanding. As an antidote to the liberal capitalist and proto-social scientific stereotypes mentioned earlier, a regard for republican language has some clear advantages. Yet Haakonssen ((ed.) 1988) is surely right to ask why we need to go beyond the categories of natural jurisprudence, with its well-argued moral criteria for judging positive laws. In Smith's case this approach issued in a 'science of the legislator or statesman' capable of providing prudential guidance to legislators anxious to act on invariable principles under changing circumstances. It also enabled him to locate the source of the most common departures from the principles of natural justice, those cases in domestic law where men imposed unjust laws on women, where 'the interest of government' could pervert a constitution, and where 'the interest of particular orders of men who tyrannize the government' had warped 'the positive laws of the country from what natural justice would prescribe' (Smith 1978: 146–7; 1976b: 340–1). Smith's science licensed a programme of reform by legislators willing to adjust existing laws, policies and institutions, as circumstances allowed, to deal with an imperfect world peopled by agents only too ready to pursue their interests at the expense of public good. Haakonssen (1993) has also raised another pertinent question to which as yet no answer seems forthcoming from the modern proponents of republican ideals: apart from the invocation of virtue as an institutional precondition for republican life, what new moral theory, in addition to the liberal idea of equal freedom under the law, is being proposed?

Speaking solely as an historian, though not without an interest in the assistance history can provide to modern debates, I would like to suggest a challenge which the organisers of these studies of the European republican heritage would be only too pleased to accept. Whatever might be said of the early modern period, the idea of a single heritage seems difficult to sustain by the end of the eighteenth century and beyond. The brief remarks above on Constant and Say suggest the complications of the post-revolutionary story in France, and there are also arguments in favour of a separate development of republican themes in England after 1790 (Philp 1998). Clearly, some elements in the heritage continued well beyond the point where these volumes end, but if we are to bridge the gap between them and the world we now inhabit, detailed consideration of the nineteenth- and twentieth-century republican experience, especially in large commercial states such as America and France, is essential. Expressed in those terms that became relevant during this period, we need to consider the relationship between republicanism and such potent political developments as liberalism, representative democracy, industrial capitalism and socialism. Neither Hume nor Smith was able to come to terms with even the earliest stages of this experience. What Smith offers, however, is the best attempt, for its time, to provide some hypotheses concerning the problems of reconciling commercial realities with republican hopes.

Bibliography

Primary Sources

A Continuation of the Narrative being the Last and Final Dayes Proceedings of the High Court of Justice 1649, London.

Abbt, Thomas 1766, *Vom Verdienste*, Goslar and Leipzig [reprint Königstein, 1978].

Addison, Joseph and Sir Richard Steele 1710/11, in *The Spectator*: no. 4 (5 March 1710/11); no. 9 (10 March 1710/11); no. 10 (12 March 1710/11).

Akta sejmikowe województwa krakowskiego (Local Assembly Acts from the Voivodeship of Krakow) 1953, vol. II, ed. A. Przyboś, Krakow.

Alamos de Barrientos, Baltasar 1990, *Discurso político al rey Felipe III al comienzo de su reinado* [1598], ed. M. Santos, Barcelona.

Allen, P. S. 1926, *Opus epistolarum Des. Erasmi Roterodami*, vol. VI, Oxford.

Alsted, Johann Heinrich 1990, 'Politica', in Alsted, *Encyclopaedia* [1630], ed. Wilhelm Schmidt-Biggemann, vol. III, Stuttgart, pp. 1218–1447.

Althusius, Johannes 1611, *Civilis conversationis libri duo recogniti, & aucti. methodice digesti et exemplis sacris et profanis passim illustrati*, Hanover.

  1932, *Politica, methodice digesta et exemplis sacris et profanis illustrata*, 3rd edn [1614], ed. Carl Joachim Friedrich, Cambridge, Mass.

Andreae, Johann Valentin 1972, *Christianopolis* [1619], ed. Richard van Dülmen, Stuttgart.

Anon. 1568, *Complainte de la désolée terre du Pais Bas*, n.p.

  1579, *Cyuile and Vncyuile Life*, London.

  1584, *A Breefe Discourse, Declaring and Approuing the Necessarie and Inuiolable Maintenance of the Laudable Customs of London*, London.

  1606, 'Libera respublica – absolutum dominium – rokosz', in Czubek (ed.) 1918: II.

  1740, *Plain Truth or, downright Dunstable: a poem; containing the author's opinion of the sale of poetic and prose performances. With some critical thoughts concerning Horace and Virgil, etc.*, London.

  1823, 'Eidgenössische Gesandtschaft an Cromwell im Jahre 1653', in Balthasar (ed.) 1823.

Aristotle 1598, *Aristotles Politiques, or Discourses of Government*, trans. I. D., London.

  1988, *The Politics*, ed. Stephen Everson, Cambridge.

  2000, *The Nicomachean Ethics*, trans. Roger Crisp, Cambridge.

311

Arnisaeus, Henning 1615, *De republica seu reflectionis politicælibri II*, Frankfurt.

Ascham, Anthony 1649, *Of the Confusions and Revolutions of Governments*, London.

Ashley, Robert 1947, *Of Honour*, ed. Virgil B. Heltzel, San Marino.

Augustine 1928–9, *De civitate dei, Libri XII*, ed. B. Dombart and A Kalb, 2 vols., Leipzig.

Averani, Giuseppe 1721, *Mémoire sur la liberté de l'état de Florence*, Florence.

[Aylmer, John] 1559, *An Harborowe for Faithfvll and Trewe Svbiectes*, Strasborowe [London].

Bacon, Francis 1730, *Francisci Baconis . . . Opera Omnia*, ed. John Blackbourne, 4 vols., London.

    1857–74, *The Works of Francis Bacon . . . Letters and Life*, ed. J. Spedding *et al.*, 14 vols., London.

Balguy, John 1726, *A Letter to A Deist*, London.

Balthasar, J. A. (ed.) 1823, *Helvetia. Denkwürdigkeiten für die XXII Freistaaten der Schweizerischen Eidgenossenschaft*, vol. I, Zurich.

Barbon, Nicholas 1690, *A Discourse of Trade*, London.

Barnave, Antoine 1988, *De la révolution et de la constitution* [1791], Grenoble.

Barston, John 1576, *Safegarde of Societie*, London.

Baynes, Roger 1577, *The Praise of Solitarinesse, Set down in the Form of a Dialogue, Wherein Is Conteyned, a Discourse Philosophical, of the Lyfe Actiue, and Contemplatiue*, London.

Beacon, Richard 1996, *Solon His Follie, or a Politique Discourse touching the Reformation of Common-weales Conquered, Declined or Corrupted* [1594], ed. Clare Carroll and Vincent Carey, Binghamton.

Beattie, James 1770, *An Essay on the Nature and Immutability of Truth, in Opposition to Sophistry and Scepticism*, Edinburgh.

Beccaria, Cesare 1984, *Dei delitti e delle pene* [1764], ed. G. Francioni, *Edizione nazionale delle Opere di Cesare Beccaria*, vol. I, Milan.

Bendicho, Vicente 1991, *Chronica de la muy ilustre, noble y leal ciudad de Alicante* [1640], ed. M. L. Cabanes and C. Mas, Alicante.

Bentivoglio, Guido 1631, *Relationi del cardinal Bentivoglio* [1629], Paris.

    1640, *Della guerra di Fiandra, descritta dal cardinal Bentivoglio* [Cologne, 1632–9], Venice.

    1983, *Relatione delle Provincie Unite* [1632], ed. S. Mastellone and E. O. G. Haitsma Mulier, Florence.

Berkeley, George, Bishop of Cloyne 1948, *The Works of George Berkeley*, vol. I: . . . *The Theory of Vision Vindicated* [1733], ed. A. A. Luce and T. E. Jessop, London.

1950 *The Works of George Berkeley*, vol. III: *Alciphron, or The Minute Philosopher* [1732], ed. A. A. Luce and T. E. Jessop, London.

Bertram, Bonaventure 1574, *De politia Judaica, tam civili quam ecclesiastica, iam inde a suis primordijs repetita*, Geneva.

Bertrand, Jean 1760, in Société économique de Berne (ed.) 1760–73, vol. I.

Besold, Christoph 1622, *De consilio politico*, Tübingen.

    1626a, *Operis politici: Variis digressionibus philologicis & juridicis illustrati, editio nova*, Strasbourg.

    1626b, *Principium et finis politicæ. Hoc est, Dissertationes duæ, quarum una prægognita politices proponit; altera de republica curanda agit*, in Besold 1626a.

    1626c, *Dissertatio politico-iuridica, de majestate in genere*, in Besold 1626a.

Bethel, Slingsby 1668, *The World's Mistake in Oliver Cromwell*, London.

Bezstronne zastanowienie się nad projektowaną ustawą następstwa tronu w Polszcze . . . [1789], n.p.

Bianchi, Vendramino 1710, *An Account of Switzerland and the Grisons*, London.

Biesius, Nicolaus 1556, *De Republica libri quatuor, quibus universa de moribus Philosophia continetur*, Antwerp.

Blancas, Jerónimo 1878, *Comentarios de las cosas de Aragón* [1588], trans. M. Hernández, Zaragoza.

Blandy, William 1581, *The Castle, or Picture of Pollicy Shewing forth Most Liuely, the Face, Body and Partes of a Commonwealth*, London.

Boccaccio, Giovanni 1967, *De mulieribus claris* [?1361], Verona (vol. [x] of *Tutte le opere di Giovanni Boccaccio*, general editor Vittore Branca).

Boccalini, Traiano 1615, *Pietra del paragone politico tratta del monte Parnaso. Dove si toccano i governi delle maggiori Monarchie dell'Universo* [1614], Cosmopoli.

   1948, *Ragguagli di Parnaso e scritti minori* [1612], ed. L. Firpo, Bari.

Bodin, Jean 1961, *Les six livres de la république* [1576] Aalen (reprint of edition of 1583).

Bolingbroke, Henry St John, Viscount 1733, *The Freeholder's Political Catechism*, London.

   1754, *Works*, ed. David Mallet, London.

   1997, *Political Writings*, ed. David Armitage, Cambridge.

Boncza-Tomaszewski, D. 1791, *Nad Konstytucją i rewolucją dnia 3 maja uwagi*, n.p.

Bonfadio, Giuseppe 1611, *De civilis administrationis optima forma disputatio, adversus oppugnantes aristocratiam*, Padua.

Bonstetten, Karl Victor 1997, *Bonstettiana. Briefkorrespondenzen Karl Viktor von Bonstettens und seines Kreises*, vol. VI, Berne.

Borde, Charles 1753, *Discours sur les avantages des sciences et des arts*, Geneva.

Bosch, Andreu 1974, *Summari, índex o epítome dels admirables y nobilíssims títols de honor de Cathalunya, Rosselló i Cerdanya* [1628], facsimile, Barcelona.

Botero, Giovanni 1597–8, *Le relationi universali*, Venice.

   1990, *Della ragion di stato e Delle cause della grandezza delle città* [1598], Bologna.

Bouillé, Marquis de 1822, *Mémoires du Marquis de Bouillé*, 2nd edn, Paris.

Bourne, William 1578, *A Booke Called the Treasure for Traueilers*, London.

Bozza, T. 1949, *Scrittori politici italiani dal 1550 al 1650*, Rome.

[Braham, Humfrey] 1555, *The Institucion of a Gentleman*, London.

Brissot de Warville, Jacques Pierre 1782, *De la vérité*, Neufchâtel.

   1784, in *Journal du lycée de Londres*, nos. 2 and 3.

Brutus, Stephanus Junius 1994, *Vindiciae contra tyrannos: il potere legittimo del principe sul popolo e del popolo sul principe* [1579], ed. and trans. S. Testoni Binetti, Turin.

Bürger, Gottfried August 1905, 'Die Republik England' [1793], in *Sämtliche Werke*, vol. VI, Berlin.

Burgersdijk, Franco 1668, *Idea politica* [1644], ed. Georgius Hornius, Leiden.

Burgh, James 1761, *The Art of Speaking, etc.*, London.

Burke, Edmund 1887, *An Appeal from the New to the Old Whigs* [1791], in *The Works of the Right Honourable Edmund Burke*, vol. III, London.

   1899, *Three Letters Addressed to a Member of the Present Parliament on the Proposals for Peace with the Regicide Directory of France* [1797], in *The Works of the Right Honourable Edmund Burke*, 12 vols., vol. V, London.

1981, *Speech on Fox's East India Bill* [1783], in *The Writings and Speeches of Edmund Burke*, vol. V: *India: Madras and Bengal 1774–1785*, ed. P. J. Marshall, Oxford, pp. 378–451.

1987, *Reflections on the Revolution in France* [1790], ed. J. G. A. Pocock, Indianapolis.

1991, *First Letter on a Regicide Peace* [1795], in *The Writings and Speeches of Edmund Burke*, vol. IX: (1) *The Revolutionary War 1794–1797*, (2) *Ireland*, ed. R. B. McDowell, Oxford, pp. 44–119

Busius, Paulus 1627, *De republica libri tres* [Franeker, 1613], Frankfurt am Main.

Bystrzonowski, W. 1730, *Polak sensat w liście, w komplemencie polityk, humanista w dyskursie . . .*, Lublin (unpaginated).

Calça, Francisco 1588, *De Catalonia liber primus*, Barcelona.

Campana, Cesare 1602, *Della guerra di Fiandra*, Vicenza.

Campbell, John 1753, *The Present State of Europe*, London.

Case, John 1593, *Sphaera ciuitatis; hoc est; reipvblicae recte ac pie secvndvm leges administrandae ratio*, Frankfurt.

Cassander, George 1847, *Oratio in laudem urbis Brugensis* [1541], ed. C. Carton, Ghent.

Castiglione, Baldesar 1967, *The Book of the Courtier* [1528], Harmondsworth.

Castrillo, Alonso de 1958, *Tractado de república* [1521], Madrid.

Cebà, A. 1825, *Il cittadino di repubblica* [1617], Milan.

Chabrit, Pierre 1783, *De la monarchie française ou de ses lois*, Bouillon.

Chantreau, Pierre-Nicolas 1790, *Dictionnaire national et anecdotique*, Politicopolis [Paris].

Charles I 1999, *XIX. Propositions Made By both Houses of Parliament, to the Kings most Excellent Majestie: With his Majesties Answer thereunto*, in Malcolm (ed.) 1999: I, 145–78.

Child, Sir Josiah 1692, *A New Discourse of Trade*, London.

Cicero 1534, *The Thre Bookes of Tullyes Offyces*, trans. Robert Whittinton, London.

1556, *Thre bokes of duties, to Marcus his sonne, turned oute of latine into english, by Nicolas Grimalde*, London.

1558, *Thre bookes of duties, to Marcus his sonne, turned out of latine into english, by Nicolas Grimalde. Wherunto the latine is adjoyned*, London.

1913, *De officiis*, ed. and trans. Walter Miller, London.

1923, *Pro Cnaeo Plancio*, London.

1926, *Philippics*, ed. and trans. Walter C. A. Ker, London.

1928, *De re publica et De legibus*, ed. and trans. Clinton Walker Keyes, London.

1942, *De Oratore. De Fato. Paradoxa Stoicorum. De Partitione Oratoria*, trans. H. Rackham, Cambridge, Mass. (Loeb edition).

1988, *De republica et De legibus*, Cambridge, Mass. (Loeb edition).

1989, *Pro Caelio. De provinciis consularibus. Pro Balbo*, trans. J. H. Freese, Cambridge, Mass. (Loeb edition).

1991, *On Duties*, ed. and trans. M. T. Griffin and E. M. Atkins, Cambridge.

Clavière, Etienne 1788, *De la foi publique envers les créanciers de l'état*, London.

1790, in *Courier de Provence*, 9 (160, 27–30 June), pp. 120–8.

Cobbett, William 1819, *A Grammar of the English Language in a Series of Letters . . .*, London.

Condillac, Etienne Bonnot de 1973, *Essai sur l'origine des connaissances humaines* [1746], ed. Jacques Derrida, Paris.

    1980, *Le Commerce et le gouvernement* [1776], Geneva.

Condorcet, Jean-Marie Antoine Nicolas Caritat de 1788, *Lettres d'un bourgeois de New Haven à un citoyen de Virginie sur l'inutilité de partager le pouvoir législatif entre plusieurs corps*, Paris.

    1790, 'Sur l'admission des femmes au droit de cité', *Journal de la société de 1789*, 3 July, pp. 121–30.

    1847, 'Discours sur la nomination et la destitution des commissaires de la trésorerie nationale et des membres du bureau de comptabilité' [1792], in *Œuvres*, ed. A. Condorcet O'Connor and M. F. Arago, vol. XII, Paris.

    1986, *Sur les élections et autres textes*, ed. Olivier de Bernon, Paris, pp. 203–72.

Considerations for the Commons in This Age of Distractions 1642, London.

Constant, Benjamin 1819, 'De la liberté des anciens comparée à celle des modernes' (speech to the Athénée Royal de Paris, February 1819), in Constant, *De la conquête et de l'usurpation*, Paris, 1986.

    1988, 'The Liberty of the Ancients Compared with that of the Moderns' [1819], in *The Political Writings of Benjamin Constant*, ed. Biancamaria Fontana, Cambridge, pp. 309–28.

Contarini, Gasparo 1543, *De magistratibus et republica venetorum*, Paris.

    1599, *The Commonwealth and Government of Venice, Written by the Cardinal Gasparo Contarini and Translated out of Italian into English by Lewes Lewkenor*, London.

    1626, *De republica Venetorum libri quinque* . . . Lugd. Batauorum [Leiden].

    1628, *De Republica Venetorum libri quinque*, 2nd edn, Lugd. Batavorum [Leiden].

Contarini, N. 1982, 'Delle istorie veneziane . . .', in Benzoni and Zanato (eds.) 1982.

Contarini, Pier Maria 1990, *Compendio universal di republica* [1602], ed. Vittorio Conti, Florence.

Cook, John 1649, *King Charles His Case*, London.

    1652, *Monarchy No Creature of God's Making*, London.

Coornhert, D. V. 1575, *Comedie van Israel vertoonende Israels zonden, straffinghe, Belydinghe, Ghebedt, Beteringe ende verlossinge. Wt het thiende Capit. Iudicum. Als een claere spiegele der tegenwoordige tijden*, n.p.

Cope, Esther S., with Willson H. Coates (eds.) 1977, *Proceedings of the Short Parliament of 1640*, The Royal Historical Society, Camden Fourth Series, vol. XIX, London.

Cornwallis, William 1601, *Discovrses vpon Seneca the Tragedian*, London.

Costa, Juan 1575, *El ciudadano*, Pamplona (revised edns, Salamanca, 1578 and Zaragoza, 1584, the latter under the title *El govierno del ciudadano. Trata de cómo se ha de regir a sí, su casa y república*), Zaragoza.

Cotovicus, Ioannes 1619, *Itinerarium hierosolymitanum et syriacum; in quo variarum gentium mores et instituta Insularum, Regionum, Urbium situs, una ex prisci recentiorisque saeculi usu; una cum eventis, quae Auctori terra marique acciderunt, dilucide recensentur. Accessit synopsis reipublicae venetae*, Antwerp.

Covarrubias, Sebastián de 1993, *Tesoro de la lengua castellana o española* [1611], facsimile, Barcelona.

Croce, B. and S. Caramella (eds.) 1930, *Politici e moralisti del Seicento*, Bari.

Cromwell, Oliver 1937–47, *Writings and Speeches of Oliver Cromwell*, ed. W. C. Abbott, 4 vols., Cambridge, Mass.

Crosse, Henry 1603, *Vertues Common-wealth: Or the High-way to Honovr*, London.

Crowley, Robert 1575, *A Sermon Made in the Chappel at the Gylde Halle in London, the xxix Day of September, 1574*, London.

Cunaeus, Petrus 1980, *Sardi venales* [1610], in C. Matheeussen and C. L. Heesakkers (eds.), *Two Neo-Latin Menippean satires: Justus Lipsius, Somnium; Petrus Cunaeus, Sardi Venales*, Leiden.

  1996, *De Republica Hebraeorum – The Commonwealth of the Hebrews* (reprint of the original edition, 1617, and of the English translation, 1653), Florence.

[Czacki, T.] [1791], *O konstytucyi 3 maja 1791*, [Warsaw].

[Czapski, F.] n.d., *Senator polski współobywatelom dobrze radzący* [*ca.* 1788], n.p (unpaginated).

Czubek, Jan (ed.) 1918, *Pisma polityczne z czasów rokoszu Zebrzydowskiego 1606–1608*, vols. II and III: *Proza* (Political Writings from the Time of the Zebrzydowski Rebellion 1606–1608, vols. II and III: Prose), Krakow.

D.C., *see* De la Court

Davel, Jean Daniel Abraham 1970, 'Manifeste du major Davel', in Marianne Mercier-Campiche (ed.), *L'Affaire Davel*, Lausanne.

Davenant, Charles 1701, *An Essay upon Universal Monarchy*, in *Essays upon I. The Ballance of Power. II. The Right of Making War, Peace and Alliances. III. Universal Monarchy*, London.

  1771, *The Political and Commercial Works of Charles Davenant LL.D.*, ed. Charles Whitworth, 5 vols., London.

[De Beaufort, L. F.] 1737, *Verhandeling van de Vryheit in den Burgerstaet*, 2nd printing, Leiden and Middelburg.

De Damhoudere, Joost 1564, *De magnificentia politiae amplissimae civitatis Brugorum*, Bruges.

  1684, *Van de Grootdadigheyt der breedt-vermaerde regeringhe vande stadt Brugge*, Amsterdam.

De la Court, Johan and/or Pieter 1660 ['V.H.'], *Consideratien en exempelen van staat, omtrent de fundamenten van allerley regeringe*, Amsterdam.

  1662a ['D.C.'], *Politike discoursen, handelende in ses onderscheide boeken, van steeden, landen, oorlogen, kerken, regeeringen en zeeden*, 1st edn, Leiden.

  1662b ['D.C.'], *Politike discoursen handelende in ses onderscheide boeken, van steeden, landen, oorlogen, kerken, regeeringen, en zeeden*, 3rd edn, Amsterdam.

  1662c ['V.D.H.'], *Interest van Holland, ofte gronden van Hollands-welvaren*, Amsterdam.

  1662d ['V.H.'], *Consideratien van staat, ofte polityke weeg-schaal, waar in met veele reedenen, omstandigheden, exempelen en fabulen werd ooverwoogen, welke forme der regeeringe, in speculatie geboud op de practijk, onder de menschen de beste zy*, 3rd edn, Amsterdam.

[De la Court, Pieter] 1702, *The True Interest and Political Maxims of the Republic of Holland, Written by De Witt and other Great Men in Holland*, London.

De Pietri, F. 1634, *Dell'historia napoletana libri due*, Naples.

De Prince Vlag, Oranje Boven n.d., n.p.

[De Witt, J.] 1654, *Deductie, ofte declaratie van de Staten van Hollandt ende West-Vrieslandt . . . ingestelt ende dienende tot justificatie van 't verleenen van seeckere Acte van Seclusie, raeckende't employ vanden heere prince van Oraigne*, The Hague.

Decision of the General Confederation, Targowica, 14 May 1792 (drafted in St Petersburg) (unpaginated).

Della Porta, A. n.d., 'Causa di stravaganze. O' vero Giornale Istorico di quanto più memorabile è accaduto nelle Rivoluzioni di Napoli negl'Anni 1647 e 1648 colla discrizzione del contagio del 1656', ms.

Demosthenes 1570, *The Three Orations of Demosthenes*, trans. Thomas Wilson, London.

Diariusz sejmu i akta sejmikowe z roku 1591–1592 (Proceedings of the Seym and Local Assembly Acts from the Years 1591-1592) 1911, in *Scriptores* 1911.

Diariusze sejmów koronnych 1548, 1553 i 1570 (Proceedings of Seyms in 1548, 1553 and 1570) 1872, vol. I, ed. J. Szujski. Komisja Historyczna Towarzystwa Naukowego Krakowskiego (Historical Commission of the Science Society of Cracow), Krakow.

Diariusze sejmowe z 1597 (Proceedings of the Seym from 1597) 1907, in *Scriptores* 1907.

Diccionario de Autoridades 1990 [1726], facsimile, Madrid.

Dizionario del cittadino o sia ristretto storico teorico e pratico del commercio 1765, Naples.

Dnewnik ljubliansago sjejma 1569 goda (Proceedings of the Seym in Lublin in 1569) 1869, ed. W. Kojałowicz, St Petersburg.

Donà, Niccolò 1734-6, *Ragionamenti sul governo veneziano*, Venice.

Donzelli, G. 1970, *Partenope liberata* [1647], ed. A. Altamura, Naples.

Doria, Paolo Mattia 1710, *La vita civile e l'educazione del Principe*, Augusta [Augsburg].

  1978a, *Il politico moderno* [1740], in V. Conti, *Paolo Mattia Doria. Dalla repubblica dei togati alla repubblica dei notabili*, Florence, pp. 129-259.

  1978b, *Idea d'una perfetta repubblica* [1753], in R. Ajello *et al.* (eds.), *Politici ed economisti del primo Settecento*, Milan and Naples.

Du Luc, F. C. 1889, 'Aus den Papieren des französischen Botschafters Franz Karl du Luc', *Archiv des Historischen Vereins des Kantons Bern*, 12.

Dybikowski, J. 1987-8, 'David Williams (1738-1816) and Jacques-Pierre Brissot: Their Correspondence', *National Library of Wales Journal*, 25: 71-97, 167-90.

Ebels-Hoving, Bunna (ed.) 1981, *Jacobus Canter Dialogus de Solitudine (c. 1491)*, Munich.

Erasmus, Desiderius 1986, 'The Education of a Christian Prince/*Institutio principis christiani*', trans. and annot. Neil M. Cheshire and Michael J. Heath, in *Collected Works of Erasmus*, vol. XXVII: *Literary and Educational Writings 5*, Toronto.

Escolano, Gaspar 1610–11, *Década primera de la historia de la insigne y coronada ciudad y reyno de Valencia*, Valencia (facsimile edn, Valencia, 1972).

Fabricius, Jacob 1631, *Einunddreissig Kriegsfragen. Von dem itzigen erbärmlichen Kriege in Deutschland*, Stettin.

Feder, Johann Georg Heinrich 1782, *Untersuchungen über den menschlichen Willen*, Lemgo.

Felltham, O. 1652, *A Brief Character of the Low Countries. Being Three weeks of Observations of the Vices and Vertues of the Inhabitants*, London.

Ferguson, Adam 1756, *Reflections previous to the Establishment of a Militia*, London.

  1757, *The Morality of Stage-Plays Seriously Considered*, Edinburgh.

  1766, *Analysis of Pneumatics and Moral Philosophy*, Edinburgh.

1768, *Versuch über die Geschichte der bürgerliche Gesellschaft*, trans. C. F. Jünger, Leipzig.

1769, *Institutes of Moral Philosophy: For the Use of Students in the College of Edinburgh*, Edinburgh.

1772, *Fergusons Grundsätze der Moralphilosophie*, trans. Christian Garve, Leipzig.

1773, *Institutes of Moral Philosophy, for the Use of Students in the College of Edinburgh*, 2nd edition revised and corrected, Edinburgh.

1776, *Remarks on a Pamphlet Lately Published by Dr. Price*, London.

1783, *The History of the Progress and Termination of the Roman Republic*, London.

1792, *Principles of Moral and Political Science, Being Chiefly a Retrospect of Lectures delivered in the College of Edinburgh*, Edinburgh.

1966, *An Essay on the History of Civil Society* (1767), ed. Duncan Forbes, Cambridge.

1995, *An Essay on the History of Civil Society* [1767], ed. Fania Oz-Salzberger, Cambridge.

1996a, 'Of the Separation of Departments, Profesions [*sic*] and Tasks Resulting from the Progress of Arts in Society', in Ferguson 1996b: 141–51.

1996b, *Collection of Essays*, ed. Y. Amoh, Kyoto.

Fernández Medrano, Juan 1602, *República mixta*, Madrid.

Ferne, John 1586, *The Blazon of Gentrie*, London.

Ferrarius, Johannes 1556, *De republica bene instituenda . . .*, Basel.

Fletcher, Andrew 1997a, *Political Works*, ed. J. Robertson, Cambridge.

1997b, 'A Discourse Concerning Government with Relation to Militias' [1697], in Fletcher 1997a.

Floyd, Thomas 1600, *The Picture of a Perfit Common Wealth*, London.

Fontanella, Francesc 1641, *Occident, eclipse, obscuretat, funeral*, Barcelona.

Foord, John 1582, *Synopsis politica*, London.

Forbonnais, François Véron de 1755, *Examen des avantages et des désavantages de la prohibition des toiles peintes*, Paris.

Fortescue, Sir John 1997, *On the Laws and Governance of England*, ed. Shelley Lockwood, Cambridge.

Foscarini, Marco 1752, *Della letteratura veneziana*, Padua.

1983, *Della perfezione della repubblica veneziana* [1722], ed. L. Ricaldone, Milan.

Franklin, Julian H. (ed. and trans.) 1969, *Constitutionalism and Resistance in the Sixteenth Century: Three Treatises by Hotman, Beza, and Mornay*, New York.

Fredro, A. M. 1660, 'Responsum in gratiam cuiusdam sermonis privati, bonone fiat Reipublicae Polonae, ubi non pluralitas vocum, verum consensus ponderatur', in *Scriptorum seu togae et belli notationum fragmenta*, Gedani.

1668, 'Punctum primum de potentia populi', in *Militarium seu axiomatum belli et harmoniam togae accomodatorum libri duo*, Book 1, Amsterdam.

Furió Ceriol, Fadrique 1978, *El concejo y consejeros del príncipe* [1559], ed. H. Mechoulan, Madrid.

Galanti, Giuseppe Maria 1782, *Elogio del signor abate Antonio Genovesi* [1772], 2nd edn, Florence.

1779, *Discorso dell'avvocato Giuseppe Maria Galanti intorno alla costituzione della società ed al governo politico, preceduto dall'Elogio del segretario fiorentino*, Naples.

Galiano, Ferdinando 1750, *Della moneta*, Naples.

Garat, Dominique Joseph 1784, Review of Chabrit 1783, in *Mercure de France*, 6 March, pp. 9–27 and 10 April, pp. 58–75.

Gardiner, Samuel Rawson (ed.) 1958, *Constitutional Documents of the Puritan Revolution*, Oxford.

Garnett, George (ed. and trans.) 1994, *Vindiciae, contra tyrannos: or Concerning the Legitimate Power of a Prince over the People, and of the People over a Prince* [1579], Cambridge.

Garve, Christian 1772, 'Anmerkungen', in Ferguson 1772.

Genovesi, Antonio 1766, *Diceosina o sia della filosofia del giusto et dell'onesto*, Naples.
    1768–70, *Lezioni di commercio o sia di economia civile*, 2 vols., Naples.

Gerhard, Johann 1885, *Loci theologici* [Jena 1610–22], ed. F. Frank, Leipzig.

Giannotti, Donato 1540, *Libro della republica de' Viniziani*, Rome.
    1631, *Dialogi de repub. venetorum cum notis et lib. singulari de forma eiusdem reip.*, Lugd. Batav. [Leiden].

Gibbon, Charles 1604, *The Order of Eqvalitie*, Cambridge.

Gibbon, Edward 1952, *Miscellanea Gibboniana*, ed. G. R. de Beer, G. A. Bonnard and L. Junod, Lausanne.

Gilabert, Francisco 1888, 'Respuesta hecha al tratado, relación y discurso historial que Antonio de Herrera hace . . .', in Francisco Gurrea, conde de Luna, *Comentarios de los sucesos de Aragón en los años 1591 y 1592*, Madrid.

Gilbert, Humphrey 1869, 'Queene Elizabethes Achademy', in *Early English Text Society*, Extra Series, vol. III.

Giraffi, A. 1844, *Masaniello* [1647], Brussels.

Giustiniani, Pompeo 1609, *Della guerra di Fiandra libri* VI, Antwerp.

Godwin, William 1985, *An Enquiry Concerning Political Justice . . .* [1793], ed. Isaac Kramnick, Harmondsworth.
    1993, *The Enquirer* [1797], in *Political and Philosophical Writings*, ed. Mark Philp, vol. V: *Educational and literary writings*, ed. Pamela Clemit, London.

Goethalsius, Franciscus 1566, *De foelice et infoelice republica, ad senatum Brugensem*, Louvain.

Goguet, François 1758, *De l'origine des lois, des arts et des sciences, et de leurs progrès chez les anciens peuples*, 3 vols., Paris.

Goodwin, John 1649, Υβριϛτοδικαι: *The Obstructours of Justice*, London.

Gordon, Thomas 1972, *The Conspirators, or, the Case of Catilina* [1721], in *Factions No More. Attitudes to Party in Government and Opposition in Eighteenth Century England*, ed. J. A. W. Gunn, London.

Goslicius, Laurentius Grimaldus (Goślicki, Wawrzyniec) 1598, *The Covnsellor. Exactly Pourtraited in Two Bookes*, trans. anon., London.
    1568, *De optimo senatore*, Venice.

Gouges, Olympe de 1791, 'La Déclaration des droits de la femme et de la citoyenne (à la Reine)', in *Écrits politiques (1788–1791)*, Paris, 1993.

Gournay, Jacques Vincent de 1983, *Traité sur le commerce de Josiah Child avec les Remarques inédites de Vincent de Gournay* [1753], ed. T. Tsuda, Tokyo.

Gournay, Marie de Jars de 1993, *Egalité des hommes et des femmes; Grief des dames; suivis du Proumenoir de Monsieur de Montaigne* [1622], ed. Constant Venesoen, Geneva.

Graffenried, E. von 1762, in Société économique de Berne (ed.) 1760–73, vol. 1.

Grapheus, Cornelius 1550, *De seer wonderlijcke schoone triumphelijcke incompst van den hooghmogenden prince Philips prince van Spaignen, Caroli des vijfden Keysers sone*, Antwerp.

Greene, Robert 1590, *The Royal Exchange. Contayning Sundry Aphorismes of Phylosophie, and Golden Principles of Morrall and Naturall Quadruplicities*, London.

Greville, Fulke 1965, *The Remains*, ed. G. A. Wilkes, Oxford.

Grondwettige Herstelling van Nederlands Staatswezen, zo voor het algemeen Bondgenootschap, als voor het Bestuur van elke byzondere Provincie, etc. 1784–6, 2 vols., Amsterdam.

Grotius, Hugo 1610, *Liber de antiquitate reipublicae Bataviciae*, Leiden.

  1614, *Decretum illustrium ac potentum ordinum Hollandiae et West-Frisiae pro pace ecclesiarum, muntium Sacrae Scripturae, auctoritate, et conciliorum, antiquorum patrum … testimonijs*, Utrecht.

  1622, *Verantwoordinghe van de wettelijcke Regieringh van Hollandt*, Paris.

  1625, *De iure belli ac pacis*, Paris.

  1647, *De imperio summarum potestatum circa sacra*, Paris.

  1738, *The Rights of War and Peace*, London.

  1868, *De iure praedae commentarius* [1604], ed. H. G. Hamaker, The Hague.

  1928–2001, *Briefwisseling*, ed. P. C. Molhuysen *et al.*, 17 vols., 's-Gravenhage.

  1950, *De iure praedae commentarius. Commentary on the Law of Prize and Booty* [1604], vol. 1, ed. Gwladys L. Williams and Walther H. Zeydel, Oxford and London.

  1984, '*De republica emendanda*: A Juvenile Tract by Hugo Grotius on the Emendation of the Dutch Polity', ed. Arthur Eyffinger *et al.*, *Grotiana*, new series, 5: 66–121.

  1994, 'Commentarius in theses XI' in Peter Borschberg, *Hugo Grotius 'Commentarius in theses XI': An Early Treatise on Sovereignty, the Just War, and the Legitimacy of the Dutch Revolt*, Berne, pp. 206–83.

Guazzo, Stefano 1586, *The Ciuile Conuersation*, trans. G[eorge] Pettie and Barth. Young, London.

  1993, *La civil conversazione* [1574], ed. A. Quondam, Ferrara.

Guicciardini, Francesco 1983, *Considerazioni intorno ai Discorsi del Machiavelli*, in N. Machiavelli, *Discorsi sopra la prima deca di Tito Livio*, Turin, pp. 519–84.

Guicciardini, Lodovico 1612, *Beschryvinghe van alle de Nederlanden anderssins ghenoemt Neder-Duytslandt*, trans. by Cornelius Kiliaan, Amsterdam.

Gundling, Nicolaus Hieronymus 1734, *Ausführlicher Discours über das Natur- und Völkerrecht*, Frankfurt and Leipzig.

Guyomar, Pierre 1793, 'Le Partisan de l'égalité politique entre les individus, ou problème très important de l'égalité en droits et de l'inégalité en fait', *Archives Parlementaires*, 73: 591–9.

Hammond, Henry 1644, *Of Resisting the Lawfull Magistrate under Colour of Religion*, Oxford.

  1649, *To the Right Honourable, the Lord Fairfax, and His Councell of Warre: the Humble Addresse of Henry Hammond*, London.

Harrington, James 1737, *The Oceana of James Harrington, Esq. and his other Works with an Account of his Life Prefix'd*, ed. John Toland, Dublin.

  1977, *Political Works*, ed. J. G. A. Pocock, Cambridge.

1980, *Works. The Oceana and other Works. With an Account of his Life by John Toland*, Aalen [2nd reprint of the edn of London, 1771].

1992, *The Commonwealth of Oceana* [1656] and *A System of Politics* [1661?], ed. J. G. A. Pocock, Cambridge.

Harris, J. 1744, *Three Treatises on Art*, London.

Hartley, T. E. (ed.) 1981–95, *Proceedings in the Parliaments of Elizabeth I*, 3 vols. London.

Harvey, Gabriel 1913, *Marginalia*, ed. G. C. Moore Smith, Stratford.

Harward, Simon 1599, *Three Sermons vpon Some Portions of the Former Lessons Appointed for Certaine Sabbaths*, London.

Henzi, Samuel 1823, 'Samuel Henzi's und seiner Mitverschworenen Denkschrift über den politischen Zustand der Stadt und Republik Bern im Jahre 1749', in Balthasar (ed.) 1823.

Herbert, William 1887, *Croftus sive de Hibernia liber* [1588], London.

Heron, Haly, 1579, *A Newe Discourse of Morall Philosophie, Entituled the Kayes of Counsaile*, London.

Hobbes, Thomas 1649, *Elemens philosophiqves du citoyen. Traicté politiqve, où les fondemens de la societé civile sont dècouverts*, trans. Samuel Sorbière, Amsterdam.

1668, *Thomæ Hobbes Malmesburiensis Opera philosophica, quæ Latine scripsit, omnia*, Amsterdam.

1840, *Of Liberty and Necessity: A Treatise* [1654], in Sir William Molesworth (ed.), *The English Works of Thomas Hobbes*, vol. VI, London.

1969, *Behemoth or The Long Parliament*, ed. Ferdinand Tönnies, 2nd edn, introd. M. M. Goldsmith, London.

1976, *Thomas White's 'De mundo' Examined*, trans. Harold Whitmore Jones, London.

1983a, *De cive: The Latin Version*, ed. Howard Warrender, Oxford.

1983b, *De cive: The English Version*, ed. Howard Warrender, Oxford.

1990, *Behemoth or the Long Parliament*, ed. Ferdinand Tönnies, introd. Stephen Holmes, Chicago and London.

1996, *Leviathan, Or The Matter, Forme, & Power of a Common-Wealth Ecclesiasticall and Civill*, ed. Richard Tuck, Cambridge.

1998, *On the Citizen*, ed. and trans. Richard Tuck and Michael Silverthorne, Cambridge.

Holbach, Paul-Henri Thiry, baron d' 1773, *La Politique naturelle ou discours sur les vrais principes du gouvernement*, vol. I, London.

1776, *Ethocratie, ou Le Gouvernement fondé sur la morale*, Amsterdam.

1820, *La Morale universelle ou les devoirs de l'homme fondés sur la nature*, Paris.

1994, *Système social ou principes naturels de la morale et de la politique* [1773], Paris.

Hotman, François 1721, *Franco-Gallia* [1573] . . . *Translated by the Author of the Account of Denmark* [Molesworth], London.

1977, *La Gaule française* [1574], Paris (facsimile of French translation, Cologne) (first Latin edn, 1573).

Huber, Ulrich 1694, *De jure civitatis* [1672], 3rd edition, Franeker.

Hume, David 1948, 'Hume's Early Memoranda, 1729-1740: The Complete Text', ed. Ernest Campbell Mossner, *Journal of the History of Ideas*, 9: 492–518.

1963, 'Of the Rise and Progress of the Arts and Sciences' [1742], in *Essays Moral, Political and Literary*, London.

1985a, *Essays Moral, Political and Literary* [1777], ed. Eugene F. Miller, Indianapolis.

1985b, 'Of the Origin of Government [1742]', in Hume 1985a.

1994, *Political Essays*, ed. Knud Haakonssen, Cambridge.

Humphrey, Lawrence 1563, *The Nobles or of Nobilitye*, London.

Hurd, Richard 1762, *Moral and Political Dialogues with Letters on Chivalry and Romance*, London and Cambridge.

Husbands, Edward, T. Warren and R. Best (eds.) 1642, *An Exact Collection Of all Remonstrances, Declarations, Votes, Orders, Ordinances, Proclamations, Petitions, Messages, Answers, and other Remarkable Passages betweene the Kings most Excellent Majesty, and his High Court of Parliament beginning at his Majesties return from Scotland, being in December 1641, and continued untill March the 21, 1643*, London.

Hutcheson, Francis 1729, *Hibernicus's Letters. A Collection of Letters and Essays on Several Subjects Lately Published in a Dublin Journal*, 2 vols., London and Dublin (with continuous pagination).

Hutchinson, Lucy 1973, *Memoirs of the Life of Colonel Hutchinson*, ed. James Sutherland, Oxford.

Il cittadino fedele. Discorso breve della giusta, generosa e prudente Risoluzione del Valoroso, e Fedelissimo Popolo di Napoli per liberarsi dall'insopportabili gravezze impostegli da Spagnuoli [Naples, 1647], in Villari (ed.) 1994: 41–54.

Imperato, F. 1604, *Discorso politico intorno al regimento delle piazze della Città di Napoli*, Naples.

[Ireton, Henry] 1648, *A Remonstrance of His Excellency Thomas Lord Fairfax, Lord Generall of the Parliament Forces, and of the Generall Councell of Officers*, London.

Iselin, Isaak 1768, *Geschichte der Menschheit*, 2nd edn, Zurich.

1770a, *Vermischte Schriften*, Zurich.

1770b, Review of Ferguson, *An Essay on the History of Civil Society*, in *Allgemeine deutsche Bibliothek*, 11: 154–68.

1772, *Versuch über die gesellige Ordnung*, Basle.

1777, Review of Smith, *Wealth of Nations*, *Allgemeine deutsche Bibliothek*, 31: 586–9.

1779, in *Allgemeine deutsche Bibliothek*, 38: 297–303.

Journal of the House of Commons.

Jubbes, John n.d., *An Apology*, London.

Junius, Franciscus (François du Jon) 1602, *De politiae Mosis observatione*, Leiden.

K[empe], W[illiam] 1588, *The Education of Children in Learning: Declared by the Dignitie, Vtilitie, and Method thereof*, London.

Kant, Immanuel 1784, *Idee zu einer allgemeinen Geschichte in weltbürgerlicher Absicht*, in *Kant's gesammelte Schriften*, Berlin, 1902.

1795, *Zum ewigen Frieden*, Berlin.

Karwicki, S. [*ca.* 1709], 'De ordinanda Republica', ms, n.p.

Katechizm narodowy 1791 1791, Warsaw (unpaginated).

Keckermann, Bartholomeus 1608, *Systema disciplinae politicae*, Hanover.

Knipschild, Philipp 1687, *Tractatus politico-historico-juridicus de civitatum imperialium iuribus et privilegiis* [1657], Ulm.

Kołłataj, Hugo 1788–9, *Do Stanisława Małachowskiego . . . anonima listów kilka*, Warsaw, vols. i–iii.

1790, *Prawo polityczne narodu polskiego*, Warsaw.

Konarski, S. 1754, *De viro honesto et bono cive ab ineunte aetate formando*, Warsaw.

1760–3, *O skutecznym rad sposobie albo o utrzymywaniu ordynaryjnych sejmów*, Warsaw, vols. i–iv.

König, M. Reinhard 1619, *Disputationum politicarum methodice*, Giessen.

Krótkie rzeczy potrzebnych z strony wolności, a swobód polskich zebranie, przez tego który dobrze życzy ojczyźnie swojej uczynione roku 1587 12 Februarii 1859 [1587], ed. K. J. Turowski, Krakow.

Kunicki, W. 1645, *Obraz szlachcica polskiego*, Krakow.

La Beaumelle, Laurent Angliviel 1997, *Mes pensées ou Le qu'en dira-t-on* [1751], ed. C. Lauriol, Geneva.

La Roche, Sophie 1793, *Erinnerungen aus meiner dritten Schweizerreise*, Offenbach.

Labenette (ed.) 1791, *Le Journal des droits de l'homme*, thirty octavo issues, 28 July to 28 August.

Lampredi, Giovanni M. 1756, *Saggio sopra la filosofia degli antichi Etruschi*, Florence.

1760, *Del governo civile degli antichi Toscani e delle cause della loro decadenza*, Lucca.

Leendertz, P. (ed.) 1924, *Het Geuzenliedboek. Uitgegeven uit het nalatenschap van E. T. Kuiper*, Zutphen, 2 vols.

Leibniz, Gottfried Wilhelm 1966, *Nouveaux Essais sur l'entendement humain* [1765], Paris.

Lemka, Jerzy 1608, *O Rzeczypospolitej* . . . (About the Commonwealth), n.p.

Les Corts generals de Pau Claris. Dietari o procés de Corts de la Junta General de Braços 1976, ed. B. de Rubí, Barcelona.

Leszczyński, S. [*ca.* 1743], *Głos wolny wolność ubezpieczający*, Nancy.

Lettera di un milanese a un napolitano amico suo, in Conti (ed.) 1984: 45–8.

Lettera scritta da un personaggio napolitano agli ordini del regno di Napoli nella quale da loro una breve istruttione per formare la nuova Repubblica, in Villari (ed.) 1994: 85–100.

Levy, Darline Gay, Harriet Branson Applewhite and Mary Durham Johnson (eds.) 1979, *Women in Revolutionary Paris 1789–1795. Selected Documents Translated with Notes and Commentary*, Urbana and London.

Lhomond, Charles-François 1779, *De viris illustribus*, Paris.

Libera respublica – absolutum dominium – rokosz [1606], in Czubek (ed.) 1918: 407.

Liebenthal, Christian 1652, *Collegium politicum* [Giessen, 1619], Amsterdam.

Lipsius, J. 1589, *Politicorum sive civilis doctrinae libri sex*, Leiden.

Livy 1600, *The Romane Historie*, trans. Philemon Holland, London.

1919, *Ab urbe condita*, Books i and ii, trans. and ed. B. O. Foster, London.

[Tite-Live] 1957, *History of Rome* [*Histoire romaine*], trans. Eugène Lasserre, Paris, vol. vii.

Locke, John 1963, *A Letter Concerning Toleration* [1689], rev., ed. and introd. Mario Montuori, The Hague.

Lottini, G. 1941, *Avvedimenti civili* [1574], ed. G. Mancini, Bologna.

Lubomirski, S. 1699, *De vanitate consiliorum*, Warsaw.

Ludlow, Edmund 1894, *Memoirs*, ed. C. H. Firth, 2 vols., Oxford.

1978, *A Voyce from the Watch Tower*, ed. B. Worden, London.

Lyly, John 1868a, *Euphues: The Anatomy of Wit* [1579], ed. Edward Arber, London.

1868b, *Euphues and his England* [1580], ed. Edward Arber, London.

Mably, Gabriel Bonnot de 1776, *Le Droit public de l'Europe fondé sur les traités*, 3 vols., Geneva.

1794–5, *Collection complète des œuvres*, vol. I: *Observations sur l'histoire de France* [1765], Paris.

1972, *Des droits et des devoirs du citoyen*, ed. Jean-Louis Lecercle, Paris.

1977a, *Œuvres* [1794–5], 15 vols., Aalen.

1977b, *Observations sur le gouvernement et les lois des Etats-Unis d'Amérique* [1784], in Mably 1977a, vol. VIII, 339–485.

1977c, *Observations sur l'histoire de France* [1765], in Mably 1977a, vols. I and II.

1977d, *De la législation ou principes des lois* [1774], in Mably 1977a, vol IX.

1977e, *Notre gloire ou nos rêves* [1779], in Mably 1977a, vol. XIII.

1977f, *De l'étude de l'histoire, à Monseigneur Le Prince de Parme* [1775], in Mably 1977a, vol. XII.

Machiavelli, Niccolò 1680, *The Works of the Famous Nicholas Machiavel*, trans. Henry Neville, London.

1760, *Opere inedite di Niccolò Machiavelli*, London [*recte* Lucca] ('edizione Lampredi').

1768, *Opere di Niccolò Machiavelli*, 8 vols., London.

1772, *Tutte l'opere di Niccolò Machiavelli segretario e cittadino fiorentino con una prefazione di Giuseppe Baretti*, 3 vols., London.

1782, *Opere di Niccolò Machiavelli*, 6 vols., Florence.

1960, *Il Principe* [1532] e *Discorsi sopra la prima deca di Tito Livio* [1518], ed. S. Bertelli, Milan.

1964, *Legazione e commissarie*, ed. Sergio Bertelli, 3 vols., Milan.

1965a, *Il teatro e gli scritti letterari*, ed. Franco Gaeta, Milan.

1965b, *Machiavelli: The Chief Works and Others*, trans. Allan H. Gilbert, 3 vols., Durham, N.C.

1979, *Ritracto delle cose della Magna* [1509], in *Opere*, ed. Sergio Bertelli, Verona.

1984, *Discorsi sopra la prima deca di Tito Livio*, ed. Giorgio Inglese, Milan.

1985, *The Discourses*, Harmondsworth.

1988, *Florentine Histories*, trans. Laura F. Banfield and Harvey C. Mansfield, Jr., Princeton.

1989, *The Chief Works and Others*, trans. Allan Gilbert, vol. I, Durham, N.C. and London.

1989, *The Prince*, ed. Russell Price and Quentin Skinner, Cambridge.

1994, *Selected Political Writings*, ed. and trans. David Wootton, Indianapolis and Cambridge.

Mackintosh, Sir James 1851, *The Miscellaneous Works*, London.

Madison, James, Alexander Hamilton and John Jay 1987, *The Federalist Papers* [1787–8], ed. Isaac Kramnick, Harmondsworth.

Malcolm, Joyce Lee (ed.) 1999, *The Struggle for Sovereignty: Seventeenth-Century English Political Tracts*, 2 vols., Indianapolis.

Mandeville, Bernard de 1714, *The Fable of the Bees, or Private Vices, Publick Benefits*, London.

Mariana, Juan de 1981, *La dignidad real y la educación del rey* [*De rege et regis institutione*, 1599], ed. L. Sánchez Agesta, Madrid.

Martí Viladamor, Francisco 1995, *Noticia universal de Cataluña* [1640], ed. X. Torres, in *Escrits polítics del segle XVII*, Vic.

Martínez del Villar, Miguel 1980, *Tratado del patronato, antigüedades, govierno y varones ilustres de la ciudad y comunidad de Calatayud y su arcedianato* [1598], Calatayud, facsimile, Zaragoza.

Masson de Pezay, A. F. J. 1771, *Les Soirées helvétiennes, alsaciennes et franch-comtoises*, Amsterdam.

Mazzei, Filippo 1976, *Researches on the United States* [1788], trans. and ed. Constance D. Sherman, Charlottesville.

Meiners, Christoph 1788, *Briefe über die Schweiz*, Berlin.

Melanchthon, Philipp 1951–61, *Werke*, vols. I–III, ed. Robert Stupperich, Gütersloh.

Melon, Jean-François 1843, *Essai politique sur le commerce* [1734], in Eugène Daire (ed.), *Economistes et financiers au XVIIIe siècle*, Paris.

Merbury, Charles 1581, *A Briefe Discovrse of Royall Monarchie, as of the Best Common Weale*, London.

Merola, Jeroni (1587), *República original sacada del cuerpo humano*, Barcelona.

Micraelius, Johannes 1644, *Syntagma historiarum ecclesiae omnium*, Stettin.
    1654, *Regia politici scientia*, Stettin.

Milton, John 1953–82, *Complete Prose Works of John Milton*, general ed. Don M. Wolfe, 8 vols., New Haven.
    1982, 'Outlines for Tragedies', in Milton 1953–82: VIII, 539–85.
    1991a, *Political Writings*, Cambridge.
    1991b, *The Tenure of Kings and Magistrates*, in *Political Writings*, ed. Martin Dzelzainis, Cambridge.

Mirouer des femmes vertueuses, ensemble la patience Griselidis par laquelle est démontrée l'obédience des femmes vertueuses; Hystoire admirable de Jeanne Pucelle 1547, Paris.

Modrzewski, Andrzej Frycz 1953, *Opera omnia*, vol. I: *Commentariorum de republica emendanda libre quinque* [1551], ed. Kazimierz F. Kumaniecki, Warsaw.

Moheau, Jean-Baptiste 1778, *Recherches et considérations sur la population de la France*, Paris.

Molesworth, Robert 1694, *Account of Denmark . . . in the Year 1692*, London.
    1738, *An Account of Denmark, As it was in the Year 1692* [1694], 4th edn, London.

Molhuysen, P. C. (ed.) 1928, *Briefwisseling van Hugo Grotius. Eerste deel, 1597–17 Augustus 1618*, The Hague.

Mommsen, Theodor and Paul Krueger (eds.) 1970, *Digesta*, in *Corpus iuris civilis*, 4 vols., Zurich.

[*Moniteur*] 1847, *Réimpression de l'ancien Moniteur depuis la réunion des Etats Généraux jusqu'au Consulat (mai 1789–novembre 1799)*, vol. I, Paris.

Montaigne, Michel de 1842, *The Complete Works of Michel de Montaigne, Comprising the Essays*, ed. W. Hazlitt, London.

[Montalembert, marquis de] 1789, *Première collection de petitions, d'écrits et de mémoires presentés à la Nation française et à ses représentants aux Etats-Généraux*, Paris.

Montano Benito [Montanus Benedictus], Arias 1575, *David. Hoc est virtutis exercitatissimae probatum Deo spectaculum, ex David pastoris militis ducis exulis ac prophetae exemplis*, Antwerp.
    1592, *De varia republica, sive commentaria in librum Judicum*, Antwerp.

Montchrestien, Antoine de 1889, *Traicté de l'oeconomie politique* [1615], ed. Théophile
    Funck-Bruntano, Paris.
Montesquieu, Charles de Secondat, baron de 1721, *Lettres persanes*, in Montesquieu
    1949–51.
    1734, *Considérations sur les causes de la grandeur des Romains et de leur décadence*, in
    Montesquieu 1949–51.
    1748, *De l'esprit des lois*, in Montesquieu 1949–51, vol. II.
    1752, *Reflections on the Causes of the Rise and Fall of the Roman Empire*, 2nd edn,
    London.
    1949–51, *Œuvres complètes*, ed. R. Caillois, Paris.
    1989, *The Spirit of the Laws* [*De l'esprit des lois*, 1748], trans. Anne M. Cohler, Basia
    Carolyn Miller and Harold Samuel Stone, Cambridge.
'Moralizacja' nad stanem Rzeczypospolitej po śmierci Augusta III, albo projekt do
    ustanowienia formy rządów Polski i do uszczęśliwienia całej ojczyzny
    Rzeczypospolitej' [*ca*. 1760], PAU Library (Krakow), ms no. 320.
Morellet, Abbé 1758, *Réflexions sur les avantages de la libre circulation des toiles peintes en
    France*, Paris.
Möser, Justus, 1964, *Justus Mösers sämtliche Werke*, Abteilung 3: *Osnabrückische Geschichte
    und historische Einzelschriften*, vol. XII, 1: *Osnabrückische Geschichte, Allgemeine
    Einleitung* [1768], ed. Paul Göttsching, Oldenburg.
Moyle, Walter 1969, *Essay upon the Constitution of the Roman Government* [*c*. 1699], in
    Robbins (ed.) 1969: 201–61.
Mulcaster, Richard 1581, *Positions . . . Necessarie for the Training vp of Children*, London.
Müller, Johannes von 1810–19, *Johannes von Müller sämmtliche Werke*, Tübingen.
Muratori, Lodovico Antonio 1964, *Primi disegni della Repubblica letteraria d'Italia esposti
    al pubblico da Lamindo Pritanio* [1704], in *Opere*, ed. G. Falco and F. Forti, Milan and
    Naples.
Naprawa Rzeczypospolitej do elekcyi nowego króla [1573], ed. K. J Turowski, Krakow, 1859.
Nedham, Marchamont 1652, *Mercurius Politicus*, no. 108, 24 June–1 July.
    1656, *The Excellencie of a Free State*, London.
    1657, *Mercurius Politicus*, April.
    1969, *The Case of the Commonwealth of England Stated* [1650], ed. P. Knachel,
    Charlottesville.
N[esbit], E. 1601, *Caesars Dialogve or a Familiar Communication Containing the First
    Institution of a Subiect, in Allegiance to His Soueraigne*, London.
Novalis (Friedrich Leopold, Baron von Hardenberg) *ca*. 1795–6, *Philosophische Studien*, in
    Schriften, ed. Richard Samuel, Darmstadt, vol. II: 104–296.
[Oglethorpe, James] 1732, *Select Tracts Relating to Colonies*, London.
Olivares, Gaspar de Guzmán, Conde-Duque de 1978–80, *Memoriales y cartas del conde
    duque de Olivares*, ed. J. H. Elliott and J. F. de la Peña, 2 vols., Madrid.
Oncken, August 1886, *Der ältere Mirabeau und die Oekonomische Gesellschaft in Bern*,
    Berne.
Opaliński, L. [1641], *Rozmowa plebana z ziemianem*, in *Pisma polskie*, ed. L. Kamykowski,
    Warsaw, 1938.
    1959, 'Obrona Polski przeciw Janowi Barclayowi' [*Polonia defensa contra Joannem
    Barclaium*, 1648], in L. Opaliński, *Wybór pism*, ed. S. Grzeszczuk, Wrocław

OPH 1762–3, *The Parliamentary or Constitutional History of England*, 24 vols., London
('*The Old Parliamentary History*').

Orzechowski, Stanisław 1858, *Dyalog albo rozmowa około exekucyi Polskiej Korony* [*Rozmowa albo dialog akolo egzekucyjej Polskiej Korony*, 1563], ed. J. K. Turowski, Krakow.

    1972, *Wybór pism* (Selected Works), ed. J. Starnawski, Wrocław.

Paine, Thomas 1969, *Rights of Man* [1791–2], Harmondsworth.

    1989, *The Rights of Man Part I* [1791–2], in *Political Writings*, ed. Bruce Kuklick, Cambridge, pp. 49–143.

Palm-Aelders, Etta 1791, *Appel aux Françoises sur la régénération des moeurs, et nécessité de l'influence des femmes dans un gouvernement libre*, Paris (facsimile in *Les Femmes dans la Révolution Française*, vol. II, Paris, 1982, text no. 33).

Parker, Henry 1648, *Of a Free Trade*, London.

    1651, *Scotlands Holy War*, London.

    1933, *Observations upon some of his Majesties Late Answers and Expresses*, in *Tracts on Liberty in the Puritan Revolution 1838–1647*, ed. William Haller, New York.

    1999, *The Case of Shipmony Briefly Discoursed*, in Malcolm (ed.) 1999: I, 93–125.

Paruta, Paolo 1657, *Politick Discourses* [1599], trans. Henry, Earl of Monmouth, London.

    1943, *Discorsi politici nei quali si considerano diversi fatti illustri e memorabili di principi e di repubbliche antiche e moderne divisi in due libri* [1599], ed. G. Candeloro, Bologna.

    1964, *Della perfezione della vita politica* [1572], in Widmar (ed.) 1964.

    1982, *Historia vinetiana* [1605?], in Benzoni and Zanato (eds.) 1982.

Patrizi, Francesco 1576, *A Moral Methode of Ciuile Policie*, trans. Richard Robinson, London.

Pauw, Charles de 1788, *Réflexions philosophiques sur les Grecs*, 2 vols., Berlin.

Pellini, P. 1664, *Dell'historia di Perugia parte prima* [e seconda] [1627], Venice.

Pellissery, Roch 1776, *Le Caffé politique d'Amsterdam ou entretiens d'un françois, d'un hollandois et d'un cosmopolite sur les divers intérêts économiques et politiques de la France, de l'Espagne et de l'Angleterre*, 2 vols., Amsterdam.

    1792, *Lettres de M. de Pellissery, prisonnier onze ans et deux mois à la Bastille et treize mois à Charenton*, Paris.

Pérez de Mesa, Diego 1980, *Política o razón de estado* [*ca.* 1632], ed. L. Pereña and C. Baciero, Madrid.

[Peski, W.] [*ca.* 1671], *Domina palatii regina libertas*, ed. J. Dębiński, *Rozne mowy publiczne, sejmików i sejmowe*, [Częstochowa], 1727.

[Peter, Hugh] 1648, *An Abridgment of the Late Remonstrance of the Army*, London.

Petrycy, Sebastian 1605, *Przydatki do Polityki Arystotelesowej* (Addenda to Aristotle's *Politics*), Krakow.

Piasecki, Paweł 1972, 'Responsum de absoluto dominio' [1631–2], ed. W. Czapliński, in *Archiwum Literackie* (Literary Archive), vol. XVI: *Miscelanea staropolskie* (Old-Polish Miscellany),4, Wrocław.

Pilati di Tassulo, Carlo Antonio 1767, *Di una riforma d'Italia: o sia dei Mezzi di riformare i più cattivi costumi e le più perniciose leggi d'Italia*, Villafranca.

    1777, *Voyages en différens pays de l'Europe en 1774, 1775 & 1776*, La Haye.

Pisan, Christine de 1982, *The Book of the City of Ladies* [1405], New York.

    1986, *Le Livre de la cité des dames* [1405], trans. and introduced by Eric Hicks and Thérèse Moreau, Paris.

Pivati, Gianfrancesco 1723, *Del perfetto governo della Serenissima repubblica veneta*, Padua.

Plato 1941, *The Republic of Plato*, ed. F. M. Cornford, Oxford.

Plutarch [Plutarque] 1538, *Recueil de haults & nobles faictz de plusieurs femmes vertueuses escript premièrement en grec par Plutarque et maintenant traduct en Françoys – A tres noble et tres haulte dame Madame Marguerite de France, fille du Roi nostre sire*, Paris.

   1968, *Plutarch's Moralia*, vol. III, trans. Frank Cole Babbitt, London and Cambridge, Mass.

Polybius 1979, *The Rise of the Roman Empire*, trans. Ian Scott-Kilvert, Harmondsworth.

   1989, *The Histories*, Cambridge, Mass. (Loeb edition).

Pope, Alexander 1738, *The Epilogue to the Satires* [reprint London and New Haven, 1953].

Pou[l]lain de la Barre, François 1671, *De l'éducation des dames pour la conduite de l'esprit dans les sciences et dans les moeurs*, Paris.

   1984, *De l'égalité des deux sexes* [1673], Paris (English translation by 'A.L.', *The Woman as Good as the Man*, London,1677).

Price, John 1649, *Clerico-Classicum, Or, The Clergi-allarum to a Third War*, London.

Priestley, Joseph 1762, *Rudiments of English Grammar, . . . with Observations on Style*, London.

Proceedings of the Convocation Sejm 1648, in *Jakuba Michałowskiego wojskiego lubelskiego a później kasztelana bieckiego księga pamiętnicza* (Memoires of Jakub Michałowski, *tribunus* of Lublin and later Castellan of Biecz), Krakow, 1864

Proceedings of the Coronation Seym 1633, in Raczyński Library, Poznań, ms 17.

Proceedings of the Election Sejm 1587, in *Dyjariusze sejmowe R. 1587. Sejmy konwokacyjny i elekcyjny* (Proceedings of the Seym in 1587: Convocation and Election Seyms), in *Scriptores* 1887.

Proceedings of the Extraordinary Seym 1613, in Archiwum Główne Akt Dawnych (The Main Archive of Old Acts), Radziwiłł Archive VI 11-48, Warsaw.

Proceedings of the Seym 1646, in Jagiellonian Library, Krakow, ms 49.

Przestroga braterska [1733], n.p. (unpaginated).

Ptolemy of Lucca 1997, *On the Government of Princes: De regimine principum*, trans. James M. Blythe, Philadelphia.

Pufendorf, Samuel 1660 *Elementa jurisprudentiae universalis*, The Hague.

   1672, *De jure naturae et gentium*, Lund (translations cited from *De jure naturae et gentium/The Law of Nature and Nations*, New York and London, 1964, 2 vols.).

   1976, *Die Verfassung des Deutschen Reiches* [*De statu imperii Germanici*, 1667], ed. Horst Denzer, Stuttgart.

Quesnay, François, 1958 'Hommes' [1757], in Quesnay, *François Quesnay et la physiocratie*, Paris.

Radzewski, F. 1743, *Kwestie politycznie obojętne*, n.p.

'Ragionamento di Tomaso Aniello Generalissimo per eccitare il suo Popolo Napolitano alla libertà', 1994, in Villari (ed.) 1994: 67–72.

Ramée, Pierre de la (Petrus Ramus) 1964, *Dialectique* [1555], ed. Michel Dassonville, Geneva.

Reasons why this Kingdome ought to Adhere to the Parliament 1642, London.

Remonstrance in Defence of the Lords and Commons in Parliament, A 1642, London.

Representation of the Judgements of Ministers of the Gospell within the Province of London, A Serious and Faithfull, 1649, London.

Ribadeneyra, Pedro de 1952, *Tratado de la religión y virtudes que ha de tener el príncipe christiano* [1595], Madrid.

Richardson, Samuel 1649, *An Answer to the London Ministers Letter*, London.

Robbins, Caroline (ed.) 1969, *Two English Republican Tracts*, Cambridge.

Rogers, Thomas 1576, *A Philosophicall Discourse, Entituled, the Anatomie of the Minde*, London.

Rousseau, Jean-Jacques 1755a, *Discours sur l'origine et les fondements de l'inégalité parmi les hommes* ['Second Discourse'], in Rousseau 1959–95, vol. III.

    1755b, 'Economie politique', in Rousseau 1959–95, vol. III.

    1758, *Lettre à d'Alembert*, in Rousseau 1959–95, vol. V.

    1761, *Julie, ou la nouvelle Héloïse*, in Rousseau 1959–95, vol. II.

    1762a, *Du contrat social*, in Rousseau 1959–95, vol. III.

    1762b, *Emile*, in Rousseau 1959–95, vol. IV.

    1959–95, *Œuvres complètes*, 5 vols., Paris.

Rushe, Arthur 1566, *A President for a Prince*, London.

Rushworth, John 1692, *Historical Collections. The Third Part; in Two Volumes. Containing the Principal Matters which happened from the Meeting of the Parliament, November the 3d. 1640: to the End of the Year 1644*, London.

Saavedra Fajardo, Diego 1976, *Empresas políticas: Idea de un príncipe político-cristiano* [1640], ed. Q. Aldea, 2 vols., Madrid.

Sadler, John 1649, *The Rights of the Kingdom*, London.

Saige, Guillaume-Joseph 1775, *Catéchisme du citoyen, ou Eléments du droit public français, par demandes et par réponses*, Geneva.

Sala, Gaspar 1640, *Proclamación católica a su majestad Piadosa Felipe el Grande*, Barcelona.

    1995, *Secrets públics* [1641], ed. E. Serra, in *Escrits polítics del segle XVII*, Vic.

Sallust 1608, *The Two most worthy and Notable Histories which remaine unmained to Posterity: (viz:) The Conspiracie of Cateline, undertaken against the government of the Senate of Rome, and The Warre which Iugurth for many years maintained against the same State*, trans. Thomas Heywood, London.

    1931, *Bellum Catilinae* in *Sallust*, ed. and trans. J. C. Rolfe, London.

Sandoval, Prudencio de 1955, *Historia de la vida y hechos del Emperador Carlos V* [1618], Madrid.

Sansovino, Francesco 1562, *Delle cose notabili che sono in Venetia*, Venice.

    1581, *Venetia città nobilissima et singolare*, Venice.

    1590, *The Quintesence of Wit, Being a Corrant Comfort of Conceites, Maximes, and Politicke Deuises*, trans. [Robert Hitchcock], London.

Sarroca, Josep 1995, *Política del comte d'Olivares, contrapolítica de Catalunya i Barcelona* [1641], in *Escrits polítics del segle XVII*, ed. E. Serra, Vic.

Schlatter, R. B. (ed.) 1975, *Hobbes' Thucydides*, New Brunswick.

Schlegel, Friedrich 1797a, 'Versuch über den Begriff des Republikanismus', *Deutschland*, 3: 10–41.

    1797b, 'Kritische Fragmente', *Lyceum der schönen Künste*, 1, 2, no. 65.

Schröder, Wilhelm von 1713, *Vom absoluten Fürstenrecht*, in Wilhelm von Schröder, *Fürstliche Schatz- und Rentkammer, nebst seinem nothwendigen Unterricht vom Goldmachen*, 3rd edn, Leipzig.

    1719, *Disqvisitio politica vom absoluten Fürstenrecht*, Wolfenbüttel.

Schubart, C. F. D. 1776, *Deutsche Chronik*, 3: 321–5 (reprinted in Jost Hermand (ed.), *Von deutscher Republik 1775–1795: Texte radikaler Demokraten*, Frankfurt am Main, 1975, pp. 37–9).

Scott, Sir Walter (ed.) 1809–15, *The Somers Tracts*, 13 vols., London.

Scriptores rerum Polonicarum 1887, vol. XI, ed. A. Sokołowski, Krakow.

1907, vol. XX, ed. E. Barwiński, Krakow.

1911, vol. XXI, ed. E. Barwiński, Krakow.

Scriverius, Petrus, 1636, *Beschrivinge van Out Batavien, Met de Antiquiteyten vandien. Mitsgaders D'Afbeeldinge, Afcomst ende Historie der Edelen Hooghgeboren graven van Hollant, Zeelant ende Vrieslant etc: Als oock, Een Corte Beschrivinghe der Nederlansche Oorlogen, beginnende vanden Aenvang der Nederlanse beroertè tot den Iare 1635*, Amsterdam.

Ségur, L. P. (ed.) 1802, *Politique de tous les cabinets de l'Europe pendant les règnes de Louis XV et de Louis XVI*, 3 vols., Paris.

Sepúlveda, Juan Ginés 1963, *Del reino y de los deberes del rey* [1573], ed. A. Losada, Madrid.

Settala, Ludovico 1930, *Della ragion di stato* [1627], in Croce and Caramella (eds.) 1930: 43–141.

Sgualdi, Vincenzo 1634, *Aristocratia conservata*, Venice.

Shaftesbury [Cooper, Anthony Ashley, 3rd earl of] 1711, *Characteristics of Men, Manners, Opinions, Times*, 3 vols., London.

Sidney, Algernon 1772, *Sydney on Government*, London.

1990, *Discourses concerning Government* [1698], ed. Thomas G. West, Indianapolis.

1996, *Court Maxims*, ed. Hans W. Blom, Eco Haitsma Mulier and Ronald Janse, Cambridge.

Siemek, K. 1632, *Civis bonus*, Krakow.

Sieyès, Emanuel-Joseph 1788, 'Essai sur les privilèges', in *Qu'est-ce que le Tiers-Etat*, Paris, 1982.

1985a, 'Dire sur la question du véto royal' [August 1789], in Sieyès 1985c.

1985b, 'Préliminaires de la constitution' [1789], in Sieyès 1985c.

1985c, *Ecrits politiques*, ed. Robert Zapperi, Paris.

Sigonius, C. 1582, *De Republica Hebraeorum*, Bononiae [Bologna].

Sinner de Ballaigues, J.-R. 1853, *Berne au XVIIIe siècle. Extrait d'un volume inédit du Voyage dans la Suisse occidentale (1781)*, Berne.

Skarga, Piotr 1972, *Kazania sejmowe* (Sermons Delivered in the Seym) [1597], ed. J. Tazbir, Wrocław.

Smith, Adam 1976a, *Wealth of Nations* [1776], ed. A. S. Skinner and R. H. Campbell, Oxford.

1976b, *Theory of Moral Sentiments* [1759], ed. D. D. Raphael and A. L. Macfie, Oxford.

1978, *Lectures on Jurisprudence* [1762–3, 1766], ed. R. L. Meek, D. D. Raphael and P. G. Stein, Oxford.

1980, *Essays on Philosophical Subjects* [1795], ed. W. P. D. Wightman, J. C. Bryce and I. S. Ross, Oxford.

1983, *Lectures on Rhetoric and Belles Lettres* [1762–3], ed. J. C. Bryce, Oxford.

1987, *Correspondence*, ed. E. C. Mossner and I. S. Ross, Oxford.

[Smith, Thomas] 1960, *Discourse of the Commonweal of the Realm of England* [1549], ed. Mary Dewar, Charlottesville.

    1982, *De republica Anglorum* [1583], ed. Mary Dewar, Cambridge.

Smythe, John 1595, *Instrvctions, Observations, and Orders Mylitarie*, London.

Société économique de Berne (ed.) 1760–73, *Mémoires et observations recueillies par la Société Oeconomique de Berne*, Zurich (1760-1) and Berne (1762–73).

Spence, Thomas 1775, *The Grand Repository of the English Language . . .* , Newcastle upon Tyne.

Spinoza, Baruch de 1951a, *Theologico-Political Treatise* [1670], in Spinoza 1951c: 1–279.

    1951b, *Political Treatise* [*ca.* 1675], in Spinoza 1951c: 279–387.

    1951c, *A Theologico-Political Treatise and A Political Treatise* [1670; *ca.* 1675] trans. R. H. M. Elwes, New York.

    1958, *The Political Works of Spinoza*, ed. A. G. Wernham, Oxford.

    1991, *Tractatus theologico-politicus* [1670] (English trans. of Gebhardt edition), Leiden.

    1994, *Politisches Traktat. Tractatus politicus* [*ca.* 1675], ed. Wolfgang Bartuschat, Hamburg.

Staël, Madame de 1788, *Lettres sur le caractère et les écrits de J.-J. Rousseau*, in *Œuvres complètes de Madame la Baronne de Staël-Holstein*, Geneva, 1967.

    1814, *Letters on the Writings and Character of J. J. Rousseau*, London.

Stanyan, Abraham 1714, *An Account of Switzerland*, London.

Starkey, Thomas 1989, *A Dialogue between Pole and Lupset*, ed. T. F. Mayer, Camden Society, 4th ser., vol. 37.

Starowolski, Szymon 1650, *Reformacyja obyczajów polskich*, Krakow.

    1991a, *Robak sumienia złego człowieka niebogobojnego i o zbawienie niedbałego* [*ca.* 1648] (The Worm Gnawing on the Bad Conscience of a Person Impious and Negligent of Redemption), in Starowolski 1991c.

    1991b, *Reformacya obyczajów polskich* [1650] (Reformation of Polish Customs), in Starowolski 1991c.

    1991c, *Wybór pism* (Selected Works), ed. I. Lewandowski, Wrocław.

Staszic, Stanisław 1787, *Uwagi nad życiem Jana Zamoyskiego*, Warsaw.

    [1790], *Przestrogi dla Polski z teraźniejszych politycznych Europy związków i z praw natury wypadajace*, [Warsaw].

Steiger, Carl Friedrich 1952, 'Rede über die Errichtung der ausländischen Finantzen des Hohen Standes', *Berner Zeitschrift für Geschichte und Heimatkunde*, 10.

Stockwood, John 1584, *A Verie Godlie and Profitable Sermon of the Necessitie, Properties and Office of a Good Magistrate*, London.

Tacitus 1591, *The Ende of Nero and Beginning of Galba. Fower Bookes of the Histories of Cornelius Tacitus. The Life of Agricola*, trans. Henry Savile, Oxford.

    1598, *The Annales of Cornelius Tacitus. The Description of Germanie*, trans. Richard Grenewey, London.

    1728, *The Works of Tacitus . . . To which are Prefixed, Political Discourses Upon that Author*, trans. Thomas Gordon, 2 vols., London.

    1925, *The Histories*, Books I–III, ed. and trans. Clifford H. Moore, London.

Thelwall, John 1808, *Mr Thelwall's Plan and Terms of Tuition etc. Institution for the Cure of Impediments of Speech, Instruction of Foreigners, Cultivation of Oratory, English Composition and Polite Literature, and the Preparation of Youth for the More Liberal Departments of Active Life*, London.

Thomas, William 1551, *An Argument, Wherein the Apparaile of Women is both Reproved and Defended*, n.p.

1549, *Historie of Italy*, London.

1550, *Rules of Italian Grammar with a Dictionarie*, London.

Timpler, Clemens 1611, *Philosophiae practicae pars tertia et ultima complectens politica integram libris v*, Hanover.

Tindal, Matthew 1709, 'Of the Liberty of the Press' [1698], in *Four Discourses . . .*, London, pp. 291–329.

Toland, John 1696, *Christianity not Mysterious . . .*, London [reprint London, 1995].

1698a, 'The Life of Milton', in *A Complete Collection of the . . . Works of John Milton*, London.

1698b, *The Militia Reform'd . . .*, London.

1701a, *Anglia libera: or the Limitation and Succession of the Crown of England Explain'd and Asserted*, London [reprint New York, 1979].

1701b, *The Art of Governing by Partys . . .*, London.

1704, *Letters to Serena* [reprint Stuttgart and Bad Cannstatt, 1964].

1709, *Adeisidaemon, sive Titus Livius a superstitione vindicatus . . . Annexae sunt ejusdem Origines Judaicae . . .*, Hagae-Comitis [The Hague].

1717a, *The State-Anatomy of Great Britain . . .*, 4th edn, London.

1717b, *The Second Part of the State Anatomy . . .*, London.

1718, *Nazarenus: or, Jewish, Gentile, and Mahometan Christianity*, London.

1720, *Tetradymus. Containing I. Hodogus . . . II. Clidophorus . . . III. Hypatia . . . IV. Mangoneutes . . .*, London.

1726, *A Collection of Several Pieces . . . With Some Memoirs of his Life and Writings*, 2 vols., London.

1751, *Pantheisticon: or, the Form of Celebrating the Socratic Society . . .*, London.

1965, *Gründe für die Einbürgerung der Juden in Grossbritannien und Irland*. English text, intro., trans. and comment by H. Mainusch, Stuttgart.

1999, *Nazarenus and Other Texts*, ed. Justin A. I. Champion, Oxford.

Tooke, John Horne 1786–1805, *Epea pteroenta, or, the Diversions of Purley*, 2 vols., London.

Trenchard, John, and Thomas Gordon 1995, *Cato's Letters: Or, Essays on Liberty, Civil and Religious, and Other Important Subjects* [1720–3], ed. Roland Hamowy, 2 vols., Indianapolis.

Treuer, Gottlieb Samuel 1719, *Wilhelm Frey Herrn von Schrödern 'Desquisitio politica vom absoluten Fürsten-Recht' mit nöthigen Anmerkungen versehen, welche derselben gefährliche Irrthümer deutlich entdecken und solches practendierte Recht gründlich untersuchen*, Leipzig and Wolfenbüttel.

1720, *Logomachias in iuris naturae doctrina dissertatio*, Helmstedt.

Tristan, Flora 1840, *Promenades dans Londres*, Paris.

Tscharner, N. E. 1769, 'Ueber die Nothwendigkeit der Prachtgesetze in einer freyen Stadt', in Isaak Iselin (ed.), *Ueber die Nothwendigkeit der Prachtgesetze in einem Freystaate*, Zurich.

Tscharner, V. B. 1782, 'Bern', in G. E. Haller and V. B. Tscharner (eds.), *Historische, geographische und physikalische Beschreibung des Schweizerlandes*, vol. I, Berne.

Turgot, Anne-Robert Jacques 1970, 'Fondation' [1757], in *Ecrits économiques*, Paris.

Tutini, C. 1754, *Dell'origine e fundazion de' Seggi di Napoli . . .* [1642], Naples.

[Twynne, Thomas] 1576, *The Schoolemaster, or Teacher of Table Philosophie*, London.

V. D. H., V. H. [Van den Hove], *see* De la Court

Valerius, Adrianus 1626, *Neder-landtsche gedenck-clanck: kortelick openbarende de voornaemste geschiedenissen van de seventhien Neder-Landsche provintien, 't sedert den aenvang der inlandsche beroerten ende troublen, tot den iare 1625*, Haarlem.

Valerius, Cornelius 1571, *The Casket of Iewels*, trans. J[ohn] C[harlton], London.

Valkenier, Petrus 1675, *'t Verwerd Europa, ofte politijke en historische beschryvinge der waare fundamenten en oorsaken van de oorlogen en revolutien in Europa, voornamentlijk in en omtrent de Nederlanden zedert den jaare 1664 gecauseert door de gepretendeerde Universeele Monarchie der Franschen*, Amsterdam

Van Aitzema, L. 1652, *Herstelde leeuw of discours over 't gepasseerde in de Vereenigde Nederlanden in 't Jaer 1650 ende 1651*, Amsterdam.

Van den Enden, Franciscus 1992, *Vrye Politijke Stellingen en Consideratien van Staat* [1665], ed. Wim Klever, Amsterdam.

Van den Vondel, J. 1612, *Passcha ofte de Verlossinge Israels uit Egypten*, Amsterdam.
    1620, *Hierusalem verwoest. Treurspel*, Amsterdam.

Van Gelderen, Martin (ed.) 1993, *The Dutch Revolt, 1555–1590*, Cambridge.

Vauvilliers, 1769, *Examen historique et politique du gouvernement de Sparte, ou lettre à un ami sur la législation de Lycurgue, en réponse aux doutes proposés par M. de Mably contre l'ordre naturel et essentiel des sociétés politiques*, Paris.

Verri, Pietro 1964, *Della economia politica* [1771], in *Del piacere e del dolore*, ed. R. De Felice, Milan.

Vico, G. B. 1953, *Principi di scienza nuova* [1744], in *Opere*, ed. F. Nicolini, Milan and Naples.
    1974, *De uno universi iuris principio et fine uno* [1721–2], in P. Cristofolini (ed.), *Opere giuridiche*, Florence.

Villari, R. (ed.) 1994, *Per il re o per la patria. La fedeltà nel Seicento*, Rome and Bari.

Vindication of the Parliament And their Proceedings, The. Or, Their Military Designe prov'd Loyall and Legall. A Treatise 1642, London.

Vitoria, Francisco de (1960), *Relectio De potestate civili* [1557], in *Obras de Francisco de Vitoria*, ed. T. Urdanoz, Madrid.

Volumina legum 1859, vol. I, ed. J. Ohryzko, St Petersburg.

Vowell alias Hooker, John [1575], *Orders Enacted for Orphans and for Their Portions within the Citie of Exceter*, London.

Voyer de Paulmy, René Louis de, marquis d'Argenson 1852–67, *Journal et mémoires*, ed. E. Rathéry, 9 vols., vol. IX, Paris.

Vranck, François 1993, 'Short Exposition of the Right Exercised from All Old Times by the Knighthood, Nobles and Towns of Holland and Westvriesland for the Maintenance of the Liberties, Rights, Privileges and Laudable Customs of the Country' [1587], in Van Gelderen (ed.) 1993: 227–38.

[Vreede, Pieter] 1783, *Waermond en Vryhart. Gesprek over de Vryheid der Nederlandren; en den Aert der Waere Vryheid*, n.p.

Walshe, Edward 1545, *The Office and Duety in Fighting for our Countrey*, London.

Walthard, B. L. (ed.) 1773, *Patriotische Reden, gehalten vor dem hochlöblichen aussern Stande der Stadt Bern*, Berne.

Warburton, Bishop William 1977, *A View of Lord Bolingbroke's Philosophy in 4 Letters to a Friend* [1754], New York.

Warszewicki, Krzysztof 1588, *Paradoxa*, Prague.
    1598, *De optimo statu libertatis*, Krakow.

Wattenwyl, A. L. von 1765, *Rede eines Eidgenossen von der Glückseligkeit der Unterthanen unter einer freien Regierung*, Berne.

Wentworth, Peter 1598, *A Pithie Exhortation to Her Maiestie for Establishing Her Svccessor to the Crowne*, n.p.

Werdenhagen, Johann Angelus von 1632, *Introductio universalis in omnes republicas, sive Politica Generalis*, Amsterdam.

Whitelocke, Bulstrode 1853, *Memorials of the English Affairs*, 4 vols., Oxford.

Wicksted [John Churchill] 1717, *An Ode for the Year MDCCVII to the King*, London (reprinted in Weinbrot 1978).

Widmar, B. (ed.) 1964, *Scrittori politici del '500 e '600*, Milan.

Williams, David 1789, *Letters on Political Liberty and the Principles of the English and Irish Projects of Reform Addressed to a Member of the House of Commons*, 3rd edn, London.

Wolan, Andrzej 1572, *De libertate Politica sive Civili*, Krakow.
    [1606], *O wolności Rzeczypospolitej albo szlacheckiej*, ed. J. K. Turowski, Krakow, 1859.

Wollstonecraft, Mary 1790, *A Vindication of the Rights of Men, in a Letter to the Right Honourable Edmund Burke; Occasioned by his Reflections on the Revolution in France*, in Wollstonecraft 1994: 1–62.
    1792a, *A Vindication of the Rights of Woman: With Strictures on Political and Moral Subjects*, 2nd edn, London.
    1792b, *Défense des droits des femmes, suivie de quelques considérations sur des sujets politiques et moraux*, Paris.
    1792c, *A Vindication of the Rights of Woman: With Strictures on Political and Moral Subjects*, in Wollstonecraft 1994: 63–283.
    1794, *An Historical and Moral View of the Origin and Progress of the French Revolution; and the Effect it Has Produced in Europe*, in Wollstonecraft 1994: 285–371.
    1994, *Political Writings*, ed. Janet Todd, Oxford.
    1995, 'A Vindication of the Rights of Men', in *A Vindication of the Rights of Men and A Vindication of the Rights of Woman*, ed. Sylvana Tomaselli, Cambridge, pp. 1–64.

Wolne zdanie wolnego szlachcica, na które ten chuba gniewać się bedziem kto się gniewa na wolność [1733], n.p.

Woudhuysen, H. R. and David Norbrook (eds.) 1992, *The Penguin Book of Renaissance Verse*, London.

Wren, Matthew 1657, *Considerations upon Mr Harrington's Oceana*, London.

Young, Arthur 1769, *Letters Concerning the Present State of the French Nation*, London.

Zabarella, Jacobo 1985, 'De Methodis' [1578], in Cesare Vasoli (ed.), *Jacobi Zabarellae De methodis libri quator, Liber de Regressu*, Bologna.

Zaborowski, Stanisław 1507, *Tractatus de natura iurium*, n.p.

Zamoyski, Jan [1605], *Pisma polityczne z czasów rokoszu Zebrzydowskiego*, in Czubek (ed.) 1918.

Zastanowienie sie nad nową Konstytucją polską [1791], n.p. (unpaginated).

Zebrzydowski, Mikoł aj 1918, *Apologia szlachcica polskiego* [1607] (Apology of a Polish Nobleman), in Czubek (ed.) 1918: III.

Zinzendorf, Karl Graf von 1936, 'Bericht des Grafen Karl von Zinzendorf über seine handelspolitische Studienreise durch die Schweiz 1764', *Basler Zeitschrift für Geschichte und Altertumskunde*, 35.

Zuccolo, L. 1930, *Della ragion di Stato* [1621], in Croce and Caramella (eds.) 1930: 25–41.

Secondary Literature

Adair, Douglass 1957, ' "That Politics May Be Reduced to a Science": David Hume, James Madison and the Tenth Federalist', *Huntington Library Quarterly*, 20: 343–60.

Albareda, Joaquim 1993, *Els catalans i Felip V. De la conspiració a la revolta (1700–1705)*, Barcelona.

Aldea, Quintín 1986–91, *España y Europa en el siglo XVII. Correspondencia de Saavedra Fajardo*, 2 vols., Madrid.

Aldridge, Alfred Owen 1951, *Shaftesbury and the Deist Manifesto*, Philadelphia.

Amelang, James S. 1982, 'Le oligarchie di Barcellona nella prima Età Moderna. Studio comparativo', *Studi Storici*, 23: 583–602.

    1986, *Honored Citizens of Barcelona. Patrician Culture and Class Relations, 1490–1714*, Princeton.

    1998, *The Flight of Icarus. Artisan Autobiography in Early Modern Europe*, Stanford.

Amoh, Yasuo 1990, 'Adam Ferguson and the American Revolution', *Kochi University Review*, 37: 55–87.

Appleby, J. O. 1984, *Capitalism and a New Social Order*, New York.

Arendt, Hannah and Karl Jaspers 1985, *Briefwechsel 1926–1969*, Munich.

Armitage, David 1992, 'The Cromwellian Protectorate and the Languages of Empire', *The Historical Journal*, 35: 531–55.

    1995, 'John Milton: Poet Against Empire', in Armitage, Himy and Skinner (eds.) 1995: 206–25.

    1997, 'A Patriot for Whom? The Afterlives of Bolingbroke's Patriot King', *Journal of British Studies*, 36: 397–418.

Armitage, David, Armand Himy and Quentin Skinner (eds.) 1995, *Milton and Republicanism*, Cambridge.

Arnade, Peter 1996, *Realms of Ritual. Burgundian Ceremony and Civic Life in Late Medieval Ghent*, Ithaca.

Ascheri, M. 1997, 'Intervento al seminario su "Continuità e discontinuità nella storia d'Italia" ', *Le carte e la storia*, 3.

Backvis, C. 1960, 'Comment les Polonais du XVIe siècle voyaient l'Italie et les Italiens', *Annuaire de l'Institut de Philologie et d'Histoire Orientales et Slaves*, 15: 240 ff.

Baker, Keith Michael 1990a, *Inventing the French Revolution: Essays on French Political Culture in the Eighteenth Century*, Cambridge.

1990b, 'A Classical Republican in Eighteenth-Century Bordeaux: Guillaume-Joseph Saige', in Baker 1990a: 128–54.

1990c, 'Fixing the French Constitution', in Baker 1990a: 252–305.

Baldini, A. E. (ed.) 1995, *Aristotelismo politico e ragion di Stato. Atti del convegno internazionale di Torino, 11–13 febbraio 1993*, Florence.

Balibar, Etienne 1985, *Spinoza et la politique*, Paris.

Barber, Sarah 1998, *Regicide and Republicanism. Politics and Ethics in the English Revolution*, Edinburgh.

Bartuschat, Wolfgang 1992, *Spinozas Theorie des Menschen*, Hamburg.

Bäschlin, Conrad 1913, *Die Blütezeit der Ökonomischen Gesellschaft in Bern. 1759–1766*, Laupen.

Becher, Ursula 1978, *Politische Gesellschaft*, Göttingen.

Behme, Thomas 1995, *Samuel von Pufendorf: Naturrecht und Staat. Eine Analyse und Interpretation seiner Theorie, ihrer Grundlagen und Probleme*, Göttingen.

Beiser, Frederick C. 1992, *Enlightenment, Revolution, and Romanticism: The Genesis of Modern German Political Thought 1790–1800*, Cambridge, Mass.

Bellamy, R. (ed.) 1990, *Victorian Liberalism: Nineteenth-Century Political Thought and Practice*, London.

Benítez, Miguel 1996, *La Face cachée des Lumières: recherches sur les manuscrits philosophiques clandestins de l'âge classique*, Paris.

Bennett, James 1830, *The History of Tewkesbury*, Tewkesbury.

Benzoni, G. and T. Zanato (eds.) 1982, *Storici e politici veneti del Cinquecento e del Seicento*, Milan and Naples.

Berlin, Isaiah 1969, 'Two Concepts of Liberty' [1958], in Berlin, *Four Essays on Liberty*, Oxford, pp. 118–72.

1979, 'The Originality of Machiavelli', in Berlin, *Against the Current: Essays in the History of Ideas*, ed. Henry Hardy, London, pp. 25–79.

Berry, Christopher 1997, *Social Theory of the Scottish Enlightenment*, Edinburgh.

Berti, Silvia *et al.* (eds.) 1996, *Heterodoxy, Spinozism, and Free Thought in Early-Eighteenth-Century Europe. Studies on the 'Traité des Trois Imposteurs'*, Dordrecht.

Besselink, L. 1988, 'The Impious Hypothesis Revisited', *Grotiana*, new series, 9: 3–63.

Biasatti, F. 1990, ' "Libertas" e "philosophari" nel *Tractatus theologico-politicus*', in Biasatti, *Prospettive su Spinoza*, Frieret, pp. 97–110.

Birely, R. 1990, *The Counter-Reformation Prince. Anti-Machiavellianism or Catholic Statecraft in Early Modern Europe*, Chapel Hill and London.

Blanchet, Régis and Danlot, Pierre 1996, *John Toland (1670–1722), un des modernes. Quand une pensée oubliée du xviiie siècle devient nécessaire au xxie siècle*, Rouvray.

Blickle, Peter (ed.) 1997, *Resistance, Representation and Community*, Oxford.

Blockmans, W. P. 1983, 'Bürger, Bürgertum – Südliche und Nordliche Niederlande', in *Lexicon des Mittelalters*, Munich, pp. 1019–21.

1988, 'Alternatives to Monarchical Centralization: The Great Tradition of Revolt in Flanders and Brabant', in Koenigsberger (ed.) 1988: 153–5.

1997, 'The Impact of Cities on State Formation: Three Contrasting Territories in the Low Countries, 1300–1500', in Blickle (ed.) 1997: 256–71.

Blom, Hans 1988, 'Virtue and Republicanism. Spinoza's Political Philosophy in the Context of the Dutch Republic', in Koenigsberger (ed.) 1988.

   1993, 'The Moral and Political Philosophy of Spinoza', in *The Routledge History of Philosophy*, vol. IV: *The Renaissance and Seventeenth Century Rationalism*, London.

   1995, *Morality and Causality in Politics. The Rise of Materialism in Dutch Seventeenth-Century Political Thought*, Rotterdam and Utrecht.

Blom, Hans W. and I. W. Wildenberg (eds.) 1986, *Pieter de la Court in zijn tijd. Aspecten van een veelzijdig publicist. Voordrachten gehouden op het De la Court Symposium, Erasmus Universiteit Rotterdam, 26 april 1985*, Amsterdam and Maarssen.

Bloom, E. A. and L. Bloom 1971, *Joseph Addison's Sociable Animal in the Market Place, on the Hustings and in the Pulpit*, Providence.

Bock, Gisela, Quentin Skinner and Maurizio Viroli (eds.) 1990, *Machiavelli and Republicanism*, Cambridge.

Boles, Laurence Huey, Jr. 1997, *The Huguenots, the Protestant Interest, and the War of the Spanish Succession, 1702–14*, New York.

Bonfatti, Emilio 1979, *La 'Civil conversazione' in Germania*, Udine.

Borrelli, G. 1993, *Ragion di stato e Leviatano. Conservazione e scambio alle origini della modernità politica*, Bologna.

   1995, 'Aristotelismo politico e ragion di stato in Italia', in Baldini (ed.) 1995: 181–99.

Bos, E. P. and H. A. Krop (eds.) 1993, *Franco Burgersdijk (1590–1635). Neo-Aristotelianism in Leiden*, Amsterdam and Atlanta.

Boulton, J. T. 1963, *The Language of Politics in the Age of Wilkes and Burke*, London.

Bouwsma, W. J. 1968, *Venice and the Defense of Republican Liberty*, Berkeley and Los Angeles.

Bouza, Fernando 1994, 'Entre dos reinos, una patria rebelde. Fidalgos portugueses en la monarquía hispánica después de 1640', *Estudis*, 20: 83–103.

Bozzolo, Carla 1967, 'Il Decameron come fonte del *Livre de la cité des dames* de Christine de Pisan', in Franco Simone (ed.), *Miscellanea di studi e ricerche sul quattrocento francese*, Turin.

Bradshaw, B. 1991, 'Transalpine Humanism', in Burns and Goldie (eds.) 1991: 95–132.

Brett, Annabel S. 1997, *Liberty, Right and Nature. Individual Rights in Later Scholastic Thought*, Cambridge.

Brewer, John D. 1986, 'Adam Ferguson and the Theme of Exploitation', *The British Journal of Sociology*, 37: 461–78.

   1989, 'Conjectural History, Sociology and Social Change in Eighteenth Century Scotland: Adam Ferguson and the Division of Labour', in D. McCrone, S. Kendrick and P. Straw (eds.), *The Making of Scotland: Nation, Culture and Social Change*, Edinburgh, pp. 13–30.

Brugge 1998, *Brugge en de Renaissance. Van Memling tot Pourbus*. Exhibition catalogue, Memling-Museum, Bruges.

Buijnsters, P. J. 1991, *Spectatoriale geschriften*, Utrecht.

Bunte, W. 1984, *Joost van den Vondel und das Judentum*, Frankfurt am Main.

Burgess, Glenn 1990, 'Contexts for the Writing and Publication of Hobbes's *Leviathan*', *History of Political Thought*, 11: 675–702.

1992, *The Politics of the Ancient Constitution: An Introduction to English Political Thought, 1603–1642*, London.

1996, *Absolute Monarchy and the Stuart Constitution*, London.

Burke, Peter 1966, 'A Survey of the Popularity of Ancient Historians, 1450–1700', *History and Theory*, 5: 135–52.

1995, *The Fortunes of the Courtier: The European Reception of Castiglione's 'Cortegiano'*, Cambridge.

Burns, J. H. and Mark Goldie (eds.) 1991, *The Cambridge History of Political Thought, 1450–1700*, Cambridge.

Burtt, Shelley 1992, *Virtue Transformed, Political Argument in England, 1688–1740*, Cambridge.

Cameron, W. J. 1961, *New Light on Aphra Behn*, Auckland.

Campbell, R. H and A. S. Skinner (eds.) 1982, *The Origins and Nature of the Scottish Enlightenment*, Edinburgh.

Campbell, T. D. 1982, 'Francis Hutcheson: "Father" of the Scottish Enlightenment', in Campbell and Skinner (eds.) 1982: 167–85.

Campos Boralevi, L. 1996, Introduction to P. Cunaeus, *De republica Hebraeorum – The Commonwealth of the Hebrews* (reprint of the original edition and of the English translation), Florence.

1997, 'Per una storia della *Respublica Hebraeorum* come modello politico', in V. I. Comparato and E. Pii (eds.), *Dalle 'Repubbliche' elzeviriane alle ideologie del '900*, Florence, pp. 17–33.

Capitani, François de 1982, 'Die Antike im schweizerischen Staatsdenken des 18. Jahrhunderts', in Ernest Giddey (ed.), *Vorromantik in der Schweiz?*, Freiburg.

Carey, Vincent 1996a, 'Introduction, part I: Richard Beacon's Irish experience', in Beacon 1996: xxiii–xxvi.

1996b, 'Richard Beacon's *Solon His Follie* (1594): Classical Sources, Text, and Context in the Conquest of Ireland', *The European Legacy*, 1: 207–13.

Carlson, A. J. 1993, '*Mundus muliebris*, the World of Women Reviled and Defended, *ca.* 195 BC and AD 1551', *Sixteenth-Century Journal*, 24, 3.

Carrive, Paulette 1995, 'Les Convictions politiques de John Toland', *Revue de Synthèse*, 2–3: 231–57.

Carter, J. J. and J. H. Pittock (eds.) 1987, *Aberdeen and the Enlightenment*, Aberdeen.

Casey, James 1979, *The Kingdom of Valencia in the Seventeenth Century*, Cambridge.

1995, 'Patriotism in Early Modern Valencia', in Kagan and Parker (eds.) 1995.

1999a, *Early Modern Spain. A Social History*, London and New York.

1999b, ' "Una libertad bien entendida": Los valencianos y el estado de los Austrias', *Manuscrits*, 17: 237–52.

Castiglione, D. 2000, ' "That Noble Disquiet": Meanings of Liberty in the Discourse of the North', in Collini, Whatmore and Young (eds.) 2000: 48–67.

Cauchies, J. M. 1994, 'La Signification politique des entrées princières dans les Pays-Bas: Maximilien d'Autriche et Philippe le Beau', *Publication du Centre Européen d'Etudes Bourguignonnes*, 34: 19–35.

Centre d'Etudes et de Recherche d'Histoire des Idées Politiques (ed.) 1996, *L'Influence de l'antiquité sur la pensée politique européenne*, Aix-en-Provence.

Cervelli, Innocenzo 1974, *Machiavelli e la crisi dello stato veneziano*, Naples.

Champion, Justin A. I. 1992, *The Pillars of Priestcraft Shaken. The Church of England and its Enemies, 1660–1730*, Cambridge.

1995, 'John Toland: The Politics of Pantheism', *Revue de Synthèse*, 2–3: 259–80.

1996, 'Legislators, Impostors, and the Politic Origins of Religion: English Theories of "Imposture" from Stubbe to Toland', in Berti *et al.* (eds.) 1996: 333–56.

2000, 'Toleration and Citizenship in Enlightenment England: John Toland and the Naturalization of the Jews, 1714–1753', in Grell *et al.* (eds.) 2000: 133–56.

Cherchi, Gavina 1985, *Satira ed enigma: due saggi sul Pantheisticon di John Toland*, Lucca.

Claeys, Gregory 1993, 'From True Virtue to Benevolent Politeness: Godwin and Godwinism revisited', in *Empire and Revolutions*, Proceedings of the Folger Institute Center for the History of British Political Thought, vol. VI, Washington, D.C., pp. 187–225.

Cochrane, E. 1981, *Historians and Historiography in the Italian Renaissance*, Chicago and London.

Coleman, Janet 2000, *A History of Political Thought. From the Middle Ages to the Renaissance*, Oxford.

Collini, Stefan, Richard Whatmore and Brian Young (eds.) 2000, *Economy, Polity and Society: British Intellectual History, 1750–1950*, Cambridge.

Collinson, Patrick 1987, 'The Monarchical Republic of Queen Elizabeth I', *Bulletin of the John Rylands Library*, 69: 394–424.

1990, *De Republica Anglorum Or, History with the Politics Put Back*, Cambridge.

1993, 'The Elizabethan Exclusion Crisis and the Elizabethan Polity', *Proceedings of the British Academy*, 84: 51–92.

1994, *Elizabethan Essays*, London.

Comparato, V. I. 1985, 'Pietro Giannone e la rivoluzione napoletana del 1647', in *L'età dei lumi. Studi sul Settecento europeo in onore di Franco Venturi*, vol. II, Naples, pp. 793–835.

1998a, 'Barcelona y Nápoles en la búsqueda de un modelo político: analogías, diferencias, contactos', in *Actes del IV Congrés d'Història Moderna de Catalunya*, in *Pedralbes*, 18, 2: 439–52.

1998b, 'La repubblica napoletana del 1647/48: partiti, idee, modelli politici', *Il pensiero politico*, 31.

Condren, Conal 1994, *The Language of Politics in Seventeenth-Century England*, London.

Consoli, J. P. 1992, *Giovanni Boccaccio, An Annotated Bibliography*, New York and London.

Conti, V. 1983, *Le leggi di una rivoluzione. I bandi della repubblica napoletana dall'ottobre 1647 all'aprile 1648*, Naples.

1984, *La rivoluzione repubblicana a Napoli e le strutture rappresentative (1647–1648)*, Florence.

1997, *Consociatio civitatum. Le repubbliche nei testi elzeviriani (1625–1649)*, Florence.

1998, 'Modelli repubblicani nel primo seicento', *Filosofia politica*, 12: 57–65.

Conti, V. (ed.) 1993, *Le ideologie della città europea dall'Umanesimo al Romanticismo*, Florence.

Costa, Jaume, Artur Quintana and Eva Serra 1991, 'El viatge a Münster dels germans Josep i Francesc Fontanella per a tractar les paus de Catalunya', in

B. Schlieben-Lange and A. Schönberger (eds.), *Polyglotte Romania. Homenatge a T. D. Stegman*, Frankfurt, pp. 257–94.

Costantini, C. 1978, *La repubblica di Genova nell'età moderna*, Turin.

Cozzi, G. 1963–4, 'Cultura politica e religione nella "pubblica storiografia" veneziana del '500', *Bollettino dell'Istituto di storia della società e dello stato veneziano*, 5–6: 215–94.

Crawford, Patricia 1977, ' "Charles Stuart, That Man of Blood" ', *Journal of British Studies*, 16: 41–61.

Cristofolini, Paolo (ed.) 1995, *L'Hérésie spinoziste: La discussion sur le* Tractatus theologico-politicus, *1670–1677, et la réception immédiate du spinozisme: Actes du Colloque international de Cortona, 10–14 avril 1991 / The Spinozistic Heresy: The Debate on the* Tractatus theologico-politicus, *1670–1677, and the Immediate Reception of Spinozism: Proceedings of the International Cortona Seminar, 10–14 April 1991*, Amsterdam and Maarssen.

Cromartie, Alan 1995, *Sir Matthew Hale 1609–1676*, Cambridge.

   1999, 'The Constitutionalist Revolution: The Transformation of Political Culture in Early Stuart England', *Past and Present*, 163: 76–120.

Cropsey, J. 1957, *Polity and Economy: An Interpretation of the Principles of Adam Smith*, The Hague.

   1975, 'Adam Smith and Political Philosophy', in Skinner and Wilson (eds.): 132–53.

Curto, Diogo R. 1988, *O discurso político em Portugal (1600–1650)*, Lisbon.

Dahm, Karl-Wilhelm, Werner Krawietz and Dieter Wyduckel (eds.) 1988, *Politische Theorie des Johannes Althusius*, Berlin.

Daniel, Stephen H. 1984, *John Toland. His Methods, Manners, and Mind*, Kingston and Montreal.

Davids, Karel and Jan Lucassen (eds.) 1995, *A Miracle Mirrored. The Dutch Republic in European Perspective*, Cambridge.

Davie, George 1981, *The Scottish Enlightenment*, London.

Davis, Colin 1981, 'Pocock's Harrington: Grace, Nature and Art in the Classical Republicanism of James Harrington', *Historical Journal*, 24, 3.

   1990, 'Cromwell's Religion', in John Morrill (ed.), *Oliver Cromwell and the English Revolution*, London.

   1993, 'Against Formality: One Aspect of the English Revolution', *Transactions of the Royal Historical Society*, 6th series, 3.

De Dios, Salustiano 1996–7, 'El absolutismo regio en Castilla durante el siglo XVI', *Ius Fugit*, 5–6: 53–236.

De Jongste, J. A. F. 1977–83, 'Een bewind op zijn smalst. Het politieke bedrijf in de jaren 1727–1747', in *Algemene Geschiedenis der Nederlanden*, 15 vols., Haarlem, vol. IX.

De Mattei, R. 1979, *Il problema della 'Ragion di Stato' nell'età della Controriforma*, Milan and Naples, 2 vols.

De Michelis, F. 1967, *Le origini storiche e culturali del pensiero di Ugo Grozio*, Florence.

De Wall, Heinrich 1992, *Die Staatslehre Johann Friedrich Horns (ca. 1629–1665)*, Aalen.

Deane, Seamus 1988, *The French Revolution and Enlightenment in England 1789–1832*, Cambridge, Mass., and London.

Decavele, Johan 1975, *De dageraad van de Reformatie in Vlaanderen (1520–1565)*, Verhandelingen van de Koninklijke Academie voor Wetenschappen, Letteren en Schone Kunsten van België, 37.76, Brussels.

Del Bagno, I. 1993, *Legum doctores. La formazione del ceto giuridico a Napoli tra Cinque e Seicento*, Naples.

Del Negro, P. 1986, 'Proposte illuminate e conservazione nel dibattito sulla teoria e la prassi dello stato', in G. Arnaldi and M. Pastore Stocchi (eds.), *Storia della cultura veneta. Il Settecento*, vol. v/2, Venice.

Den Uyl, Douglas J. 1983, *Power, State, Freedom*, Assen

Denzer, Horst 1972, *Moralphilosophie und Naturrecht bei Samuel Pufendorf. Eine geistes- und wissenschaftsgeschichtliche Untersuchung zur Geburt des Naturrechts aus der Praktischen Philosophie*, Munich.

Diaz, F. 1973, 'L'Idea repubblicana nel Settecento italiano fino alla Rivoluzione francese', in Diaz, *Per una storia illuministica*, Naples, pp. 423–63.

Dockès-Lallement, N. 1996a, 'Mably et l'institution de la société spartiate', in Centre d'Etudes et de Recherche d'Histoire des Idées Politiques (ed.) 1996: 229–58.

1996b, 'La Réponse de Vauvilliers à l'enthousiasme laconophile de Mably', in Centre d'Etudes et de Recherche d'Histoire des Idées Politiques (ed.) 1996: 259–91.

Dreitzel, Horst 1970, *Protestantischer Aristotelismus und absoluter Staat. Die 'Politica' des Henning Arnisaeus (ca. 1575–1636)*, Wiesbaden.

1988, 'Der Aristotelismus in der politischen Philosophie Deutschlands im 17. Jahrhundert', in Eckhard Kessler, Charles H. Lohr and Walter Sparn (eds.), *Aristotelismus und Renaissance. In memoriam Charles B. Schmitt*, Wiesbaden, pp. 163–92.

1989, 'Ständestaat und absolute Monarchie in der politischen Theorie des Reiches in der frühen Neuzeit', in Georg Schmidt (ed.), *Stände und Gesellschaft im Alten Reich*, Wiesbaden, pp. 19–50.

1991, *Monarchiebegriffe in der Fürstengesellschaft. Semantik und Theorie der Einherrschaft in Deutschland von der Reformation bis zum Vormärz*, Cologne, Weimar and Vienna.

1992, *Absolutismus und ständische Verfassung in Deutschland. Ein Beitrag zu Kontinuität und Diskontinuität der politischen Theorie in der frühen Neuzeit*, Mainz.

Dufour, Alfred 1991, *Droits de l'homme, droit naturel et histoire. Droit, individu et pouvoir de l'Ecole du Droit naturel à l'Ecole du Droit historique*, Paris.

Dupont, Florence 1989, *La Vie quotidienne du citoyen romain sous la République, 509–27 av. J.C.*, Paris.

Duprat, Catherine 1994, 'Don et citoyenneté en l'An II, les vertus du peuple français', in Michel Vovelle (ed.), *Révolution et république, l'exception française*, Paris.

Durand, Y. 1973, *Les Républiques au temps des monarchies*, Paris.

Duso, Giuseppe 1996, 'Una prima esposizione del pensiero politico di Althusius: La dottrina del patto e la costituzione del regno', *Quaderni Fiorentini per la Storia del Pensiero Giuridico Moderno*, 25: 65–126.

1999, 'Il governo e l'ordine delle consociazioni: la *Politica* di Althusius', in Giuseppe Duso (ed.), *Il Potere. Per la Storia della Filosofia politica moderna*, Rome, pp. 77–94.

Dybikowski, J. 1993, *On Burning Ground: An Examination of the Ideas, Projects and Life of David Williams*, Oxford.

Dyck, Andrew R. 1996, *A Commentary on Cicero, De officiis*, Ann Arbor.

Dzelzainis, Martin 1989, 'Milton, Macbeth, and Buchanan', *The Seventeenth Century*, 4: 55–66.

1995, 'Milton's Classical Republicanism', in Armitage, Himy and Skinner (eds.) 1995.

Dzięgielwski, J. 1993, 'Stan szlachecki w zyciu publicznym Rzeczypospolitej w pierwszym stuleciu po unii lubelskiej', in A Sucheni-Grabowska and A. Dybkowska (eds.), *Tradycje polityczne dawnej Polski*, Warsaw.

Eberle, Friedrich and Theo Stammen (eds.) 1989, *Die Französische Revolution in Deutschland: Zeitgenössische Texte deutscher Autoren*, Stuttgart.

Ehrard, Jean 1997, 'Le Corps de Julie', *L'Invention littéraire au XVIIIe siècle: fiction, idées, société*, Paris, pp. 101–16.

Elliott, J. H. 1963, *The Revolt of the Catalans (1598–1640)*, Cambridge.

1973, 'England and Europe: a Common Malady?', in C. Russell (ed.), *The Origins of the English Civil War*, London.

1986, *The Count-Duke of Olivares. The Statesman in an Age of Decline*, New Haven and London.

1993, 'Catalunya dins d'una Europa de monarquies compostes', in *Actes del Tercer Congrés d'Història Moderna de Catalunya*, in *Pedralbes*, 13, 1: 11–23.

1994 *Lengua e imperio en la España de Felipe IV*, Salamanca.

Ellis, Harold A. 1998, *Boulainvilliers and the French Monarchy: Aristocratic Politics in Early Eighteenth-Century France*, Ithaca.

Emery, Christopher Ralph 1967, 'The Study of Politics in the Netherlands in the Early Eighteenth Century', Dissertation, London.

Erämetsä, Erik 1961, *Adam Smith als Mittler englisch-deutscher Spracheinflüsse. The Wealth of Nations*, Helsinki.

Eyffinger, Arthur 1984, 'Introduction', in Grotius 1984: 5–56.

Fauré, Christine 1997, 'Des droits de l'homme aux droits de la femme, une conversion intellectuelle difficile', in Fauré (ed.), *Encyclopédie politique et historique des femmes*, Paris, pp. 209–10 (English translation: 'From the Rights of Man to the Rights of Woman: A Difficult Intellectual Conversion', in Fauré (ed.) 2002).

Fauré, Christine (ed.) 2002, *Political and Historical Encyclopedia of Women*, Chicago.

Feingold, Mordechai 1997, 'The Humanities', in Nicholas Tyacke (ed.), *The History of the University of Oxford*, vol. IV: *Seventeenth-Century Oxford*, Oxford, pp. 211–357.

Fernández Albaladejo, Pablo 1990, 'León de Arroyal: Del "sistema de rentas" a la "buena constitución"' in E. Fernández de Pinedo (ed.), *Haciendas forales y hacienda real. Homenaje a D. Miguel Artola y D. Felipe Ruiz Martín*, Bilbao, pp. 95–111.

1992, *Fragmentos de monarquía*, Madrid.

1996, ' "Observaciones políticas": Algunas consideraciones sobre el lenguaje político de Francisco Martínez Marina', *Initium. Revista Catalana d'Història del Dret*, 1: 691–714.

1997, 'Católicos antes que ciudadanos. Gestación de una "política española" en los comienzos de la Edad Moderna', in Fortea (ed.) 1997: 103–27.

Fernández Albaladejo, Pablo (ed.) 1997, *Monarquía, imperio y pueblos en la España Moderna*, Alicante.

Fernandez-Santamaria, J. A. 1977, *The State, War and Peace. Spanish Political Thought in the Renaissance, 1516–1559*, Cambridge.

1997, *La formación de la sociedad y el origen del estado. Ensayos sobre el pensamiento político español del Siglo de Oro*, Madrid.

Ferro, Víctor 1987, *El dret públic català. Les institucions de Catalunya fins el decret de la Nova Planta*, Vic.

Fink, Zera 1945, *The Classical Republicans*, Urbana.

Firpo, L. 1965, *Traduzioni dei 'Ragguagli' di Traiano Boccalini*, Florence.

Flammermont, Jules 1899, 'J.-L. Favier, sa vie et ses écrits', *La Révolution française*, 38: 161–84, 258–76, 314–35, 411–62.

Fontana, Alessandro, Francesco Furlan and Georges Saro (eds.) 1997, *Venise et la Révolution française: les 470 dépêches des ambassadeurs de Venise au Doge, 1786–1795*, Paris.

Fontana, Biancamaria (ed.) 1994, *The Invention of the Modern Republic*, Cambridge.

Forbes, Duncan 1966, 'Introduction', in Ferguson 1966: xiii–xli.

   1975a, *Hume's Philosophical Politics*, Cambridge.

   1975b, 'Sceptical Whiggism, Commerce, and Liberty', in Skinner and Wilson (eds.) 1975: 179–201.

   1982, 'Natural Law and the Scottish Enlightenment', in Campbell and Skinner (eds.) 1982: 186–204.

Fortea, José Ignacio 1990, *Monarquía y Cortes en la Corona de Castilla. Las ciudades ante la política fiscal de Felipe II*, Salamanca.

   1997, 'Entre dos servicios: la crisis de la hacienda real a fines del siglo XVI', *Studia Historica. Historia Moderna*, 17: 63–90.

Fortea, José Ignacio (ed.) 1997, *Imágenes de la diversidad. El mundo urbano en la Corona de Castilla (s. XVI–XVIII)*, Santander.

France, Peter 1992, *Politeness and its Discontents: Problems in French Classical Culture*, Cambridge.

Franklin, Julian H. 1991, 'Sovereignty and the Mixed Constitution: Bodin and his Critics', in Burns and Goldie (eds.) 1991: 298–328.

Friedeburg, Robert von 1998, 'Reformed Monarchomachism and the Genre of the "politica" in the Empire: The *Politica* of Johannes Althusius in its Constitutional and Conceptual Context', *Archivio della Ragion di Stato*, 6: 127–53.

   1999, *Widerstandsrecht und Konfessionskonflikt. Notwehr und Gemeiner Mann im deutsch-britischen Vergleich 1530–1669*, Berlin.

   2000, 'Welche Wegscheide in die Neuzeit? Lutherisches Widerstandsrecht, "Gemeiner Mann" und konfessioneller Landespatriotismus zwischen "Münster" und "Magdeburg" ', *Historische Zeitschrift*, 270: 561–616.

   2001, 'In Defence of *Patria*: Resisting Magistrates and the Duties of Patriots in the Empire from the 1530s to the 1640s', *The Sixteenth Century Journal*, 32: 357–82.

Friedeburg, Robert von and Wolfgang Mager 1996, 'Learned Men and Merchants: The Growth of the Bürgertum', in Sheilagh Ogilvie (ed.), *Germany. A New Social and Economic History*, vol. II, London, pp.164–95.

Frijhoff, Willem Th. M. 1981, *La Société néederlandaise et ses gradués, 1575–1814*, Amsterdam

Fuidoro, I. 1994, *Successi historici raccolti dalla sollevatione di Napoli dell'anno 1647*, ed. A. M. Giraldi and M. Raffaeli, introd. R. Villari, Milan.

Fukuda, Arihiro 1997, *Sovereignty and the Sword. Harrington, Hobbes, and Mixed Government in the English Civil Wars*, Oxford.

Furet, François 1992, *Revolutionary France, 1770–1880*, trans. Antonia Nevill, Oxford.

Furet, François and Mona Ozouf (eds.) 1992, *Le Siècle de l'avènement républicain*, Paris.

Gabba, Emilio 1995, 'Adam Ferguson e la storia di Roma' in Gabba, *Cultura classica e storiografia moderna*, Bologna, pp. 73–97.

Galasso, G. 1994, 'Una ipotesi di "blocco storico" oligarchico-borghese nella Napoli del Seicento: i "Seggi" di Camillo Tutini fra politica e storiografia', in G. Galasso, *Alla periferia dell'impero. Il Regno di Napoli nel periodo spagnolo (secoli XVI–XVII)*, Turin, pp. 247–69.

Garin, E. 1966, *Storia della filosofia italiana*, Turin.

Gauchet, Marcel 1989, *La Révolution des droits de l'homme*, Paris.

Gaudemet, Jean 1959, 'Le Statut de la femme dans l'empire romain', in *La Femme, Publication de la Société Jean Bodin*, Brussels.

Gautier, Claude 1992a, 'Ferguson ou la modernité problematique', in Adam Ferguson, *Essai sur l'histoire de la société civile* [1767; trans. M. Bergier, 1783], Paris, pp. 5–94.

  1992b, 'De la liberté chez les modernes: Ferguson, critique de la modernité', *Droits*, 8: 125–40.

Gawlick, Günther and Lothar Kreimendahl 1987, *Hume in der deutschen Aufklärung. Umrisse eine Rezeptionsgeschichte*, Stuttgart and Bad Cannstatt.

Gelabert, Juan E. 1997a, 'Tráfico de oficios y gobierno de los pueblos de Castilla (1543–1643)', in L. A. Ribot and L. de Rosa (eds.), *Ciudad y mundo urbano en la Epoca Moderna*, Madrid.

  1997b, 'Ciudades en crisis: Castilla, 1632–1650', in Fortea (ed.) 1997: 447–73.

Gellner, Ernest 1994, 'Adam Ferguson', in Gellner, *Conditions of Liberty. Civil Society and Its Rivals*, London.

  1996, 'Adam Ferguson and the Surprising Robustness of Civil Society', in E. Gellner and C. Cansino (eds.), *Liberalism in Modern Times. Essays in Honour of José G. Merquior*, Budapest, pp. 119–31.

Gentles, Ian 1991, 'The Impact of the New Model Army', in Morrill 1991: 84–103.

  1992, *The New Model Army in England, Ireland and Scotland, 1645–1653*, Oxford.

Geuna, Marco 1998, 'La tradizione repubblicana e i suoi interpreti: famiglie teoriche e discontinuità concettuali', *Filosofia politica*, 12: 101–32.

Geurts, P. A. M. 1956, *De nederlandse opstand in de pamfletten 1566–1584*, Nijmegen.

Geyl, P. 1948–59, *Geschiedenis van de Nederlandse Stam*, 3 vols., Amsterdam and Antwerp.

  1971, 'Het stadhouderschap in de partijliteratuur onder De Witt', in P. Geyl, *Pennestrijd over staat en historie. Opstellen over de Vaderlandse Geschiedenis aangevuld met Geyl's Levensverhaal (tot 1945)*, Groningen, pp. 3–71

Gierke, Otto 1913, *Das deutsche Genossenschaftsrecht*, vol. IV: *Die Staats- und Korporationslehre der Neuzeit. Durchgeführt bis zur Mitte des siebzehnten, für das Naturrecht bis zum Beginn des neunzehnten Jahrhunderts*, Berlin.

Giesey, Ralph A. 1968, *If not, not. The Oath of the Aragonese and the Legendary Laws of Sobrarbe*, Princeton.

Gil, Xavier 1995, 'Aragonese Constitutionalism and Habsburg Rule: The Varying Meanings of Liberty', in Kagan and Parker (eds.) 1995.

1996, 'Visión europea de la monarquía española como monarquía compuesta, siglos XVI y XVII' in C. Russell and J. Andrés Gallego (eds.), *Las monarquías del Antiguo Régimen, ¿monarquías compuestas?*, Madrid, pp. 65–95.

Gilbert, Felix 1969, 'Machiavelli e Venezia', *Lettere Italiane*, 21: 389–98.

1976, Review of [Pocock 1975,] *The Machiavellian Moment, Times Literary Supplement*, 19 March, pp. 307–8.

Giuntini, Chiara 1979, *Panteismo e ideologia repubblicana: John Toland (1670–1722)*, Bologna.

Goldie, Mark 1991, 'The Scottish Catholic Enlightenment', *Journal of British Studies*, 30: 20–62.

1992, 'Common Sense Philosophy and Catholic Theology in the Scottish Enlightenment', *Studies on Voltaire and the Eighteenth Century*, 302: 281–320.

1993, 'Priestcraft and the Birth of Whiggism', in Phillipson and Skinner (eds.) 1993.

González Alonso, Benjamín 1980, 'La fórmula "obedézcase, pero no se cumpla" en el derecho castellano de la edad media', *Anuario de Historia del Derecho Español*, 50: 469–87.

1981, *Sobre el estado y la administración de la Corona de Castilla en el Antiguo Régimen*, Madrid.

Goodin, R. and P. Pettit (eds.) 1993, *A Companion to Political Philosophy*, Oxford.

Grafton, Anthony 1991, 'Humanism and Political Theory', in Burns and Goldie (eds.) 1991.

1996, Review of Burke 1995, *London Review of Books*, 22 August 1996.

Grafton, Anthony and Lisa Jardine 1986, *From Humanism to the Humanities. Education and the Liberal Arts in Fifteenth- and Sixteenth-Century Europe*, Cambridge, Mass.

Grau, Ramon and Marina López 1979, 'Capmany', in F. Artal (ed.), *Ictineu. Diccionari de les ciències de la societat als Països Catalans (s. XVIII–XX)*, Barcelona.

Gregory, Tullio 1998, '*Libertinisme érudit* in Seventeenth-Century France and Italy: The Critique of Ethics and Religion', *The British Journal for the History of Philosophy*, 6, 3: 323–49.

Grell, Ole Peter *et al.* (eds.) 2000, *Toleration in Enlightenment Europe*, Cambridge.

Groenhuis, G. 1977, *De Predikanten*, Groningen.

1981, 'Calvinism and National Consciousness: The Dutch Republic as the New Israel', in A. C. Duke and C. A. Tamse (eds.), *Britain and the Netherlands*, vol. VII, The Hague, pp. 118–33.

Groupe de Recherches Spinozistes 1992, *L'Ecriture Sainte au temps de Spinoza et dans le système spinoziste*, vol. IV, Paris.

Grześkowiak-Krwawicz, A. 1985, 'Publicystyka polska lat 1772–1792 o angielskim systemie rządow', *Przegląd Humanistyczny*, 5–6.

1990, *Publicystyka stanisławowska o modelu rządow monarchii francuskiej*, Wrocław.

1994, 'Rara avis czy wolni wsrod wolnych?', in L. Kądziela, W. Kriegseisen and Z. Zielinska (eds.), *Trudne stulecia. Studia z dziejów XVII I XVIII wieku*, Warsaw.

Grzybowski, Konstanty 1959, *Teoria reprezentacji w Polsce epoki Odrodzenia* (Theory of Representation in Poland in the Epoch of the Renaissance), Warsaw.

Guerci, Luciano 1979, *Libertà degli antichi e libertà dei moderni: Sparta, Atene e i 'philosophes' nella Francia del '700*, Naples.

Guggisberg, Kurt 1951, 'Daniel von Fellenberg (1736–1801). Beiträge zur bernischen Kulturgeschichte', *Berner Zeitschrift für Geschichte und Heimatkunde.*

Guy, John 1993, 'The Henrician Age', in Pocock (ed.) 1993: 13–46.

1995a, 'Introduction: The 1590s: The Second Reign of Elizabeth I', in John Guy (ed.), *The Reign of Elizabeth I: Court and Culture in the Last Decade*, Cambridge, pp. 1–19.

1995b, 'The Rhetoric of Counsel in Early Modern England', in Dale Hoak (ed.), *Tudor Political Culture*, Cambridge, pp. 292–310.

Haakonssen, Knud 1981, *The Science of a Legislator: The Natural Jurisprudence of David Hume and Adam Smith*, Cambridge.

1993, 'Republicanism', in Goodin and Pettit (eds.) 1993: 568–74.

1996, *Natural Law and Moral Philosophy: From Grotius to the Scottish Enlightenment*, Cambridge.

Haakonssen, Knud (ed.) 1988, *Traditions of Liberalism: Essays on John Locke, Adam Smith, and John Stuart Mill*, [St Leonards, New South Wales].

Hackett, Helen 1995, *Virgin Mother, Maiden Queen. Elizabeth I and the Cult of the Virgin Mary*, Basingstoke.

Haitsma Mulier, Eco 1980, *The Myth of Venice and Dutch Republican Thought in the Seventeenth Century*, Assen.

1987, 'The Language of Seventeenth-century Republicanism in the United Provinces: Dutch or European?', in Pagden (ed.) 1987: 179–95.

Haitsma Mulier, Eco and Wyger Velema (eds.) 1999, *Vrijheid. Een geschiedenis van de vijftiende tot de twintigste eeuw.* Serie Nederlandse begripsgeschiedenis 2, Amsterdam.

Hammerstein, Notker 1982, *Jus und historie*, Göttingen.

Hammerstein, Notker (ed.) 1995, *Staatslehre der frühen Neuzeit*, Frankfurt.

Hampsher-Monk, Iain 1988, 'Rhetoric and Opinion in the Politics of Edmund Burke', *History of Political Thought*, 9, 3.

Hardenberg, H. 1962, *Etta Palm, een Hollandse Parisienne 1743–1799*, Assen.

Harpham, E. 1984, 'Liberalism, Civic Humanism and the Case of Adam Smith', *American Political Science Review*, 78, 3: 764–74.

Hartog, F. 1993, 'La Révolution française et l'antiquité: avenir d'une illusion ou cheminement d'un quiproquo?', in Situations de la démocratie: M. Gauchet, P. Manent and P. Rosanwallon (eds.), *La Pensée politique*, Paris, pp. 30–61.

Head, Randolph C. 1995, *Early Modern Democracy in the Grisons*, Cambridge.

Heinemann, F. H. 1952, 'John Toland and the Age of Reason', *Archiv für Philosophie*, 4: 35–66.

Hellmuth, Eckhart (ed.) 1990, *The Transformation of Political Culture: England and Germany in the Late Eighteenth Century*, Oxford.

Hendrix, H. 1995, *Traiano Boccalini fra erudizione e polemica. Ricerche sulla fortuna e bibliografia critica*, Florence.

Hernández, Mauro 1997, 'Cuando el poder se vende: venta de oficios y poder local en Castilla, siglos XVII y XVIII', in J. Alvarado (ed.), *Poder, economía, clientelismo*, Madrid.

Hernández, Ramón 1995, *Francisco de Vitoria. Vida y pensamiento internacionalista*, Madrid.

Hexter, J. H. 1969, *On Historians*, London.

Hill, C. 1993, *The English Bible and the Seventeenth-Century Revolution*, London.

Hill, Lisa 1996, 'Anticipations of 19th and 20th Century Social Thought in the Work of Adam Ferguson', *Archives Européennes de Sociologie*, 37: 203–28.

1997, 'Adam Ferguson and the Paradox of Progress and Decline', *History of Political Thought*, 18: 677–706.

Hirschmann, A. O. 1980, *Les Passions et les intérêts*, Paris.

Hirst, Derek 1975, *The Representative of the People?*, Cambridge.

Hofmann, Hasso 1974, *Repräsentation. Studie zur Wort- und Begriffsgeschichte von der Antike bis zum 19. Jahrhundert*, Berlin.

1988a, 'Der spätmittelalterliche Rechtsbegriff der Repräsentation in Reich und Kirche', *Der Staat*, 21: 523–45.

1988b, 'Repräsentation in der Staatslehre der Frühen Neuzeit', in Dahm *et al.* (eds.) 1988: 513–42.

Holmes, Geoffrey 1986, *Politics, Religion and Society in England 1679–1742*, London.

Holmes, Richard 1990, *Coleridge: Early Visions*, Harmondsworth.

Honig, Bonnie 1992, 'Toward an Agonistic Feminism: Hannah Arendt and the Politics of Identity', in J. Butler and J. W. Scott (eds.), *Feminists Theorize the Political*, New York, pp. 215–35.

Honig, Bonnie (ed.) 1995, *Feminist Interpretations of Hannah Arendt*, University Park.

Hont, Istvan 1987, 'The Language of Sociability and Commerce: Samuel Pufendorf and the Theoretical Foundations of the "Four-Stages Theory" ', in Pagden (ed.) 1987: 253–76.

Hont, Istvan and Michael Ignatieff 1983, 'Needs and Justice in The Wealth of Nations', in Hont and Ignatieff (eds.) 1983: 1–44.

Hont, Istvan and Michael Ignatieff (eds.) 1983, *Wealth and Virtue. The Shaping of Political Economy in the Scottish Enlightenment*, Cambridge.

Hook, A. and R. B. Sher (eds.) 1995, *The Glasgow Enlightenment*, East Linton.

Höpfl, H. 1982, *The Christian Polity of John Calvin*, Cambridge.

Huet, Busken C. 1882, *Het Land van Rembrandt*, 2 vols., Haarlem.

Hughes, Michael 1992, *Early Modern Germany, 1477–1806*, London.

Huiskamp, M. 1991, 'Openbare lessen in geschiedenis en moraal. Het Oude Testament in stadhuizen en andere openbaren gebouwen', in Tuempel *et al.* (eds.) 1991: 134–55.

Hunt, Lynn 1995, *Le Roman familial de la Révolution française*, Paris [translation of *The Family Romance of the French Revolution*, 1992].

IJsewijn, Jozef 1975, 'The Coming of Humanism to the Low Countries', in H. A. Oberman and T. A. Brady (eds.), *Itinerarium Italicum. The Profile of the Italian Renaissance in the Mirror of its European Transformations, Dedicated to P. O. Kristeller*, Leiden.

Im Hof, Ulrich 1967, *Isaak Iselin und die Spätaufklärung*, Berne and Munich.

Iñurritegui, José María 1998, *La gracia y la república. El lenguaje político de la teología católica y el príncipe cristiano de Pedro de Ribadeneyra*, Madrid.

Iofrida, Manlio 1983, *La filosofia di John Toland. Spinozismo, scienza e religione nella cultura europea fra '600 e '700*, Milan.

Israel, Jonathan 1995, *The Dutch Republic. Its Rise, Greatness, and Fall 1477–1806*, Oxford.

2000, 'Spinoza, Locke and the Enlightenment Battle for Toleration', in Grell *et al.* (eds.) 2000: 102–13.

2001, *Radical Enlightenment. Philosophy and the Making of Modernity 1650–1750*, Oxford.

Jacob, Margaret 1981, *The Radical Enlightenment. Pantheists, Freemasons, and Republicans*, London.

Jago, Charles 1995, 'Taxation and Political Culture in Castile, 1590–1640', in Kagan and Parker (eds.) 1995.

James, Susan 1997, *Passion and Action. The Emotions in Seventeenth-Century Philosophy*, Oxford.

Jardine, Lisa and Grafton, Anthony 1990, ' "Studied for Action": How Gabriel Harvey Read his Livy', *Past and Present*, 129: 30–78.

Jarque, Encarna 1994, 'La oligarquía urbana de Zaragoza en los siglos XVI y XVII: estudio comparativo con Barcelona', *Revista Jerónimo Zurita*, 69–70: 147–67.

Jeanroy, A. 1922, 'Boccace et Christine de Pisan: le *De claris mulieribus*, principale source du *Livre de la cité des dames*', *Romania*, 48.

Jones, Howard 1998, *Master Tully. Cicero in England*, Nieukoop.

Jordan, Constance 1987, 'Woman's Rule in Sixteenth-century British Political Thought', *Renaissance Quarterly*, 40: 421–51.

Kagan, Richard L. 1995, 'Clio and the Crown: Writing History in Habsburg Spain', in Kagan and Parker (eds.) 1995: 73–99.

1998, '*Urbs* and *civitas* in Sixteenth- and Seventeenth-century Spain', in D. Buisseret (ed.), *Envisioning the City. Six Studies in Urban Cartography*, Chicago and London.

Kagan, Richard L. and Geoffrey Parker (eds.) 1995, *Spain, Europe and the Atlantic World. Essays in Honour of John H. Elliott*, Cambridge.

Kalyvas, Andreas and Ira Katznelson 1998, 'Adam Ferguson Returns. Liberalism through a Glass, Darkly', *Political Theory*, 26: 173–97.

Kaplan, Yosef 2000, *An Alternative Path to Modernity: The Sephardi Diaspora in Western Europe*, Leiden.

Kelsey, Sean 1997, *Inventing a Republic. The Political Culture of the English Commonwealth 1649–1653*, Manchester.

Kettler, David 1965, *The Social and Political Thought of Adam Ferguson*, Columbus.

1977, 'History and Theory in Ferguson's *Essay on the History of Civil Society*: a Reconsideration', *Political Theory*, 5: 437–60.

Klein, Lawrence E. 1984, 'The Third Earl of Shaftesbury and the Progress of Politeness', *Eighteenth-Century Studies*, 18: 186–214.

1989, 'Liberty, Manners and Politeness in Early Modern England', *Historical Journal*, 32: 583–605.

1993a, 'Shaftesbury, Politeness and the Politics of Religion', in Phillipson and Skinner (eds.) 1993.

1993b, 'The Political Significance of "Politeness" in Early Eighteenth-Century Britain', in Schochet (ed.) 1993.

1994, *Shaftesbury and the Culture of Politeness*, Cambridge.

Klein, S. R. E. 1995, *Patriots Republikanisme. Politieke Cultuur in Nederland (1766–1787)*, Amsterdam.

Klippel, Diethelm 1990, 'The True Concept of Liberty. Political Theory in Germany in the Second Half of the Eighteenth Century', in Hellmuth (ed.) 1990: 447–66.

Knuttel, W. P. C. 1889–1920, *Catalogus van de pamflettenverzameling berustende in de Koninklijke Bibliotheek, 1486–1853*, 7 vols., The Hague.

Koebner, Richard, and Helmut Dan Schmidt 1964, *Imperialism: The Story and Significance of a Political Word, 1840–1960*, Cambridge.

Koenigsberger, H. G. 1997, 'Republicanism, Monarchism and Liberty', in R. Oresko, G. C. Gibbs and H. M. Scott (eds.), *Royal and Republican Sovereignty in Early Modern Europe. Essays in Memory of Ragnhild Hatton*, Cambridge.

Koenigsberger, H. G. (ed.) 1988, *Republiken und Republikanismus im Europa der frühen Neuzeit*, Munich.

Konopczyński, W. 1930, *Le 'liberum veto': Etude sur le développement du principe majoritaire*, Paris.

  1966, *Polscy pisarze polityczni xviii wieku*, Warsaw.

Kossmann, E. H. 1960, *Politieke theorie in het zeventiende-eeuwse Nederland*, Amsterdam.

  1963, *In Praise of the Dutch Republic: Some Seventeenth-century Attitudes*, London.

  1985, 'Dutch Republicanism', in *L'età dei Lumi. Studi storici sul Settecento europeo in onore di Franco Venturi*, 2 vols., Naples, vol. 1, pp. 453–86 (reprinted in E. H. Kossmann, *Politieke theorie en geschiedenis. Verspreide opstellen en voordrachten*, Amsterdam, 1987, pp. 211–33).

Kramnick, I. 1990, *Republicanism and Bourgeois Radicalism: Political Ideology in Late Eighteenth-Century England and America*, Ithaca.

Krieger, Leonard 1957, *The German Idea of Freedom. History of a Political Tradition*, Chicago and London.

Kühlmann, Wilhelm 1994, 'Zum Profil des postreformatorischen Humanismus in Pommern', in Wilhelm Kühlmann and Horst Langer (eds.), *Pommern in der frühen Neuzeit*, Tübingen, pp. 101–23.

Labourdette, Jean-François 1990, *Vergennes. Ministre principal de Louis XVI*, Paris.

Landmann, Julius 1903, *Die auswärtigen Kapitalanlagen aus dem Berner Staatsschatz im xviii. Jahrhundert*, Zurich.

Lamont, William 1969, *Godly Rule*, London.

Langen, August 1974, 'Der Wortschatz des 18. Jahrhunderts', in Friedrich Maurer and H. Rupp (eds.), *Deutsche Wortgeschichte*, vol. ii, 3rd edn, Berlin and New York.

Larrère, Catherine 1979, 'Les Typologies des gouvernements chez Montesquieu', in Michel Bellot-Antony *et al.* (eds.), *Etudes sur le xviiie siècle*, Clermont-Ferrand, pp. 87–103.

  1988, 'Rousseau, la forêt, le champ, le jardin', in A. Cadoret (ed.), *Chassez le naturel . . .* , Paris.

  1992, *L'Invention de l'économie au xviiie siècle*, Paris.

  1994, 'Droit et mœurs chez Montesquieu', *Droits*, 19: 11–22.

  1997, 'Le Gouvernement de la loi est-il un thème républicain?', *Revue de synthèse*, 4th series, 2–3: 237–58.

Lasio, D. di 1993, *Il pensiero politico di d'Holbach: Pregiudizi, diritti e privilegi*, Bari.

Lecanuet, R. P. 1895, *Montalembert, sa jeunesse*, Paris.

Leduc-Lafayette, D. 1974, *Le Mythe de l'antiquité chez J.-J. Rousseau*, Paris.

Leeb, I. L. 1973, *The Ideological Origins of the Batavian Revolution. History and Politics in the Dutch Republic 1747–1800*, The Hague.

Lefort, Claude 1992, 'Foyers du républicanisme', in Lefort, *Ecrire. A l'épreuve du politique*, Paris, pp. 181-208.

Letwin, W. 1988, 'Was Adam Smith a Liberal?', in Haakonssen (ed.) 1988: 65-80.

Levack, Brian P. 1973, *The Civil Lawyers in England 1603-1641: A Political Study*, Oxford.

Lever, J. W. 1980, *The Tragedy of State*, London.

Levin, Carole 1994, *'The Heart and Stomach of a King': Elizabeth I and the Politics of Sex and Power*, Philadelphia.

　　1998, ' "We Shall Never Have a Merry World while the Queene Lyveth": Gender, Monarchy, and the Power of Seditious Words', in Walker (ed.) 1998: 77-95.

Link, Christoph 1979, *Herrschaftsordnung und bürgerliche Freiheit. Grenzen der Staatsgewalt in der älteren deutschen Staatslehre*, Vienna, Cologne and Graz.

Lock, F. P. 1985, *Burke's Reflections on the Revolution in France*, London.

Loraux, Nicole 1984, *Les Enfants d'Athéna: idées athéniennes sur la citoyenneté et la division des sexes*, Paris.

Löther, Andrea 1994, 'Bürger-, Stadt- und Verfassungsbegriff in frühneuzeitlichen Kommentaren der Aristotelischen *Politik*', in Reinhart Koselleck and Klaus Schreiner (eds.), *Bürgerschaft. Rezeption und Innovation der Begrifflichkeit vom Hohen Mittelalter bis ins 19. Jahrhundert*, Stuttgart, pp. 239-73.

Lunenfeld, Marvin 1989, *Keepers of the City. The* corregidores *of Isabella I of Castile, 1474-1504*, Cambridge.

Lurbe, Pierre 1990, 'Le Spinozisme de John Toland', in Olivier Bloch (ed.), *Spinoza au xviiie siècle*, Paris, pp. 33-74.

　　1995a, '*Clidophorus* et la question de la double philosophie', *Revue de Synthèse*, 2-3: 379-98.

　　1995b, 'Le Christianisme au miroir de l'islam dans le *Nazarenus* de John Toland', *Dix-huitième siècle*, 27: 335-47.

Lutz, Heinrich 1987, *Das Ringen um die deutsche Einheit und kirchliche Erneuerung*, Frankfurt.

McCullough, Peter E. 1998, 'Out of Egypt: Richard Fletcher's Sermon before Elizabeth I after the Execution of Mary Queen of Scots', in Walker (ed.) 1998: 118-49.

MacGillivray, R. 1974, *Restoration Historians and the English Civil War*, The Hague.

Maciszewski, Jarema 1986, *Szlachta polska i jej państwo* (Polish Nobility and their State), 2nd edition, Warsaw.

Mackenney, Richard 1989, *The City-State, 1500-1700. Republican Liberty in an Age of Princely Power*, Basingstoke and London.

McLaren, A. N. 1996, 'Delineating the Elizabethan Body Politic: Knox, Aylmer and the Definition of Counsel 1558-88', *History of Political Thought*, 17: 224-52.

McMurrin, S. M. (ed.) 1986, *The Tanner Lectures on Human Values*, Cambridge, vol. vii.

McNamara, P. 1998, *Political Economy and Statesmanship: Smith, Hamilton and the Foundation of the Commercial Republic*, DeKalb.

Mager, Wolfgang 1990, 'République', *Archives de Philosophie du Droit*, 35: 257-73.

Malcolm, Noel 1991, 'Hobbes and Spinoza', in Burns and Goldie (eds.) 1991.

Malherbe, Michel 1995, 'La Raison polémique chez John Toland', *Revue de Synthèse*, 2-3: 357-78.

Maranini, G. 1974, *La costituzione di Venezia* [1931], vol. II, Florence.

Maravall, José Antonio 1979, *Las Comunidades de Castilla. Una primera revolución moderna*, Madrid.

1997, *Teoría del estado en España en el siglo XVII*, Madrid.

Marshall, Geoffrey 1954, 'David Hume and Political Scepticism', *Philosophical Quarterly*, 4: 247–57.

Masson, Frédéric 1908, *Le Sacre et le couronnement de Napoléon*, Paris.

Mastellone, S. 1972, *Venalità e antimachiavellismo in Francia 1572–1610*, Florence.

1983, Introduction to Bentivoglio 1983.

1985, 'I repubblicani del Seicento e il modello politico olandese', *Il pensiero politico*, 18: 145–63.

1986, *Storia del pensiero politico europeo*, vol. I, Turin.

1993, 'La città europea come spazio politico dal Quattrocento al Settecento', in Conti (ed.) 1993: 3–16.

Maurer, Michael 1987, *Aufklärung und Anglophilie in Deutschland*, Göttingen and Zurich.

Maurer, Wilhelm 1967–9, *Der junge Melanchthon*, 2 vols., Göttingen.

Mayer, Thomas F. 1989, *Thomas Starkey and the Commonweal*, Cambridge.

Méchoulan, Henry 1991, *Être juif à Amsterdam au temps de Spinoza*, Paris.

Meier, Ulrich 1996, 'Vom Mythos der Republik', in Andrea Loether *et al.* (eds.), *Mundus in imagine*, Munich, pp. 345–88.

Meinecke, F. 1970, *L'idea della ragion di stato nella storia moderna* [1924], Florence.

Mendle, Michael 1985, *Dangerous Positions: Mixed Government, the Estates of the Realm, and the Making of the Answer to the XIX Propositions*, Alabama.

1993, 'Parliamentary Sovereignty: a Very English Absolutism', in Phillipson and Skinner (eds.) 1993: 97–119.

1995, *Henry Parker and the English Civil War: The Political Thought of the Public's 'privado'*, Cambridge.

Michalski, J. (ed.) 1984, *Historia sejmu polskiego*, Warsaw.

Milgate, M. and C. B. Welch (eds.) 1989, *Critical Issues in Social Thought*, London.

Minowitz, P. 1993, *Profits, Priests, and Princes: Adam Smith's Emancipation of Economics from Politics and Religion*, Stanford.

Möller, Horst 1989, *Fürstenstaat oder Bürgernation. Deutschland 1763–1815*, Berlin.

Montag, Warren 1999, *Bodies, Masses, Power: Spinoza and his Contemporaries*, London and New York.

Montluzin, Emily Lorraine de 1988, *The Anti-Jacobins 1798–1800*, Basingstoke.

Moore, James 1988, 'Natural Law and the Pyrrhonian Controversy', in P. Jones (ed.), *Philosophy and Science in the Scottish Enlightenment*, Edinburgh, pp. 20–38.

1990, 'The Two Systems of Francis Hutcheson', in Stewart (ed.) 1990.

Moore, James and Michael Silverthorne 1983, 'Gershom Carmichael and the Natural Jurisprudence Tradition in Eighteenth-Century Scotland' in Hont and Ignatieff (eds.) 1983: 73–87.

1984, 'Natural Sociability and Natural Rights in the Moral Philosophy of Gershom Carmichael', in V. Hope (ed.), *Philosophers of the Scottish Enlightenment*, Edinburgh, pp. 1–12.

Moorman van Kappen, O. 1986, 'Iets over ons oud-vaderlandse stadsburgerschap', *Gens Nostra*, 41: 180–92.

Mörke, Olaf 1995 'The Political Culture of Germany and the Dutch Republic: Similar Roots, Different Results', in Karel Davids and Jan Weassen (eds.), *A Miracle Mirrored. The Dutch Republic in European Perspective*, Cambridge, pp. 135–72.

  1997, *'Stadtholder' oder 'Staatholder'? Die Funktion des Hauses Oranien und seines Hofes in der politischen Kultur der Republik der Vereinigten Niederlande im 17. Jahrhundert*, Münster and Hamburg.

Morreale, Margherita 1959, *Castiglione y Boscán. El ideal cortesano en el Renacimiento español*, 2 vols., Madrid

Morrill, John 1993, *The Nature of the English Revolution*, London.

Morrill, John (ed.) 1991, *The Impact of the English Civil War*, London.

Mosse, George L. 1950, *The Struggle for Sovereignty in England*, East Lancing.

Mout, Nicolette 1988, 'Ideales Muster oder erfundene Eigenart. Republikanische Theorien während des niederländischen Aufstands', in Koenigsberger (ed.) 1988: 169–94.

Muir, Edward 1984, *Il rituale civico a Venezia nel Rinascimento*, Italian trans., Rome.

Mülinen, W. F. von 1900, 'Daniel Fellenberg und die Patriotische Gesellschaft in Bern', *Neujahrsblatt des Historischen Vereins des Kantons Bern*.

Muller, J. W. (ed.) 1902, *Woordenboek der Nederlandsche Taal*, vol. III, Leiden.

Musi, A. 1989, *La rivolta di Masaniello nella scena politica barocca*, Naples.

Nanke, Cz. 1907, *Szlachta wołyńska wobec Konstytucji 3 Maja*, Lvov.

Nelson, J. R. 1987, *Liberty and Property: Political Economy and Policy-Making in the New Nation, 1789-1812*, Baltimore.

Nippel, Wilfried 1980, *Mischverfassungstheorie und Verfassungsrealität in Antike und früher Neuzeit*, Stuttgart.

Nitschke, Peter 1995, *Staatsraison kontra Utopie*, Stuttgart and Weimar.

Norbrook, David 1984, *Poetry and Politics in the English Renaissance*, London.

  1999, *Writing the English Republic: Poetry, Rhetoric and Politics 1627-1660*, Cambridge.

Nussbaum, Martha C. 1986, *The Fragility of Goodness. Luck and Ethics in Greek Tragedy and Philosophy*, Cambridge.

Nuzzo, E. 1995, 'Crisi dell'aristotelismo politico e ragion di Stato. Alcune preliminari considerazioni metodologiche e storiografiche', in Baldini (ed.) 1995: 11–52.

Oestreich, G. 1982, *Neostoicism and the Early Modern State*, Cambridge.

Ogonowski, Z. 1992, 'Nad pismami A. M. Fredry w obronie liberum veto', in *Filozofia polityczna w Polsce XVII wieku i tradycje demokracji europejskiej*, Warsaw.

Olivieri, Luigi (ed.) 1983, *Aristotelismo veneto e scienza moderna*, Padua.

Ong, Walter J., S. J. 1983, *Ramus, Method, and the Decay of Dialogue*, Cambridge, Mass. and London.

Opaliński, E. 1983, 'Postawa szlachty polskiej wobec osoby królewskiej jako instytucji w latach 1587-1648', *Kwartalnik Historyczny*, 90.

  1995, *Kultura polityczna szlachty polskiej w latach 1587-1652* (Political Culture of the Polish Nobility in the Years 1587-1652), Warsaw.

Osmond, Patricia J. 1993, 'Sallust and Machiavelli: From Civic Humanism to Political Prudence', *Journal of Medieval and Renaissance Studies*, 23: 407–38.

Othmer, Sieglinde C. 1970, *Berlin und die Verbreitung des Naturrechts in Europa. Kultur- und sozialgeschichtliche Studien zu Jean Barbeyracs Pufendorf-Übersetzung und eine Analyse seiner Leserschaft*, Berlin.

Outram, Dorinda 1989, *The Body and the French Revolution. Sex, Class and Political Culture*, New Haven.

Oz-Salzberger, Fania 1995a, *Translating the Enlightenment. Scottish Civic Discourse in Eighteenth-Century Germany*, Oxford.

  1995b, 'Introduction', in A. Ferguson, *An Essay on the History of Civil Society*, ed. F. Oz-Salzberger, Cambridge, pp. vii–xxv.

Paganini, Gianni 1998, 'Haupttendenzen der clandestinen Philosophie', in Jean-Pierre Schobinger (ed.), *Grundriss der Geschichte der Philosophie. Die Philosophie des 17. Jahrhunderts*, vol. I, Basel, pp. 121–95.

Pagden, Anthony (ed.) 1987, *The Language of Political Thought in Early Modern Europe*, Cambridge.

Palladini, Fiammetta 1978, *Discussioni seicentesche su Samuel Pufendorf: scritti latini 1663–1700*, Bologna.

  1989, 'Is the *socialitas* of Pufendorf really anti-Hobbesian?', Unpublished Paper for the Conference 'Unsocial Sociability, Modern Natural Law and the 18th-Century Discourses of Politics, History and Society', Max-Planck-Institut für Geschichte, Göttingen, 26–30 June.

Palmer, Gesine 1996, *Ein Freispruch für Paulus. John Tolands Theorie des Judenchristentums. Mit einer Neuausgabe von Tolands 'Nazarenus' von Claus-Michael Palmer*, Berlin.

Pangle, T. 1988, *The Spirit of Modern Republicanism: The Moral Vision of the American Founders and the Philosophy of Locke*, Chicago.

Pardos, Julio A. (unpublished paper), on A. Capmany.

  1995, 'Virtud complicada', in Ch. Continisio and C. Mozzarelli (eds.), *Repubblica e virtù. Pensiero politico e monarchia cattolica fra XVI e XVII secolo*, Rome, pp. 77–92.

Parker, H. T. 1937, *The Cult of Antiquity and the French Revolutionaries*, Chicago.

Parkinson, George 1984, 'Spinoza on Freedom of Man and Citizen', in Z. Pelczynski and J. Gray (eds.), *Conceptions of Liberty in Political Philosophy*, London.

Pasquino, Pasquale 1994, 'The Constitutional Republicanism of Emmanuel Sieyès', in Fontana (ed.) 1994: 107–17.

Patterson, Annabel 1997, *Early Modern Liberalism*, Cambridge.

Paulys Realencyclopädie der classischen Altertumswissenschaft 1931, Stuttgart.

Pawiński, Adolf 1978, *Rządy sejmikowe w Polsce 1572–1795 na tle stosunków województw kujawskich* (The Rule of Local Assemblies in Poland 1572–1795 against a Background of Relations in the Voivodeships of Kujawy), 2nd edn, Warsaw.

Peltonen, Markku 1994, 'Classical Republicanism in Tudor England: The Case of Richard Beacon's *Solon His Follie*', *History of Political Thought*, 15: 469–503.

  1995, *Classical Humanism and Republicanism in English Political Thought 1570–1640*, Cambridge.

Perrot, Jean-Claude 1992, 'Les Economistes, les philosophes et la population: multiples bienfaits d'une erreur', in Perrot, *Une histoire intellectuelle de l'économie politique. XVIIe–XVIIIe siècle*, Paris.

Pesante, Maria Luisa 1995, 'La teoria stadiale della storia e l'analisi economica. Adam Smith', *Annali della Fondazione Luigi Einaudi*, 29: 249–85.

Pettit, Philip 1993, 'Liberalism and Republicanism', *Australian Journal of Political Science*, 28, Special Issue, pp. 162–89.

1997, *Republicanism. A Theory of Freedom and Government*, Oxford.

Peyer, Hans Conrad 1978, *Verfassungsgeschichte der alten Schweiz*, Zurich.

Phan, Marie-Claude 1975, 'Les Déclarations de grossesse en France (xvie–xviiie siècles), essai institutionnel', *Revue d'histoire moderne et contemporaine*, January–March.

1980, 'Les Amours illégitimes à Carcassonne, 1676–1786, d'après les déclarations de grossesse et les procédures criminelles', Doctoral Thesis, Paris.

Phillipson, Nicholas 1981, 'The Scottish Enlightenment', in R. Porter and M. Teich (eds.), *The Enlightenment in National Context*, Cambridge, pp. 19–40.

1987, 'Politics, Politeness and the Anglicisation of Early Eighteenth Century Scottish Culture', in R. Mason (ed.), *Scotland and England 1286–1815*, Edinburgh, pp. 226–46.

1989, *Hume*, London.

1993a, 'Politeness and Politics in the Reigns of Anne and the Early Hanoverians', in Pocock (ed.) 1993: 211–45.

1993b, 'Politics and Politeness in the Philosophy of David Hume', in Schochet (ed.) 1993.

1993c, 'Propriety, Property and Prudence: David Hume and the Defence of the Revolution', in Phillipson and Skinner (eds.) 1993: 302–20.

Phillipson, Nicholas and Quentin Skinner (eds.) 1993, *Political Discourse in Early Modern Britain*, Cambridge.

Philp, M. 1998, 'English Republicanism in the 1790s', *Journal of Political Philosophy*, 6, 3: 235–62.

Piacente, G. B. 1861, *Le rivoluzioni del Regno di Napoli negli anni 1647–1648 e l'assidio di Piombino e Portolongone*, Naples.

Pincus, Steven 1996, *Protestantism and Patriotism. Ideologies and the Making of English Foreign Policy 1650–1668*, Cambridge.

Pitkin, Hanna Fenichel 1984, *Fortune Is a Woman. Gender and Politics in the Thought of Niccolò Machiavelli*, Berkeley.

Pleij, Herman 1994, 'The Rise of Urban Literature in the Low Countries', in Erik Kooper (ed.), *Medieval Dutch Literature in its European Context*, Cambridge, pp. 62–77.

Pocock, J. G. A. 1971a, 'Time, History and Eschatology in the Thought of Thomas Hobbes', in Pocock, *Politics, Language and Time*, New York.

1971b, *Politics, Language and Time: Essays on Political Thought and History*, New York.

1972, 'Custom and Grace, Form and Matter', in Martin Fleisher (ed.), *Machiavelli and the Nature of Political Thought*, New York.

1975, *The Machiavellian Moment. Florentine Political Thought and the Atlantic Republican Tradition*, Princeton.

1977, 'Introduction', Harrington 1977.

1982, 'The Problem of Political Thought in the Eighteenth Century. Patriotism and Politeness' (with replies by E. H. Kossmann and E. O. G. Haitsma Mulier), *Theoretische Geschiedenis*, 9: 3–36.

1983, 'Cambridge Paradigms and Scotch Philosophers: A Study of the Relations between the Civic Humanist and the Civil Jurisprudential Interpretation of Eighteenth-century Social Thought', in Hont and Ignatieff (eds.) 1983: 235–52.

1985a, *Virtue, Commerce, and History: Essays on Political Thought and History, Chiefly in the Eighteenth Century*, Cambridge.

1985b, 'Virtues, Rights, and Manners: A Model for Historians of Political Thought', in his *Virtue, Commerce, and History*, Cambridge, pp. 37–50.

1987a, 'Betweeen Gog and Magog: The Republican Thesis and *Ideologia Americana*', *Journal of the History of Ideas*, 48: 325–46.

1987b, 'Spinoza and Harrington: An Exercise in Comparison', *Bijdragen en Mededelingen Betreffende de Geschiedenis der Nederlanden*, 102, 3, pp. 435–49.

1987c, *The Ancient Constitution and the Feudal Law: A Reissue with a Retrospect*, Cambridge.

1994a, 'Machiavelli and the Rethinking of History', *Il pensiero politico*, 27, 2.

1994b, 'England's Cato: the Virtues and Fortunes of Algernon Sidney', *Historical Journal*, 37, 4.

Pocock, J. G. A. (ed.) 1993 (with Gordon Schochet and Lois G. Schwoerer), *Varieties of British Political Thought, 1500–1800*, Cambridge.

Price, Mary Bell and Lawrence Marsden Price 1934, *The Publication of English Humaniora in Germany in the Eighteenth Century*, Berkeley.

Probyn , Clive T. 1991, *The Sociable Humanist: The Life and Works of James Harris 1709–1780*, Oxford.

Procacci, G. 1965, *Studi sulla fortuna del Machiavelli*, Rome.

Puigdomènech, Helena 1988, *Maquiavelo en España. Presencia de sus obras en los siglos xvi y xvii*, Madrid.

Quaglioni, D. 1991, 'The Legal Definition of Citizenship in the late Middle Ages', in A. Mohlo, K. Raaflaub and J. Emlen (eds.), *City States in Classical Antiquity and Medieval Italy*, Stuttgart, pp. 155–66.

1993, ' "Civitas": appunti per una riflessione sull'idea di città nel pensiero politico dei giuristi medievali', in Conti (ed.) 1993: 59–76.

Queller, D. E. 1987, *Il patriziato veneziano. La realtà contro il mito*, Italian trans., Rome.

Raeff, Marc 1983, *The Well-Ordered Police State*, London and New Haven.

Rahe, Paul 1994, *Republics Ancient and Modern*, vol. ii: *New Modes and Orders in Early Modern Political Thought*, Chapel Hill.

Raskolnikoff, N. 1990, *Des Anciens et des modernes*, Paris.

Rawls, John 1993, *Political Liberalism*, New York.

Rawson, E. 1966, *The Spartan Tradition in European Thought*, Oxford.

Raynaud, Philippe 1989, 'Les Femmes et la civilité: aristocratie et passions révolutionnaires', *Le Débat*, 57.

Reinhardt, Volker 1995, 'Machiavellis helvetische Projektion. Neue Überlegungen zu einem alten Thema', *Schweizerische Zeitschrift für Geschichte*, 45.

Remus, D. 1992, 'Zur systematischen Bedeutung des Freiheitsbegriffs in der Philosophie Spinozas', D. Phil. Dissertation, Hamburg.

Riley, Denise 1988, '*Am I that Name?' Feminism and the Category of 'Women' in History*, Minneapolis.

Riley, Patrick C. 1986, *The General Will Before Rousseau: The Transformation of the Divine into the Civic*, Princeton.

Robertson, John 1983a, 'Scottish Political Economy beyond the Civic Tradition', *History of Political Thought*, 4: 451–82.

   1983b, 'The Scottish Enlightenment at the Limits of the Civic Tradition', in Hont and Ignatieff (eds.) 1983: 137–78.

   1985, *The Scottish Enlightenment and the Militia Issue*, Edinburgh.

   1990, 'The Legacy of Adam Smith: Government and Economic Development in the *Wealth of Nations*' in Bellamy (ed.) 1990: 15–41.

   1993, 'Universal Monarchy and the Liberties of Europe: David Hume's Critique of an English Whig Doctrine', in Phillipson and Skinner (eds.) 1993: 349–73.

Roeck, Bernd 1984, *Reichssystem und Reichsherkommen. Die Diskussion über die Staatlichkeit des Reiches in der politischen Publizistik des 17. und 18. Jahrhunderts*, Stuttgart.

Rokkan, Stein 1973, 'Cities, States and Nations', in S. M. Eisenstadt and Stein Rokkan (eds.), *Building States and Nations*, vol. 1, London, pp. 73–97.

Rorty, R., J. B. Schneewind and Q. Skinner (eds.) 1984, *Philosophy in History*, Cambridge.

Rosa, M. 1964, *Dispotismo e libertà nel Settecento: interpretazioni repubblicane di Machiavelli*, Bari.

Rosanvallon, Pierre 1992, *Le Sacre du citoyen*, Paris.

Rosenblatt, Helena 1997, *Rousseau and Geneva: From the* First Discourse *to the* Social Contract, *1749–1762*, Cambridge.

Rosenthal, M. A. 1997, 'Why Spinoza Chose the Hebrews: The Exemplary Function of Prophecy in the Theological-Political Treatise', *History of Political Thought*, 17, 2 (Summer).

Rostworowski, E. 1976, 'Republikanizm polski i anglosaski w XVIII wieku', *Miesięcznik Literacki*, 8.

Rowen, Herbert H. 1972, *The Low Countries in Early Modern Times. A Documentary History*, New York.

   1978, *John de Witt, Grand Pensionary of Holland, 1625–1672*, Princeton.

   1988, *The Princes of Orange. The Stadholders in the Dutch Republic*, Cambridge.

   1994, 'The Dutch Republic and the Idea of Freedom', in Wootton (ed.) 1994: 310–40.

Rubiés, Joan Pau 1996, 'La idea del gobierno mixto y su significado en la crisis de la Monarquía Hispánica', *Historia Social*, 24: 57–81.

Rubinstein, Nicolai 1991, 'Italian Political Thought, 1450–1550', in Burns and Goldie (eds.) 1991.

Rudé, George (ed.) 1967, *Robespierre*, Englewood Cliffs.

Ruiz Ibáñez, José Javier 1996, 'Sujets et citoyens: les relations entre l'état, la ville, la bourgeoisie et les institutions militaires municipales à Murcie (XVI–XVII siècle)', in M. Boone and M. Prak (eds.), *Statuts individuels, statuts corporatifs et statuts judiciaires dans les villes européennes (moyen âge et temps modernes)*, Leuven and Apeldoorn.

   1999, *Felipe II y Cambrai: el consenso del pueblo. La soberanía entre la práctica y la teoría política (1595–1677)*, Madrid.

Ruiz, Teofilo F. 1994, *Crisis and Continuity. Land and Town in Late Medieval Castile*, Philadelphia.

Russell, Conrad 1990, *The Causes of the English Civil War*, Oxford.

Salmon, J. H. M. 1959, *The French Religious Wars in English Political Thought*, Oxford.
  1996, 'The Legacy of Jean Bodin: Absolutism, Populism or Constitutionalism?',
    History of Political Thought, 17: 500–22.
Sánchez Marcos, Fernando 1998, 'The Future of Catalonia. A *sujet brûlant* at the Münster
    Negotiations', in H. Duchhardt (ed.), *Der Westfälische Friede*, Munich, pp. 273–91.
Sanderson, John 1989, *'But the People's Creatures': The Philosophical Basis of the English
    Civil War*, Manchester.
Santing, Catrien 1995, 'Liberation from the Trivial Joke: Dutch Renaissance Educators
    and their Cultural and Socio-political Objectives', in J. W. Drijvers and A. A.
    MacDonald (eds.), *Centres of Learning. Learning and Location in Pre-Modern Europe and
    the Near East*, Leiden, pp. 315–28.
Sapiro, Virginia 1992, *A Vindication of Political Virtue. The Political Theory of Mary
    Wollstonecraft*, Chicago.
Sasso, Gennaro 1967, 'Polibio e Machiavelli: costituzione, potenza, conquista', in Sasso,
    Studi su Machiavelli, Naples, pp. 223–80.
Saxonhouse, Arlene W. 1985, *Women in the History of Political Thought. Ancient Greece to
    Machiavelli*, New York.
Schama, S. 1987, *The Embarrassment of Riches. An Interpretation of Dutch Culture in the
    Golden Age*, London.
Scheible, Heinz 1997, *Melanchthon. Eine Biographie*, Munich.
Schiff, Mario 1978, *La Fille d'alliance de Montaigne* [1910], Geneva.
Schilling, Heinz 1986, 'The Reformation and the Rise of the Early Modern State', in
    James D. Tracy (ed.), *Luther and the Modern State in Germany*, Ann Arbor, pp. 21–30.
  1992, 'Dutch Republicanism in its Historical Context', in Schilling, *Religion, Political
    Culture and the Emergence of Early Modern Society, Essays in German and Dutch History*,
    Leiden, etc., pp. 413–27.
Schindling, Anton 1989, 'Nürnberg', in Anton Schindling and Walter Ziegler (eds.), *Die
    Territorien des Reiches im Zeitalter der Reformation und Konfessionalisierung. Land und
    Konfession 1500–1650*, vol. I: *Der Südosten*, Münster, pp. 32–42.
Schlumbohm, Jürgen 1973, *Freiheitsbegriff und Emanzipazionsprozeß. Zur Geschichte eines
    politischen Wortes*, Göttingen.
Schmidt-Biggemann, Wilhelm 1983, *Topica Universalis. Eine Modellgeschichte
    humanistischer und barocker Wissenschaft*, Hamburg.
Schneewind, J. B. 1998, *The Invention of Autonomy: A History of Modern Moral Philosophy*,
    Cambridge.
Schneppen, Heinz 1960, *Niederländische Universitäten und deutsches Geistesleben von der
    Gründung der Universität Leiden bis ins späte 18. Jahrhundert*, Münster.
Schochet, Gordon 1992, 'John Locke and Religious Toleration', in Lois G. Schwoerer
    (ed.), *The Revolution of 1688–89. Changing Perspectives*, Cambridge, pp. 147–64.
Schochet, Gordon (ed.) 1993, *Politics, Politeness and Patriotism*, Washington, D.C.
Schoeffer, I. 1977, 'The Batavian Myth during the Sixteenth and Seventeenth
    Centuries', in J. S. Bromley and E. H. Kossmann (eds.), *Britain and the Netherlands*,
    vol. V, The Hague, pp. 78–101.
Schröder, Winfried 1989, 'Pantheismus', in Joachim Ritter and Karlfried Gründer
    (eds.), *Historisches Wörterbuch der Philosophie*, vol. VII, Darmstadt, pp. 59–63.

Schutte, G. J. 1979, 'Willem IV en Willem V', in C. A. Tamse (ed.), *Nassau en Oranje in de Nederlandse geschiedenis*, Alphen aan den Rijn, pp. 187–93.

Scorza, R. A. 1991, 'A Florentine Sketchbook: Architecture, *apparati* and the Accademia del Disegno', *Journal of the Warburg and Courtauld Institutes*, 54: 172–85.

Scott, Jonathan 1988, *Algernon Sidney and the English Republic*, Cambridge.

    1993, 'The Rapture of Motion: James Harrington's Republicanism', in Phillipson and Skinner (eds.) 1993: 139–63.

    1994, 'The Law of War: Grotius, Sidney, Locke and the Political Theory of Rebellion', in Simon Groenveld and Michael Wintle (eds.), *Britain and the Netherlands*, vol. XI: *The Exchange of Ideas*, Zutphen: 115–32.

    1996, 'The Peace of Silence: Thucydides and the English Civil War', in Miles Fairburn and W. H. Oliver (eds.), *The Certainty of Doubt: Essays in Honour of Peter Munz*, Wellington.

    1997, Review of Wootton (ed.) 1994, in *Parliamentary History*, pp. 243–6.

    2000a, *England's Troubles: Seventeenth-century English Political Instability in European Context*, Cambridge.

    2000b, Review of Arihiro Fukuda, *Sovereignty and the Sword: Harrington, Hobbes and Mixed Government in the English Civil Wars*, in *English Historical Review*, 2.

Scott, W. R. 1900, *Francis Hutcheson*, Cambridge.

Sellers, M. N. S. 1994, *American Republicanism: Roman Ideology in the United States Constitution*, New York.

    1998, *The Sacred Fire of Liberty: Republicanism, Liberalism and the Law*, New York.

Séris, Jean-Pierre 1994, *Qu'est-ce que la division du travail? Ferguson*, Paris.

Serra, Eva 1991, '1640: La revolució política. La implicació de les institucions', in E. Serra (ed.), *La revolució catalana de 1640*, Barcelona.

Sheehan, James 1989, *German History 1770–1869*, Oxford.

Shephard, Amanda 1994, *Gender and Authority in Sixteenth-Century England: The Knox Debate*, Keele.

Sher, Richard B. 1985, *Church and University in the Scottish Enlightenment. The Moderate Literati of Edinburgh*, Edinburgh.

    1989, 'Adam Ferguson, Adam Smith, and the Problem of National Defense', *Journal of Modern History*, 61: 240–68.

Sher, Richard B. and Jeffrey R. Smitten (eds.) 1990, *Scotland and America in the Age of Enlightenment*, Princeton.

Shklar, Judith 1964, *Legalism*, Cambridge, Mass.

    1978, Review of Harrington 1977, *Political Theory*, 6 (November): 558–61.

    1990, 'Montesquieu and the New Republicanism', in Bock, Skinner and Viroli (eds.) 1990: 265–79.

Silvano, G. 1993, *La 'Republica de' Viniziani'. Ricerche sul repubblicanesimo veneziano in età moderna*, Florence.

Simon Tarrés, Antoni 1999, *Els orígens ideològics de la revolució catalana de 1640*, Barcelona.

Simon, Jocelyn 1968, 'Dr Cowell', *Cambridge Law Journal*, 26: 260–72.

Simonutti, Luisa 1995, 'Premières réactions anglaises au *Traité théologico-politique*', Paolo Cristofolini (ed.) 1995: 123–37.

1996, 'Spinoza and the English Thinkers. Criticism on Prophecies and Miracles: Blount, Gildon, Earbery', in Van Bunge and Klever (eds.) 1996: 191–211.

Skinner, A. S. and T. Wilson (eds.) 1975, *Essays on Adam Smith*, Oxford.

Skinner, Quentin 1974a, 'Conquest and Consent: Thomas Hobbes and the Engagement Controversy', in G. E. Aylmer (ed.), *The Interregnum: The Quest for Settlement 1646–1660*, London.

1974b, 'The Principles and Practice of Opposition: The Case of Bolingbroke versus Walpole', in Neil McKendrick (ed.), *Historical Perspectives. Studies in English Thought and Society*, London, pp. 93–128.

1978, *The Foundations of Modern Political Thought*, 2 vols., Cambridge.

1981, *Machiavelli*, Oxford.

1983, 'Machiavelli on the Maintenance of Liberty', *Politics*, 18: 3–15.

1984, 'The Idea of Negative Liberty: Philosophical and Historical Perspectives', in Rorty, Schneewind and Skinner (eds.) 1984: 193–221.

1986, 'The Paradoxes of Political Liberty', in McMurrin (ed.) 1986: 225–50.

1987, 'Sir Thomas More's Utopia and the Language of Renaissance Humanism', in Pagden (ed.) 1987: 123–57.

1988a, 'Meaning and Understanding', in Skinner 1988c: 29–67.

1988b, 'Some Problems in the Analysis of Political Thought and Action', in Skinner 1988c: 97–118.

1988c, *Meaning and Context: Quentin Skinner and his Critics*, ed. and introd. by James Tully, Princeton.

1989, 'The State', in Terence Ball, James Farr and Russell Hanson (eds.), *Political Innovation and Conceptual Change*, Cambridge, pp. 90–131.

1990a, 'The Republican Ideal of Political Liberty', in Bock, Skinner and Viroli (eds.) 1990: 293–309.

1990b, 'Thomas Hobbes on the Proper Signification of Liberty', *Transactions of the Royal Historical Society*, 40: 121–51.

1990c, 'Machiavelli's *Discorsi* and the Pre-humanist Origins of Republican Ideas', in Bock, Skinner and Viroli (eds.) 1990: 121–41.

1996, *Reason and Rhetoric in the Philosophy of Hobbes*, Cambridge.

1998, *Liberty before Liberalism*, Cambridge.

Smith, David L. 1991, 'The Impact on Government', in Morrill 1991: 32–49.

Smith, Nigel 1994, *Literature and Revolution in England, 1640–1660*, New Haven.

Smith, O. 1984, *The Politics of Language 1791–1819*, Oxford.

Snow, Vernon F. 1977, *Parliament in Elizabethan England. John Hooker's Order and Usage*, New Haven.

Soly, H. 1984, 'Plechtige intochten in de steden van de Zuidelijke Nederlanden tijdens de overgang van Middeleeuwen naar Nieuwe Tijd: communicatie, propaganda, spektakel', *Tijdschrift voor Geschiedenis*, 97: 341–61.

Sommerville, Johann P. 1996, 'English and European Political Ideas in the Early Seventeenth Century: Revisionism and the Case of Absolutism', *Journal of British Studies*, 35: 168–94.

1999, *Royalists and Patriots: Politics and Ideology in England 1603–1640*, London.

Sorkin, David 1996, *Moses Mendelssohn and the Religious Enlightenment*, London.

Stadter, P. A. 1965, *Plutarch's Historical Methods and Analysis of the* Mulierum Virtutes, Cambridge, Mass.

Steiger, Christoph von 1954, *Innere Probleme des bernischen Patriziates an der Wende zum 18. Jahrhundert*, Berne.

Stewart, M. A. 1987, 'John Smith and the Molesworth Circle', *Eighteenth-Century Ireland*, 2.

Stewart, M. A. (ed.) 1990, *Studies in the Philosophy of the Scottish Enlightenment*, Oxford.

Stimson, S. 1989, 'Republicanism and the Recovery of the Political in Adam Smith', in Milgate and Welch (eds.) 1989: 91–112.

Stollberg-Rillinger, Barbara 1999,*Vormünder des Volkes? Konzepte landständischer Repräsentation des alten Reiches*, Berlin.

Stolleis, Michael 1988, *Geschichte des öffentlichen Rechts in Deutschland*, vol. 1: *Reichspublizistik und Policeywissenschaft 1600–1800*, Munich.

Stolleis, Michael (ed.) 1983, *Hermann Conring (1606–1681). Beiträge zum Leben und Werk*, Berlin.

Stolleis, Michael (ed.) 1995, *Staatsdenker in der Frühen Neuzeit*, 3rd edn, Munich.

Stoye, E. 1954, *Vincent Bernard de Tscharner. A Study of Swiss Culture in the Eighteenth Century*, Fribourg.

Strengholt, L. 1984, Review of A. den Besten, *Het Wilhelmus*, 1983, *Tijdschrift voor Nederlandsche taal- en letterkunde*, 100: 237–8.

Strumia, A. 1991, *L'immaginazione repubblicana. Sparta e Atene nel dibattito filosofico-politico dell'età di Cromwell*, Florence.

Sucheni-Grabowska, A. 1994, 'Obowiązki i prawa królów polskich w opiniach pisarzy Odrodzenia', in *Między monarchią a demokracją. Studia z dziejów Polski*, Warsaw.

   1997, 'The Origin and Development of the Polish Parliamentary System through the End of the Seventeenth Century', in S. Fiszman (ed.), *Constitution and Reform in Eighteenth-Century Poland*, Bloomington.

Sullivan, Robert E. 1982, *John Toland and the Deist Controversy. A Study in Adaptations*, Cambridge, Mass.

Sullivan, Vickie 1994, 'The Civic Humanist Portrait of Machiavelli's English Successors', *History of Political Thought*, 15, 2.

Szczucki, Lech (ed.) 1978, *700 lat myśli polskiej. [2], Filozofia i myśl społeczna* XVI *wieku* (700 Years of Polish Thought. [2], Philosophy and Social Thought XVI Century), Warsaw.

Taranto, D. 1995, 'Per un repertorio bibliografico delle scritture politiche italiane della seconda metà del Seicento', *Archivio della Ragion di Stato*, 3: 5–56.

Taylor, Miles 1991, '*Imperium et Libertas*? Rethinking the Radical Critique of Imperialism during the Nineteenth Century', *Journal of Imperial and Commonwealth History*, 19: 1–23.

Tazbir, J. 1991, 'Węgrzy jako symbol i przestroga w literaturze staropolskiej', *Odrodzenie i Reformacja w Polsce*, 36: 147–96.

Tega, W. 1978, 'D'Holbach e l'utopia della riforma', in P. Casini (ed.), *La politica della ragione, Studi sull'illuminismo francese*, Bologna, pp. 273–315.

Tenenti, Alberto 1987, 'Il potere dogale come rappresentazione', in Alberto Tenenti, *Stato: un'idea, una logica. Dal Comune italiano all'assolutismo francese*, Bologna.

Thomas, Yan 1990, 'La Division des sexes en droit romain', in Georges Duby and
   Michelle Perrot (eds.), *Histoire des femmes*, vol. 1, Paris.
Thompson, I. A. A. 1992, *War and Society in Habsburg Spain*, Aldershot.
   1995, 'Castile, Spain and the Monarchy: The Political Community from *patria natural*
   to *patria nacional*', in Kagan and Parker (eds.) 1995: 125–59.
   1997, 'Patronato real e integración política en las ciudades castellanas bajo los
   Austrias', in Fortea (ed.) 1997: 475–96.
Tilmans, Karin 1992, *Historiography and Humanism in Holland in the Age of Erasmus*,
   Nieuwkoop.
Todd, Margo 1987, *Christian Humanism and the Puritan Social Order*, Cambridge.
Toffanin, G. 1972, *Machiavelli e il 'Tacitismo'. La politica storica al tempo della contrariforma*,
   Naples.
Torras Ribé, Josep M. 1983, *Els municipis catalans de l'Antic Règim, 1453–1808*,
   Barcelona.
Torres, Xavier 1995, 'Pactisme i patriotisme a la Catalunya de la Guerra dels Segadors',
   Recerques, 32: 45–62.
   1997, 'Dinasticismo y patriotismo en la Cataluña de la Guerra de los Segadores:
   el testimonio de un zurrador barcelonés', in Fernández Albaladejo (ed.) 1997:
   395–408.
Treue, Wilhelm 1951, 'Adam Smith in Deutschland: Zum Problem des "Politischen
   Professors" zwischen 1776 und 1810', in W. Conze (ed.), *Deutschland und Europa:
   Festschrift für Hans Rothfels*, Düsseldorf, pp. 101–33.
Tribe, Keith 1988, *Governing Economy: The Reformation of German Economic Discourse
   1750–1840*, Cambridge.
Tricomi, Albert 1989, *Anticourt Drama in England 1603–1642*, Charlottesville.
Tuck, Richard 1979, *Natural Rights Theories: Their Origin and Development*, Cambridge.
   1985, 'Warrender's *De cive*', *Political Studies*, 33: 308–15.
   1991, 'Grotius and Selden', in Burns and Goldie (eds.) 1991: 499–529.
   1993, *Philosophy and Government, 1572–1651*, Cambridge.
Tuempel, Ch. *et al.* (eds.) 1991, *Het Oude Testament in de Schilderkunst van de Gouden Eeuw*,
   Amsterdam.
Underdown, David 1971, *Pride's Purge: Politics in the Puritan Revolution*, Oxford.
Utz, Hans 1959, *Die Hollis-Sammlung in Bern. Ein Beitrag zu den englisch-schweizerischen
   Beziehungen in der Zeit der Aufklärung*, Berne.
Van Bunge, Wiep and Wim Klever (eds.) 1996, *Disguised and Overt Spinozism around 1700.
   Papers Presented at the International Colloquium held at Rotterdam, 5–8 October 1994*,
   Leiden.
Van de Klashorst, G. O. 1986, ' "*Metten schijn van monarchie getempert*". De verdediging
   van het stadhouderschap in de partijliteratuur, 1650–1686', in Blom and
   Wildenberg (eds.) 1986: 93–136.
   1999, 'De ware vrijheid, 1650–1672', in Haitsma Mulier and Velema (eds.) 1999:
   157–85.
Van de Klashorst, G. O., E. O. G. Haitsma Mulier and H. W. Blom (eds.) 1986,
   *Bibliography of Dutch Seventeenth-Century Political Thought. An Annotated Inventory,
   1581–1710*, Amsterdam and Maarssen.

Van der Coelen, P. 1991, 'Thesauri en Trezoren. Boeken en bundels met oudtestamentische prenten', in Tuempel *et al.* (eds.) 1991: 168–93.

Van der Heijden, M. C. A. (ed.) 1967–72, *Die tyrannie verdrijven. Godsdienst . . . in de 16e en 17e eeuw*, in *Spectrum van de nederlandse letterkunde*, 25 vols., Utrecht and Antwerp.

Van Gelderen, Martin 1986, 'A Political Theory of the Dutch Revolt and the *Vindiciae contra tyrannos*', *Il Pensiero politico*, 19: 163–81.

  1990, 'The Machiavellian Moment and the Dutch Revolt: the Rise of Neostoicism and Dutch Republicanism', in Bock, Skinner and Viroli (eds.) 1990: 205–23.

  1992, *The Political Thought of the Dutch Revolt 1555–1590*, Cambridge.

  1998, 'Contested Kingship. Conceptions of Monarchy and Civil Power in Spanish and Dutch Political Thought, 1555–1598, in J. Martínez Millán (ed.), *Felipe II. Europa y la Monarquía Católica*, Madrid, pp. 365–77.

  1999, 'From Domingo de Soto to Hugo Grotius. Theories of Monarchy and Civil Power in Spanish and Dutch Political Thought', *Il pensiero politico*, 32, 2: 186–205.

Van Kley, Dale (ed.) 1989, *The French Idea of Freedom: The Old Regime and the Declaration of Rights of 1789*, Stanford.

Van Tijn, Th. 1956, 'Pieter de la Court. Zijn leven en zijn economische denkbeelden', *Tijdschrift voor Geschiedenis*, 69: 304–70.

Vanderjagt, Arjo 1981, '*Qui sa vertu Anoblist*'. *The Concepts of noblesse and chose publicque in Burgundian Political Thought*, Groningen.

Vasoli, Cesare 1968, *La dialettica e la retorica dell'Umanesimo. 'Invenzione' e 'Metodo' nella cultura del xv e xvi secolo*, Milan.

  1988, 'The Renaissance Concept of Philosophy', in Charles B. Schmitt, Quentin Skinner, Eckhard Kessler and Jill Kraye (eds.), *The Cambridge History of Renaissance Philosophy*, Cambridge, pp. 57–74.

Veen, Theo Johannes 1976, *Recht en nut. Studien over en naar aanleiding van Ulrik Huber (1636–1694)*, Groningen.

  1985, '*De lege regia*: Opmerkingen over de interdependentie van geschiedsbeschouwing, politieke theorie en interpretatie van Romeins recht bij Ulrik Huber', in G. Th. Jensma, F. R. Smit and F. Westra (eds.), *Universiteit te Franeker: Bijdragen tot de geschiedenis van de Friese Hogeschool*, Leeuwarden, pp. 321–34.

Vega, J. A. 1989a, 'Feminist Republicanism. Etta Palm-Aelders on Justice, Virtue and Men', *History of European Ideas, Special Issue on Women and the French Revolution*, 10, 3: 333–51.

  1989b, 'Luxury, Necessity, or the Morality of Men. The republican discourse of Etta Palm-Aelders', in *Les Femmes et la Révolution Francaise. Actes du Colloque*, vol. 1, Toulouse, pp. 363–70.

  1991, 'Etta Palm, une Hollandaise à Paris', in Willem Frijhoff and Rudolf Dekker (eds.), *Le Voyage révolutionnaire*, Hilversum, pp. 49–57.

  1996, 'Feminist Discourses in the Dutch Republic at the End of the Eighteenth Century', *Journal of Women's History*, 8, 2: 130–51.

  2000, 'Sade's libertijnse republiek. Over pornografische parabels en esthetische politiek', *Jaarboek voor Vrouwengeschiedenis*, 20: 109–33.

Vega, Judith A. and Rudolf M. Dekker 2002, 'Women and the Dutch Revolutions of the Late Eighteenth Century', in Fauré (ed.) 2002.

Velema, W. R. E. 1987, 'God, de deugd en de oude constitutie. Politieke talen in de eerste helft van de achttiende eeuw', *Bijdragen en Mededelingen betreffende de Geschiedenis der Nederlanden*, 102: 476–97.

　　1997, 'Republican Readings of Montesquieu. The Spirit of the Laws in the Dutch Republic', *History of Political Thought*, 18: 43–63.

　　1998, 'From the Rule of Law to Popular Sovereignty: The Concept of Liberty in the Dutch Republic, 1780–1787', *Zeitschrift für historische Forschung. Vierteljahresschrift zur Erforschung des Spätmittelalters und der frühen Neuzeit*, 21: 69–82.

Venturi, Franco 1970, *Utopia e riforma nell'Iluminismo*, Turin.

　　1971, *Utopia and Reform in the Enlightenment*, Cambridge.

　　1990, *La Repubblica di Venezia (1761–1797)*, vol. v/2 of Venturi, *Settecento riformatore: L'Italia dei Lumi*, Turin.

Verdam, J. 1911, *Middelnederlandsch Woordenboek*, The Hague.

Vermij, Rienk H. 1996a, 'The English Deists and the *Traité*', in Berti *et al.* (eds.) 1996: 241–57.

　　1996b, 'Matter and Motion: Toland and Spinoza', in Van Bunge and Klever (eds.) 1996: 275–88.

Vidal-Naquet, P. 1990, 'La Formation de l'Athènes bourgeoise', in P. Vidal-Naquet, *La Démocratie grecque vue d'ailleurs*, Paris.

Viejo, Julián 1997, 'Ausencia de política. Ordenación interna y proyecto europeo en la monarquía católica de mediados del siglo XVII', in Fernández Albaladejo (ed.) 1997: 615–29.

Vierhaus, Rudolf 1987a, *Deutschland im 18. Jahrhundert: Politische Verfassung, soziales Gefüge, geistige Bewegungen*, Göttingen.

　　1987b, 'Montesquieu in Deutschland: Zur Geschichte seiner Wirkung als politischer Schriftsteller im 18. Jahrhundert', in Vierhaus 1987a: 7–32.

　　1990, 'The Revolutionizing of Consciousness. A German Utopia?', in Hellmuth (ed.) 1990: 561–77.

Villanueva, Jesús 1994, 'Francisco Calça y el mito de la libertad originaria de Cataluña', *Revista Jerónimo Zurita*, 69–70: 75–87.

　　1995, 'El debat sobre la constitució de l'observança a les Corts catalanes de 1626–1632', *Manuscrits*, 13: 247–72.

Villari, R. 1967, *La rivolta antispagnola a Napoli. Le origini (1585–1647)*, Bari.

　　1987, *Elogio della dissimulazione. La lotta politica nel Seicento*, Rome and Bari.

Villiers, Baron Marc de 1910, *Histoire des clubs de femmes et des légions d'Amazones 1793–1848–1871*, Paris.

Viroli, Maurizio 1988, *Jean-Jacques Rousseau and the 'Well-Ordered Society'*, trans. D. Hanson, Cambridge.

　　1990, 'Machiavelli and the Republican Idea of Politics', in Bock, Skinner and Viroli (eds.) 1990: 143–71.

　　1992, *From Politics to Reason of State: The Acquisition and Transformation of the Language of Politics, 1250–1600*, Cambridge.

　　1994, *Dalla politica alla ragion di stato. La scienza del governo tra XIII e XVII secolo*, Rome.

1995, *For Love of Country. An Essay on Patriotism and Nationalism*, Oxford.

1998, *Machiavelli*, Oxford.

Wälchli, Karl Friedrich 1964, 'Niklaus Emanuel Tscharner. Ein Berner Magistrat und ökonomischer Patriot 1727–1794', *Archiv des Historischen Vereins des Kantons Bern*, 48.

Walder, Ernst 1944, 'Machiavelli und die virtù der Schweizer', *Schweizer Beiträge zur Allgemeinen Geschichte*, 2.

Walker, Julia M. (ed.) 1998, *Dissing Elizabeth: Negative Representations of Gloriana*, Durham: Duke University Press.

Walker, Mack 1971, *German Home Towns: Community, State, General Estate, 1648–1871*, Ithaca.

Walther, Manfred 1985, 'Die Transformation des Naturrechts in der Rechtsphilosophie Spinozas', *Studia Spinozana*, 1: 73–104.

1992, 'Institution, Imagination und Freiheit bei Spinoza. Eine kritische Theorie politischer Institutionen', in Manfred Göhler (ed.), *Zu einer Theorie politischen Institutionen*, Neuwied, pp. 246–75.

1993, 'Philosophy and Politics in Spinoza', *Studia Spinozana*, 9: 49–57.

1996, 'Kommunismus und Vertragstheorie. Althusius – Hobbes – Spinoza – Rousseau oder Tradition und Gestaltwandel einer politischen Erfahrung', in Peter Blickle (ed.), *Theorien kommunaler Ordnung in Europa*, Munich, pp. 127–62.

Walzer, M. 1985, *Exodus and Revolution*, New York.

Waszek, Norbert 1985, 'Bibliography of the Scottish Enlightenment in Germany', *Studies on Voltaire and the Eighteenth Century*, 230.

Weinbrot, Howard D. 1978, *Augustus Caesar in 'Augustan England': The Decline of a Classical Norm*, Princeton.

Werminghoff, Albert 1921, *Conrad Celtis und sein Buch über Nürnberg*, Freiburg.

Weston, Corinne Comstock 1965, *English Constitutional Theory and the House of Lords 1556–1832*, London.

Whaley, Joachim 1985, *Religious Toleration and Social Change in Hamburg, 1529–1819*, Cambridge.

Whatmore, R. 1998, 'The Political Economy of Jean-Baptiste Say's Republicanism', *History of Political Thought*, 19, 3: 439–56.

Wickwar, W. H. 1968, *Baron d'Holbach: A Prelude to the French Revolution*, New York.

Wildenberg, Ivo W. 1986, *Johan & Pieter de la Court (1622–1660 & 1618–1685). Bibliografie en receptiegeschiedenis. Gids tot de studie van een oeuvre*, Amsterdam and Maarssen.

Wilhelm, Uwe 1995, *Der deutsche Frühliberalismus. Von den Anfängen bis 1789*, Frankfurt.

Willoweit, Dietmar 1995, 'Juristische Argumentation in den Werken von Rechtskonsulenten mindermächtiger Stände', *Blätter für deutsche Landesgeschichte*, 131: 189–202.

Winch, Donald 1978, *Adam Smith's Politics: An Essay in Historiographic Revision*, Cambridge.

1983, 'Adam Smith's "Enduring Particular Result": A Political and Cosmopolitan Perspective', in Hont and Ignatieff (eds.) 1983: 253–69.

1992, 'Adam Smith: Scottish Moral Philosopher as Political Economist', *The Historical Journal*, 35, 1 (March): 91–113.

1996, *Riches and Poverty: An Intellectual History of Political Economy, 1760–1834*, Cambridge.

Winters, Peter Jochen 1995, 'Althusius' in Stolleis (ed.) 1995: 29–51.

Wirszubski, Chaim 1950, Libertas *as a Political Idea at Rome during the Late Republic and Early Principate*, Cambridge.

Wokler, Robert 1995, *Rousseau*, Oxford.

Wolin, S. 1960, *Politics and Vision: Continuity and Innovation in Western Political Thought*, Boston.

Woodhouse, A. S. P. (ed.) 1938, *Puritanism and Liberty*, London.

Wootton, David (ed.) 1994, *Republicanism, Liberty and Commercial Society 1649–1776*, Stanford.

Worden, Blair 1977, *The Rump Parliament 1648–1653*, Cambridge.

1981, 'Classical Republicanism and the Puritan Revolution', in Hugh Lloyd-Jones, Valerie Pearl and Blair Worden (eds.), *Essays in Honour of H. R. Trevor-Roper*, London.

1985, 'Providence and Politics in Cromwellian England', *Past and Present*, pp. 55–99.

1990, 'Milton's Republicanism and the Tyranny of Heaven', in Bock, Skinner and Viroli (eds.) 1990: 225–45.

1991a, 'English Republicanism', in Burns and Goldie (eds.) 1991: 443–75.

1991b, 'The Revolution of 1688–9 and the English Republican Tradition', in Jonathan I. Israel (ed.), *The Anglo-Dutch Moment*, Cambridge, pp. 241–77.

1994a, 'Ben Jonson among the Historians', in Kevin Sharpe and Peter Lake (eds.), *Culture and Politics in Early Stuart England*, Basingstoke, pp. 67–89.

1994b, 'Part 1', in Wootton (ed.) 1994: 45–193.

1994c, 'Republicanism and the Restoration', in Wootton (ed.) 1994: 139–93.

1995a, 'Milton and Marchamont Nedham', in Armitage, Himy and Skinner (eds.) 1995.

1995b, ' "Wit in a Roundhead": The Dilemma of Marchamont Nedham', in Susan Amussen and Mark Kishlansky (eds.), *Political Culture and Cultural Politics in Early Modern England*, Manchester.

1996, *The Sound of Virtue: Philip Sidney's* Arcadia *and Elizabethan Politics*, New Haven.

1999a, 'Favourites on the English Stage', in Lawrence Brockliss and J. H. Elliott (eds.), *The World of the Favourite*, New Haven.

1999b, 'Politics in *Catiline*: Jonson and his Sources', in Martin Butler (ed.), *Re-presenting Ben Jonson*, Basingstoke.

1999c, Review of Norbrook 1999, *Times Literary Supplement*, 29 January.

2001, *Roundhead Reputations. The English Civil Wars and the Passions of Posterity*, London.

Wright, Johnson Kent 1994, 'National Sovereignty and the General Will', in Van Kley (ed.) 1994: 199–233.

1997, *A Classical Republican in Eighteenth-Century France: The Political Thought of Mably*, Stanford.

Wyduckel, Dieter 1996, 'Die Vertragslehre Pufendorfs und ihre rechts- und staatstheoretischen Grundlagen', in Fiammetta Palladini and Gérald Hartung (eds.),

Samuel Pufendorf und die europäische Frühaufklärung. Werk und Einfluß eines deutschen Bürgers der Gelehrtenrepublik nach 300 Jahren (1694–1994), Berlin, pp. 147–65.

Wykes, David L. 1990, 'The Tercentenary of the Toleration Act of 1689: A Cause for Celebration?', in E. J. Furcha (ed.), *Truth and Tolerance. Papers from the 1989 International Symposium on Truth and Tolerance, McGill University*, Montreal, pp. 60–82.

Zapalac, Kristin E. S. 1990, *'In His Image and Likeness'. Political Iconography and Religious Change in Regensburg, 1500–1600*, Ithaca.

Zielińska, Z. 1991, *'O sukcesyi tronu w Polszcze', 1787–1790*, Warsaw.

Zorn, Wolfgang 1976, 'Die soziale Stellung der Humanisten in Nürnberg und Augsburg', in Otto Herding and Robert Stupperich (eds.), *Die Humanisten in ihrer politischen und sozialen Umwelt*, Boppardt.

Zwitzer, H. L. (ed.) 1987, *Joan Derk van der Capellem, Aan het Volk van Nederland. Het patriottisch program uit 1781*, Amsterdam.

Contributors

DAVID ARMITAGE is the James R. Barker Chair of Contemporary Civilization (2002–5) at Columbia University, New York, USA.

HANS ERICH BÖDEKER is Senior Research Fellow at the Max-Planck-Institut für Geschichte, Göttingen, Germany.

LEA CAMPOS BORALEVI is Professor of History at the University of Florence, Italy.

VITTOR IVO COMPARATO is Professor of Modern History at the University of Perugia, Italy.

VITTORIO CONTI is Professor of History at the University of Florence, Italy.

MARTIN DZELZAINIS is Reader in Renaissance Literature and Thought, Department of English, Royal Holloway, University of London, England.

CHRISTINE FAURÉ is Directrice de recherche of the Centre de Recherches Politiques de la Sorbonne, Université Paris I, which is part of the Centre National de la Recherche Scientifique (CNRS).

ROBERT VON FRIEDEBURG is Professor of History at the Erasmus University, Rotterdam, The Netherlands.

MARCO GEUNA is Professor of History of Political Philosophy at the University of Milan, Italy.

XAVIER GIL is Professor of Early Modern History at the University of Barcelona, Spain.

ANNA GRZEŚKOWIAK-KRWAWICZ is Research Fellow at the Institute of Literary Research of the Polish Academy of Sciences, Warsaw.

IAN HAMPSHER-MONK is Professor of Political Theory at the University of Exeter, England.

BELA KAPOSSY was assistant to the Professor for the History of Political Thought at the University of Lausanne and is in charge of a research project for the Swiss National Science Foundation on 'The Patriotic and Economic Societies of Berne in European Context (1759–1766)'.

367

Catherine Larrère is Professor of Philosophy at the University of Bordeaux 3, France.

Edward Opaliński is Research Fellow at the Institute of History of the Polish Academy of Sciences, Warsaw.

Fania Oz-Salzberger is Senior Lecturer at the School of History and at the Law Faculty, University of Haifa, Israel.

Markku Peltonen is Senior Lecturer in History at the University of Helsinki, Finland.

Eluggero Pii was Professor of History at the University of Florence, Italy

Jonathan Scott is Carroll Amundson Professor of British History at the University of Pittsburgh, USA.

Quentin Skinner is the Regius Professor of Modern History at the University of Cambridge and a Fellow of Christ's College, Cambridge, England.

Michael Sonenscher is a Fellow and Director of Studies in History at King's College, Cambridge, England.

Jean Fabien Spitz is Professor of Philosophy at the Sorbonne, University of Paris 1, France.

Karin Tilmans is Lecturer of History at the University of Amsterdam and manager of the Dutch postgraduate school for cultural history, the Huizinga Institute.

Martin Van Gelderen is Professor of Intellectual History at the University of Sussex, England.

Judith A. Vega is lecturer in Social and Political Philosophy at the University of Groningen, The Netherlands.

Wyger Velema is Lecturer of Modern History at the University of Amsterdam, The Netherlands.

Donald Winch is Research Professor in the Graduate Research Centre in the Humanities at the University of Sussex, England.

Blair Worden is Professor of Early Modern History at the University of Sussex and currently British Academy Research Professor, England.

Johnson Kent Wright is Associate Professor of History at Arizona State University, Tempe, USA.

Simone Zurbuchen is Research Fellow at the Centre for European Enlightenment Studies in Potsdam, Germany, She also teaches philosophy at the universities of Zurich and Potsdam.

Index of Names of Persons

This index includes the names of all persons, including modern scholars, mentioned in the text and in the footnotes. Figures in **bold type** refer to extended passages (including chapters and sections).

Index of Subjects

Figures in **bold type** refer to extended passages (including chapters and sections).

DATE DUE
